SOCIAL SCIENCE IN
CHRISTIAN PERSPECTIVE

SOCIAL SCIENCE IN CHRISTIAN PERSPECTIVE

Paul A. Marshall
and Robert E. VanderVennen
Editors

UNIVERSITY
PRESS OF
AMERICA

LANHAM/NEW YORK/LONDON

Copyright © 1988 by

University Press of America,® Inc.

4720 Boston Way
Lanham, MD 20706

3 Henrietta Street
London WC2E 8LU England

Printed in the United States of America

British Cataloging in Publication Information Available

Library of Congress Cataloging-in-Publication Data

Social science in Christian perspective / Paul A. Marshall and Robert
E. VanderVennen, Editors.
p. cm.—(Christian studies today)
Papers presented originally at a conference held at the Institute for Christian
Studies, Toronto, in July, 1978.
"Co-published by arrangement with the Institute for Christian
Studies, Toronto, Ontario, Canada"—T.p. verso.
Includes bibliographical references.
1. Social sciences—Religious aspects—Christianity—Congresses.
I. Marshall, Paul A., 1948–   . II. VanderVennen, Robert E.
III. Institute for Christian Studies. IV. Series.
BR115.S57S65   1988
261.5—dc 19   88–20482 CIP
ISBN 0–8191–7103–4 (alk. paper)
ISBN 0–8191–7104–2 (pbk. : alk. paper)

All University Press of America books are produced on acid-free paper.
The paper used in this publication meets the minimum requirements of American
National Standard for Information Sciences—Permanence of Paper for Printed
Library Materials, ANSI Z39.48–1984.

Social Science in Christian Perspective
is the
1988 Robert Lee Carvill Memorial Book
and is
thankfully dedicated to the memory of
Bernard Zylstra
organizer of the
1978 International Social Sciences Conference
and
original editor of this volume

Contents

Preface

The papers in this volume were presented originally at a conference held at the Institute for Christian Studies, Toronto, in July 1978. Ten years is a long delay in publication, even allowing for the rhythms of much modern scholarship. In this case the delay is explained by the original editor's struggle with cancer. In 1986 Bernard Zylstra died and the present editors took over his responsibilities.

In the course of time these papers arrived on my desk with a note asking for my recommendation concerning possible publication. The appearance of the book reflects, *inter alia*, my positive assessment of their worth. Certainly much has been lost over the years: despite some updating, some of the papers address matters which are no longer centers of discussion in their field and, of course, none of the papers deal with the most recent literature.

Nevertheless, despite these problems, these papers are well worth publishing, either individually or as a collection. The reason that they deserve a wide audience is that they embody an overall approach to the social sciences that is relatively unknown, theoretically penetrating, and not well illustrated by any other volume currently in English. This is the approach described by Hendrik Hart in the Introduction as an attempt to achieve what he calls "an inner reformation of the sciences," a Christian effort to rework science from the inside out. In this view the relation of religion and science is not one of separate realms, nor is it merely that we can study religion by means of the sciences. It is not the notion that religion can provide ethical guidelines for science, nor that science can be a "tool" for religious people. Rather it is the view that the history, the sociology, the structure, the very conceptual makeup of the sciences reflect deep-seated patterns of commitment which can properly be called religious. Hence the authors, all committed Christians, are here seeking to work out their Christian faith in the actual practice of science, even in their science's most technical aspects. This is the trait that distinguishes these essays and this book.

Such an approach is represented elsewhere, such as, for instance, in David Lyon's *Sociology and the Human Image* (Downers Grove: InterVarsity Press, 1985), Alan Storkey's *Christian Social Perspective* (Leicester: Inter-Varsity Press, 1979), and Nicholas Wolterstorff's *Until Justice and Peace Embrace* (Grand Rapids: Eerdmans, 1983), but this present collection covers a much wider range of fields and is aimed at a more specialized and professional audience. It is intended to allow us to observe the actual practise of arguing Christian social science.

As is the hallmark of "inner reformation" approach, the book opens with a somewhat philosophic introduction by Hendrik Hart, who seeks to explain what the essays try to do. From there we go on to "social theory" in the essays of Elaine Botha, Richard Mouw, Johan van der Vyver, and Paul Marshall, which attempt to deal with paradigmatic and methodological questions. Thence, we move to particular fields of social inquiry: sociology, economics, politics, and technology. In each of these cases the subsection begins with a theoretical overview of the field (Strauss, Cramp, Haan, Skillen) which tries to lay bare the field's underlying assumptions and concepts and which sets the stage for essays on more focused topics —David Lyon on secularization, Maarten Vrieze on the sociology of knowledge, Bas Kee on the capital debate, George Monsma on welfare economics, and Egbert Schuurman on systems.

I am thankful to the late Bernard Zylstra and to Mark Okkema who did most of the earlier editing as well as to Betty Polman, Alice de Koning, and Ruth Bruinsma who typed, proofed, and copyedited, and to Jim Prall who helped us transfer this to the computer. Thanks also to Carroll Guen and Willem Hart who prepared this manuscript for final publication. Special praise must go to Bob Vander Vennen, Director of Education Services at the Institute for Christian Studies, who coordinated the editing and production with unfailing diligence and patience. The Institute itself has graciously provided financial assistance for the publication. Finally, I would like to thank the contributors themselves: they have waited patiently for this to appear (or perhaps some just forgot about it) and kindly have consented to let some of their older work be published even though their own knowledge and thinking may have moved beyond what is represented here.

Paul Marshall
Toronto, February 1988

INTRODUCTION
The idea of
an inner reformation
of the sciences
Hendrik Hart

The papers in this volume have more in common than their
focus on the social sciences. They share a common concern with
what people in a neo-Calvinian tradition have called "the inner
reformation of the sciences." Some authors enthusiastically
accept the idea of such reformation and have worked with it for
a long time. Others are skeptical of it and relate to it for the first
time here. Since none of the papers addresses the idea of an
inner reformation of scholarship explicitly, I will do so in this
introductory paper.

I will explain and clarify this notion of an inner reformation of science by discussing its origins, its meaning as implemented in certain useful concepts, and its potential in the
future. After a brief introduction of the idea I will give a short
historical sketch, outline some contributions of two contemporary thinkers, suggest some ideas of my own, and offer a critical
assessment of the tradition's future.

Introduction
From the beginning of the Christian religion, we know of believers aware of a connection between their faith and their
scholarship. For some it means shielding their faith from the
influences of intellectual endeavors. For others the reverse
seems more appropriate. They seek to align their faith with the
most recent givens of modern thought. And between these
extremes we find many other nuances of the relationship.

Most of the reflection on Christian scholarship has been
focused on the relation between faith and reason. Some see
reason based on faith, others as leading to faith. Some think
faith must account to reason, others believe reason should
eliminate faith. Scholars in the inner reformation tradition
believe that conversion in Jesus Christ is in principle total,
radical, and integral; that nothing in the life of the convert can
be left outside of the scope of allegiance to Jesus as Lord of

creation. Since all humans have both beliefs and concepts, these scholars argue that both the beliefs of faith and the concepts of reason ought to be subjected to the rule of the gospel.

Thus adherents of the inner reformation tradition believe that science or scholarship, as the systematic rational formation and use of precise and intricate networks of concepts called theories, must fall within the scope of conversion. At the same time they believe that science traditionally found its roots in soil foreign to the gospel—in-*isms* like rationalism, objectivism, scientism, and positivism. As a result these adherents believe that Christians active in scientific disciplines ought to celebrate their conversion by letting their faith have its effect in those disciplines. They should work in science for continuing reformation, changing science radically from within, pulling its roots out of its traditionally idolatrous soil and transplanting them in the soil of the gospel. This tradition calls for a radical, total, and integral reformation of the entire scientific enterprise.

At the same time people who support the inner reformation tradition affirm that science must maintain its own nature. An inner reformation does not seek to destroy science or make it unrecognizable. The need for reformation arises when science departs from its own nature and pretends to take on the structures of final truth and authoritative revelation. Science is certainly necessary in our culture, but in a radically reformed fashion.

Within the inner reformation tradition people regard this need for scientific reformation as a contemporary cultural priority. Scientific reform should not be just a hobby or an interesting pastime for certain gifted people; it is a core issue in the survival of our culture. It is important for Western culture, for our expanding and integrating world, and for the Christian church.

General historical context
When we survey the broad cultural background of the idea of an inner reformation of the sciences, we reach all the way back to the early struggles between the Christian church and other cultural powers in Western civilization. The church presented faith in divine revelation as the channel for hearing the ultimate voice of authority in human experience. This stance brought it into conflict with other voices making similar claims. We remember the ancient conflicts between church and state and

between faith and reason.[1] But the radical antithesis between the light of the gospel and the darkness of sin was often misunderstood by the early church. As a result many believers who reflected on faith in relation to reason resolved the tensions and conflicts by means of dualisms. They made attempts to retain the ultimacy of both faith and reason. Various strategies were used for this, such as synthesis between faith and reason, accommodation of the one to the other, or divisions of territory in which one authority would hold sway in one area of life, while a different one would rule in another area.

These dualistic solutions of the conflict between faith and reason as ultimate authorities caused serious misunderstandings of the rightful authority of analysis and of the rightful claims of the academic disciplines. In time these misunderstandings led to the doctrine of the autonomy of reason.[2] This doctrine implied at the very least that reason was not subject to any authority except its own. But soon enough it also took on a much more sweeping interpretation, namely, that all of human experience is subject to the authority of reason. Valid experience is rational experience. Consequently, rationality and scientific endeavor could not be submitted to the redemptive authority of God's revelation in Jesus. Instead, the academy grew to be the place where biblical authority was authoritatively rejected. Thus, scholarship came to be rooted in soil that was in principle hostile to the roots of the Christian religion.

But the dualisms were never the only approach. If we go as far back as Augustine we find his conviction that the light of the gospel is truly accepted whenever those who walk by it contend with the forces of darkness and attempt to live all of their life by that light. The forces of darkness have *de*formed reality; the light of the gospel must *re*form it. Since human life and the rest of reality are of one piece, no authority, not that of reason either, is possible or legitimate outside of the gospel.

This approach to conflicts between Christian faith and other powers may be called reformational. It seeks to *re*form through faith whatever has become *de*formed by its having been withdrawn from the authority of divine revelation. Whatever has been so withdrawn must be reformed from within by being brought to an integral fit within the radical wholeness of human life and the rest of reality.[3] The original condition of reality is not the broken world we know, but a shalom-filled creation. The gospel calls us to serve Jesus in restoring that original creation.[4]

Within the Protestant Reformation this view of the Christian religion was prominent in the work of John Calvin, who understood it to imply that synthesis and accommodation are not viable approaches to the conflict between the authority of the gospel and other voices of ultimacy. This led him to an explicit denial of the autonomy of reason and one may say that the inner reformation tradition in science originates in Calvin's approach to the authority of reason.[5]

It would not be correct, however, to say that the inner reformation tradition as a specific tradition began with John Calvin.[6] Though it appeals to Calvin, it did not arise until half a century ago.[7] It had its immediate origins in a nineteenth-century neo-Calvinian revival in the Netherlands, more specifically in the work of Abraham Kuyper, one of the people influenced by that revival.[8] Kuyper was particularly concerned to give public expression to the sovereign lordship of Christ in all areas (Kuyper's spheres) of human society.[9]

Early Kuyperians tried to follow the path of obedience to the gospel in the academy in an academically respectable way. At first they primarily just confessed this obedience and worked out a theological rationale. The first generation did not succeed in embodying it in a general scholarly approach. Later explicit theoretical elaboration of the meaning of Christ's sovereign lordship within scholarship is especially related to the philosophical work of second-generation Kuyperians at the Free University of Amsterdam.[10] This work sparked a neo-Kuyperian movement which on the North American continent became known as the reformational movement.[11] It is within this neo-Kuyperian movement that we find the expression "inner reformation of the sciences" and it is this movement's articulation of the relation between faith and learning to which I refer as the inner reformation tradition.

I will now sum up how adherents of this tradition see the interrelation of the gospel and academic study.[12] In the first place, they insist that no fundamental conflict between irreconcilable spiritual directions can be legitimately resolved by effecting a synthesis between the conflicting traditions. They acknowledge no division of ultimate authority between different territories. Science, too, has only one supreme authority—the authority that has been given to Jesus. Secondly, they believe this supreme authority must become manifest differently in the different areas of human life. A theory and a confession, a legal code and a moral code, a system of government and an economic order must all in their own way embody their subjection to the authority of Christ. A theory thus has its own proper authority which it can and ought to maintain over against other forms of authority. The government has authority, but not to dictate scientific truth. The economy has an authority all its own, but not to determine morality. However, although theory has authority of its own, it does not have autonomy. In the third place, people in this tradition believe philosophical reflection and awareness are necessary for the enterprise of inner reformation in order to contribute critical foundational perspectives, interdisciplinary coherence, and integral wholeness to the academic community. A comprehensive paradigm, model, or framework to guide the reformation of the sciences will enhance theoretical cohesion among scholars and disciplines; provided, of course, the philosophical reflection is designed to make these contributions. Fourthly, adherents insist that inner reformation is in principle a legitimate program for all the disciplines, not just for the humanities or social sciences, nor just for religion or moral analysis. The idea of the inner reformation of the sciences is a comprehensive idea. This leads to a fifth characteristic, the conviction that the inner reformation needs organized communal expression. Without the normal channels of the academy, that is, lectures, conferences, journals, societies, and institutions, the work of the inner reformation is bound to fail. Private hobby or individual inspiration would only prevent the formation of a genuine tradition. Finally, people working within this tradition aim for actual, concrete, practical differences and effects within the disciplines. They aim to go beyond matters of attitude or interpretation to an actual penetration of the disciplines with distinctive concepts and paradigms.

Some Examples
To summarize: within the inner reformation tradition we find scholars calling for total, radical, and integral change in the sciences. They understand this change not just in terms of a restructuring of theories but also in terms of religious redirection. Further, they believe it is not enough to witness to Christ's lordship among individual academics. They envision concrete conceptual penetration into the academic community through

concerted effort. Can this be more than a mere idea or ideal? In order to suggest that it can be, I will discuss briefly some philosophical contributions made by two neo-Kuyperians, namely, Herman Dooyeweerd and Nicholas Wolterstorff.[13]

God's sovereignty. Though what Dooyeweerd and his sympathizers have said on this point is clearly within the long established Calvinian tradition, their emphasis on God's sovereignty has led to renewed attention to the scholar's inability to say things about God with theoretical precision and certitude. In Dooyeweerd's thought, the sovereign God is not only the God who alone rules and guides the world, but also the God whose sovereignty transcends our ability to formulate theories about God. We cannot encapsulate God within our theoretical comprehension. Still, we can know God dependably. But such reliable knowledge is the knowledge of faith rather than of reason. A theological system tends to obscure that the God who is known and trusted is also the God who is mysterious and surprising. This contribution by Dooyeweerd leads to a critical openness in all our theorizing. No theoretical concept can ever lay claim to finality or eternity, not even a concept about something God reveals to us.[14] Social science must never come with theories about society or human relations which pretend absolute normativity linked to the divine nature or to divine revelation.[15]

Spiritual direction. God's guidance of creation from origin to destiny through the Spirit gives a direction to our lives and to history. So does the guidance of evil spirits. Dooyeweerd sharply distinguished this direction and consequently our own spirituality from the structures[16] of things. At the same time he saw these structures as the vehicle or pathway of spiritual direction.[17] Direction can only be the direction of structures; structures can only be structures of direction. This view makes it possible to distinguish between the question of good and evil as a different question from that of actual and concrete social structures. Good structures can be taken in an evil direction. Denatured structures can be redirected for good. Different views of social structures cannot by themselves constitute a difference between good and evil. The difference between monarchy and parliamentary democracy cannot be that as structure the one is necessarily good and the other naturally evil. Systems are good and evil primarily from the point of view of their spiritual direction.[18]

Order and subjectivity. The world manifests structures. Their origin lies in creation's being subjected to divine principles of origin. The divinely ordained order of creation, to which the actual creation is subjected, provides for a structured creation. This order is invariant and enduring. It is this divine order[19] which the Spirit follows and calls us to obey as creation moves to its destiny. A spiritual development which leads to structures that do not have their origin in the divine order of creation cannot ultimately lead to anything good.

Thus, though good and evil are not themselves structural matters, not all structures are necessarily paths to the good or for the good. Structure is not the same as direction. But at the same time we cannot address the one without the other. Structure and direction are integrally interwoven. A capitalist society as concrete society manifests a structural system as well as a spiritual direction. An evaluation of its reality must pay attention to all of its sides. The actual empirical structures of that society are never just the presence of the divinely ordained creation order, but a subjectively shaped structuration under the guidance of some spirit.

Time.[20] The world is thoroughly temporal and developing. God's Word and Spirit transcend creation in that they sovereignly and eternally mold and direct creation. But their presence in creation is always a presence in ever changing and developing subjectivity. God calls creation to move, change, grow, and develop. Newness and change are gifts of God, indications that the world is on the move toward its destiny. For that reason the theory of the order of creation is not properly used if it leads to static and conservative interpretations of social structures.

Religion. When used as a technical concept, the word *religion* refers to the radical, total, and integral concentration of all of creation in the human self. The state of the universe is at any one time determined in part by human obedience or disobedience by this question: Has the human community responded responsibly to God's Word and Spirit or irresponsibly to the pseudorevelation of an evil spirit? Evil spirits contend with

God through the human community. God brings redemption through the human community. That is what Dooyeweerd means by religion.[21] Religion nevertheless determines history only in part. God is faithful to maintain the order of creation and to guide creation to its true destiny through the renewed human community in the new Adam. The church is the first fruit of that renewal. This view of religion implies that no human problems can be religiously neutral. Hence the pursuit of the inner reformation of science.

Irreducibility. The concept of a creation order for created reality implies that the inviolable invariance of that order requires us to respect the ultimate integrity of different kinds of order. Different kinds of order cannot be reduced to one another. We must not interpret a subject as an object or mistake a subject-object relation for a part-whole relation. We must beware that functions of one kind (e.g., the organic functions of living things) must not be confused with functions of another kind (e.g., the mechanical functions of material things). We must respect entities as wholes. They are different from the totality of the functions they have. The creation is a fundamental unity in its origin in the one God. But it is also radically and irreducibly varied and diverse. God calls creation to be one in spirit and multiple in its structures.

Society. Dooyeweerd incorporates all of the above concepts in his concept of human society. Society is first of all a total, religious, communal category. Human society as a totality cannot be reduced to being a state, or an economy, or even a church. At the same time we cannot have society unless it develops into states, economies, churches, and so forth. And these various functionally different social realities cannot be reduced to one another. A state is not an economy; a church is not a therapeutic group.

For people in the inner reformation tradition who work with these admittedly very philosophical concepts, the important thing is that these concepts are viewed as originating in an interpretation of fundamental biblical teachings and as leading to specific interpretations of reality, including social reality. This tradition, therefore, has given every indication that the idea of inner reformation is a possibility, that is, biblical principles via philosophical frameworks can lead to an interpretation of categories of social reality that lead to changes in social theory.[22]

But to find oneself within the inner reformation tradition one need not be a Dooyeweerdian. Nicholas Wolterstorff's *ReasonWithin the Bounds of Religion*[23] clearly demonstrates an attempt to redirect the theoretical enterprise from within, though without the use of the concepts and categories developed by Dooyeweerd. Wolterstorff, too, has developed a number of theoretical approaches that can concretely help us in facing the task of theoretical reorientation.[24] I will draw attention here to two concepts of his that are of special significance for the sciences. One is his concept of the different kinds of beliefs; the other is his concept of shalom in practice.

Theory of beliefs. Wolterstorff distinguishes between data beliefs, data background beliefs, and control beliefs. Data beliefs are the beliefs we form about our world as we focus on certain realities and try to get to know them. Data background beliefs are beliefs we have already formed about our world. They function as the assumed context when we form data beliefs. Control beliefs direct us to make choices when we form data beliefs or compose theories which incorporate data and background beliefs.

Control beliefs, then, play a fundamental role when we accept or reject a theory. Among these control beliefs we find beliefs of our fundamental Christian commitment.[25] They function in such a way that when data beliefs or data background beliefs come into conflict with beliefs of commitment we often are inclined to reject such data or data background beliefs or the theory which leads to them.

Wolterstorff's theory of beliefs contributes significantly to the program of the inner reformation of the sciences. He clearly distinguishes between data and data beliefs. He thus accentuates the subjective component in all our factual knowledge and makes it impossible for us to claim absolute certainty or objectivity for our information. We ourselves have formed our beliefs. This does not mean our beliefs cannot be true. They can be and must be. But they are not true without their subjective and historical components.

In a second significant contribution, Wolterstorff insists that specific beliefs can and do function in all three ways. Whether or not a belief is a new data belief, an assumed background belief, or a deeply rooted control belief depends in part on how it functions in a theory. We may focus on atomic particles to form data beliefs about them. We may also assume beliefs about atomic particles as background beliefs when forming a theory about genetic transmission via DNA. And we may be so committed to the ultimacy of atomic particles that our beliefs about them control our rejection of anything but material reality as real. And the same is true about beliefs we may have as a result of our belonging to Jesus. We may sometimes critically focus on them, sometimes assume them, and sometimes find them helping us reject a theory or accept something otherwise quite unbelievable.

A third concept of significance in Wolterstorff's theory is that since our beliefs themselves can at any time function as data, or as background, or as control, it is clear that beliefs themselves give us no ultimate clue as to what our control beliefs should be. Our ultimate commitment which underlies its specific belief content, rather than the specific beliefs that may articulate this content, ultimately shapes our decision as to which of our beliefs will at a given moment function as control beliefs.[26]

Shalom in practice. With his theory of beliefs Wolterstorff has articulated an important conviction within the inner reformation tradition, namely, that we are responsible for our beliefs. It is therefore no wonder that after he developed this theory a decade ago and after further reflections on the relation between theory and praxis he gave more thought to the concept of control in the formation of theories. He had already concluded that rational beliefs could not be ultimate even in their own formation. He now also concluded that theory, rather than controlling praxis, must itself be controlled by its service to praxis. In our present sociohistorical situation we must direct theory by asking what beneficial effects it will have for bringing peace and justice to our world. We can focus the religious direction of the scholarly enterprise of our day if we concentrate on our world's outcry for shalom. This focus must not merely set our agenda in terms of what theories we propose to work on. It must internally shape the whole theoretical enterprise.

In this further articulation Wolterstorff gives evidence of his commitment to the belief of the inner reformation tradition that there can be no separation between our faith and other dimensions of our experience and world. The inner reformation tradition rejects a faith-reason separation, a church-state separation, a secular-sacred separation. Without the inner integration of our faith within the other areas (Wolterstorff's reason within the bounds of religion), we shall on the one hand have a faith out of touch with those areas and probably for that reason a dead or conservative faith, while on the other hand we shall have areas of life undirected by our faith and probably for that reason in conflict with biblical directives.

Further Contributions
The complexity of science is vast and the inner reformation tradition is young and supported by a small community. For that reason I am encouraged by even the few examples I have been able to mention as fruits of this tradition. But we need to accomplish much more to give the tradition viability in the contemporary world of scholarship. An example of an area needing more attention is that of unresolved controversies about polarities: fact-value, objective-subjective, reason-faith, and others. Too often the discussions among Christians in science center on having to choose for one or the other. The inner reformation tradition helps us to see the poles as the opposite ends of continuous lines, or as the sides of correlations. This helps us to understand the controversies and to resolve them by viewing them as accents on a continuum or in a correlation, rather than as oppositions or alternatives. I shall look at some of these polarities now.

Objective universal fact or subjective individual value? Suppose we see one task of science as the formation of theories and we take theories to be the conceptual abstraction and articulation of general structures. Then we can see a double relationship at work. On the one hand there is the correlation of subjective, empirical reality and the divine order of creation. In the structures of things we analyze, we see evidence of order within empirical reality. With the methods of analysis or conceptual inquiry we arrive at concepts, propositions, laws, and theories. In these we have isolated the general structures concrete reality displays as a result of its subjection to divine order. On the other hand there is the continuum of reality which at one end presents us with the more or less simple, precise, and mechanical world of mathematics and physics, while at the other end we have the bewilderingly complex, fluid, dynamic world of ethics and theology. These are not opposite poles, but ends of a spectrum. In between are such worlds as those studied in the life sciences, psychology, aesthetics, semantics and logic, sociology, economics, and law.

In this double relationship of a correlation related to a continuum we can understand some of the accents in science. As science moves deeper and deeper into the structures of reality toward the order of creation, theories become simpler, more universal, and more permanent. This is not more true when we talk about the principles of physics than when we talk about principles of human society. The law symbolized by $E=mc^2$ is neither more nor less simple, universal, or permanent than the law that human beings must be just in order to survive. On the other hand, as science in its investigation of structures comes closer and closer to the subjective, empirical, historical realities that exhibit these structures, the theories become more complex, less general in scope, and more relative. This is true for certain physical theories just as much as for economic theory.

We can also see now that as our investigations approach the ultimate limits of human experience they become more and more characterized by controversy, urgency, subjectivity, relevance, and religiosity. And the more we attend to the ultimate functional foundations of all reality, the more detached, common, and objective we appear to be. The upshot is that the more accurate and quantitative we can be, the less meaningful our work appears, even though it increases in shared reliability. And the more exciting our work, the more subjective and individual our certainty.

But all of this, I wish to stress, is relative: "the more, the less" is the operative concept, rather than "either this or that." The theorist as well as the reality about which we theorize have a variety of limits. These limits or extremes of a spectrum also show up in our theories. And they show up more visibly as we move toward them, while they recede from visibility as we move away from them. But none completely disappear, nor do any appear in full clarity by themselves. From universal principle, to statistical generalization, to frequent tendency we move in a continuum which can be a continuum only when the ends remain connected.

Neutral theory and biased practice? Some of us so strongly oppose belief in neutrality that we overreact to verificationism and objectivism. However, science in its formation of theories always aims at what is common and universal in empirical reality. Therefore science *appears* objective, neutral, and aloof from practice. These features of science can easily be misinterpreted—and they have been. But they are simply a function of the scientific experience of structures that are common and universal. Commonality and universality carry their testimony with them in the work of the scientist who investigates them. At the same time, true science understood as a subjective and historical human activity cannot just simply and wholly *be* neutral, or objective, or beyond practice. If the structures laid bare in theory are genuine structures of created reality, they are structures of and for the practice of human life. They can be real only in the practice of human life. And we can test our concepts of them only in that practice. The most abstract structures, if real, are eminently practical in their own meaning. And genuine science cannot but be practical.

Abstract theory or relevant practice? At heart, the true method of science is always the method of analysis: abstraction, generalization, conceptualization, and articulation by means of comparison and contrast, argument and conclusion, naming and definition. There is no conflict here with the confession that genuine analysis has its roots in the gospel. This recognition of the character of science simply supports and confirms that science has the specific authority of analysis and that the scientist must therefore observe the authority of analysis. No theoretician may violate analytic canons. No interpretation of our confession may violate the requirements of genuine science if, indeed, we also confess that science is itself real and genuine only when it heeds the order of creation. We must do full justice to the fact that science is predominantly analytic.

But science, though predominantly analytic, is also more than analytic. And its predominant components must be thoroughly and integrally interwoven with the "more" in science. However, science would perish if this integration would undo its universality, its distance from concrete realities, or its aloofness from life's immediacies. Adherents of the inner reformation tradition will have to give full honor to science's analytic character if a reformation is to be achieved.

Science and religion. Many traditions in science exemplify the need for reform, but none as clearly as that tradition which reduces the fullness of what knowledge is to that kind of knowing which is characteristic of science, namely, analytic, conceptual, theoretical knowing. That tradition, by also making that sort of knowing autonomous in or even determinative of human experience, has been mainly responsible for rejecting faith as knowing and for denying revelation as truth. In this way the oldest, most pervasive, and most influential tradition on knowing in our culture misformed our understanding of analysis and science and denatured our understanding of truth, faith, and knowing.

One consequence of this history has been a rivalry between faith and reason. This rivalry was fundamentally a clash between two faiths and two ultimate claims to authority. So it is important to realize that the dominant Western tradition about theory is not just a theory. It is a theory religiously committed to itself. It is a faith commitment to theory in which theory takes on revelatory qualities. Its claims do not pit theory against religion, but religion against religion, with the qualification that the religion of theory is uncritical with respect to its own status.

It is important to understand the nature of this uncritical attitude. If someone is committed to theory as ultimate, for that person all knowledge which does not meet the standards of theoretical knowledge is pseudo knowledge. But knowledge informed by a commitment to theory cannot meet its own standards. It cannot theoretically meet the demands for verification of its own ultimacy and autonomy. I cannot verify my belief that only verified knowledge is real knowledge.[27]

When people in the inner reformation tradition criticize the dominant tradition in theory, they do not merely criticize a rival theory with a theory of their own. Rather, they approach a rival religious tradition with a call for religious redirection. In the context of that religious meeting of minds it is crucial that within the inner reformation tradition the traditional notions of truth, knowledge, and certainty be examined with the utmost rigor and dedication. This is not a philosophical luxury. These notions are for the most part still almost entirely unexamined assumptions for many theorists. Their assumption in the disciplines makes it impossible to ask attention for alternative approaches to traditional theories, for these alternatives cannot be evaluated unless there is a prior willingness to entertain alternative notions of knowledge, truth, and certainty.

Evaluation

Should we try to develop a Christian tradition in scholarship? This question can be resolved into three questions, and each concerns the role of science and of Christian believers in our culture: (1) Does science still present itself, in one way or another, as a cultural priority? (2) Do scientists still follow traditions whose need for spiritual reorientation is a cultural priority in our day? and (3) Do Christian believers in the academy show any competence in bringing redemptive redirection to the sciences?

I can make a case for answering all three questions affirmatively. But the opposite is also possible. We can make both cases. And for that reason when we answer these questions we need to make a choice, a decision. In the face of conflicting evidence, how do we choose? In the 1978 version of this paper, I was pessimistic and skeptical. But events in the intervening years have consolidated the positive elements in my evaluation that were also present earlier. In the general climate surrounding reflection on theory, we see that objectivity, neutrality, and rationalistic arrogance have made place for more awareness of relativity, subjectivity, the role of fundamental perspectives, and the contribution to knowledge of other than rational elements. Christian academics seem more interested, more serious, and more numerous than a number of years ago. So my choice is for stressing the evidence that supports answering the three questions positively.

I believe science is still a formidable force in our culture. It still presents itself credibly to millions as the reliable source of knowledge and truth. And since science plays this role by largely ignoring anything but physical reality and logical methods, that is, since the truth it presents is still a version of rational naturalism, science continues to lead our culture astray and to present as knowledge a disjointed conglomerate of information leading to increasing lack of wisdom and judgment. Christians in this situation give more and more evidence of moving in a different direction and of making a difference in doing so.

But even if we do choose to answer our questions positively, other obstacles present themselves. Are there enough people? Are they and can they be in touch with each other? Are the resources available? Here too, I now believe, cautiously hopeful answers can be given. Christian institutions of higher learning have begun to cooperate nationally and internationally. Scholars in various branches have banded together in societies. Journals and conferences are on the increase.

At a time when a new sense of community is perhaps being forged, when ties are still fragile, and the emergence of a common mind still suffers from clashing traditions and too vague a sense of what brings us together, it will not be helpful to move too fast and to be overly definite and determinate. Each contributing group and each individual will contribute most by being humble and open-minded, by listening to others and being eager to serve. Perhaps one thing could help us move ahead. I have in mind our attempt to understand, know, and experience what it means that the overwhelming influence of the scholarly tradition has always made people opt for rational naturalism, for autonomous secularity, for human emancipation from spirituality and transcendence as sources of authority and truth. What does it mean to be spiritual in science? What would it take to open science up to other dimensions of reality besides those of matter and reason? And what might the effects be? These, it seems to me, are crucial realities to face. And many are preparing themselves to face them. So perhaps there is yet another opportunity in our time to forge a redemptive Christian presence in the world of scholarship, still time to redirect one of the most important forces of modern culture.

Notes

1. Augustine and Tertullian proposed different solutions to the faith-reason conflict. Augustine struggled with the relationship and came to different conclusions at different times in his life, including more than one position even during his Christian period. (On this see the unpublished paper "Through Philosophy to Faith: Augustine's Evolution Reconsidered" by Leo C. Ferrari of St. Thomas University in Frederiction, New Brunswick, read at the 1985 meeting of the Canadian Philosophical Association in Montreal.) Tertullian became famous for his contemptuous "Jerusalem and Athens" approach, in which the one can have nothing to do with the other.

2. Perhaps the earliest crystallization of the struggle in the form of this doctrine is found in the work of John Scotus Eriugena. This means that it took till the ninth century before the authority struggle began to be settled in favor of reason. But the struggle itself is as old as Paul's letters to the Christians of Corinth.

3. For a recent treatment of this way of being a Christian believer see the analysis of world formative religion in Nicholas Wolterstorff, *Until Justice and Peace Embrace* (Grand Rapids: Eerdmans, 1983).

4. This characterization of the gospel is as old as Paul's formulation of it in Colossians 1:15-20. Though the idea is prominent in the inner Reformation tradition, it is not limited to Reformed or even Protestant Christian traditions. For a powerful contemporary Roman Catholic treatment, see Matthew Fox, *Original Blessing: A Primer in Creation Spirituality* (Santa Fe: Bear & Company, 1983).

5. See Hendrik Hart, Johan van der Hoeven, and Nicholas Wolterstorff, eds., *Rationality in the Calvinian Tradition* (Lanham, MD: University Press of America, 1983).

6. People often do not sufficiently understand the complexity and variety of Christian views on the relevance of faith to academic pursuits. When I say the inner Reformation tradition is historically "specific," I mean more specific than Calvinian approaches to reason in general. The latter, in turn, are more specific than world reformative approaches in general. And these, again, are only one trend in the variety of approaches found within the Christian tradition.

7. The first public and institutional embodiments are the publication of Herman Dooyeweerd's *Wijsbegeerte der Wetsidee* (later translated and published as *A New Critique of Theoretical Thought*, even though a more literal translation of the original Dutch title would have been "Philosophy of the cosmonomic idea," by which Dooyeweerd meant to indicate his fundamental Calvinian conviction that the entire creation is subjected to the cosmic law of the sovereign Creator, God, and that, consequently, nothing in creation has any original authority) and the organization of the Association for Calvinist Philosophy, both in 1935.

8. For a recent treatment of Kuyperian influences in contemporary North America, see George Marsden's contribution in Alvin Plantinga and Nicholas Wolterstorff, eds., *Faith and Rationality: Reason and Belief in God* (Notre Dame, IN: University of Notre Dame Press, 1983).

9. Kuyper's leadership gave rise to Christian labor unions, political parties, and institutions of higher learning. At least three such institutions arose on three continents more than a century ago: the Free University of Amsterdam (Europe), the Potchefstroom University for Christian Higher Education (Africa), and Calvin College of Grand Rapids, Michigan (North America).

10. Dirk Hendrik Theodoor Vollenhoven and Herman Dooyeweerd are the authors of this philosophical approach. Both received appointments at the Free University in 1928, from which they did not retire till the 1960s. See C.T. McIntire, ed., *The Legacy of Herman Dooyeweerd* (Lanham, MD: University Press of America, 1985).

11. Characteristically, publicly organized manifestations were again in the fields of labor (Christian Labour Association of Canada), politics (Citizens for Public Justice), and education (Institute for Christian Studies and Curriculum Development Centre), all based in Toronto, Canada.

12. I assume that my summary covers all neo-Kuyperians and not only the followers of Dooyeweerd among them. It includes a "common sense Calvinian" like Nicholas Wolterstorff, who as a neo-Kuyperian will recognize this summary as one he shares, even though he is not in the Amsterdam school of Calvinian philosophy.

13. I chose Dooyeweerd because his work is undoubtedly to date the most magisterial, comprehensive, and influential elaboration of an articulate philo-

sophical position within the tradition. I chose Wolterstorff to demonstrate that to develop fruitful and penetrating philosophical ideas within the tradition one does not need to subscribe to the ideas of Dooyeweerd in particular or to those of the Amsterdam school in general. Others could have been chosen, such as D. H. T. Vollenhoven, C. Van Til, H. Stoker, H. Runner, or A. Plantinga. Vollenhoven concentrated in the history of philosophy and is, therefore, less suitable to provide examples. Further, none of his work is in English. His pioneering work in historiographical methodology, however, remains fruitful for those who continue to use it. Van Til's distinctive work is almost exclusively theological. Stoker has had little influence even though he has been very original. Runner has been very influential but has published no original work. Plantinga's work has been mostly polemical and apologetic.

14. Precisely this point is at issue in Donald R. Hettinga's critique of Paul Marshall, *Thine Is the Kingdom* (Basingstoke: Marshall, Morgan, & Scott, 1984). See "Frameworks for Politics," *The Banner* (September 9, 1985): 20.

15. Neither Dooyeweerd nor some of his followers in the social sciences have themselves always honored this principle. Via the theory of creation ordinances, Dooyeweerd's theories have often been interpreted — also by himself — as faithful renditions of God's very will.

16. The structure of a thing, for Dooyeweerd, is the typical interrelation of its properties and relations.

17. We are directed through structures. The Spirit of God directs history along the paths of the Word of God.

18. That systems and structures are nevertheless not neutral affairs will become evident from the next paragraph on order and subjectivity.

19. In the Dooyeweerdian tradition, this order is often referred to as the Word of God in Scripture. Consequently, Dooyeweerd's distinction between structure and direction in the world is an interpretation of the Bible's distinction between Word and Spirit.

20. Dooyeweerd's concept of time is his point of entry to deal with the goodness of change, history, and relativity without falling into the temptation of relativism or historicism. A temporal world, for Dooyeweerd, is a world called to change within a framework of order.

21. Religion is, therefore, not the same as faith for Dooyeweerd. Faith is a term that refers to one human function among many. Whether or not one's faith (which all humans have) is true depends on one's religion, that is, on whether or not one is totally, integrally, and radically incorporated within a community that seeks to be shaped by God's Word as it seeks to follow God's Spirit.

22. Though I shall not do so here, one can demonstrate that all interpretations of fundamental social categories, via philosophical frameworks, are rooted in spiritual principles, among which we often find apostate principles. I would need to do this, however, to complete an argument for the legitimacy of the claim that theory requires inner reformation.

23. Nicholas Wolterstorff, *Reason within the Bounds of Religion* (Grand Rapids: Eerdmans, 1976).

24. Besides the book just mentioned, the most relevant publications are the Introduction to *Faith and Rationality* (cited in note 8 above) and the chapter on theory in *Until Justice and Peace Embrace* (cited in note 3 above).

25. Even though Wolterstorff does in no way depend on Michael Polanyi's work, his threefold distinction of data, data background, and control beliefs

has a remarkable resemblance to Polanyi's focal, tacit, and commitment dimensions of knowing. See Michael Polanyi, *Personal Knowledge: Towards a Post-critical Philosophy* (London: Routledge & Kegan Paul, 1958).

26. See also Hendrik Hart, "The Articulation of Belief: A Link between Rationality and Commitment," in *Rationality in the Calvinian Tradition*, cited in note 5 above).

27. Alvin Plantinga aptly refers to this as the self-referential incoherence of commitment to reason as basic foundation.

Objectivity under attack: rethinking paradigms in social theory - a survey
M. Elaine Botha

The myth of neutrality

The greatest superstition of our time is the belief in the ethical neutrality of science. Even the slogan of ethical neutrality itself implies a programme and a credo. Wolfgang Köhler, one of the greatest psychologists of our time, searched all his life for the "place of value in a world of facts" — the title of the book in which he summed up his personal philosophy. But there is no need to search for such a place because the values are diffused through all the strata of the various sciences, as the invisible bubbles of air are diffused in the waters of a lake, and we are the fish who breathe them in all the time through the gills of intuition. Our educational establishment, from the departments of physics through biology and genetics, up to the behavioural and social sciences, willy-nilly imparts to the students a Weltanschauung, *a system of values wrapped up in a package of facts. But the choice of the shape of the package is determined by its invisible content; or to change the metaphor, our implicit values provide the non-Euclidian curvature, the subtle distortion of the world of facts.*[1]

This quotation which states very frankly that scientific neutrality in the sphere of science is a myth, reflects a variety of symptoms of a certain sort that are now prevalent in different fields of science. What the symptoms in question indicate is that there is a clear reorientation taking place in the attitude of neutrality to science. The fact that the quotation is part of a lecture delivered during a Nobel symposium is certainly not without significance. The exposure of the neutrality postulate as a myth has already taken place in the philosophy of science, and is now making its impact on practically all the natural and social sciences.

This movement in a fundamentally new direction is taking place in practically all disciplines. It is interesting to note that the discussion concerning neutrality, objectivity, freedom from values, and engagement in science has advanced far enough to lead to a radical rethinking of the basic paradigms in social theory in general. The paradigms under discussion involve such questions as the accepted model of science instrumental in most disciplines, the relationship between facts and values, the problem of theory and practice, and the role of ideology in science.

When Christian social scientists are confronted with these developments, they face quite a dilemma. The neutrality postulate, which until recently was one of the practically unassailable strongholds of science, has been subjected to heavy criticism both from within and from without. The result—and this is what Christian social scientists must face up to—is that the former enemy of Christian scholarship has been defeated by combatants who could be regarded as strange bedfellows for the Christian scholar. The heavy attack after all came from assailants outside the circle of Christian scholarship.

This attack, which has made its impact felt over a wide spectrum of disciplines and has exposed the positivistic foundations of the basic model of science long operative in those disciplines, has caused such a breakthrough that the positivistic foundations of science can now be said to have been radically undermined. In social science in general, the result has been a deep awareness of a crisis which has resulted in a radical rethinking of the basic paradigms in use.

The discovery that the supposed enemy has apparently ceased its opposition and, furthermore, that a good part of the attack was carried out by scholars who certainly do not share the fundamental viewpoint of the Christian scholar gives rise to a serious question: Is the Christian scholar's equipment adequate to cope with the new problems posed by the crisis of social science and the reorientation of social theory?

My goal in this paper is to touch on the main contours of the new direction in social science. Specific attention will be given to the developments within the philosophy of science that were instrumental in the new developments within the social sciences. Some of the fundamental problems in this area have already been dealt with by scholars from the reformational tradition, but the contributions that have made to date still seem few and far between.

Positivism as a target

Stephen Toulmin[2] is of the opinion that the developments within the philosophy of science, in some strange sense, serve as a litmus paper by which one can determine the nature of the changes in direction that have taken place in the sciences during the past decade. He affirms that there is a clear change of focus in the philosophy of science and that this change became manifest in virtually all the disciplines, especially in the course of the 1960s. The contributing factors that eventually culminated in these developments can be traced back to the original roots of positivism and empiricism, but they are mainly reactions to the neopositivist model of science that developed during the early twentieth century.

At the turn of the century, practically all of the sciences manifested a strong tendency toward a formal, natural scientific model of theory and concept formation. This model of science was primarily ahistorical and was directed mainly at the formal aspects of science; logical propositions and the conceptual structure of scientific theories, as well as abstractly mathematical formulae and models, were characteristic of this development, which Toulmin speaks of aptly as the "Formalist revolution."[3]

Across the whole spectrum of the sciences, from logic through mathematics to the social sciences and even to the arts, the core of the intellectual task was defined in static, structural, ahistorical, and—wherever possible—mathematical terms.[4] In the philosophy of science this development was precipitated by way of an attempt to completely eradicate all subjective elements on the one hand, which meant on the other hand that a systematic effort had to be made to prove that science is objective. Philosophers of science therefore concerned themselves primarily with the analysis of the formal structure and system of scientific thought, giving priority to questions of logical justification. Scientific discoveries, conceptual renewal, and the growth of scientific knowledge were considered of secondary importance—or even totally irrelevant.

It was in the context of this state of affairs that a change of direction came about. In this paper I will deal with the provocation that led to the change, the nature of the change itself, and the shift of focus with regard to various theoretical points of conflict. The past decade was characterized by a revolution in the philosophy of science. In this revolution, the new approach

claims totally new insights into the structure and nature of
scientific theory and its development. It also introduces new
solutions to traditional problems within the theory of science.[5]
    What is it these new theories are actually opposed to?
    Shapere characterizes the rebellion as "the revolt against
positivism."[6] The brand of positivism against which the revolt
is directed is logical positivism or neopositivism, which is a
twentieth century variation of the older, more familiar positivism of Auguste Comte. Logical positivism as a scientific school
of thought, is indebted to the "Vienna Circle" (*Wiener Kreis*).[7]
However, the opposition is also directed toward a conception
of science that is strongly influenced by positivism in general
and logical positivism in particular. The so-called standard
view of science or the received view of scientific theories that
resulted from logical positivist approach will be discussed in a
later context.[8]
    In the general empirical and positivistic conception of
science, science is viewed as an institution for the acquisition of
true knowledge about nature. Observation and experiment lay
the groundwork for acquiring this knowledge. The process of
scientific research starts with the collection of data through
observation and experiments. Relying on such data, the scientist reaches laws of nature by way of induction, generalization,
abstraction, and idealization. Those laws of nature are regarded as present in nature itself, where they are discovered by
the observer. Scientific examiners, then, are guided in their
work by their experience; they function mainly as passive registering instruments.[9]
    It is clear that such a view of science leaves very little scope
for reflection on the validity of the methods used or their relevance. The primary concern will be the eradication of all speculative or metaphysical elements that cannot be forced into the
mold of sense experience. In the preceding section, I pointed to
"positivism" as the target at which the revolution in the philosophy of science was particularly aimed. But it takes little
argument to show that "positivism" is hard to define; as a
movement it has been dynamic rather than static and has taken
on different forms in different historical contexts.
    Habermas summarizes Comte's philosophy of science in
the form of a set of rules all covered by the term *positive*.
Included among the rules are the following:
    1. The basic rule is that all knowledge has to prove itself

through sense certainty of systematic observation that secures intersubjectivity.

2. Methodological certainty is just as important as sense certainty. The reliability of scientific knowledge is guaranteed by unity of method.

3. The demand for precision in knowledge is warranted only by the formally cogent construction of theories that allow the deduction of law-like hypotheses.

4. There is demand for the utility of knowledge in order to ensure technical control over nature and society by means of science. What is necessary is a unification of theories, and acquaintance with laws which allow both explanation of facts and the possibility of their prediction.

5. Knowledge is, in principle, incomplete and relative to the nature of the positive spirit. Scientific knowledge does not pretend to know the absolute reality and is not, like metaphysics, the knowledge of ultimate origins.[10]

Positivism can also be summed up in the three basic tenets formulated by von Wright.[11] For many of the social sciences, these tenets have to a great extent influenced the conception of what constitutes a respectable scientific discipline.

The first tenet is methodological monism or the idea of the unity of scientific method amid the diverse subject matter of scientific investigation. The second tenet is that the exact natural sciences—especially mathematical physics—set a methodological ideal or standard by which to measure the degree of development and perfection achieved by the other sciences, including the humanities. The third tenet is a characteristic view of scientific explanation as "causal." More specifically, this involves the subsumption of individual cases under hypothetically assumed general laws of nature, including "human nature." It is remarkable that even though few Anglo-Saxon thinkers have been positivists in the strict sense of either Comtean positivism or logical positivism, the positivist temper has had a profound influence upon them all the same. According to Bernstein, the positivist temper basically recognizes only two models for legitimate knowledge—the empirical or natural sciences and the formal disciplines such as logic and mathematics.[12] Anything that cannot be reduced to either of these two models and does not satisfy the severe standards set by such disciplines is to be regarded with suspicion. Historically, mainstream social scientists have come to view their own disciplines through the spectacles of positivism. Not only was positivism in its Comtean guise built into practically all the social science disciplines as a cornerstone of their epistemology, but the influence of logical positivism soon dismantled the grand edifice of social and political philosophy, with the result that the subject matter of the social and political sciences was sorted out into a triad of empirical, definitional, or meaningless components.

Logical positivism contributed to a conception of science in which science was seen as a system of statements that are related to one another as axiomatic systems of conceptual pyramids built up according to the principle of noncontradiction.[13] The core of the problem was how these scientific language systems were anchored in reality. The Vienna Circle's famous discussion of so-called protocol sentences, in which Carnap, Neurath, and Zilsel participated in 1932-33, is a clear example of this.

In logical positivism the emphasis gradually shifted to the justification of scientific theories, the so-called "context of justification." Because of this development, the content of research and the genesis of scientific theories were regarded as subordinate to the central problem of the justification of scientific theories and the legitimation of those theories. This focus also brought the problem of the verification of scientific theories to the foreground.

The philosophy of science was seen as a kind of formal logic that concerned itself primarily with the formal sides of scientific theories and with the reconstruction of the logic of scientific findings; it was not to concern itself, however, with the content of these formally logical tenets. The difference between the so-called "context of discovery" and the "context of justification," which was originally formulated by Hans Reichenbach,[14] now served as an important point of departure. The lack of interest in the history of the sciences must be viewed against this background. When the formal and logical facets of the scientific results are regarded as primary, it stands to reason that the contents of science—and therefore also the history of the practice of science—will be of less importance.

The other pole of this school of thought (that of logical empiricism), laid especially heavy emphasis on the necessity of grounding these formalized theories in empirical reality or experience. To carry this grounding out, the familiar distinction between observational and theoretical terms was introduced.[15] Observational terms would be directly grounded in experience, while theoretical terms would be bound to empirical proofs via scientific hypotheses. It hardly needs to be demonstrated that on this level of scientific work all contact with the reality with which science is ultimately concerned is gradually lost. This distinction between observational and theoretical terms has become known as the "two-tier view of science."[16] Furthermore, logical positivism has long proclaimed that the natural scientific methodology is a model for the social sciences—with the ideal of the "Idea of a Unified Science" in the background.

Historical background to the "received view" of scientific theories
The so-called standard view of science was a response to the prevalent scientific attitude of the late nineteenth century, which was a blend of Comtean positivism, materialism, and mechanism. According to mechanistic materialism, science can present a picture of the world that is firmly based on empirical inquiry rather than philosophical speculation. The materialistic-mechanistic point of view was followed by the neo-Kantian philosophy of science which saw the task of science as the dicovery of the general form or structure of sensations. The task of science is to discover the structure of the ideal world—the structures of phenomena which are not structures of the thing-in-itself.

Other schools also reacted against this mechanistic-materialistic worldview. Mach's intial neo-Kantian position was gradually modified; what emerged was a neo-positivist position in which he came to reject any a priori elements in the constitution of our knowledge of things. Mach argued that science is no more than a conceptual reflection on facts of which elements are contents of consciousness provided by sensation. Scientific statements must be empirically verifiable, which implies that all empirical statements in scientific theory must be capable of being reduced to statements about sensations.

With the gradual acceptance of quantum physics and the new physics of Einstein, the position of materialistic mechanism was undermined. The focus on causality and determinism was replaced by the notions of chance and indeterminacy which had a profound effect on the existing view of science. As a result of this change, a crisis developed in the conception of science prevalent at that time. This crisis caused the philosophy of science to develop along different lines, including the lines of thought that later became known as the Berlin School (associated with Hans Reichenbach) and the Vienna Circle (associated with Moritz Schlick). The conception of science developed on the foundations of logical positivism eventually became known as the "standard conception of science" or the "received view" or "orthodox view" of scientific theories. The members of the Vienna Circle were opposed to the introduction of any metaphysical entities in science and philosophy. The original version of the "received view" of scientific theories, according to Suppe (1974), reads basically as follows: A scientific theory is to be axiomatized in mathematical logic. The terms of the logical axiomatization are to be divided into three types: (1) logical and mathematical terms, (2) theoretical terms, and (3) observational terms which are given a phenomenal or observational interpretation. The axioms of the theory are formulations of scientific law; they specify relationships holding between theoretical terms. Theoretical terms are merely abbreviations for phenomenal descriptions; that is to say, they are descriptions involving only observational terms. Thus the axiomatizations must include various explicit definitions for the theoretical terms in the form $Tx \equiv Ox$, where "T" is a theoretical term and "O" is an observational term. Such explicit definitions are called "correspondence rules," since they coordinate theoretical terms with corresponding combinations of observational terms. The observation terms refer to specified phenomena or phenomenal properties, and the only interpretation given to theoretical terms is their explicit definition provided by the correspondence rules.[17]

The "received view" of scientific theories provided a means of avoiding the introduction of metaphysical entities. Since metaphysical entities are not phenomenal or observational entities, the terms used to describe them cannot be observation terms. Therefore they must be theoretical terms. However, since theoretical terms are allowed only if they can be provided with correspondence rules to give them an explicit phenomenal definition, no objectionable, metaphysical entities can be introduced into scientific theories.

If the "received view" could eliminate the introduction of objectionable entities in scientific theories, why could it not be extended to philosophy and to all discourse? The advocates of the "received view" could see no reason why it could not. Therefore, under the influence of Wittgenstein's doctrine of logically perfect language, they broadened the "received view" into a general doctrine of cognitive significance: the only meaningful discourse was discourse conducted in terms of phenomenal language or that used terms that were abbreviations for expressions in phenomenal language. Any assertions that failed to meet these requirements were branded metaphysical nonsense.

All cognitively significant discourse about the world had to be empirically verifiable. Under the original version of the "received view," all assertions of a scientific theory are reducible to assertions in protocol language about phenomenal experience. Thus the problem of the verification of assertions was reduced to the question of how observation language and protocol language assertions are to be verified. Different theses were advanced in response to this question, including the proposal that the observation language or protocol language would be either (1) a sense-datum language that would provide a phenomenalistic characterization of experience, or (2) either a physicalistic language or a thing language in which one speaks of material things and ascribes observable properties to them.

Physicalism ultimately won the day: the observational terms in the "received view" were interpreted as referring to material things and observable properties. The verification of physicalistic assertions was taken to be nonproblematic. As the Vienna Circle further investigated the nature of scientific knowledge, the "received view" underwent considerable modification and evolution.

Allied with the "received view" is the conception of the growth of knowledge in which scientific progress and development are seen as cumulative. Science establishes theories which, if highly confirmed, are accepted, and continue to be accepted without much danger of subsequent disconfirmation. The development of science consists in the extension of such theories to wider scopes, in the development of new, highly confirmed theories for related domains, and in the incorporation of confirmed theories into more comprehensive theories. Science is thus a cumulative enterprise in which old successes are extended and augmented by new successes. Old theories are not rejected or abandoned after they have been accepted; they are simply superseded by more comprehensive theories to which they are reduced.[18]

What are the basic elements of this "received view"? Scheffler outlines them as follows: this point of view, departing from the idea of the objectivity of science, regards science as a systematic, public undertaking controlled by logical and empirical facts with the formulation of truth about the natural world as the purpose of the undertaking. In general, this truth universally pursued is expressed in the laws of nature "which tell us what is always and everywhere the case."[19]

It is observation that supplies the required empirical facts, the hard phenomenal data we try to grasp by means of our lawlike hypotheses. The ultimate purpose of those hypotheses is to account, in one way or another, for the lawlike character of nature or reality. The laws the scientist is confronted with and tries to account for can be divided into two groups: (1) observational or experimental laws, and (2) theoretical laws. Observational laws generalize on the basis of data available to the senses, and then they mold this knowledge in the form of language that refers to objects and processes perceived. Theoretical laws, by contrast, are expressed in a more abstract idiom and cannot, as in the case of laws of observation, be subjected to the test of direct inspection and experiment. "Their function is not to generalize observed phenomena, but rather to explain the laws which themselves generalize the phenomena."[20]

Scheffler views the attack on the standard view of science as a serious threat to the objectivity of science.[21] The new philosophy of science is an even greater threat, for no appeal can possibly be made to common states of affairs that make the veracity or tenability of a theory possible. What is worse still, according to Scheffler, is that in this process the distinction between the logic of discovery and the logic of the justification of scientific theories falls away.[22] Reality as an independent factor, reality as independent of human observation, disappears; every point of view, every new theory, creates is own reality, as it were.[23] In this respect the comparability and reconciliation of theories becomes an important and decisive factor, confronting us with the problem "incommensurability."[24]

So far I have discussed only a few main points in the development of logical positivism. These points will serve as a broad framework against which the most significant resistance movement in the new philosophy of science can be highlighted and understood. My purpose in the rest of this paper is to offer an overview one of the most important schools that has contributed to the change of direction of philosophy of science in general, a school that has exerted an appreciable influence on the basic paradigms in social scientific theory.

The revolt against positivism

It was a new discipline, namely, the history of science or historiography of science, that contributed the most to the fierce onslaught on the ramparts and stronghold of logical positivism.[25] Insofar as the logical empiricists were truly concerned with the history and development of science, the role played by the history of science was seen primarily as contributing to scientific progress by bringing about development through the accumulation of knowledge.

The turning point in the philosophy of science was brought about by the "new philosophy of science," with Stephen Toulmin, N. R. Hanson, P. K. Feyerabend, and T. S. Kuhn as its most important representatives.[26] Toulmin's *Philosophy of Science*, published in 1953, heralded the new movement, although related conceptions are found in the earlier publications of Michael Polanyi and R. G. Collingwood.[27]

It is important to note that there were also other currents of thought (for example, phenomenology and neo-Marxism) that contributed toward the undermining of the basic statements of positivism, each in its own way. However, because the logical positivist model of science served as a model for so many other disciplines and still continues to do so in many fields, I will devote my attention primarily to the impact that the so-called Historical school of Kuhn *cum suis* had on the basic conceptions of the logical positivist philosophy of science. Another reason for restricting this paper to the influence of the Historical school is that its criticism of the basic assumptions of the standard view of science has affected the basic assumptions of many of the social sciences and given rise to an effort of radically reformulating the basic scientific paradigm of many of the social sciences.

It is ironic that Kuhn's work became one of the most important means by which the groundwork of the logical positivist conception of science was undermined, for his book was published in a well-known series of the logical positivist movement: "The International Encyclopaedia of Unified Science."[28] Kuhn, Toulmin, Hanson, and Feyerabend, whose ideas were instrumental in the change in philosophy of science, shared the following characteristic interests: (1) a strong interest in the history of the sciences, (2) an acknowledgment that presuppositions play a decisive role in all scientific theories, and (3) in general, a revolt against the view that science can be fully formalized.

The presuppositions that play a role in science differ from one tradition, theory, or school of thought to another. These differing philosophical backgrounds and paradigms function as spectacles through which the scientist views the facts of reality. They determine the questions addressed to reality, give meaning to the facts that are investigated, and in a certain sense even determine what the facts will be.[29]

Because these presuppositions, which are embedded in philosophical backgrounds, are so decisive in scientific theories, not only the logical form of scientific theories but also the content of specific theories must be investigated. A second problem posed by this new approach to science is whether all scientists can be said to share a communal point of departure in reality itself or at least share a common observation language that could facilitate the comparison and evaluation of theories.

The "new philosophy of science"[30] focused attention on the fact that the distinction between the context of discovery and the context of justification contributed to an atrophied view of science in which only the formal, logical aspects of the process were brought into the discussion; the important factors, the ones that governed the context of discovery in scientific endeavor were not for epistemology to deal with. Long before the observational-theoretical distinction—the well-known cornerstone of the positivist theory of science—started to crumble, a few philosophers of science had already come to the conclusion that Reichenbach's thesis[31] that epistemology was concerned only with the context of justification was at fault; in particular, it was wrong with regard to science.

The idea took root that what is required is a new kind of analysis of theories, an analysis that concerns itself with the epistemic factors governing the discovery, genesis, development, and acceptance or rejection of theories. Such an analysis would have to pay careful attention to the idea that science is practiced from within a conceptual perspective that to a great extent determines which questions are worth investigating and which types of answers are acceptable. The conceptual perspective provides a way of thinking about a class of phenomena in such a manner that it defines the legitimate problems and delimits the standards for solving them in an acceptable way. Such a perspective is intimately linked to the scientist's language, which conceptually shapes the way he or she experiences the world. What this implies is that science is practiced from within a worldview *(Weltanschauung)* or lifeworld *(Lebenswelt)*; the task of the philosophy of science is the analysis of these different worldviews. Such an approach would then have to pay considerable attention to the historical development of the various worldviews and the sociological factors that shaped the various theories. One can easily see that this approach advocated by the Historical school in the philosophy of science is incompatible with many of the most basic postulates of the neopositivist conception of science as formulated in the standard conception of scientific theories.[32]

Despite substantive differences in position and development, the worldview analyses proposed by Feyerabend, Hanson, Toulmin, Kuhn, and others present remarkably similar views of science. According to Suppe, [33] their accounts of how these analyses contribute to the scientific enterprise all have as their core some version of the following three theses:

1. Observation is theory-laden. The *Weltanschauung* determines how one views, describes, or interprets the world. Hence adherents of different theories will observe different things when they view the same phenomena.

2. Meanings are theory-dependent. The descriptive terms (both theoretical and observational) used by a science undergo a shift in meaning when they are incorporated into, or used in conjunction with, a theory. Thus the principles of a theory help determine the meanings of the terms occurring in them. The meanings of such terms will therefore vary from theory to theory. Changes in theory result in changes in meaning.

3. Facts are theory-laden. What counts as a fact is determined by the *Weltanschauung* associated with a theory. As such, there is no neutral set of facts for assessing the

relative adequacy of a theory. That theory must be assessed according to standards set by its *Weltanschauung*.

The result of these developments is that whereas all metaphysics was once regarded as a foreign field outside the bounds of science, it has now come to be regarded as an integral part of science. Ontology and worldview have been recognized as ineradicable components embedded in all scientific theories.[34] Of the four most important figures of the Historical school in the philosophy mentioned above, Thomas Kuhn merits special attention. Even though Kuhn states explicitly that his theory is not applicable to social science, he is the one who has had the strongest recognizable influence on social science. Moreover, he has also made a definite contribution to the change of direction in the scientific theories that underlie the structure of many social sciences. Kuhn, in short, is exceptionally important; he is regarded as one of the most fervent adversaries of the traditional, standard view of science.

Thomas Kuhn and the "standard view of science"
Kuhn's book *The Structure of Scientific Revolutions*, published in 1962, exerted a remarkable influence on the entire change of direction in the philosophy of science.[35] Until the publication of this book, the controversy in which logical positivism was enveloped was a fight within the closed circle of its adherents. Because of Kuhn's book, the fight suddenly spread into ever-widening circles beyond the philosophy of science. Soon natural scientists and social scientists of all sorts became involved.

The representatives of the Historical school were quite well versed in the problems of the sphere of the natural sciences. The material they extracted to prove their theses came primarily from these disciplines. Those ideas or theses then found their way into the social sciences by way of Kuhn's book, accompanied by the new model of the structure of science which Kuhn *cum suis* propagated.

In a nutshell, Kuhn's conception amounts to this: scientists, in the ordinary practice of science, are incorporated by virtue of their training, tradition, and education into some specific scientific tradition that is supported by some paradigm or other accepted by the particular scientific community within which they work.[36] This Kuhn calls "normal science." A crisis and scientific revolution can take place in the course of the development of the science, as an older paradigm is replaced by a newer one. Kuhn states: "Scientific revolutions are noncumulative episodes in which an older paradigm is replaced in whole or in part by an incompatible new one."[37] Such a paradigm consists of a strong network of commitments—conceptual, theoretical, instrumental, and methodological—and it includes quasi-metaphysical commitments. A paradigm includes implicit theoretical and methodological assumptions that make the selection, evaluation, and criticism of facts possible. One factor that can give rise to the development of a "crisis" in normal science is the rise of anomalies, that is, phenomena that can no longer be solved or explained by means of the old paradigm.

A discipline that still finds itself in a preparadigmatic phase[38] undergoes a struggle between conflicting paradigms. However, the moment a particular paradigm becomes dominant, the large variety of paradigms disappears. The one leading paradigm then becomes the basis on which facts are selected and problems are formulated. This development is characterized as a "revolution." After the "revolution," "normal" science resumes its practice on the basis of the new paradigm.

Kuhn's theory about the structure of science poses many problems that merit consideration. I will not discuss all those problems here, for my main goal in this paper is to explore the influence of Kuhn and of the Historical school in general. Because of that influence, many social sciences have been forced into what could be called a paradigmatic crisis, especially with regard to their basic model of the nature of science.

Kuhn uses the term *paradigm* in a variety of ways. There are three main connotations of the term that can be distinguished:

1. Metaphysical paradigms: the fact that reality is viewed in a new way.

2. Sociological paradigms, which imply that a new theory or approach in a science is universally acknowledged as a scientific achievement by the scientific community concerned.

3. Artefact or "construct" paradigms, in which the paradigm provides science with a new set of tools by means of which research can be conducted.

Later Kuhn defined the term *paradigm* more precisely. He chose to use the concept of a "disciplinary matrix,"[39] which consists of roughly four components:

1. Symbolic generalizations.

2. Shared commitments to beliefs.

3. Values that provide natural scientists with a sense of community.

4. Exemplars. This is what he now chooses to mean by the term *paradigm*. He uses the term to refer to the concrete solutions that students encounter right from the start of their scientific education.

The process whereby scientists shift from one paradigm to another is called a "conversion." Kuhn uses the familiar psychological concept of a "Gestalt switch" to illustrate this process. He maintains that scientists can adhere to only one theory or paradigm at a time. However, if scientists should choose to approach the same (?) facts by way of a different paradigm, all they will actually see is the same (?) image in the light of the new or second theory.[40]

This problem of conceptual change—as well as the idea that the observation of facts is theory-laden, which is bound up with it—has subsequently become of primary importance not only in the philosophy of science but also in a variety of other disciplines.

In a certain sense every theory or scientific system is interwoven with a network or family or system of concepts that are interrelated in a particular way. Whereas philosophers of science, from the beginning of this century, were primarily interested in investigating the logical form as well as the logical consistency and coherence of scientific statements, it gradually became apparent that there was an equally important matter in need of investigation, namely, the willingness of some scientists to sacrifice a logically consistent and coherent system of concepts for a different system of concepts that in turn could be investigated from a logical and formal point of view.

All of a sudden, this phenomenon of the change of concepts and systems of concepts and their related hypotheses seems to have become a question of vital importance. What actually happened here was that the dynamics of historical change in scientific theories became a relevant problem within the theory of science.

The subsequent transition from an analysis of logical structures to the analysis of scientific developments is indeed the most important change of direction that has taken place within the philosophy of science and the various disciplines influenced by the basic conceptions of the philosophy of science. The main reason why this development is so significant is that it represents a direct attack on the "standard view of science."

Kuhn's contributions can be traced directly and indirectly in the social sciences—directly in a variety of social sciences that have ventured on a paradigm search that at times gives one the impression of paradigmatic confusion, and indirectly in the fact that his views have contributed remarkably to the demise of the basic model of science fundamental to most mature natural sciences and many social sciences. Disregarding for the moment Kuhn's influence on the history and sociology of science, we would have to say that sociology seems to be the one social science in which his ideas enjoy abundant attention. In this connection the work of Friedrichs is noteworthy. In his book, *A Sociology of Sociology*, the outlines of Kuhn's theory with regard to scientific change are applied and worked out.[41] In practically all other social sciences (that is, political science, anthropology, education, economics, and history), Kuhn's concepts have been actively implemented. An interesting phenomenon worthy of mention in this respect is that in many disciplines it is difficult to determine at a superficial glance to what extent the science concerned actually understood Kuhn's intention and the whole transition that took place in the philosophy of science! Sometimes the idea of a paradigm is implemented in a typically empiricopositivistic manner, so that one gets the impression that the frantic search for "facts" has been replaced by an even more frantic search for paradigms! In a certain respect, this represents a weakness in Kuhn's theory. He emphasized the existence and historical development of paradigms without providing criteria for justification of the content or the truth of the paradigm. In that sense Kuhn's contribution does indeed create the impression of a certain relativism with respect to the final criteria by which the truth of a theory could be determined, and this in turn strengthens the impression that truth is ultimately what is sanctioned by the elite within a scientific community.[42]

Therefore it is exceptionally important to differentiate between (1) the direct influence of Kuhn's theory on the various disciplines as a result of the transition within the philosophy of science and (2) the mere application of his theory of the revolutionary development of science. It is also necessary to distinguish clearly between a general tendency toward the unmasking of the idea of neutrality and value freedom on the one hand, and on the other hand the objectivity that developed without the above-mentioned factors influencing these developments in any way. Kuhn and the Historical school represent only one group among many schools of thought that have influenced this tendency by way of their contributions.

In this paper I will illustrate the recent change of focus in certain disciplines. Those disciplines are not just indebted to Kuhn for their change in focus; it was also because of internal scientific factors that they developed in the direction of value commitment and the acknowledgement that facts are theory-laden. It is interesting to note that in these types of disciplines, Kuhn's theory is lavishly applied in order to describe the trend or change underway in science.

The above-mentioned developments within the philosophy of science itself and also within various disciplines are not the only ones of which we should take note. It is also important to be aware that in many disciplines, different new schools are developing that have one characteristic in common—the revolt against positivism in general, or the revolt against important positivist elements in the older theories of science that have long been at the root of the dominant conception of science in most of those disciplines. It is globally possible, then, to identify certain common developments within the philosophy of science, the various disciplines, and historical developments within society and culture, developments within which a recognizable relationship is manifest.[43]

We live in an age in which it has been declared that we have reached the end of ideology.[44] Therefore, against the developments sketched above, it is quite understandable that the fact that the intrinsic "ideological" nature of science has surfaced on all sides is a cause of much concern on the part of social scientists who adhere to the outdated ideal of objectivity and neutrality. Apart from these developments within the sphere of the philosophy of science, social science—more specifically, sociology—has experienced a severe crisis in which the most basic assumptions of its scientific edifice have been thoroughly questioned.

The state of the social sciences
When reference is made to the change of focus that took place in the philsophy of science and in the various disciplines that were directly or indirectly influenced by these developments, one gets the impression that the calm and uniform history of the social sciences was at one point suddenly interrupted by the infiltration of ideas from the area of philosophy of science. This impression, however, does not tally with reality. Positivism in its many variations was the only continuous thread that more or less bound the majority of the social sciences together. A historical survey of the development of the social sciences soon makes it clear that this part of the structural edifice of science was subject to crises and states of turmoil from the very beginning of its development.

In a discussion of the social sciences in 1956, Kimpton diagnosed the crisis of the social sciences as an inability to clearly outline and define their boundaries. It is striking that although the sociology departments of most American universities date from the beginning of this century, there was already talk of a crisis in the social sciences shortly after their establishmen—to be precise, approximately twenty years later.[45]

Kimpton, writing in *The State of the Social Sciences*, published in 1956 on the occasion of the celebration of the twenty-fifth anniversary of the Social Science Research Building in Chicago, was of the opinion that the social sciences probably find themselves in the same position as the natural sciences during the time of Paracelsus in the 16th century—on the boundary between science and pseudo-science.[46] The crisis of the social sciences, as he saw it, was that it appeared that no feasible solution had been found for the methodologically correct relation between theory and experience. Kimpton believed that the social sciences still found themselves in a stage of development in which facts were collected indiscriminately: the unsurveyable mass of data would be correlated and statistically processed without any important conclusions and without any important interpretation of the facts on the basis of a theory.

Part of the crisis is a certain type of attitude characteristic of the social sciences, an attitude in which the fact-value dichotomy and the subject-object dichotomy, the heritage of the positivistic approach to the social sciences, is treated as an infallible doctrine. In recent years there has been a complete change, so that the social sciences have developed an eye for the problem of scientific rationality, or, to put it in Kimpton's words, they see the necessity of a correct relationship between facts and theory.

Michael Polanyi was certainly one of the most prominent representatives of present-day philosophers of science who made the sharpest attack on the false separation between facts and value and the relations between facts and theories. Kuhn was one of Polanyi's students.

Polanyi's accent on the personal element in all knowledge is the source of his radical criticism of any and all attempts to make too sharp a distinction between fact and value, and subject and object. He maintains that the knower has a reserve of "tacit knowledge" of which he or she is conscious.[47] This knowledge of the knower, which cannot be proved, lies at the root of the explicit knowledge of people. Polanyi's acknowledgment of the unity of the process of knowledge leads him to stress that science is not to deal solely with facts, just as morality, religion and literature do not deal solely with values.

The crisis diagnosed by Kimpton in the 1950's does not seem to have been solved in the past decade; rather, it has been intensified by some penetrating questioning of certain basic assumptions central to the foundation of the social sciences. Cornelis[48] shows that this crisis of the social sciences has a clearly epistemological character. The scientific thinking of social scientists has been rendered problematic. He points out the following facets of what he takes to be the problem:

1. The manner in which sociology collects its empirical data has been thoroughly questioned.

2. The freedom of values as a traditional official ideology of the social sciences has been declared a myth.

3. The social commitment and engagement of science and knowledge has been heavily emphasized.

4. The realization of the necessity of a critical examination of the presuppositions of sociology and the social sciences has won and more and more ground and has led to the development of the idea of a "sociology of sociology."

In some social scientific disciplines, the crisis manifested itself in the form of a questioning of the social scientific theoretical model of science as coined by logical positivism and logical empiricism. In other disciplines the same problem cropped up —but then by way of external and internal factors, as stated earlier.

In order to illustrate more specifically what I have been arguing up to this point, I will focus attention on certain developments within sociology.

The crisis of sociology
The concept of a "crisis" already seems to have become quite familiar within the scientific vocabulary of sociology. Although the points of view on the nature and content of the crisis differ, there seems to be general agreement that there is in fact a crisis within the confines of this discipline.[49] The American and German variants of Western sociology are not fully agreed on the nature and scope of the crisis, but there are points of contact between them all the same. The common factors present in the analyses of the crisis presented by German and American sociology respectively is a disillusionment with the idea of science's value freedom and objectivity. The two variants of Western sociology also share a growing consciousness of the social engagement of sociology. A superficial glance at the titles of articles in most sociological periodicals provides enough proof of this tendency. Think, for example, of the articles of Gouldner and Gray.[50] The title of the latter article speaks for itself: "Value-free Sociology: A Doctrine of Hypocrisy and Irresponsibility."

German sociology
Recent developments in German sociology show a neo-Marxist phase immediately following an initial antipathy toward positivism.[51] In 1968, the important year of the student riots, the German sociologists gathered together. It was symptomatic of the emotionally violent times in which the congress took place that the sociologists actually came to blows by the time of their

departure. The theme of the congress was "Late Capitalism or Industrial Society" (*Spätkapitalismus oder Industriegesellschaft*). This theme—and the congress itself—occasioned a violent confrontation between the representatives of the different points of view. In any case this meeting signalled the climax of the neo-Marxist influence on sociology.[52]

After this remarkable meeting of the German sociologists, it was not until 1974, six years later, that another such congress was held in Kassel, Germany. At this congress it became apparent that the pluralism of sociological theories had become the burning question, along with the problem of the comparison of theories. The occasion for this discussion was an article by Karl-Otto Hondrich.[53] Hondrich's article served as the basis for a forum on points of departure for a theory concerning the comparison of theories. Hondrich tried to reconcile the different theories with one another by reducing them to a common denominator. Systems theory was chosen to fill the role of common denominator. Although all sorts of interesting points came to light in the discussion, it became evident that the problems at the core of sociology are the questions of so-called sociological universals and the nature of scientific theories. As I see it, these two questions are the most important problems not only in the history of the social sciences but also in the current crisis of sociology and discussions with regard to the crisis of sociology. Christian scholarship should turn its attention to these problems if it has any hope of bending these sciences in a normative direction.

In the history of German sociology, other crises preceded the above-mentioned crisis. Among them were the "battle over method" (*Methodenstreit*) and the "battle over value judgments" (*Werturteilstreit*).[54] The controversy just before the two milestones of 1968 and 1974 was the well-known "battle over positivism" (*Positivismusstreit*). This struggle, which dates from 1961 and is earlier, I shall discuss here because a number of important figures and trends confronted one another in this conflict, figures and currents that join in the revolt against positivism in one way or another.

In a certain sense, it is misleading to characterize this struggle as the "battle over positivism" since none of the participants can be branded a full-blown positivist. The writings of Popper, Adorno, Habermas, and Albert, compiled in the well-known book *The Positivist Dispute in German Sociology* date from the "Arbeitstagung der Deutschen Gezellschaft für Soziologie" held in Tubingen in 1961.

There are indeed certain affinities between Popper's position and the positivist view, but for more than half a century he was one of the most violent critics of positivism. Moreover, Popper objected to being classified with the neopositivists.[55] Adorno concerned himself chiefly with the manner in which empirical investigation functions in practice. He subjected the concept of fact to subtle analysis, reaching the conclusion that fact-gathering sociologists achieve nothing more than the duplication of the alienation of people in society. By simply registering opinions without taking into consideration the circumstances under which those opinions were formed, social science winds up leading to a duplication of the ills of society rather than an alleviation of those ills.

Popper, on the other hand, dealt primarily with methodological views and developed a "criticistic theory of knowledge." All theories are preliminary, he maintained, and no theory is immune to rational criticism. The social sciences can best be advanced by solutions to problems and by the development of theories that prove capable of withstanding penetrating criticism.

This controversy was taken a step further between Jürgen Habermas and Hans Albert, a pupil of Popper. The discussion between these two revolved around the questions concerning the "context of discovery" and the "context of justification" of theories. Habermas maintained that the problem of scientific rationality must be understood in the broader context of historical and social relationships. Albert, on the other hand, was interested in Popperian problems connected with the justification of scientific statements. It is clear that the neo-Marxist complaint about science's lack of societal and political involvement greatly expanded the scope of the crisis in the social sciences, specifically sociology. The problem of freedom from values was superseded by the problem of scientific relevance, which in turn brought aspects of the socialization and politicization of the social sciences into the scope of the controversy.

The most important contribution to the crisis of social science and sociology made by both Marxists and neo-Marxists was the unmasking of the ideological character of the thesis that science is value free.

American sociology

In Gouldner's important work, *The Coming Crisis of Western Sociology*, the crisis in Western society is related to the crisis of American culture, society, and politics of the past decades. What Gouldner says about the functionalism of Talcott Parsons, which served as the model for Western and American sociology, is that it primarily gave a *description* of American society.[56] Thereby it contributed to the scientific sanctioning of the status quo. The central concept of his functionalism was the concept of order, which implied that disorder is subordinate to order and that any form of disfunctioning would be set right by the built-in stabilizing tendencies of the structure of society. There was no specific prescriptive task for science in this process.

The crisis of Western sociology, according to Gouldner, is the crisis of the conservative establishment sanctioned by the functionalism of Parsons.[57] It is the crisis of science and technical know-how made available in order to maintain the status quo. In opposition to this sanctioning effect, the newer theories demand a critical attitude—one in which the basic assumptions of society are criticized. Gouldner accentuated another facet of the crisis: with the rise of the welfare state, functionalism, which was then the Western form of sociology, found itself in a curious position. On the one hand, functionalism served as the handmaiden of the welfare state, for it was the "official" analyzer cf the static order of the status quo; on the other hand, it was involved in dramatic social changes manifested in the growth of the welfare state. Functionalism was a sociology of *order*, but it was now confronted with the problem of *change*. This situation was aggravated by the fact that the growth of the welfare state caused great sums of money to become available for research in the social sciences. The result was that the social sciences were in a certain sense theoretically unprepared for the demands made by society and the problems of the society in which it was to go about its work. Therefore Gouldner states that the new methodological model that developed in sociology during the past decade did not come about as a result of some theoretical interaction with new data; rather,

> what has happened is that old data and old problems have, largely for reasons exogenuous both to the theory and research of sociology, come to be assigned new value,

significance, and reality. In short, the relationship between the technostructure and the infrastructure of sociology has changed and has become increasingly tension-laden largely because of changes in the latter. This, primarily, is why major theoretical changes are now occurring and impending.[58]

From the main lines in the argument of this paper, it should be apparent by now that the social sciences are currently in a developmental crisis which has had the effect of forcing practically all practitioners to a radical rethinking of the basic paradigms fundamental to research in the social sciences. If the historical roots of these developments had been taken into consideration, the breakup of the rather shaky relationship between facts and values, theory and practice, and ideology and theory could have been predicted.

Historical roots of a "broken marriage"
The current conceptual and scientific dilemmas characteristic of most of the disciplines in the social sciences are the outcome of a long historical development. The logical positivism of the early twentieth century was one of the most important culminations of that development. The distinction between normative and empirical theory, the dichotomy between facts and values, and the divorce between theory and practice have suddenly become highly relevant issues through the contributions of critical, dialectical, and neo-Marxist social scientists and philosophers who focussed on the value relevance and engagement of scientific endeavor. These developments were strengthened by the contribution of the Historical school with its sharp attack on the idea of the objectivity of science.

The premature divorce of facts and values, theory and practice, and empirical and normative theory can be traced back to at least the seventeenth century.[59] The epistemological paradigm coined by Bacon, Descartes, Hobbes, Locke, Newton, and others is characterized by Spragens as the "objectivist" tradition.[60] This paradigm with its three parallel dichotomies has been maintained most persistently and consistently within the schools of positivism and behaviorism. In fact, this epistemological paradigm still influences virtually all the social sciences insofar as they have not been undermined, on the one hand by the impact of the new philosophies of science and on the other hand by the critical, phenomenological, and other schools with their focus on the necessity of engagement in the scientific enterprise.

The legacy of the objectivist-epistemological paradigm was brought about by various factors. One of the most important of them is surely the physicalistic-mechanistic worldview with its relentless reduction of reality into a single homogeneous plane. This assumption of the homogeneity of the world brings with it corollary linguistic and methodological prescriptions. The unidimensional ontological construct basic to this approach calls for a methodological linguistic ccounterpart which Spragens speaks of as "semantic conflation."[61] The effect of this semantic conflation is the reduction of the multidimensionality of the meaning of a term to a unidimensional language game on the basis of a presupposed cosmological homogeneity.

This development, which took place under the influence of the seventeenth-century mechanization of the scientific worldview, also led to other adverse effects, effects that became more pronounced under the influence of logical positivism and its ideal of linguistic and logical clarity. The appropriate usage of the term is claimed by the lingual analyst—who then subtly posited a significant ontological thesis under the guise of assuring terminological clarity.

As we take these historical roots of the objectivist epistemological paradigm into consideration, we must not overlook two other scientific traditions: Kantianism and neo-Kantianism. The false dichotomy was substantially influenced by Weber, in particular. Weber's value freedom thesis accentuated the necessity of eradicating all political and ethical value judgments in scientific work. The traces of the original Kantian dichotomy between theoretical and practical reason are quite apparent here.[62]

A Christian alternative?

The question that arises from the analysis of these developments is whether the Christian social scientist can furnish Christian alternatives to the anomalies created by the objectivist epistemological paradigm. It is quite clear that a Christian approach to the basic questions posed by these developments within the social sciences should direct its reformational attacks at the spiritual roots of the current crisis in social science and sociology in particular.

Much has already been done in this respect. From the perspective of Herman Dooyeweerd's philosophy of the cosmonomic idea, James Olthuis has developed a position that treats at least one aspect of the triad of dichotomies characteristic of the crisis of the social sciences, namely, the fact-value dichotomy.[63] The problem posed by critical sociologists and philosophers concerned with the necessity of acknowledging the integration of theoretical and practical knowledge contains aspects of scientific endeavor that are of fundamental importance for the development of an alternative, Christian, normative direction within the social sciences. The same could be said of the work done on the relationship between ideology and methodology. Wolterstorff's contribution concerning the relationship between faith and theory has given us important directional indications as to the ways in which religious, metaphysical, and philosophical presuppositions actually function within the scientific enterprise.[64] Still, many questions remain.

One important question is whether the fundamental change in the epistemological paradigm of the social sciences brought about by the influence of the schools mentioned above also affects the so-called domain assumptions of the various social sciences in any way. If it is true that the basic epistemological paradigm is expressed in scientific terms that reflect its lack of multidmensionality, then it is quite clear that the ontological premises of sciences built on this paradigm are very much in need of revision. What implications would this have, for example, for the encyclopedic problem of the social sciences?

Another question is the problem or set of problems implied by the developments concerning value engagement. The awareness of value engagement in the social sciences has led to a strong current in the direction of the politicization of society. Value engagement is being interpreted as *political* value involvement. This raises the question as to the boundaries of political values and with it the question as to the nature of the *social* and the *political* world. This problem becomes even more acute when it is realized that the methodological basis of these sciences, in which the physicalist-causal approach with its heavy emphasis on mathematical quantification and logical symbolization has been thoroughly questioned, has led to a distorted representation of social and political reality.

These developments within the social sciences confront the Christian social scientist with the task of reformationally redefining not only the basic epistemological tenets of the social sciences but especially the ontological assumptions and methodological approaches characteristic of these aspects of reality.

Notes

1. Arthur Koestler, "Rebellion in a Vacuum," in *The Place of Values in a World of Facts*, ed. Arne Tiselius and Sam Nilsson (Stockholm: Almquist & Wiskell, 1970), 222-23.

2. Stephen Toulmin, "Rediscovering History," *Encounter* 36 (January 1971, no. 1): 53.

3. This Formalist revolution was part of the antimetaphysical stance of both positivism in general and logical positivism.

4. Toulmin, 56.

5. See D. Shapere, "Meaning and Scientific Change," in *Mind and Cosmos: Essays in Contemporary Science and Philosophy*, ed. Robert G. Colodny (Pittsburgh: University of Pittsburgh Press, 1966), 42 and Theodore Kisiel, "New Philosophies of Science in the U.S.A.," *Zeitschrift für Allgemeine Wissenschaftstheorie* 5 (1974, no.1): 139.

6. Shapere, 41.

7. The most important representatives of this school include M. Schlick, O. Neurath, R. Carnap, E. Nagel, C. Hempel, H. Reichenbach, and L. Von Mises. The school also includes members of the Minnesota Circle, such as Feigl and Brodbeck, who have implemented these conceptions in the social sciences.

8. See Israel Scheffler, *Science and Subjectivity* (Indianapolis: Bobbs-Merrill, 1967), 7-15 and 67-68 and Frederick R. Suppe, ed., *The Structure of Scientific Theories* (Urbana: University of Illinois Press, 1974).

9. See Klaus Holzkamp, "Wetenschaptheoretische Vooronderstellingen van een Kritisch-emancipatorische Psychologie," in *Het Neopositivisme in de Sociale Wetenschappen: Analyse, Kritiek, Alternatieven*, ed. L. W. Nauta (Amsterdam: Van Gennep, 1975), 345.

10. Jürgen Habermas, *Knowledge and Human Interests*, trans. Jeremy J. Shapiro (Boston: Beacon Press, 1971), 74-78.

11. George H. von Wright, *Explanation and Understanding* (London: Routledge & Kegan Paul, 1971), 4.

12. Richard J. Bernstein, *The Restructuring of Social and Political Theory* (New York: Harcourt, Brace, & Jovanovich, 1976), 15.

13. Holzkamp, 347.

14. Hans Reichenbach, *Experience and Prediction* (Chicago: University of Chicago Press, 1938), chapter 1 of section 1.

15. Scheffler, 47-53 (cited in note 8 above).

16. See Suppe, 6-118 (cited in note 8 above); Herbert Feigl, "The Orthodox View of Theories: Remarks in Defense as Well as Critique," in *Analyses of Theories and Methods of Physics and Psychology*, ed. Michael Radner and Stephen Winokur (Minneapolis: University of Minnesota Press, 1970), 3-16; and Clark G. Hempel, "On the 'Standard Conception' of Scientific Theories," in *Analysis of Theories and Methods of Physics and Psychology*, ed. Michael Radner and Stephen Winokur (Minneapolis: University of Minnesota Press, 1970), 142-63.

17. Suppe, 12.
18. Suppe, 55-56.
19. Scheffler, 8 (cited in note 8 above).
20. Scheffler, 8.
21. Scheffler, 12.
22. Scheffler, 17.
23. Scheffler, 19.
24. T. S. Kuhn, "Reflections on My Critics," in *Criticism and the Growth of Knowledge*, ed. Imre Lakatos and Alan Musgrave (Cambridge, Eng.: Cambridge University Press, 1970), 232, 266, 274-77.
25. See Shapere, 37 (cited in note 5 above).
26. See Shapere, 50; and Kisiel, 139 (cited in note 5 above).
27. See R. G. Collingwood, *An Essay on Metaphysics* (Oxford: Clarendon Press, 1940), chapters 4-6 . In Collingwood's conception the "absolute presuppositions fulfill the same function as paradigms. Also see Jay Newman, "Metaphysics and Absolute Presuppositions," *Man and World* 6 (1973): 280ff. and Leon J. Goldstein, rev. of *Mind, History and Dialectic: The Philosophy of R. G. Collingwood* by Louis O. Van Mink and *Collingwood and the Reform of Metaphysics: A Study in the Philosophy of Mind* by Lionel Rubinoff, *Man and World* 6 (1973): 84.
28. T. S. Kuhn, *The Structure of Scientific Revolutions* (Chicago: University of Chicago Press, 1973). Kuhn's *Structure* first came out in 1962, but it was revised in light of criticisms of his position. References here are to the revised and enlarged 1973 edition.
29. In this connection see the views of Alexander Koyre, S. Palter, and S. Toulmin.
30. See Kisiel, 138 (cited in note 5 above).
31. Reichenbach, 6-7 (cited in note 14 above).
32. See Suppe, 132 (cited in note 8 above).
33. Suppe, 191.
34. See J. O. Wisdom, "Scientific Theory: Empirical Content, Embedded Ontology and Weltanschauung," *Philosophy and Phenomenological Research* 33 (1972-73): 75-76.
35. See Feigl, 3-16 (cited in note 16 above); Hempel, 142-63 (cited in note 16 above); and Scheffler, 7-15 and 67-68 (cited in note 8 above).
36. Kuhn later defined "paradigm" more concisely, and he replaced the older conception of paradigm with "disciplinary matrix."
37. Kuhn, *Structure*, 91 (cited in note 28 above).
38. This phrase of Kuhn's refers to the social and natural sciences in their early development. Later he typified these sciences as "proto-sciences," that is, sciences still developing into mature science.
39 Kuhn, *Structure*, 182; and Kuhn "Reflections," 271-72 (cited in note 24 above).
40. Kuhn, *Structure*, 111, 150.
41. This publication is representative of a stream of literature that assiduously tries to implement Kuhn's views in the various disciplines. Kuhn himself admits that the literature has become so vast that it is impossible to cope with it all. See *Paradigms and Revolutions*, ed. Gary Gutting (Notre Dame: University of Notre Dame Press, 1980). My data-retrieval search for the period from 1970 to 1973 produced so many titles and references, I could not read all the

material.

42. See N. T. van der Merwe, "Paradigm, Science, and Society," *Koers* 4, 5, and 6 (1975): 328.

43. See Toulmin, 53 (cited in note 2 above).

44. See Daniel Bell, *The End of Ideology: On the Exhaustion of Political Ideas in the Fifties* (Glencoe, Ill.: Free Press, 1960).

45. Lawrence A. Kimpton, "The Social Sciences Today," in *The State of the Social Sciences*, ed. Leonard D. White (Chicago: University of Chicago Press, 1956), 348-52.

46. Harvard, one of the oldest departments of sociology in the United States, was only established in 1929.

47. Michael Polanyi, *The Tacit Dimension* (New York: Doubleday, 1966).

48. Arnold Cornelis, "De Crisis in de Social Wetenschappen. Het Probleem der Vooronderstellingen," *Mens en Maatschappij* 48 (1973, no.2): 151-86.

49. See Alvin W. Gouldner, *The Coming Crisis of Western Sociology* (New York: Basic Books, 1970) and S. N. Eisenstadt with M. Curelaru, *The Form of Sociology: Paradigms and Crises* (New York: Wiley, 1976).

50. Gray, "Value-free Sociology: A Doctrine of Hypocrisy and Irresponsibility," *Sociological Quarterly* 9 (1969, no.2): 176-85; and Gouldner, "Anti-Minotaur: The Myth of a Value-Free Sociology," *Social Problems* 9 (1962, no.3): 201-13.

51. See P. Schnabel, "De Duitse Sociologie Tussen Theorie en Praxis," *Sociologische Gids* 75 (1975, no. 1): 48.

52. See Theodor W. Adorno et al., *The Positivist Dispute in German Sociology*, trans. Glyn Adey and David Frisby (London: Heinemann, 1976).

53. See L. W. Nauta, ed., *Het Neopositivisme in de Sociale Wetenschappen: Analyse, Kritiek, Alternatieven* (Amsterdam: Van Gennep, 1975).

54. See Reiner F. Beerling, *Sociologie en Wetenschapscrisis* (Meppel: Boom, 1959).

55. See note 52 above.

56. Gouldner, 331, 354 (cited in note 49 above).

57. Gouldner, 369.

58. Gouldner, 370.

59. See Thomas A. Spragens, *The Dilemma of Contemporary Political Theory: Toward a Post-behavioral Science of Politics* (New York: Dunellen, 1973), 10.

60. Spragens, 27.

61. Spragens, 42.

62. See Cornelis, 174 (cited in note 48 above).

63. James H. Olthuis, *Facts, Values and Ethics* (Assen: Van Gorcum, 1969), 182ff.

64. See Nicholas Wolterstorff, *Reason within the Bounds of Religion* (Grand Rapids: Eerdmans, 1976).

Reflections on individualism I
Richard J. Mouw

My interest in individualism has been partially stimulated by the conviction that this is an important concern for North American conservative evangelicals. Some of us who have been critical of certain common strands of evangelical social thought also have been fond of arguing that a biblically faithful evangelical social conscience is inhibited by the widespread influence of individualism. I, for one, have argued this point many times.

Because I have frequently insisted on this point, I was recently caught off guard when I was the one accused of being an individualist—once in a friendly argument about soteriology with an European Barthian, and once in a not-so-friendly argument about human rights with an Afrikaner philosopher. These were, for me, unsettling experiences. Having found out what it is like for the shoe to be on the other foot, I began to suspect that the term "individualism" is not always used in a clear and precise manner. I vowed that I would attempt to find a clearer definition of that label. This discussion is a modest first step in that direction.

The attempt to understand what people mean by "individualism" is complicated by several factors. First, the label has a rich multidisciplinary life. It appears in a variety of discussions and attaches itself to a number of different modifiers: religious individualism, ecclesiological individualism, political individualism, economic individualism, sociological individualism, ontological individualism, methodological individualism, and epistemological individualism.

Second, in any one of these contexts the label is applied to a number of seemingly disparate viewpoints and emphases. Take, for example, the discussions of religious individualism. If we gather all the claims that have been made as to which brands of Christianity are individualistic, we are confronted with a startling array. For example, it has been argued that the

entire Old Testament is hostile to individualism; others insist
that there are clear individualistic themes in the Old Testament
—Jeremiah is regularly referred to as the first biblical individualist. Some insist that one or another New Testament writer is
to be distinguished from the others by his individualism, as in
the title of an article by a New Testament scholar: "The Individualism of the Fourth Gospel." Others are convinced that the
entire New Testament, in contrast to the Old, is individualistic.
It has been argued that the primitive Judeo-Christian tradition
is to be credited with introducing individualism into Western
thought. Some see individualism as emerging in late Medieval
Catholicism. Others view the Reformation as an individualistic
reaction against Catholicism. Some argue that though the Reformation itself was not essentially individualistic, Calvinism
was, while others insist that Luther was the individualistic
deviant among the Reformers. Others see individualism as
having been spawned by the Anabaptists. It has been suggested that Calvinism was not individualistic, but that it degen-
erated into such in Puritanism. Similarly, it is argued that
Pietism is an individualistic aberration of Lutheranism. Still
others have insisted that neither Puritanism nor Pietism were
individualistic themselves, but that Evangelicalism is the individualistic heir of the Puritan and Pietist traditions. However,
some Evangelicals refuse to accept the label; they insist that
only one kind of Evangelicalism is individualistic, namely,
Fundamentalism. Some Fundamentalists, in turn, insist that
they are not individualistic, although there may be a few Fundamentalists here and there who lean in that direction.

Thus the term is applied to virtually every level. And on
each level some representatives of the accused group insist that
the term does not correctly apply to them but to the group on
the rung below.

All of this points to a third complicating factor. In different
contexts the label has different emotive and rhetorical force. As
Yehoshua Arieli points out in his study of eighteenth and
nineteenth century American political thought,[1] in past centuries the term was used by the followers of Saint-Simon as a term
of extreme ridicule, but in certain strains of American thought
it has been used as a congratulatory label. On other occasions it
is used for straightforward classification.

By its very weaknesses and inadequacies my discussion
will demonstrate some important lessons about individualism.

As should already be obvious, the topic is vast and complex; appropriately, then, this discussion is fragmentary and inconclusive. Indeed, I will focus primarily on one small area in the broad reaches of individualist thought—political individualism. Even within that limitation I will only begin to approach the subject. Let my remarks be thought of as prologomena to critical discussion by Christian theorists of political individualism. I am not even certain that the dimensions of the subject I will discuss are important or interesting to others. In that regard, then, I am going to do my own thing, proving that individualism is a very concrete and lively option.

It is not too difficult to give a formal account of political individualism. In some sense or another, it views the individual as the center of political life; it emphasizes the role of the individual human being. This does not, of course, tell us much, since there are several ways in which the individual can be considered the center of political life.

One way would have to do with a metaphysical understanding of political life. What is a society? What is a political unit, such as the state, composed of? A straightforward individualistic answer would claim that society is nothing but a group of individuals; to talk about the activities of a state is to talk about the activities of individuals.

Bill Bright, the president of Campus Crusade for Christ, seems to be making this kind of claim when he writes:

Individuals make up society, and society cannot be changed until individuals are changed. Selfishness, prejudice, hate, greed, lust, are all individual problems which become the problems of collective man and society as a whole. Our problem is solved, then, if the individual is changed, that is, if enough individuals are changed.[2]

Very few people would disagree with the claim that, in some sense or another, "individuals make up society." But Bright seems to be insisting on a special version of that claim, that society is "nothing but" a collection of individuals; hence his proposal that we can solve societal problems by dealing with each individual separately.

A metaphysical thesis of this sort has been debated in recent years in the Anglo-American philosophical discussion of the merits of "methodological individualism" versus "methodological holism."[3] The individualistic position has been defended by, among others, J. W. N. Watkins, who puts his case this way:

> [T]he ultimate constituents of the social world are individual people who act more or less appropriately in the light of their dispositions and understanding of their situation. Every complex social situation, institution, or event is the result of a particular configuration of individuals, their dispositions, situations, beliefs, and physical resources and environment. There may be unfinished or half-way explanations of large-scale social phenomena (say, inflation) in terms of other large-scale phenomena (say, full employment); but we shall not have arrived at rock-bottom explanations of such larger-scale phenomena until we have deduced an account of them from statements about the dispositions, beliefs, resources, and interrelations of individuals.... [According to the alternative view, holism] social systems constitute "wholes" at least in the sense that some of their large-scale behavior is governed by macro-laws which are essentially *sociological* in the sense that they are *sui generis* and not to be explained as mere regularities or tendencies resulting from the behavior of interacting individuals....If methodological individualism means that human beings are supposed to be the only moving agents in history, and if sociological holism means that some superhuman agents or factors are supposed to be at work in history, then these two alternatives are exhaustive.[4]

Watkins's position is obviously formulated in reaction to a view that takes social entities to possess a kind of reality "in their own right."

In his monumental work, *Suicide,* Emile Durkheim argues that such entities as groups and classes have their own psychic and moral dispositions that are to be thought of as more than the sum of individual dispositions. It is not, Durkheim insists, that a society could somehow exist even if there were no individuals. Nonetheless, the kinds of entities that are involved in "social facts" are such that two claims are true of them: first, that these entities have "a reality of a different sort from each individual considered singly"; and second, that the collective entities can act as causal factors with respect to individual states

—they can "affect the individual."[5]

Watkins is, in effect, denying each of these claims. There are no social entities with a reality distinct from individuals; therefore, "human beings are the only moving agents in history."

This dispute involves a number of difficult and complex issues that I will not explore. But one interesting strand of the discussion can be briefly noted. Joseph Agassi claims to be sympathetic to the basic thrust of Watkins's individualism, but he proposes a variation on it, which he calls "institutional individualism." On this view

> "wholes" do exist..., but they have no (distinct) interests.... An institution may have aims and interests only when people give it an aim, or act in accord with what they consider should be its interests; a society or an institution cannot have aims and interests of its own.[6]

More generally,

> institutions can be explained as inter-personal means of co-ordination, as attitudes which are accepted conventionally or by agreement. Not that an agreement was signed by those who have the attitude, but the attitude is maintained by one largely because it is maintained by many, and yet everyone is always at liberty to reconsider his attitude and change it. This idea...accords with the classical individualistic idea that social phenomena are but the interactions between individuals. Yet it does not accord with the classical individualistic-psychologistic idea that this interaction depends on individuals' aims and material circumstances alone; rather it adds to these factors of interaction the existing interpersonal means of co-ordination as well as individuals' ability to use, reform, or abolish them, on their own decision and responsibility.[7]

What does this amount to? It will be helpful to look at some examples. Contemporary critics of sexist and racist patterns often insist that patterns of sexual and racial interaction are not merely individual incidents, but that they are in some sense built into the institutionalized structures of our society. Masters and Johnson seem to be presenting a holistic account of this sort when they describe the evolution of sex roles in this way:

With sexual functioning firmly established in our culture as something apart from other natural processes, there were sexual roles to assign, sexual practices to establish, sexual restrictions to impose. All were done out of hand by an omnipotent social arbitration that communicated to the individual not only what his or her sexual patterns should be—but what it must be.[8]

It was decided—who knows by whom—that the male was the sex expert. Each of us was born into a social system in which sex roles and sexual practices were already deeply ingrained. I never consciously decided as a child that I wanted the television movies to portray John Wayne as a tough and admirable hero and my friend Irma as a stupid, sexy blond. Similarly, I was not aware of how Dagwood always controlled the finances and Dennis the Menace's mother always wore an apron. From as early as I can remember, when I heard "nurse" I pictured a woman, and when I heard "doctor" I pictured a man. And so on.

Who decided these things? Not my parents or Masters and Johnson. Masters and Johnson say that it was decided by—and they are being somewhat caustic—"an omnipotent social arbitration." Watkins would have us believe that this is wrongheaded, that these collective beliefs about sex roles are in fact nothing more than the beliefs held by individual men and women. But this hardly seems adequate. Sexism or the complex system of sex roles, sexual attitudes, prejudices, stereotypes, expectations, and myths that existed when I was born were already, in some sense, there. And they influenced me without someone sitting down and verbally articulating those beliefs to me.

This is the kind of phenomenon that Agassi is trying to account for. There are such things as institutionalized attitudes and beliefs. Beliefs can be codified, accumulated. They can come to have a kind of life of their own. But, Agassi insists, institutions come to have beliefs and aims of their own only because individuals give them beliefs and aims. For any institutional belief or aim, some individual had it first, and then it became codified, institutionalized.

This is, of course, an important concession by the individualist. He does not deny that institutions have dispositions and aims; Agassi only requires that such an aim had to be, at some time or another, invested into the institution by some individual or group of individuals.

If this modified individualism were accepted, it would be incompatible with Bill Bright's remarks, which we quoted earlier. Sin can, on this modified view, originate in individuals, but sinful aims can then come to be invested in institutions; thus there can be a kind of accumulated or codified sin. This is the issue that seems to me to be at stake in John Frame's misguided criticisms of "the Amsterdam philosophy." Frame writes:

> Sin is an *exclusively personal* category. Only a *person* can sin. Only a *person* can disobey a law of God; only a *person* can hate his creator; only a *person* can rebel against his Lord. A tree can be *affected* by sin, but it cannot sin. Thorns and thistles can ruin a garden as God's curse on man's sin, but those thorns and thistles are not *sinners*. The same is true of social institutions. A labor union may be affected by the sins of its members; but the union will not thereby be a *sinner*.[9]

Frame is insensitive to the ways in which institutions are not merely affected by sin, but can *embody* and *perpetuate* that sin. Institutional life encompasses such phenomena as books, jokes, constitutions, handbooks, role assignments, decision-making procedures, and the like. These entities are not *merely* affected by sin. They are vehicles, extended agents, and codifications of human aims and purposes. If by some miracle every member of the Teamsters Union was converted to Christianity on a single evening—say, by each watching Billy Graham on TV in the privacy of his or her own home—there would still be considerable work to do if the *union* were to be saved. Constitutions would have to be rewritten, codified expectations and processes would need to be revised, criteria for membership might have to be drastically changed, budgetary policies would need to be rescinded, and so on.

But I must raise the possibility that even the modified individualism of Agassi does not adequately account for the nature of institutions. I think that it is susceptible to a number of objections. I limit myself to a theological consideration. Since World War II a number of theologians, especially Western European theologians, have shown considerable interest in the Pauline conception of the principalities and powers. This theology of the powers has stirred considerable excitement in some quarters, where it is often hailed as a major breakthrough for the biblical theology movement.

What is interesting for our purposes are the fascinating parallels between discussions of the powers and the arguments in the methodological individualism/holism debate. Jim Wallis has correctly noticed the parallels:

> The frequent observation of sociology that institutions, structures, bureaucracies, and so on, are more than the sum of the individuals who make them up and that they often seem to have a life of their own is confirmed by the biblical insights. After years of neglect, the biblical theology of the "principalities and powers" or, simply, "the powers" is being recovered.[10]

Albert H. van den Heuvel tells us that "when Paul discussed powers, he was relating the gospel of Jesus Christ to the way the Christian faces these suprapersonal and sometimes sub-human powers" that often "seem to be very real forces" in human history, powers that

> stand for the impersonal rulers of our society—economies, propaganda, sex, public opinion, religious sentiments, racial prejudice, nationalism, or colonialism, all those things that undoubtedly exist in, influence, and sometimes dominate our lives without ever being fully visible.[11]

The most fascinating parallel to our present concerns is provided by Hendrikus Berkhof. He tells us that Paul's conception of the powers—which are "invisible higher powers" operating "in and behind...visible authorities"—should be viewed against previous rabbinic and apocalyptic writings. From that older perspective "two things were always true of the powers: (1) they are personal spiritual beings, and (2) they influence events on earth, especially events within nature."[12]

Berkhof sees Paul as modifying each of these points. First, Paul went far in the direction of depersonalizing the powers. At the very least, Berkhof argues, Paul did not view the powers as angels; and "one can even doubt whether Paul conceived the powers as personal beings." What is essential to Paul's conception is that "whether they be conceived as persons or as impersonal structures of life and society, they form a category of their own—"domicile" is in that "sphere which binds together the divine and human world."[13]

Second, instead of viewing the powers as operating primarily in nature, as in the older tradition, Paul sees their influence "as especially connected with human affairs." As created powers they are intended by God to "serve as the invisible weight-bearing substratum of the world"—they "hold life together." But because of sin a "demonic reversal...has taken place on the invisible side of creation. No longer do the powers bind man and God together; they separate them."[14] In short, the powers exert a "rebellious" influence on human social life.

The interesting parallel is this: Berkhof notes two features of the powers that are directly parallel to Durkheim's two comments on social facts: first, they exist "on their own"; and second, they influence human social consciousness.

What shall we say of this parallel? Does it provide us with a control belief that bears on the individualism/holism dispute? More specifically, does this parallel indicate that we, as Christians, are committed to a Durkheimian holism? Let us briefly consider some options.

As I see it, the kinds of biblical theological observations Berkhof is offering in his discussion of the powers are just that —observations from the point of view of biblical theology. They must be carried over into systematic theology and even further into Christian social thought where they must be subject to sifting, sorting, and interdisciplinary reflection.

From the point of view of social theory, there are at least three possible interpretations of the biblical theological themes. One possibility is this: that we take Paul to be teaching us that there are several nonhuman, but in some sense personal, agents. I think this view requires that these agents be viewed as "centers of consciousness" who are at work behind the scenes of human cultural life. We can think of these agents as fallen angels, demonic beings. They somehow control the social dimensions of the creation. Thus, when we study the designs in the socio-political arena, we are, whether we realize it or not, reckoning with their designs and purposes as well as those of human beings.

This seems to me to be the way C. S. Lewis portrays things in his fine novel *That Hideous Strength*. Mark Studdock, a naive young secular sociologist, is drawn into the plans of an Institute dedicated to totalitarian goals. He gradually becomes suspicious, long after the reader has become convinced that the Institute's purposes are malevolent. As his struggle increases he encounters an evil power that is both personal and more than human. Lewis leaves us with a vivid picture of a corporate struggle that is not merely against flesh and blood, nor against bricks and mortar.

As I have already indicated, Berkhof shies away from such a reading of the Pauline literature; Paul, he says, does not view the powers as personal agents. I am not as certain of this as Berkhof is. It is difficult to decide. Often, of course, people embrace demonology in a manner that views evil agents as whimsical. In that case the social sciences could be viewed as crude attempts to study demonic maneuverings in human culture. But one could also hold that the powers are personal forces committed to pursuing their rebellious purposes in systematic and lawlike patterns. If so, social scientific understanding might be a key ingredient in the proper rites of social exorcism.

If this personalistic option were to be defended adequately, it would require at least two arguments. First, it would have to be shown that this is what Paul thought. Then it would have to be demonstrated that we must think like Paul. I do not know whether these arguments could be successfully defended.

The other two possible interpretations share a common starting point. They both deny that Paul teaches that the powers are personal centers of consciousness. When Paul speaks of the powers in a personal manner, he is personifying or using metaphor, as he certainly seems to be doing when he speaks of death as a personal agent, as an enemy that had to be defeated by Christ. According to these views, the references to the powers are less-than-literal ways of talking about patterns of social interaction. And there are two ways of understanding these patterns: individualistically or holistically.

But this brings us back to our original discussion before we introduced the biblical references to the powers. We must, it would seem, choose between individualism and holism on extra-biblical grounds. We must first decide whether we are metaphysical individualists or holists, and then we will know how to understand Paul. This is, I think, a fairly accurate description of where the matter stands.

Of these metaphysical options, the individualism of Bright and Watkins seems to me the least plausible. Agassi's institutional individualism rightly acknowledges codified, accumulated, institutionalized beliefs and attitudes. This patternedness, which seems to have a reality of its own, is also acknowledged, obviously, by the personalistic view of the powers and by Durkheimian holism. And it is interesting that most biblical theologians who discuss the powers suggest one of these last two views. I am inclined to think that their metaphysical instincts are accurate.

We have been discussing political individualism as a metaphysical theory, as an account of what kinds of entities do, or do not, exist in the socio-political realm. There is a second way of viewing the individual as the center of political life, a way that relates to a set of issues that are more normative than metaphysical. Steven Lukes points to some of these issues when he discusses three distinct ideas associated with political individualism:

> [F]irst, a view of government as based on the (individually-given) consent of its citizens—its authority or legitimacy deriving from that consent.... Second, and allied to this, is a view of political representation as representation, not of orders or estates or social functions or social classes, but of individual interests. And third, there is a view of the purpose of government as being confined to enabling individuals' wants to be satisfied, individuals' interests to be pursued and individuals' rights to be protected, with a clear bias towards *laissez-faire* and against the idea that it might legitimately influence or alter their wants, interpret their interests for them or invade or abrogate their rights.[15]

These doctrines and emphases are distinct from the metaphysical individualism we have already discussed. Here we ask how a government, state, or civil society *ought* to act. These concerns are compatible with different metaphysical accounts of society. For example, even if there are classes that have a reality of their own, the normative individualist insists that the interests of such entities ought not to override the interests of individuals.

Lukes enumerates three fundamental political questions where the normative individualist stresses the importance of the individual: From what does a government derive its authority? What or whom do political officials properly represent? And what is the fundamental purpose of government? In each case the answer emphasizes the individual: governments derive their authority to govern from the consent of individuals; political officials are the representatives of individual concerns; and governments exist to serve the needs and interests of individuals.

Normative political individualism, then, stresses the centrality of the individual in response to at least these three questions. I do not want to follow this emphasis as it weaves its way through the intricacies of political theory, but just briefly look at this fundamental concern for the individual and his or her rights.

Ronald H. Nash has recently stated the individualist's case in a most provocative manner, defending political individualism from an avowedly Christian perspective:

Man's essential freedom and his right to exercise that freedom are his by virtue of his creation in God's image. To be truly human, to be most expressive of the image of God, man needs to be free, to be able to choose. When the state deprives man of his liberty, man loses an essential part of his humanness.[16]

Then, after bemoaning present political trends in North America, Nash concludes that "we have gotten into our present fix because we have insisted on supplanting the God-ordained supremacy of the individual person in the political order with the leviathan state."[17]

It is easy to think of critical responses to this emphasis on the "God-ordained supremacy of the individual." For one thing, it is difficult to ground this emphasis in biblical references to the image of God, as Nash attempts to do. As I have argued elsewhere,[18] there are good reasons to think that the biblical creation accounts place far greater emphasis on our sociality and communal interdependence than on our individuality.

Where, then, do we find the "God-ordained supremacy of the individual" being taught in the Scriptures? Is not the emphasis, rather, on our God-ordained cultural obligations, on our corporate involvement? And is not the chief end of a human being to glorify God as supreme? Does that glorification not involve our submission to all that God has instituted for the ordering and structuring of his creation? And is not the political order a part of that structuring? If Nash were reporting on the I-centeredness of conservative-evangelical experience, his report would be accurate. But his words hardly seem to capture the biblical picture.

These are, I think, appropriate responses to Nash's individualistic emphasis—but only as far as they go. These responses are also typical reactions of certain Christian traditions when they encounter individualistic themes in religion and politics. Roman Catholicism and Eastern Orthodoxy have relied heavily on the motif of mystical union. Calvinism—especially Dutch Calvinism—joins these two traditions with its own motif of the organism (see Afrikaner ideology).

Here Christian social thought needs to proceed very carefully and cautiously. I am convinced that we can rightly reject normative individualism, but only after we have absorbed some of its crucial emphases.

Consider, for example, a common argument against social contract theories of political obligation. The argument proceeds along these lines: political obligation cannot be grounded in a human contract that has been consented to, either implicitly or explicitly, by individuals. God has ordained that there be states and civil authorities; governments exist, then, not by the will of human beings but by the will of God. Therefore we must choose: either citizens' obligations to obey their governments are derived from their own wills or from the will of God.

I think this is much too simple. Indeed, it presents us with a false choice. Is my obligation to be faithful to my wife grounded in a human contract or agreement, or is it grounded in the will of God? Did not God ordain marriage? And are not Christians required to live in marital faithfulness as a part of a life of obedience to God? My marital obligations, then, are grounded in God's decrees.

But that cannot be the whole story. In an important sense, of course, I am obligated *to God* to live in marital fidelity—in that sense my obligation is rooted in the eternal purposes of God for his creation. But it seems obvious that in another sense, I am obligated *to my wife* to offer her my continuous fidelity.

And that obligation has a definite historical origin. I ceremonially incurred that obligation one summer evening when I pledged my fidelity to her before a gathered people.

God has ordained that there *be* marriages, and that they be characterized by loving, monogamous fidelity. But *my* obligation to live in a specific relationship to a specific person is also based on a contract or covenant with that human being. If I violate that contract, two distinct charges can be laid against me: I have disobeyed the God who ordained the institution of marriage, and I have broken a specific vow to that human being, my wife.

Does the marriage relationship, then, rest on the will of God or the wills of human beings? The answer is: both. And much the same holds for political obligations. When David became king over Israel, he was reminded of a covenant he had made with God: "...and the Lord your God said to you, 'You shall be shepherd of my people Israel, and you shall be prince over my people Israel.'" But this *vertical* obligation was complemented by a *horizontal* one: "So all the elders of Israel came to the king at Hebron; and David made a covenant with them at Hebron before the Lord..." (1 Chron. 11:2-3, RSV). It is difficult to see how a belief in the God-instituted nature of government rules out contractual agreement between government and citizens.

Similarly, if the role and authority of government is not to be understood exclusively in terms of the wishes and desires of individual citizens, it does not follow that those wishes and desires are irrelevant to the proper concerns of government. It seems to me that whatever the ultimate inadequacies of individualistic theories, we may view them as legitimate reminders of one important focus for political concern. We may have to reject the "God-ordained *supremacy* of the individual"; but we must not ignore the God-ordained *importance* of the individual.

Indeed, it may be that not all that *appears* to be individualistic can be legitimately labeled such. Consider the spirituality of black American slaves. Slavery in North America was, among other things, a direct and sustained assault on the black family: husbands were forcibly separated from wives and children from parents (not unlike conditions in certain parts of the world today, conditions that sometimes, like then, are under Calvinist sponsorship!). The black person was stripped of communal relationships, and this loss of community is poignantly expressed in black slave spirituals: "Sometimes I feel like a motherless child"; "I must walk this lonesome valley, I've got to walk it by myself"; "Soon I will be done with the troubles of the world."

The black theologian James H. Cone, in his marvelous little book *The Spirituals and the Blues*, rightly warns us not to interpret this black spirituality as individualistic:

> It is commonplace among many interpreters of black religion to account for the emphasis on the "I" in the spirituals and other black church expressions by pointing to the influence of white pietism and revivalism in the nineteenth century. But that assumption, while having some merit, is too simplistic; it does not take seriously enough the uniqueness of black religion....The existential "I" in black religion...did not have as its content the religious individualism and guilt of white religion or refer to personal conversion in those terms....The "I" of black slave religion was born in the context of the brokenness of black existence. It was an affirmation of self in a situation where the decision to be was thrust upon the slave....Thus the struggle to be both a person and a member of community was the major focus of black religion. The slave knew that an essential part of this struggle was to maintain his affirmation even—and especially—when alone and separated from his community and its support. He knew that he alone was accountable to God, because somewhere in the depth of the soul's search for meaning, he met the divine.[19]

We must keep this extremely important emphasis before us. Some of us in the Reformed tradition are inclined to argue, and rightly so, I believe, that a straightforward, unqualified social contract theory fails for two basic reasons. First, it wrongly assumes that the individual is the fundamental political unit, thus ignoring the need to distribute rights and obligations to other kinds of entities, such as families, churches, labor unions, schools, art guilds, and the like. Secondly, it fails to recognize that these other units have their own patterns of authority and that they cannot simply be subsumed under the authority of the civil state.

My own sympathies are, I repeat, with these "sphere

sovereignty" emphases. But the I-centered expressions of the
black slave, as described by James Cone, are not individualistic
denials of sphere sovereignty. They are urgent cries for help
and understanding from individuals who have not yet been
allowed to function in that diversity of spheres. The black slave
has been deprived of the ability to function as a familial being,
a wage earner, a worshiper, a student. His I-centered talk is, in
effect, an insistence that he possesses the credentials of personhood that, if recognized, would permit him to function in these
spheres. Cruelly denied recognition of that personhood by
other human beings, he is standing tall in the final court of
appeals, affirming his dignity as one created by God and
redeemed by Jesus' blood.

This is an emphasis that Helmut Gollwitzer rightly asserts
against Marxist thought:

> In Christian thought...an unprecedented, supreme accent
> is laid, as Marx suspected, but wrongly expressed it, on the
> individual life...because the content of the gospel is the
> victory of the love of God. This love is directed toward
> every man, and further, to the individual man. It does not
> isolate him, but it individualizes him in the same way as
> the love of the father and mother does with each individual
> child, however large the number of children.... For this
> love every single person is irreplaceable.[20]

Much of what we call "religious individualism"—which I
think might be more accurately described as a blend of soteri-
ological and ecclesiological individualism—is, in fact, a celebration of this sense of irreplaceability, which is often expressed beautifully, as in Wesley's hymn:

> Died He for me,
>   who caused His pain?
> For me,
>   Who Him to death pursued?
> Amazing love! How can it be?
>   That Thou, my Lord, shouldst die for me?

This celebration of God's individualizing love can be
understood by white evangelicals in a way that is analogous to
Cone's treatment of the "I" in black slave spirituality. A person

has come to realize the hopelessness of his or her individual guilt and rebellion, overwhelmed with indebtedness and a sense of spiritual bankruptcy. Then the good news breaks in: Jesus paid it all; and he paid the debt for me. I am loved by God; I am redeemed by his unsurpassed mercy. This seems to be at the heart of the Christian gospel.

But is there not more to the gospel than this? Of course. There is much more. Jesus paid the debt on behalf of the whole creation—a creation groaning for the New Age. I am called to participate in God's work of renewal, a work which requires that I deny myself and take up the cross—a cross that must be borne in the company of the redeemed. And there is much more. The gospel is more than a message about my irreplaceability. But it is not less than that.

As I view things, then, the irreplaceability of each individual is an unavoidable biblical concern. Each human being is created in God's image and each receives the call to turn from his or her present rebellion to participation in God's renewing work. God knows each individual by name and to those who do his will he promises that their names will be recorded in the Lamb's book forever.

No political official, no human government can afford to ignore the basic human, even individual, needs of those whom God knows by name. For, as the Belgic Confession says of the elect, someday "the Son of God will confess their names before God His Father and His elect angels...and their cause which is now condemned by many judges and magistrates as heretical and impious will then be known to be the cause of the Son of God"(Art.37). This, I believe, correctly describes the future vindication of many who are presently persecuted and oppressed by governments that deny basic human rights.

Nor can we afford to ignore these matters when formulating our political *theories*. With all of the recent talk among theologians about the need to understand theologies "contextually," we also would do well to understand the variety of individualisms contextually. The claim for the rights of individuals is one that can be asserted in a variety of contexts, because the rights of the individual can be bartered away for a variety of currencies. Some will attempt to absorb the individual into a class or a role; others will deny his or her interests for the sake of an emperor, a *Geist*, or a national soul; others will sacrifice the individual out of economic or racial—that is, racist

—pride, or out of a fear of communism or a concern for law and order.

To be sure, defenses of the political individual will vary. Some will view the individual as a virtual deity, a worthy pretender to the Creator's throne; others will defend the individual, not as a god, but as god*like*, a bearer of the divine image. Our Christian arguments, proddings, and preachments on this subject will differ from context to context. But in every context the Christian theorist ought to be guided by a vision of a community of individuals redeemed from polytheistic combat, spiritual and political anarchy, and a compulsive pursuit of "self-realization" to the service of a King who calls each of his subjects by name, but who calls them, nonetheless, to participate in a community whose shalom can only be realized when each member proclaims: "My only comfort in life and in death is that I am not my own. "

Those who are inspired by this Christian vision will, I fear, be accused on occasion of adhering to an individualism. This should neither surprise nor intimidate us. In one context or another that label describes a position that someone thinks overemphasizes the individual. In that case, the label never *decides* anything; it merely points out that the place or role of the individual must be discussed. Thus when Jacques Maritain accuses Martin Luther of being an individualist, he ought to be taken as highlighting a topic that must be discussed between some Roman Catholics and some Protestants. Much the same is occurring when that accusation comes from the lips of a Barth or a Vorster or a Lenin.

I do not mean to suggest that someone cannot, in one context or another, overemphasize the place or role of the individual. There are positions that I believe are individualistic. And we ought to become clearer—clearer than I have been in these prologomena—about that label "individualistic." The important thing, of course, is to better understand the proper relationship or relationships between the individual and the larger social (and political) order so that we can better call individuals and governments to conform to God's standards of justice.

Notes
1. Yehoshua Arieli, *Individualism and Nationalism in American Ideology* (Baltimore: Penguin Books, 1964), chapter 10.

2. Bill Bright, *Revolution Now!* (Arrowhead Springs, San Bernardino, Calif.: Campus Crusade for Christ, 1969), 21.

3. This debate has been carried on in a number of journals. Some of the essays in the debate have been collected in several anthologies. The best anthology on this subject is probably John O'Neill, ed., *Modes of Individualism and Collectivism* (London: Heinemann, 1973).

4. J. W. N. Watkins, "Historical Explanation in the Social Sciences," in John O'Neill, ed., *Modes of Individualism and Collectivism* (London: Heinemann, 1973), 167-68.

5. Emile Durkheim, *Suicide: A Study in Sociology* (New York: Free Press, 1951), 320.

6. Joseph Agassi, "Methodological Individualism" in John O'Neill, ed., Modes of Individualism and Collectivism (London: Heinemann, 1973), 188.

7. Agassi, 212.

8. William H. Masters and Virgina E. Johnson, *The Pleasure Bond: A New Look at Sexuality and Commitment* (New York: Bantam Books, 1976), 3.

9. John M. Frame and Leonard J. Coppes, *The Amsterdam Philosophy: A Preliminary Critique* (Phillipsburg, N.J.: Harmony press, n.d.), 48.

10. Jim Wallis, *Agenda for Biblical People* (New York: Harper & Row, 1976), 63.

11. Albert H. van den Heuvel, *These Rebellious Powers* (London: SCM Press, 1966), 24-25.

12. Hendrikus Berkhof, *Christ and the Powers* (Scottsdale, Pa.: Herald Press, 1962), 11, 14.

13. Berkhof, 18, 19, 24.

14. Berkhof, 22, 23, 24.

15. Steven Lukes, *Individualism* (New York: Harper & Row, 1973), 79-80.

16. Ronald H. Nash, "Three Kinds of Individualism," *The Intercollegiate Review* (Fall 1976), 37.

17. Nash, 40.

18. See Richard J. Mouw, *Politics and the Biblical Drama* (Grand Rapids: Eerdmans, 1976), chapter 2.

19. James H. Cone, *The Spiritual and the Blues: An Interpretation* (New York: Seabury Press, 1972), 67-68.

20. Helmut Gollwitzer, *The Christian Faith and the Marxist Criticism of Religion* (New York: Charles Scribner's Sons, 1970), 112.

Reflections on individualism II
Johan D. van der Vyver

The concept of individualism

Professor Mouw has presented a commendable analysis of the concept and meaning of "individualism." In the first place he exposed the inacccurate and ambiguous use of the term and, in the second place, he demonstrated the need for a clear understanding and consistent application of philosophical vocabulary. There is a distinct analogy between philosophical terminology and an African chameleon. If one examines the meaning of those nice sounding words commonly employed by philosophers, one finds that they often take on different shades of meaning to satisfy the subjective prejudices of the person who uses them or they designate irreconcilable concepts. The language of philosophy has therefore become known for its perplexity, ambiguity, and obscurity; and regretfully so, because philosophy should disclose the real substance and meaning of reality in theoretical terms, and the language of philosophy ought to convey the philosopher's ideas with precision and without a chance of misapprehension.

There is in this regard much to be learned from the *consistent problem-historical method* of the Amsterdam philosopher, D. H. Th. Vollenhoven.[1] Professor Vollenhoven's philosophical endeavours have basically tried to formulate a right approach to a truly scientific treatment of the history of philosophy. Preoccupied with methodology, he has designed a set of philosophical terms that characterize the various fundamental theoretical premises that have emerged from the different systems of Western thought. The great variety of theoretical opinions and statements could, according to Vollenhoven, be related to a few basic problems. Each of those problems, in turn, permitted a very limited number of fundamental points of view. Vollenhoven reserved a philosophical term to denote one fundamental answer to a basic problem of philosophy. He not only defined each term with minute precision, but he also secured a consistent use of his philosophical stock of words.

Vollenhoven related the concept of individualism to the fundamental cosmic problem of the nature and relationship between the general or universal and the singular or individual aspects of all mineral, vegetable, animal, and human substances or entities. For example, Richard Mouw is, on the one hand, an individual with very special qualities and unique characteristics that cause him to be different from all other persons. On the other hand, he is also a human being who shares certain essential attributes with all other members of the human family. How, then, do these two sides of a man relate to one another?

We could ask the same basic question about the individuality of a particular pine tree in the garden outside and its universality as part of a certain biological species, or the singularity of the green and yellow budgie in the pet shop downtown and its collective participation in the being of other feathered members of the animal kingdom.

Much has been said and written about the relationship between the uniqueness of a particular thing and the general characteristics of certain kinds of things. But the great variety of Western views can be finally reduced to one of three basic assumptions.

Individualism supposes that the cosmos consists of individual things only. Words indicating a general species are only names for collections of similar individual entities (nominalism), or they designate mental concepts that do not represent any truly existent equivalent in actual reality (conceptionalism).

Universalism does acknowledge the existence of individual substances but professes that collective phenomena in general, or certain specified collective phenomena, must always take precedence over their particular parts.

Partial universalism tries to recognize both the individual and universal aspects of things without valuing one more than the other. Partial universalism either regards the individual and universal "things" as two separate entities with the same qualities but differing in size or extent (partial universalism coupled with a macro-microcosmos theme),[2] or it views individual and universal phenomena as two distinct features in every mineral, vegetable, animal, and human entity (partial universalism coupled with the theme of form and matter).[3]

Individualism, accordingly, can be defined as that cosmological premise that regards the individual aspect of creation as primary and regards the universal side of reality as merely a general concept or a word intended to designate a collection of individual things, which do not really comprise a solidary unity or a structural whole.[4]

Kinds of individualism

Professor Mouw rightly pointed out that individualism is an encyclopedic concept with, inter alia, ecclesiological, sociological, economic, juridical, and political connotations.

He gave sufficient account of individualism in religion, pointing out, among other things, that John Frame's supposition that only individual persons can participate in sin[5] is a clear instance of an individualistic interpolation of biblical truth.

Sociological individualism expresses the view that social entities—family groups, educational institutions, sport clubs, cultural organizations, business enterprises, labor unions, political parties, national units, benevolent societies, and religious communions—are the creation of individuals, and are nothing more than the sum total of their individual members.

The well-known utilitarian, Jeremy Bentham, visualized a perfect state that tried to secure the greatest happiness of the greatest number to produce the complete happiness of all.[6] He transformed individualism into an economic doctrine.

In jurisprudence, individualism is exemplified by the supposition that a legal persona is an abstract notion or a fictitious entity composed of a collection of individuals.[7]

Political theories show the gist of individualism insofar as they assume that political power is derived from the individual subjects of the particular state, that the government represents only the people and is also answerable for its actions only to the people, and that state authority has been instituted for the sole purpose of fostering the interests of the individual members of the body politic.

Political individualism

The basic credo of political individualism can be concisely paraphrased: *salus singulorum est suprema lex* (the well-being of individuals is the highest law).

Professor Mouw has, in my opinion, exposed the onesidedness and oversimplifications of individualism and universalism (collectivism/holism). He has also indicated most convincingly that individualism and universalism are not our only options. Nor, may I add, are the two variations of partial universalism satisfactory answers to our problems. There is another alternative that avoids the typical tendency of all -isms to absolutize a particular aspect of the cosmos and that acknowledges the reality and the equal value and importance of the singularity and generality of all created substances.

From a Christian point of view, one ought to respect both the unique distinctiveness and the social involvements of all persons. And a truly Christian social theory would strike a balance between the personal privacy of the individual and his or her social responsibilities as a member of various community structures, and in particular between a private enclave of personal liberties and the juridical obligations of a person as a subject of state authority.

Contemporary political science stresses the need to restrict the competencies of the repositories of political power so as to safeguard the private life of the individual against state interference. It must, however, be emphasized that our principle of equilibrium also curtails an individual's personal freedom.

Social responsibilities of the individual
In politics a person's social responsibilities concern his or her interindividual relations with other members of the body politic as well as intraindividual relations between the state and its subjects.

Interindividual relations between different subordinates of state authority
Interindividual conflicts of interest ought, in my opinion, to be settled in accordance with the Roman-Dutch principle: *sic utere tuo ut alienum non laedas* (use what is yours so as not to injure others).

It might be noted in passing that the United States Supreme Court has devised the doctrine of preferred freedoms to cope with interindividual conflicts of interests in juridical relations.[8] This doctrine simply means that certain rights and freedoms of the individual have preference over other claims that stand in the way of absolute enjoyment of the preferred rights and freedoms. The rights and freedoms singled out for preferential treatment are those proclaimed in the First

Amendment: freedom of religion, speech, and the press, and the right to assemble peaceably and to petition the government for a redress of grievances. The rights that must yield to the preferred freedoms are especially those with an economic flavor.

The Roman-Dutch principle of *sic utere tuo ut alienum non laedas* is more in keeping with the principle of equality inherent in the traditional Aristotelian concept of justice. It is, after all, the business of the law to balance and reconcile conflicting interests into harmoniously coexistent obligations, claims, and competencies of the subjects within a particular political community or—as Immanuel Kant would put it—to determine the conditions under which the volition of one person can have its way alongside the volition of other persons under a general law of freedom.[9] If state-imposed law were to attach preferences to a particular kind of right or freedom at the expense of equally fundamental values, the equilibrium of the legal order would be thrown out of balance and injustices would consequently manifest themselves.

Intraindividual relations between the state and its subjects
Conflicts of interests within a political community are not restricted to interindividual relations of state subjects. They are also inevitable accessories of the relationship of authority and subordination between a government and the people.

In the United States such conflicts of interest are supposed to be dealt with on the basis of the doctrine of a clear and present danger. This doctrine was first introduced in the case of *Schenk v. United States*, 249 US 47 at 52 (1919), by the celebrated American Supreme Court judge, Oliver Wendell Holmes, who said:

> ...the character of every act depends upon the circumstances in which it is done....The most stringent protection of free speech would not protect a man in falsely shouting "fire" in a theatre and causing a panic. It does not even protect a man from an injunction against uttering words that may have all the effects of force....The question in every case is whether the words used are used in such circumstances and are of such a nature as to create a clear and present danger that they will bring about the substan-

tive evils that Congress has a right to prevent. It is a question of proximity and degree.

The doctrine therefore implies that the rights and freedoms of the citizen must yield to community interests when, and only when, there is a clear and present danger that their exercise will cause a wrong that state authority has a right to prevent.[10]

It is, I believe, fair to state that when appraising individual rights vis-à-vis community interests the United States Supreme Court has been consistently individualistic. It tends to transform the constitutionally protected rights and freedoms into a set of more or less absolute titles. Mr. Justice Black, perhaps the most outspoken partisan of absolute constitutional rights, definitely favored a literal interpretation of the sweeping language of the United States Constitution. He said: "I simply believe that 'Congress shall make no law' means Congress shall make no law."[11]

Roman law, expressed in the adage *salus reipublicae suprema lex* (the well-being of the state is the highest law), represents the opposite side of the coin. This maxim accounts for many injustices in the course of the history of Western civilization. It stands to reason that unless state or community interests are confined to a clearly scrutinized sphere of competencies and as long as the state feels free to extend its powers over too wide a range of self-imposed functions the *salus reipublicae* can become the excuse for state absolutism.

There is, in this regard, an important lesson to be learned from the political theory of contemporary Calvinism which defines—and restricts—the functions of the state (and consequently also the *salus reipublicae*) in terms of the particular destiny of a political community. That destiny, a postulate of creation, has been predestined by the essential structure of the state. The destiny and corresponding functions of the state must be distinguished from the typical destiny and functions of other social entities. By virtue of the comprehensive doctrine of sphere sovereignty, the competencies entrusted to state legislatures and governments ought to be confined to the state's own structural household. And the social responsibilities of individual subjects of the state ought to reach no further than the appropriate destiny of the body politic as designated by its characteristic leading or qualifying function.

Restrictions of political power

The powers and competencies of governments ought accordingly to be restricted so as to permit and even guarantee the personal freedom of the individual within the compass of his interindividual and intraindividual social responsibilities. In view of contemporary political practices, three limitations need special emphasis: the curtailment of state authority (which stems from the doctrine of sphere sovereignty), the principle of the rule of law, and the idea of human rights protection.

The doctrine of sphere sovereignty

The Calvinist doctrine of sphere sovereignty[12] is based on the premise that each and every social entity has been instituted for a specific purpose and finds its destiny within the ambit of our temporal existence as a necessary instrument of the divine providence of God. Educational institutions are by their very nature destined to further the acquisition of knowledge. Social clubs are there to animate social intercourse between people. Business enterprises are called on to pursue economic aims. Cultural organizations are entrusted with the task of promoting aesthetic achievements. Benevolent societies are designed to administer the ethical command requiring people to love their neighbors. Religious communions are charged with fostering people's faith. It is of the essence of Calvinistic sociology that the distinguishing feature or fundamental characteristic of a particular type of social entity is predetermined by its typical leading or qualifying function. Its activities ought to remain orientated to its destiny as defined by the relevant leading or qualifying function.

The principle of sphere sovereignty likewise restricts the jurisdiction of state authority to a particular sphere of competencies that exist alongside the similar sovereign spheres of other social entities, such as the church, family, university, or corporation. State absolutism manifests itself when the state encroaches on the exclusive domain of nonpolitical social entities.

The leading or qualifying function of a political community must, according to Herman Dooyeweerd, be sought in the juridical aspect of reality.[13] That leading function is expressed in a public legal relationship that unifies the government, the people, and the territory that constitutes the political community into a politico-juridical whole. The state's task is especially

to harmonize conflicting interests. This implies that state actions can, in fact, cover the entire spectrum of everyday life,
even though the social aspect affected by such state action
might fundamentally be educational, economic, aesthetic, or
religious. On the other hand, the state should not interfere in
essentially educational, economic, aesthetic, religious or other
nonpolitical matters unless a conflict of interest requires juridical intervention to maintain or restore harmony within human
society.

The doctrine of sphere sovereignty therefore demands
breathing space for all social entities operating within a particular territory. Though the doctrine is primarily concerned with
the relationship between different kinds of social structures, it
nevertheless has a bearing on the freedom of the individuals.
By honoring the sovereignty of nonpolitical communities
within its territorial borders, the state enables the individual to
exercise the right to participate in the activities of such nonpolitical communities.

The rule of law
The British constitutional lawyer, A. V. Dicey, introduced and
originally defined the concept of "rule of law" during the late
nineteenth century to denote certain fundamental rules of
English constitutional law. Dicey's notion was, however, soon
transformed by a series of interpretations into a universal
Sollensprinzip, that is, into an aggregate of directive principles
signifying what the law ought to be. Different exponents of the
concept read their own subjective predilections into the notion
of the rule of law.[14] The confusion that resulted led Sir Ivor
Jennings to compare the rule of law to an unruly horse. He said:
"If analysis is attempted, it is found that the idea includes
notions which are essentially imprecise."[15] So let me clearly
state that the meaning of rule of law ought, in my opinion, to be
restricted to the formal principle of legality, which simply
means that both the government and the subordinates of the
state should be subject to the law. The opposite of the rule of law
would be arbitrary governmental powers. Executive powers
are by definition arbitrary if government competencies are not
legally restricted or judicially controlled.

Arbitrary rule is the worst form of anarchy. The Calvinistic notion of the divine source of government authority does not
sanction arbitrary rule. Almost a century ago the British histo-

rian, Lord Acton, coined the celebrated maxim: "Power tends to corrupt; absolute power corrupts absolutely." He also added a line that is especially relevant today: "There is no worse heresy than that the office sanctifies the holder of it."[16] It stands to reason that the dignity and worth of the individual would be greatly jeopardized if the power of the government over its subjects were not sufficiently defined in legal norms.

The principle of human rights
The doctrine of human rights has many pitfalls, and each human rights theory is undoubtedly susceptible to criticism. Yet, on the whole, the general idea of this doctrine is sound. In every political community individual citizens ought to enjoy certain basic rights and fundamental freedoms without fear of state intervention.

The particular rights and freedoms that require preferential protection might, according to modern human rights theories, differ from place to place and from time to time according to what Gustav Radbruch would call *die Natur der Sache*[17] or the prevailing natural, social, and juridical circumstances. But two universal prerequisites are generally accepted.

First of all, political entities should achieve national independence in accordance with the right of peoples to self-determination. This right includes the entitlement of all adult citizens of a given political community to participate in the political processes of that community. Secondly, all citizens within a particular community should be treated equally by and before the law.

To safeguard the privileged rights and freedoms of the individual, it is usually suggested that a Bill of Rights be enacted guaranteeing the unimpeded enjoyment of those rights and freedoms and the amendment or repeal of which is to be subjected to extraordinary procedures and restricted to carefully specified circumstances. To effectively protect the human rights and fundamental freedoms, it is also essential that a body be entrusted with the substantive right of review and with competency to invalidate parliamentary legislation and governmental actions that infringe on the Bill of Rights.

Concluding remarks
Western civilization has witnessed almost every conceivable form of government, ranging from the most stringent autoc-

racy to contemporary, extreme liberal democracy and including one or two instances of anarchism. In recent years, as law-states have been transformed into welfare-states, governments have been obliged to provide various social services to promote the well-being of underprivileged, disabled, and unemployed citizens. This development coincides with the rise of socialism, which requires state control of a wide range of economic phenomena, such as labor opportunities, wages, the major sources of production, and the prices of basic commodities. This ever-increasing variety and extent of state functions and obligations underline the need to reappraise the nature and proper limits of the competencies to be entrusted to the repositories of political power.

I trust my introductory remarks show that the individual ought never to shirk from his or her social responsibilities toward the political community and that state control ought, on the other hand, never to undermine the individuality of the human person.

Notes
1. For a commendable summary of the consistent problem-historical method of Vollenhoven, see B. J. van der Walt, *Heartbeat: Taking the Pulse of Our Theological-Philosophical Heritage* (Potchefstroom: Potchefstroom University for Christian Higher Education, 1978), 5-29.
2. Plato thus regarded the state as a macrocosmic image of an individual human being.
3. Aristotle accordingly presented the individual and the universal aspects of particular things as their form and matter respectively, though he could never make up his mind whether the form of a thing represented its individual aspect and the matter represented its universal aspect, or the other way around.
4. See D. H. Th. Vollenhoven, *Geschiedenis der Wijsbegeerte* (Franeker: T. Wever, 1950), I:41:

> ...*individualisten* — stelde het individueele primair en het universeele secundair: universeel is b. v. een algemeen begrip, een woord met algemeene beteekenis en de gemeenschap in een levensverband; in dit milieu houdt men het algemeene in begrip en woord voor de vage aanduiding van een verzameling individuen, die in werkelijkheid geen eenheid is, en ziet men de levensverbanden als voortbrengselen der activiteit van individuen.

Also see I:176:
> ...de individualistische...(acht) het individueele primair, het universeele daarentegen secundair.... Het universeele beschouwt men hier dan ook slechts als resultaat der denkende, sprekende of gemeenschap stichtende activiteit van individuen: het komt slechts voor also vaagheid

bij begrippen en woorden en in de gemeenschap als resultaat der samenweking van individuen.

5. See John M. Frame and Leonard J. Coppes, *The Amsterdam Philosophy: A Preliminary Critique* (Philadelphia: Presbyterian & Reformed, 1973), 48.
6. In Charles W. Everett ed., *The Limits of Jurisprudence Defined* (New York: Columbia University Press, 1945), 113, Bentham makes a similar (individualistic) calculation of "goods" to arrive at "the greatest good of the whole community."
7. We must not confuse individualism with positivism. Positivism believes that only concrete substances exist (and such substances might include collective things), whereas individualism acknowledges the reality of individual things only (without necessarily denying the real existence of immaterial objects).

The fiction theory regarding legal personae of F. C. von Savigny was clearly inspired by a positivistic point of departure. In *System des Heutigen Romischen Recht* (Berlin: Veit, 1840-49) 2:236, von Savigny described legal personae as "ausgedehnt aufkunstliche, durch blosse Fiction angenommene Subjecte."

The same is true of the conceptionalistic construction of a legal persona by the eminent Dutch jurist, W. Zevenbergen. In *Formeele Encyclopaedie der Rechtswetenschap als Inleiding tot de Rechtswetenschap* (The Hague: n.p., 1925), 267, he states:

Rechtssubjecten zijn nooit reeel existeerende dingen of wezens: daarom bestaat er ook geen behoefte om te doen, 'alsof' ze existeeren. Rechtssubject is een gedachte. Elke rechtspersoonlikheid is iets juridisch, niet iets natuurlijks of werkelijks. Van nature zijn er menschen en dingen. Van rechtswege zijn er slechts (in dit opzicht) personen.

However, Zevenbergen's compatriot, L. J. van Apeldoorn, did clearly construct the legal persona in individualistic terms, by assuming that the rights and obligations of such a collective legal subject belong jointly to the members thereof. See, for instance, *Inleiding tot de Studie van het Nederlandse Recht*, 9th ed. (Zwolle: n.p., 1950), 143.
8. According to Wolfgang Friedmann, the doctrine of preferred freedoms originated from a footnote remark of Stone, J. in *United States* v. *Carolene Products Co.*, 304 US 144 (1938). See his *Legal Theory*, 5th ed. (London: Stevens, 1967), 149; and *Law in a Changing Society* (Berkeley: University of California Press, 1959), 18.
9. See I. Kant, *Metaphysik der Sitten*, ed. Karl Vorländer (1797, 2nd ed. Leizig: F. Meiner, 1907), 34-35, where Kant defined natural law (the law that ought to be) as "der Inbegriff der Bedingungen, unter denen die Willkur des einen mit der Willkur des anderen nach einem allgemeinen Gesetze der Freiheit zusammen vereinigt werden kann."
10. Accordingly, different sections of the Subversive Activities Act 1950 (64 Stat 987), which were intended to effectively check the activities of communists, have been declared unconstitutional in cases such as *Aptheker* v. *Secretary of State*, 378 US 500 (1964), and *United States* v. *Robel*, 389 US 258 at 262-3 (1967).

11. Hugo F. Black, *A Constitutional Faith* (New York: A. Knopf, 1969), 45.

12. For an elaborate analysis of the history, contents, and implications of this doctrine, see J.D. van der Vyver, *Die Juridiese Funksie van Staat en Kerk: 'n Kritiese Analise van die Beginsel van Soewereiniteit in Eie Kring* (Durban: Butterworths, 1972). Important aspects of the doctrine also appear in my article, "The State, the Individual and Society," *The South African Law Journal* 1977, 291ff.

13. See Herman Dooyeweerd, *A New Critique of Theoretical Thought*, 4 vols. (Philadelphia: Presbyterian & Reformed 1952-58), 3:435. For Dooyeweerd's analysis of the structure of a political community in general, see *New Critique*, 3:379ff.

14. As to the most representative interpretations of "rule of law," see Johan D. van der Vyver, *Seven Lectures on Human Rights* (Cape Town: Juta, 1976), 106ff.

15. Ivor Jennings, *The Law and the Constitution*, 5th ed. (London: University of London Press, 1963), 50.

16. Lord Acton, letter to Mendell Creighton, 5 April 1887, in John Emerich Edward Dalbert-Acton, *Essays on Freedom and Power*, selected and ed. Gertrude Himmelfarb (Boston and Glencoe, Ill.: Beacon, 1949) 364.

17. *Vorschule der Rechtsphilosophie*, 2nd ed. (Gottingen: Vandenhoeck & Ruprecht, 1959), 20-23.

Reflections on quantitative methods
Paul A. Marshall

Satan stood up against Israel, and incited David to number Israel. So David said to Joab and the commanders of
the army, "Go, number Israel, from Beer-sheba to Dan,
and bring me a report, that I may know their number." But
Joab said, "May the Lord add to his people a hundred
times as many as there are! Are they not, my lord the king,
all of them my lord's servants? Why then should my lord
require this? Why should he bring guilt upon Israel?" But
the king's word prevailed against Joab.... And Joab gave
the sum of the numbering of the people to David....But he
did not include Levi and Benjamin in the numbering, for
the king's command was abhorrent to Joab.

But God was displeased with this thing, and he
smote Israel.... So the Lord sent a pestilence upon Israel....
And David said to God, "Was it not I who gave command
to number the people? It is I who have sinned and done
very wickedly....
IChronicles 21:1-7, 14, 17 (RSV)

Introductory remarks
In the twentieth century there has been a growing emphasis on
quantification and quantitative methods in the social sciences.[1]
It is now perhaps the dominant ethos within the United States,
and its influence has spread to other countries. This emphasis
is manifested in three overlapping forms:

1. The development of methods and techniques, involving
statistical and other mathematical treatments, that study social
structures and behavior by analyzing quantitative data. This
development involves questions of statistical theory, probability theory, measurement, data analysis, causal analysis, content
analysis, polling, voting, and legislative surveys.

2. The development of theories about the nature of society
that are justified in some part by their amenability to mathe-

matical treatment. These theories are sometimes difficult to distinguish from group 1. Such theories include systems theory, group theory, cybernetic models, economic models, organizational models, general simulation models, and general behavioral theory.

3. The development of theories and models of politics based on what is often called "mathematical reasoning." These are usually simple models expressed in terms of mathematical equations. The properties of such equations are explored, and deductions made from them are tested for what they might reveal about society. This class includes game theories, rational and other decision models, and some economic models.

Critical analyses of this phenomenon tend to be of two types. One type focusses on scientism, behavioralism, and fact/value questions and then points out how methods affect our view of the world as much as do substantive theories.[2] However, this type of analysis rarely goes beyond a general critique of quantitative methods, and ignores their internal structure. The other type of analysis is usually idiographic, often considering the defects of one mathematical technique.[3] This type rarely discusses the overall nature of such methods. In general, there is little systematic analysis and evaluation of quantitative methods as such in the social sciences.[4]

This is unfortunate, as many methods often are used indiscriminately. For example, though economists are generally better trained and more sophisticated in their methods than other social scientists, the eminent economist Joan Robinson still laments that:

> Mathematical operations are performed on entities that cannot be defined; calculations are made in terms of units that cannot be measured; accounting identities are mistaken for functional relationships; correlations are mistaken for causal laws; differences are identified with changes; and one way movements in time are treated like movements to and fro in space. The complexity of models is elaborated merely for display, far and away beyond the possibility of application to reality.[5]

This matter should especially concern Christians, for these mathematical developments are in the vanguard of attempts by the social sciences to imitate the natural sciences and they often portray humanity and society without considering the reality of our freedom and responsibility. I take it that Christians oppose such a view. At the same time we should have, I trust, no problem per se with trying to observe and describe regularities in social events; nor would we object per se to counting things, even by sophisticated methods.[6] We need, then, some means of understanding quantitative methods and some means of unraveling the scientific from the merely scientistic. This paper tries to develop some guidelines for such understanding and unraveling.

Representing social things in mathematical terms

The ambiguity of "quantification". There are some curious conceptions in mathematical methodology. One is the tendency to speak of *quantifying* things. What does this term mean? It implies that a thing has been made into a quantity. Indeed, some authors speak of *"imparting* properties of numbers to phenomena."[7] But usually the thing "quantified" remains as it is, barring some experimental interaction. The investigator has only assigned some numbers to represent the thing quantified and nothing has been done to the thing itself. This is not a mere semantic quibble, for the term "quantify" obscures the fact that a number only represents a thing and tends to confer an almost alchemic quality to the procedure.

Quantification as a form of classification. It is clear that social entities—such as parties or families—are not themselves solely numerical; only numbers are that. Hence when we express social entities in terms of numbers, we are either representing the entities themselves by numbers or, a subset of this, representing them by their numerical aspects.[8]

Before we can represent something mathematically, count something, or ask "How much of a thing?" we must know what we are counting. We must first ask, "What is a thing?" For example, if you say there are three, or five, or seven political parties in a country, then you must understand what constitutes a political party before you can count them. As Karl Deutsch pointed out, "counting is repeated recognition."[9]

Expressing something by a quantity can take place only after other relevant features have been examined and compared. Only if we can say that the things in question are of a like kind, can we refer to two of them, or ten of them, or whatever.

As Studdert-Kennedy pointed out, "quantification is not a quantum jump into an independent and methodologically arcane level of thought. We are concerned with an extension of the elementary analytical activity of making distinctions, of classifying and comparing entities."[10] Expressing something in a quantitative form is always and inevitably a classification. Whether the classifications are current, accepted ones, such as measuring income in money, or are those suggested by scientific investigators themselves, they are classifications.

If a systematic comparison is neglected, then a number conveys an *implicit* classification.[11] For example, if it is said that there are four parties, then there are implicit criteria for a party such that these four are included while others are rejected. If a quantitative expression is made prematurely, then it is likely to be based on an implicit classification that is somewhat arbitrary or unrefined. Hence the conclusions are likely to be misleading. These implicit classifications are a form of a posteriori reasoning—classifications made with a view to their amenability to quantification. Jean Blondel, for example, reached the surprising conclusion that the party systems of Sweden and Italy were of similar types, an opinion at variance with the views of most authorities on comparative politics.[12] He noted that these systems contained similar numbers of parties of roughly similar sizes (measured in number of votes gathered at general elections). This counting procedure implied, for example, that Christian democratic votes are of a type with communist votes. But such votes might be quite different in kind. A Christian democrat might vote to elect a government while a communist might vote to make a country ungovernable. For some purposes it might be inaccurate to just conceive of votes as ticks on pieces of paper. Blondel appears to have added just such ticks, presumably on the grounds that they were politically important and easily countable. But this quantification did not analyze votes to ensure that they were of like types. His classification appears to have been made because of its amenability to quantification, giving a distorted view of party systems.[13]

Quantification increases neither precision nor accuracy. The Nobel Prize winner in economics, Herbert Simon, observed:

> Mathematics has become the dominant language of the natural sciences not because it is quantitative—a common

delusion—but primarily because it permits clear and rigorous reasoning about phenomena too complex to handle in words. This advantage of mathematics over cruder languages should prove of even greater significance in the social sciences, which deal with phenomena of the greatest complexity, than it has in the natural sciences.[14]

But it is debatable whether mathematics is the dominant language of the natural sciences. One could make a case for the English language. It is true that the natural sciences frequently discuss calculi and the morphology of equations, nevertheless these discussions need more than numbers so that they can refer to actual experiments and observations. Otherwise everything would be pure mathematics with no reference to anything beyond itself.[15] We should not be deluded by large quantities of mathematics into thinking that talking about formulae is the same as talking about the things that formulae refer to.

Simon seems to think that mathematics is the most accurate and precise form of representation.[16] However, quantification is partly analogous to a translation. It would be a remarkable translation that could take a "crude" term (as Simon would put it) from a language in which, after all, it was conceived and formulated and then consistently translate it into a term with more precision and accuracy. How could we get a sufficiently clear notion of the nuances of an English word to be able to establish the accuracy of its translation into mathematics? By what standards, other than mathematical, could we tell if the mathematical translation was suitable? We could not judge the clarity of the translation with more or less accuracy than our standards permitted. But if the standards for translation are expressed, not in mathematical language but in a more ordinary language, then the mathematical translation can not be judged with more or less accuracy than the terms of the ordinary language permitted. If the standards for translation are mathematical, then it is circular to argue that the mathematical translation is clearer or more accurate than the "cruder," original language.

Intelligence tests are a useful example here. The statement "A has an IQ of 140 and B has an IQ of 120" might appear to be more precise than the statement "A is more intelligent than B." However, an intelligence test is of use only if it actually reflects what we consider to be intelligence. If the scores given on a particular test did not reflect what we considered to be the intelligence of the subjects, then we would reject the test as a measure. If we found that subjects who scored 120 appeared to be as intelligent and performed as well in other circumstances as subjects who scored 140, then we would think, I trust, that the test did not have the power to discriminate at this level. Here we can see that the test codifies our perceptions of what constitutes levels of intelligence. The test will maintain its validity as long as it appears to be congruent with our perceptions of it. The test will have precision according to how sharply we can perceive intelligence. *It cannot be more precise than the criteria that we use to judge it.* Hence an intelligence test cannot be more precise about intelligence than the degree to which we can discriminate levels of intelligence.

Of course an investigator might adopt an operationalist definition of what constitutes a level of intelligence and hence assert that its most fundamental measure is an IQ test score. But in this instance it is this particular test score—a number—to which the argument about precision has shifted.[17] The argument is then that test scores are the most precise expression of test scores, which is the circularity referred to earlier.[18]

Some conclusions on quantification. We can conclude that expressing something in numerical terms should only be done after the various aspects and facets of what is being studied have been compared and their similarities and dissimilarities noted. When we have determined that certain things are alike in the relevant aspects, then we can express how much or how many of them there are. This quantification does not increase accuracy or precision.

If our mathematical expressions have been derived from such a process, and if the results of a measuring apparatus continue to reflect our conception of the relative strengths of the things being measured, then the numerical values so obtained might be considered as data suitable for analysis. We will now consider the mathematical treatment of such data.

The mathematical treatment of terms and its relation to social interactions
Mathematical treatments must reflect social relations. The applicability of mathematical calculi to social situations is part of the

larger question of applying mathematical calculi to any "real" situations. Indeed, the applicability of such calculi is sometimes thought to be cause for surprise. Some have wondered how adding two plus two in a number system gives results similar to adding two oranges to two apples. This is because mathematics is frequently regarded as a formal or logical system, "rational" in its construction. How does it happen that this "rational" system relates to and reflects the "empirical" world?[19]

However, such calculi do not necessarily reflect empirical situations; rather, they only relate to such situations in a particular and derivative way. Consider, as an example, the sort of question usually given to young children in grade school textbooks. "If one man can dig a trench in four days, how long will it take two men?" The expected answer is, of course, two days. However, as any economist can demonstrate, this is manifestly incorrect. Two men working might set up systems of cooperation, division of labor, and morale building or perhaps conflict. They might dig a trench in one and one-half days or two and one-half days. Only circumstantially will it be two days. We cannot subject a particular relation, in this case an economic one, to a mathematical treatment and expect that the consequent equations and results will necessarily reflect the real structure of the relationship.

As a further example, if one took a population in which one-third of the people earned $1,000, one-third earned $5,000, and one-third earned $15,000 and expressed the income in terms of pentiles, the results would be 1,000: 2,300: 5,000: 11,700:15,000. The real structure would be missed and the figures would tend to indicate a gradation of income.

Few social scientists would make these errors since the structure of the mathematics and its implications are relatively easy to see. However, these scientists are often unaware of the systematic structure behind the qualifications they use to guard against these errors. The qualifications, in fact, ensure that a prior knowledge of relationships within society comes to expression in the mathematics. The mathematical calculi follow the social pattern of distribution. But this point is rarely examined, and scientists simply exhort each other to be "judicious" without any systematic guidance as to what it means to be "judicious."[20] Consequently, when a complex mathematical treatment (factor analysis, regression analysis, or various forms of calculus) is used, then its implications for the nature of the data being treated and for the nature of the relations being assumed are rarely acknowledged or even known.[21]

It is technically possible, if we already know the nature and form of a social relationship, to reduce this relationship to mathematical terms and so to derive mathematical calculi that reflect the mathematical substructure of the social interplay. For example, we can study the actual behavior of the men in the trench and express it mathematically using the procedure outlined above. We can proceed from a knowledge of social factors, causes, and interrelations to a mathematical expression. But we cannot proceed from purely formal numerical relations and assume they will necessarily reflect a social situation.[22]

It appears then that the mathematical calculi used to analyze data, such as are derived from the processes outlined above, must be understood as the mathematical aspects or reductions of social relations. In this case the calculi must meet the criteria of justification which apply to the data themselves.

Social relations and the interpretation of correlations and graphs. The relation between mathematical treatments and the social interactions they purport to represent comes to the fore in discussions as to whether we should use linear or curvilinear correlation coefficients. Common statistical techniques, such as factor analysis, mainly consider linear correlations between variables.[23] But there seem to be no a priori reasons to expect that social relations will be reflected only in equations of a linear form or, even, of a curvilinear form.[24]

Because a stress on determining linear or curvilinear correlations might cause us to overlook other possible mathematical relations, graphical techniques have been suggested. It is thought that with the visual aid of a graph possible relations between the data might be suggested that would otherwise be overlooked.[25] This method at least has the advantage of suggesting mathematical reductions of social relations that are not confined to the formal simplicity of purely mathematical relations.

However, we still need prior understanding of the social nature of relations being considered, as can be shown by considering figure 1. Y and Z are two axes representing variation in two variables. The Xs mark points showing the known value of one variable when the other variable has a particular value. If the points are plotted, then it is possible to draw various lines through them that portray particular postulated mathematical relations between the data.

The line A suggests a linear relation between Y and Z that "explains" about 70% of the variance in Y and Z.[26] Line B suggests a relation between Y and Z of the form Z = Yn that "explains" about 85% of the variance of Z. Line C suggests a complex relation between Y and Z involving at least Yn and sine Y that "explains" about 98% of the variance of Z. A possible line D could suggest a very complex relation that "explains" all of the variance in Z. Such a line D is theoretically possible for any set of points.

One can select lines of varying "degrees of fit" to the points that "explain" certain amounts of variance. "Unexplained" variance is the distance of the points from these lines. It must be emphasized that we have no mathematical grounds for deciding which of these lines to choose. Yet the line we choose will purport to indicate what type of relationship, and how strong a relationship, exists between the variables.

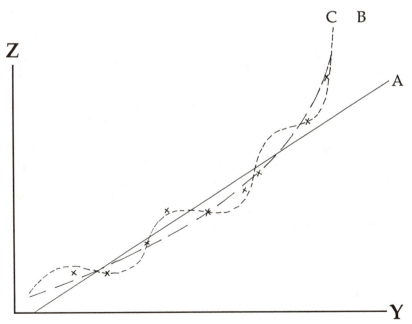

Figure 1

The literature offers two grounds for selection of a particular line. One is the criterion of parsimony, that is, select the simplest line that expresses some relation. However, this mathematical Occam's razor implies that the relationship, if any, will have a simple mathematical form. But why should we expect social relations to be like this? The use of log linear relationships (i.e., the reduction of the units of the axes to a logarithmic base so that the lines in the graph will have a visually simpler form) merely complicates this problem. It cannot solve it.

The other method of procedure, suggested by E. R. Tufte, is more to the point.[27] Tufte suggests that we consider political or social relationships first and then test various models (linear or curvilinear) until the desired "degree of fit" is achieved. He also suggests that we do not choose between a linear or another model solely on the degree of correlation; rather, we should examine the *residuals* (the variations of the data about this line) to see if there is some systematic variation around the model. These are certainly more substantive grounds for selecting a particular line and, in the light of our discussion so far, they should lead to some truly empirical results.

Tufte, however, ignores one problem. If, for example, only 50% of the covariation is accounted for by a particular line, then this might have little bearing on the actual degree of relationships between the variables because the other 50% of variation might indicate a systematic, causal relationship of a more complex mathematical form. We should certainly examine the form of the social relation itself. But we should go further than Tufte's suggestion. We should try to derive the mathematical relation by determining the *numerical aspect* of the relation.[28]

The potential heuristic value of mathematical treatments. I have stressed the need to arrive at mathematical treatments by the legitimate and argued reduction of social relations rather than assuming that particular mathematical relations adequately reflect social ones. However, particular extrapolations from simple mathematical models might have a heuristic value, as in extrapolations from game theory or group theory to party systems or group interactions. Having seen certain structures and boundaries emerge in such models, we might check to see if they operate in more complex and modally different situations. However, we should always ask, "Do such approaches reveal structures parallel to independently examined social relations?" The social relations are analytically prior to the mathematical ones and are frequently, though not always, prior in the strategy of research.

Drawing conclusions from mathematical treatments

The interpretation of coefficients. If we have discovered an apparent mathematical relation between two variables, there are still grave difficulties with interpreting a result. Lancelot Hogben gives a useful example in the field of immunology. We may suppose that (1) disease X is incurable if untreated and (2) a typical clinical trial suggests the recovery rate under treatment Y as 25% and under treatment Z as 50%. If we merely substitute treatment Z for treatment Y in order to increase the recovery rate by 25%, then our preoccupation with averages (which might be mathematical artifacts) could blind us to biological realities. We should rather ask what peculiarities are common to individuals who respond to, or fail to respond to, one or another treatment. We should search for the conditions under which we might have a recovery rate of 100%. Of course we might not be able to find these conditions or even progress beyond the 25% of Y and 50% of Z. However, these figures should not be taken a priori as a result.[29]

This example reveals the necessary priority of specifically biological analysis. The illustration can be applied to social relations with special ramifications in the matter of causality. It implies that explanations and theories of causality must be of a correct modal character.

Arthur Maass makes this point when he speaks of the political scientist Vladimir O. Key:

> Where gross data (e.g., demographic, income levels, etc.) indicate, for example, that 70% of businessmen voted one way, Key invariably asks the question why 30% did not vote their apparent economic interests; and the answer not infrequently is that the classification provided by the gross data is irrelevant.[30]

Giovanni Sartori makes a similar point when he suggests that if, typically, only a portion of the working class votes for "its" party, it begs the question to say that this represents class voting; if it did so in a mechanical way (i.e., if workers vote for a labor party because they are workers) then *all* workers should vote for the same party.[31] He maintains that at the very least we need to suggest why some workers vote their interest and some don't. This might enable us to discover the exact causes behind such voting patterns. Such an approach should be taken to all correlation coefficients.

Mathematical relations are information, not necessarily laws. Probability statements that can be made about society are generally of an "if—then" character. (For example, "If the prime minister cuts taxes, then his election chances will improve.")[32] Few researchers have claimed to be able to speak of the probability of the prime minister cutting taxes without using another "if—then" form. An absolute prediction appears almost impossible unless we limit ourselves to physical or biological causes, such as the prime minister's death. In the natural sciences, apart from astronomy perhaps, absolute predictions usually take place only in an experimental setting, to the degree that all variables are controlled except the ones under investigation. Such predictions could state "...if all else is constant," but since all else is being *held* constant the statement is not necessary. Unless we can put similar controls on a political system, such a procedure does not seem transferable.

Perhaps when researchers make predictions, they should state what must remain constant or vary only slightly for the prediction to be correct. This could help avoid the frequent predictions of the form "if nothing changes—everything will stay the same."

These questions of probability and prediction can be illustrated by insurance company actuarial tables, which are probably our most accurate social predictors. These tables appear to have a high predictive capacity about, for example, the average life expectancy of the class of married males, with two children, who drink moderately and drive twenty thousand miles a year. At least, we rarely hear about large insurance companies going bankrupt. However, their predictive capacity is limited in that such tables (and their monetary disbursements!) assume that no major social changes will occur. As the fine print indicates, a nuclear war, plague, purge or revolution, or even less important events would cause widespread changes in the tables. The tables do not indicate invariant "social laws" since they themselves can be subjected to social change.

These questions about probability and change also reveal something of the deterministic nature of relations expressed in mathematical terms, unless they are taken as pure *information* about the present or past. It is sometimes acknowledged that nonprobabilistic mathematical calculi are deterministic, but it is often held that probabilistic statements are not so. My statements are meant to apply to both classes.

For example, even if a claim is made about the probable relation between income levels and expressed political unrest, there is always the possibility of the relation being subjected to political change (such as repression that severely limits expressed political unrest). Consequently a probabilistic statement can be misleading if it is held to be a *necessary* condition to which political activity must be subordinated rather than mere information about some occurences.

A discussion of this sort is frequently considered an argument about "free will" against statistical laws.[33] This argument is an extraneous concern. What is being asserted here is merely that a probabilistic statement is unnecessarily deterministic if it is held to be a necessary relationship, unless it can be demonstrated that the particular relation cannot be subject to political change. Mathematical statements about relationships can be very useful as generalizations or as information, but they cannot be treated as social law unless we can show they are necessary conditions of society.[34]

Concluding remarks

I have outlined a scheme for considering quantitative methods in the social sciences. My primary intent has been analytical. Much of my discussion has been negative, stressing the limits on what can be done. This may leave the wrong impression that such quantitative methods are nearly useless. Hence, I would like to suggest one general reason why such methods might and should be used—a reason that is quite obvious but often overlooked.

Especially with the advent of computers mathematical treatments are useful in handling large quantities of data. It is the nature of mathematics to be concerned with quantity. Mathematical treatments are not more rigorous, precise, accurate, or unequivocal than "qualitative" methods, but they deal with numbers of things. Whenever we are faced with large amounts of data—as we usually are—then mathematical treatments are inevitable. Quantitative methods do not give us higher and more rigorous social science; they enable us to deal with quantities and large amounts of data.

One final cautionary remark. There is a major trend in our society to consider the quantitative aspects of phenomena as their only important and real aspects. In my country the Inuit (Eskimo) word for government official means "one who counts." If it is true, as I have maintained, that many of the proposed mathematical procedures and methods are seriously deficient and reductionist, then this means that our society tends to shape itself according to deficient and reductionist criteria. For example, a government might just react according to its standing in opinion polls. The potential pitfalls of mathematical treatments could then be institutionalized in a deficient society. It appears that various reductionist economic theories have already been institutionalized. In this case, then even deficient mathematical treatments might, in a superficial way at least, describe and predict our deficient social behavior. But if this continues, then, as Hannah Arendt commented, our problem might well be not that such mathematical treatments do not "work" but that they are starting to "work" all too well.

Notes

1. While most of my experience of quantitative methods is in political science, a fact reflected in many of the examples, I do not think such methods differ from those in other social sciences.
2. Cf. Herbert J. Storing, ed., *Essays on the Scientific Study of Politics* (New York: Holt, Rinehart & Winston, 1962); Pitirim A. Sorokin, *Fads and Foibles in Modern Sociology and Related Sciences* (Chicago: H. Regnery, 1956); Stanislav Andreski, *Social Science as Sorcery* (London: Andre Deutsch, 1972); Jacques Barzun, *Clio and the Doctors* (Chicago: University of Chicago Press, 1974); Bernard R. Crick, *The American Science of Politics: Its Origins and Conditions* (London: Routledge & Kegan Paul, 1959); C. W. Mills, *The Sociological Imagination* (New York: Oxford University Press, 1959); and C. Bay, "Politics and Pseudopolitics: A Critical Examination of Some Behavioral Literature," in *Behavioralism in Political Science*, ed. Heinz Eulau (New York: Atherton Press, 1969), 109-140.
3. Cf. M. Nowakowska, "The Limitations of the Factor Analytic Approach to Psychology with Special Application to Cattell's Research Strategy," *Theory and Decision* 4 (1973-74), 109-41; J. K. Lindsay, "A Critique of Scaled Variables," *Quantity and Quality* 9 (1975): 137-50; J. F. Marquette, "Standard Scores as Indices: The Pitfalls of Doing Things the Easy Way," *Midwest Journal of Political*

Science 16 (1972): 278-86; H. Nurmi, "Social Causality and Empirical Data Reduction Technique," *Quantity and Quality* 8 (1974): 159-80; H. F. Weisberg, "Dimensionland: An Excursion into Spaces," *American Journal of Political Science* 18 (1974): 743-76 and "Models of Statistical Relationship," *American Political Science Review* 68 (1974): 1638-55; J. K. Lindsay, "A Comparison of Additive and Multiplicative Models for Qualitative Data," *Quantity and Quality* 9 (1975): 43-50; D. Shields, "Statistical Explanation in Cross-Cultural Research: A Comparison of the Utility of Linear and Curvilinear Correlations," *The Sociological Quarterly* 16 (1975): 115-23; and C. E. Susmilils and W. T. Johnson, "Factor Scores for Construction Linear Composites: Do Different Techniques Make a Difference?" *Sociological Method and Research* 4 (1975): 166-88.

4. The nearest approaches are Hayward R. Alker, Jr., *Mathematics and Politics* (New York: Macmillan, 1965); T. R. Gurr, *Politimetrics* (Englewood Cliffs, N.J.: Prentice-Hall, 1972); James S. Coleman, *Introduction to Mathematical Sociology* (New York: Free Press, 1964); A. Hacker, "The Utility of Quantitative Methods in Political Science," in *Contemporary Political Science*, ed. James C. Charlesworth (New York: Free Press, 1967): 134-49; Paul F. Lazarsfeld, ed., *Mathematical Thinking in the Social Sciences* (New York: Free Press, 1954); Paul F. Lazarsfeld and Neil W. Henry, eds., *Readings in Mathematical Social Science* (Cambridge, Mass.: MIT Press, 1968); Anatol Rapoport, "Conceptualization of a System as a Mathematical Model," in *Operational Research and the Social Sciences*, ed. J. R. Lawrence (London: Tavistock, 1966): 515-29; Fred Massarik and Philburn Ratoosh, eds., *Mathematical Explorations in Behavioral Science* (Homewood, Ill.: R. D. Irwin, 1965); R. W. Bronson, "Theoretical Mathematics," R. V. Kidd, "Mathematical Models," and L. F. S. Natalicio, "Units of Measurement," *Methodology and Science* 3 (1970): 156-60; Gordon Tullock, *Toward a Mathematics of Politics* (Ann Arbor: University of Michigan Press, 1967); Anatol Rapoport, *Strategy and Conscience* (New York: Harper & Row, 1964); and David Willer, *Scientific Sociology: Theory and Method* (Englewood Cliffs, N.J.: Prentice-Hall, 1967).

5. Quoted by Robert Heilbroner, "The New Economics," *The New York Review of Books* 27 (February 21, 1980, no. 2): 20.

6. The term "mathematical" will be used interchangeably with *numerical* or *quantitative*. Formalist and Logicist schools of mathematics would maintain that mathematics could be extended beyond the manipulation of numbers. I will not take up this question but only consider *numerical, quantitative* approaches.

7. Bernard S. Phillips, *Social Research: Strategy and Tactics* (New York: Macmillan, 1966), 166-67, italics mine.

8. Cf. Herman Weyl, *Philosophy of Mathematics and Natural Science*, rev. and augm. (Princeton, N.J.: Princeton University Press, 1959), 144ff. I am using terms like "thing" or "phenomena" loosely, not in a technical sense. I am simply referring to "anything." The numerical aspect means that dimension of things that reveals itself in numerical fashion. If there are five polar bears in a cage, the numerical aspect of the polar bears is five; nothing else is said about the bears but their discrete quantity. We may also speak of their ten eyes, five noses, one hundred claws, and so forth. For a discussion of this, see Herman Dooyeweerd, *A New Critique of Theoretical Thought* 4 vols. (Philadel-

phia: Presbyterian & Reformed, 1953-58), 2:79-106.

9. Karl Deutsch, "Toward an Inventory of Basic Trends and Patterns in Comparative and International Politics," *American Political Science Review*, 54 (1960), p. 38.

10. Gerald Studdert-Kennedy, *Evidence and Explanation in Social Science: An Interdisciplinary Approach* (London: Routledge & Kegan Paul, 1975), 78. Also see chapter 4.

11. For a good discussion of this point, see G. Sartori, "Concept Misformation in Comparative Politics," *American Political Science Review* 64 (1970): 1033-53.

12. Jean Blondel, *An Introduction to Comparative Politics,* (London: Weidenfeld & Nicolson, 1969), 157ff. Also see the problems discussed by Rapoport, *Strategy*, chapters 10 and 11 (cited in note 4 above).

13. See Sartori. Also see R. A. Dahl, "The Concept of Power," *Behavioral Science* 2 (1957): 201-15, where Dahl gives each vote in a congressional roll call equal weight as he considers the concept of power. See the comments of O. Benson, "The Mathematical Approach to Political Science," in *Contemporary Political Science*, (New York: Free Press, 1967) 108-33. This point is also made by H. F. Weisberg, "Models," and with reference to economics by Wassily Leontiev, "The Problem of Quantity and Quality in Economics," in *Quantity and Quality*, ed. Daniel Lerner (New York: Free Press 1961), 117-28.

14. Herbert Simon, quoted in William Buchanan, *Understanding Political Variables* (New York: Charles Scribner's Sons, 1969), 63. Compare K. Arrow, "Mathematical Models in the Social Sciences," in *The Policy Sciences*, ed. Daniel Lerner and Harold Lasswell (Stanford, Calif.: Stanford University Press, 1951).

15. Compare Simon with this more amusing quote from Joel Cohen, "On the Nature of Mathematical Proofs," in *A Stress Analysis of a Strapless Evening Gown*, ed. Robert A. Baker (Englewood Cliffs, N.J.: Prentice-Hall, 1963), 93: Bertrand Russell has defined mathematics as the science where we n e v e r know what we are talking about nor whether what we are saying is true. Mathematics has been shown to apply widely in many other scientific fields. Hence most other scientists do not know what they are talking about nor whether what they are saying is true.

16. Cf. W. P. Shiveley, *The Craft of Political Research* (Englewood Cliffs, N.J.: Prentice-Hall, 1974), 21.

17. I have discussed this aspect of operationalism in my "Some Recent Conceptions of Operationalism and Operationalizing," *Philosophia reformata* 44 (1979): 46-68. Also see Hugh G. Petrie, "A Dogma of Operationalism in the Social Sciences," *Philosophy of the Social Sciences* 1 (1971): 145-60.

18. In a more political vein, the example can be given of political attitude scales or rank orderings of political opinion, as in Guttman scales. Cf. Glendon A. Schubert, ed., *Judicial Decision-Making* (New York: Free Press, 1963).

19. See the comments of Karl R. Popper, "Why Are the Calculi of Logic and Arithmetic Applicable to Reality?" in *Conjectures and Refutations* (New York: Basic Books, 1962), 201-14.

20. The papers of Weisberg cited above are an exception to this. In these papers Weisberg points out that any form of mathematical treatment is an expression of a model of politics.

21. Examples of this occur with respect to dimensional variance and invari-

ance. See, for example, D. K. Osborne, "On Dimensional Invariance," *Quantity and Quality* 12 (1978): 75-89. Similarly with Z scores, see P. Cutwright, "National Political Development: Measurement and Analysis," in *Politics and Social Life: An Introduction to Political Behavior*, ed. Nelson Polsby, R. A. Dentler and P. A. Smith (Boston: Houghton Mifflin, 1963), 569-83. And with whole-part relations, see Hubert M. Blalock, *Theory Construction* (Englewood Cliffs, N.J.: Prentice-Hall, 1969), 5-6. See also Marquette (cited in note 3 above).

22. A similar point is made by Carl G. Hempel in "Reduction: Ontological and Linguistic Facets," in *Philosophy, Science, and Method: Essays in Honor of Ernst Nagel*, ed. Sidney Morgenbesser, Patrick Suppes, and Morton White (New York: St. Martin's Press, 1969), 179-200. Hempel makes the point that one can, technically, reduce "downwards" in ontic modes but not "upwards."

23. "Linear" in this context means equal changes in one variable are correlated with equal changes in another variable. The changes in the latter variable may be equal to that of the first variable, or two times, or one hundred times, and so forth. Linear correlations can be contrasted with curvilinear correlation where a change in one variable may be with, for example, the square of the change in another variable.

24. Several authors now emphasize the importance of curvilinear correlations. See Lindsay, Shields, and Susmilils and Johnson (cited in note 3 above). Also see Edward R. Tufte, "Improving Data Analysis in Political Science," in *The Quantitative Analysis of Social Problems*, ed. Edward R. Tufte (Reading, Mass.: Addison-Wesley, 1970), 437-49. On the general problems involved, see J. Armstrong, "Derivation of Theory by Means of Factor Analysis, or Tom Swift and His Electric Factor Analysis Machine," *American Statistician* 21 (1967): 17-21.

25. See Tufte (cited in previous note above). In same volume, see J. W. Tukey and M. B. Wilk, "Data Analysis and Statistics: Techniques and Approaches."

26. In this context "explain" is used in the sense common in the quantitative literature. It is simply a measure of covariation and need not imply explanation (or causality) in the more usual sense. However, as the goal of maximal "explanation" (in this narrow sense) is frequently evident in the literature, it is often implied that this "explanation" has the attributes of explanation in a more usual sense. In particular cases it might do so, but there is no a priori reason why it should.

27. Edward R. Tufte, *Data Analysis for Politics and Policy*, (Englewood Cliffs, N.J.: Prentice-Hall, 1974), 65ff., 115ff.

28. This point also applies to questions of regression analysis and even to questions of linear and curvilinear correlation coefficients. Cf. K. E. Southwood, "Substitution Theory and Statistical Interaction," *American Journal of Sociology* 83 (1978): 1154-1203. Southwood shows that linear regression models can be misleading because of the possible interaction of variables.

29. Lancelot Hogben, *Statistical Theory* (New York: Norton, 1957), 341-42. Also see the comments in Tufte, *Data Analysis*, about what may be hidden in cross tabulations.

30. Arthur Maass, ed. *The Responsible Electorate: Rationality in Presidential Voting, 1936-1960* (New York: Vintage Books, 1968), Forward to Vladimer O. Key ix. Also see 40, 70.

31. G. Sartori, "From the Sociology of Politics to Political Sociology," in *Politics and the Social Sciences*, ed. Seymour M. Lipset (New York: Oxford University

112   *Social science in Christian perspective*

Press, 1969), 75ff.

32. Cf. the comments of L. C. Thurow, "Economics, 1977," *Daedalus* 106 (Fall 1977): 86-89.

33. Cf. I. Budge, "The Scientific Status of Political Science: A Comment on the Self-fulfilling and Self-defeating Prediction," *British Journal of Political Science* 3 (1973): 249; and C. Ake, "The Scientific Status of Political Science," *British Journal of Political Science* 2 (1972): 109-15.

34. Cf. A. J. Ayer, "Man as a Subject for Science," in *Philosophy, Politics and Society: a Collection*, ed. Peter Laslett and W. G. Ruciman, 3d ser. (Oxford: Basil Blackwell, 1967), 8ff. Ayer too gets into the question of "free will," but his statements about the status of generalizations are more to the point. Cf. David Hume's comment that "A man who, at noon, leaves his purse full of gold on the pavement of Charing Cross, may as well expect that it will fly away like a feather, as that he will find it untouched an hour later," quoted in Budge (see previous note above). This statement, too, is subject to political change, since, by all accounts, the expectations might be higher in Peking stations.

Philosophy and sociology
Daniel F. M. Strauss

Introduction
Sociology, from its birth at the beginning of the nineteenth century and in its subsequent growth and development as a special science, continuously stressed its fundamental dependence on philosophical presuppositions.[1] As a science of creation in its totality, philosophy explores the mutual coherence in the discernible diversity of cosmic facets. Since no special science can escape a foundational view of the relationship between the various aspects of creaturely reality, it is obvious that no special science can operate without philosophical presuppositions. Even when a special science wishes to account for its own existence, it is compelled to move outside its own universe of discourse. Special scientists, therefore, either have a philosophical vision (in which they give a critical account of their philosophical starting point), or they are uncritical victims of some particular philosophical trend in their special science.

Let us consider the basic philosophical orientations of a few modern sociologists. R. M. MacIver started his sociological thinking in 1917 by clearly distinguishing two kinds of laws: material and vital. The former is "the law of invariable concomitance or sequence, the fixed order of material nature," and the latter is revealed "in the will of the living, unstable, relative, riddled with changefulness and imperfection."[2] Subsequently, in an intermediate period, MacIver distinguished the "Physical Realm," "The Realm of Organic Being" and "The Realm of Conscious Being."[3] (These distinctions are similar to P. Sorokin's distinctions between the inorganic, the organic, and the superorganic,[4] and they are influenced by the philosophical approach of the neo-Kantian thinker H. Rickert.) In the well-known textbook of MacIver and Page entitled *Society*, the third realm is divided into civilization and culture.[5] In one of his last works, however, we note a remarkable shift in his total orientation that even cancels his original distinction between material and vital law. In line with the continuity postulate of mechanistic evolutionism, MacIver wrote:

> The line from the inorganic to the organic is continuous. The line therefore from the nonliving to the living is continuous and among the living from the simplest living forms of vegetative existence to the highest of the animal world.[6]

The development of R. Bierstedt is another striking example of such a radical shift. In a discussion of the early work of T. Parsons, *The Structure of Social Action*, Bierstedt stridently rejected the scientific value of terms like means and ends:

> The positivistic tradition...requires as the very minimum criterion of a concept that it be reducible to referents which can directly be related to sense-experience or be reached by empirical operations. Ends and means by definition fail to satisfy this criterion. They are not sensory objects to which an investigator can respond.[7]

Claiming that "concrete existential entities susceptible of sense-experience" are the "prime criterion of science," Bierstedt does not hesitate to speak of sociology as "a natural science."[8] In 1974 Bierstedt reviewed his positivism as follows:

> It is an orthodox positivistic response to Parson's theory, an assertion of the necessity of dispensing with subjective concepts in sociological inquiry, and a defense of determinism against voluntarism. At the time it was written I had fallen under the influence of George A. Lundberg, then a visitor in the Columbia department, and had read with increasing excitement all his polemical papers.[9]

Eventually, it was MacIver, among others, who led Bierstedt to "a close and critical examination" of his own position and he was finally convinced that Lundberg's radical empiricism "had solipsistic consequences and would, if taken seriously, destroy the objectivity of sociological knowledge."[10] A mere eleven years after his attack on the Parsonian means-end schema, he read a paper before the annual meeting of the Illinois Academy of Science with the title, *A Critique of Empiricism in Sociology!*[11] In this article he stressed the active role of human reason in scientific inquiry, which transcends sense-experience,[12] betraying the influence of Kant.[13]

As a last example, we take Max Weber's well-known definition of sociology's field of investigation:

> The term "sociology" is open to many different interpretations. In the context used here it shall mean that science which aims at the interpretative understanding of social behavior in order to gain an explanation of its causes, its course, and its effects.[14]

Othmar Spann reacted to this definition. He simply stated that Weber tried to combine two self-contradictory elements in his circumscription: interpretative understanding (*deutend verstehen*) and causal explanation (*ursachlich erklaren*). Interpretative understanding, for Spann, implies that one must take account of the qualitative meaning and meaning-coherence of that which is analyzed; but it never implies a causal explanation (such as the calculation of the motion of the earth in physics). Spann concludes:

> It is clear that through interpretative understanding, through taking account of the qualitative meaning of an object, every form of causality is excluded.[15]

For Spann causality merely indicates the external mechanical succession of phenomena. It concerns the totality of antecedents from which a specific phenomenon follows as its temporal consequent. Interpretative understanding, on the other hand, relates the disclosure of meaningful coherences to internal categories.[16] To illustrate this difference, Spann gives an example. When two people combat each other, its meaning is understandable as battle (*Kampf*). However, its external mechanical-causal side is merely "energy-transformation of bodily muscles," "accelerated motions of weapons," "elasticity," and "oxidation" (the sparks from the swords), and so on.[17] As a member of the Vienna Circle, Otto Neurath developed a "Sociology on a Materialist Foundation" or, as he preferred to call it, a physicalistic sociology.[18] Neurath sharply disapproved of Weber's sympathy for a "Verstehende" sociology and only approved of the complementary part of Weber's approach that emphasized causal explanation:

> He who keeps free from metaphysics, understanding [*Verstehen*] and similar strivings, can, as a sociologist, only use behavioristic phrases, as are proper in a discipline with a materialist foundation.[19]

To gain clearer insight into the philosophical background of these profound differences, we need to look at the genesis of modern sociology.

The Genesis of Modern Sociology
Theoretical reflection on human society is almost as old as philosophy itself. Since ancient Greek times philosophers speculated extensively about humans and their coexistence with other humans. Traditionally, however, these reflections were framed within general philosophy and almost always concerned the state and (especially during medieval times) the church. In Renaissance times, what Dooyeweerd called the central ground motive of nature and freedom conditioned the subsequent developments within modern humanism.[20] The ideal of free and autonomous personality (the freedom pole) aroused the urge to control reality in terms of the newly developing mathematical natural sciences. According to this (mathematical) science ideal (the nature pole), all of reality must be reduced to mathematical-physical terms that allow a causal explanation. Thomas Hobbes was subject to the humanistic science ideal when he described the state as based on a physics of human nature.[21] Hobbes was acquainted with the mechanics of Galileo, which explains Hobbes's emphasis on the kinematical motion of phenomena.

John Locke's social contract theory, a mathematical construction of human society, also starts from the humanistic ideal of science, although Locke partially exchanged the physical viewpoint for a psychological orientation. Locke proceeded in his psychologistic epistemology from separate sensory impressions and, similarly, in his mathematical construction of the state he attempted to derive everything from isolated individuals with their innate and inalienable human rights. Those rights were not given up in the contract but, as civil rights of life and property, they were protected by organized author- ity. To secure maximum civil freedom there must be a mini- mum of governmental control (the doctrine of *laissez-faire, lais- sez-passer*). The Classical school in economics (A. Smith) emu- lated Locke's idea of the state, convinced that economic life was governed by invariable laws of nature that are in harmony with individuals' pursuit of economic self-interest within the frame- work of their inalienable rights of life, liberty, and property. This development introduced for the first time a distinction between the state and civil society. Previously, theories of human society always developed within a theory of the state.

Civil society was first identified with the sphere of social- economic events, encompassing the developing class differ- ences. St. Simon was the first thinker who tried to explain the whole of society causally from the formation of classes and from the growth of class oppositions. Following R. J. Turgot's distinction of three stadia in the "natural history" of human- kind (a theological, metaphysical and positive stadium),[22] St. Simon reacted violently against the individualistic strain of the Enlightenment. He no longer saw society as a collection of in- dividuals, but as an all-encompassing organic whole (the view of organicistic universalism). And A. Comte also explicitly analyzed society universalistically, as an organic whole with its parts.

Promoted by their stress on the humanistic science ideal, these reflections on human society advanced under the flag of "social physics." Even Comte used the term *physique sociale*. In a letter to Valat (December 15, 1824), Comte for the first time used the term "sociology," although the term itself was not published before 1838.[23] In his extensive work on "Positive Philosophy," Comte gave the following account of his new term:

> I believe that at the present point I must risk this new term, which is precisely equivalent of the expression I have already introduced, *physique sociale*, in order to be able to designate by a single word this complementary part of natural philosophy which bears on the positive study of the totality of fundamental laws proper to social phenom- ena.[24]

Although Comte was faithful to the humanistic science ideal, analyzing phenomena in their simplest elements, he disliked statistics in sociology. Only after the Belgian statistician published a work in 1835 on "social physics" did Comte publish his new term "sociology." However, the atomistic analytical aim of the humanistic science ideal tended to contradict Comte's universalistic organicism. D. Martindale correctly pointed out: "Organicism and positivism should have been in tension from the start."[26]

From our brief analysis of the genesis of modern sociology, we may cull some conclusions: (1) the birth of sociology was dominated by the humanistic science ideal aimed at an exact analysis of society in terms of physical laws; (2) in a self-contradictory way, universalistic organicism was connected with this atomistic physicalistic starting point; and (3) since Comte focused on society as a whole, his sociology cannot be a truly special science (studying society only from one abstracted aspect). For that reason Comte confined his sociology within his "positive philosophy." Nonetheless, the path was now paved for the subsequent development of modern sociology as a special science. It is remarkable to note that the well-known three-stadia-law of Comte still has a descendent in the following words of D. Martindale:

> Sociology is a part of that great evolution of thought in western civilization which passes from religion through philosophy to science.[27]

We can now return to our three earlier examples. The dilemma between various realms or kinds of laws (MacIver), or between determinism and voluntarism (Bierstedt's reaction to Parsons), or between causality and understanding (in Weber's definition of sociology) can be traced back to the fundamental polar tension in the humanistic ground motive of nature and freedom. The reaction of W. Dilthey and the Baden school of neo-Kantian thought to the causal-analytical method of inquiry of the natural sciences marked an important shift toward the primacy of the personality ideal. Dilthey contrasted positivistic explanation, in his reflections on historical reason, with the new method of the cultural sciences, namely, the empathy of understanding (*Verstehen*) of spiritual reality. Only this

method, sharply separated from natural scientific explanations, could achieve a penetrating insight into the values and
aims of the teleological, spiritual world.[28]

Rickert (and Windelband) complemented the Kantian
dualism between *Sein* and *Sollen* (being and ought to be) with
their value idea. Culture, in their view, is the junction of pure
nature-reality conjoined with supratemporal, universally valid
values. Against this background they distinguished generalizing (nomothetic) natural sciences and individualizing (idiographic) spiritual sciences.[29] Subsequently, Rickert allowed for
"generalizing sciences which have the cultural domain for their
subject matter," but he considered this generality as limited by
the very nature of "a cultural value." Therefore, according to
Rickert, the "dividing line between the natural and the cultural
sciences is thereby maintained in this respect as well."[30]

This concise sketch of the reaction inspired by the humanistic personality ideal helps us evaluate the changes we have
noted in MacIver and Bierstedt. MacIver left his original affin-
ity with the ideal of personality in favor of the science ideal,
while Bierstedt followed the opposite path.

To gain a better insight into the way sociology can be
biblically reformed, we cannot bypass the basic philosophical
problem of sociology, namely, the question of its distinctive
subject matter.

The subject matter of sociology as a special science
Sociology originated as a science of human society in its totality. Then does sociology have a special scientific character with
a distinctive, limited approach? Frequently the answer is in the
negative.

> There are those, for example, who would say that sociol-
> ogy is the basic social science, of which all others are
> subdivisions. There are others who claim, with equal
> emphasis, that sociology is a specialized science of social
> phenomena, as specialized in its interests as are economics
> and political science.[31]

The first alternative is often accompanied by universalistic
undertones, as in the case of J. B. McKee:

It is possible to enlarge even further the frame of reference and view sociology as the study of society, when society is defined as the largest and most encompassing of social structures, whose diverse groups and institutions are organized with a reasonable coherence into a single entity.[32]

Sorokin wanted it both ways. According to him general sociology

is concerned with society as a genus, with the properties and relationships that are found in any society, be it a business firm, a church, a state, a club, the family, or anything else.[33]

Although sociology is "a generalizing science dealing with the socio-cultural universe as a whole," it does not mean that sociology "is an encyclopedic survey of all the social sciences or that it is a vague philosophical synthesis." Sorokin claims that in spite of its generalizing nature, "sociology remains a strictly special science." Sociology "does not attempt to do the work of the other social sciences," but just like general biology it is interested in "the properties and repeated relationships" of the "superorganic world."[34] Sorokin, nevertheless, did not even consider the crucial question of how a special science can study society as a whole without reducing those other special sciences (limiting themselves to specific aspects of society) to mere subdisciplines of sociology.

A similar problem is present in Dooyeweerd's view of sociology.

So we conclude that, as a science of human society in its total structures, positive sociology has no special scientific but only a social philosophic viewpoint. But although determined by the latter, its field of research is different from that of social philosophy.[35]

This delimitation is not clear. How can the subject matter of positive sociology be oriented to a social philosophical viewpoint but differ from the subject matter (field of research) of social philosophy?

L. von Wiese pointed out that G. Simmel was the first in
Germany to distinguish sociology from social philosophy.
Sociology was "for him a special science (*Einzelwissen-
schaft*)."[36] In line with Kant's form-matter distinction (used in
Kant's epistemology), Simmel gave an ontological explanation
of the conditions necessary for a society,[37] and he claimed that
sociology is a special science only when it "detaches by analysis
the forms of interaction or sociation from their contents."[38] In
themselves, according to Simmel,

> these materials which fill life, these motivations which
> propel it, are not social. Strictly speaking, neither hunger
> nor love, work nor religiosity, technology nor the func-
> tions and results of intelligence, are social. They are factors
> in sociation only when they transform the mere aggrega-
> tion of isolated individuals into specific forms of beings
> with and for one another, forms that are subsumed under
> the general concept of interaction.[39]

With a similar emphasis on form, Kelsen introduced his
pure jurisprudence (*reine Rechtslehre*), regarded by him as "a
geometry of the total phenomenon of law."[40] Even before
Kelsen, R. Stammler introduced the form-matter schema in
jurisprudence. The "connective will" is for him the form of a
society, only receiving stability and endurance by juridical
determination.[41]

It is clear that form as such cannot demarcate special
sciences. By pointing toward form we can arrive with equal
right at sociology (Simmel), at jurisprudence (Kelsen), or even
at both (Stammler)! How can we distinguish social forms and
juridical forms? To account for these different kinds of forms,
we first have to analyze the internal structural differences
present in the social and juridical aspects, something completely impossible with purely formal criteria!

Dooyeweerd spoke eloquently of the "internally anti-
nomic exclusivism" of the "transcendental-logical forms of
knowledge" in the epistemology of cultural sciences.

> The material (the content of experience), assumed to be
> grasped in these "forms of knowledge," was in fact out-
> lawed. The "pure theory of law" transferred this content to

sociology, psychology, and the science of history. "Formal sociology" referred it back to the other "cultural sciences," and "pure economics," "pure grammar," "pure aesthetics" or ""ethics" could not give shelter to the "historical material of experience" either.[42]

F. Znanieci agrees with Simmel and von Wiese that sociology is a special science. In spite of the fact that he employs the concept of culture as a *genus*-concept embracing various types of culture (as species), he makes an important distinction between social actions and nonsocial actions (such as religious, technical, economic, and aesthetic actions).[43] This suggestion is much more promising than trying to define sociology in terms of action theory (M. Weber, T. Parsons, and others).[44] Bierstedt even avoids the category of action:

> I would contend that no one who begins with action— either the stimulus-response of behavioristic psychology or the means-end schema of a voluntaristic psychology— can easily arrive at a notion of the social order.[45]

The action-concept is just as multivocal as the form-concept. It always stands in need of modal or typical qualifications. Modally qualified actions are, for instance, economic actions, aesthetic actions, social actions, and so forth. Typically qualified actions are those collective actions taken by a societal structure in its total organization, such as measures taken by a government, the scientific policy of a university, and so on.

I am convinced that modal abstraction is the distinctive feature of any scientific endeavor. It stands to reason that I consider it worthwhile to investigate the possibilities of a modally delimited special science of sociology. The various aspects distinguished in Reformed philosophy not only provide points of entry into the experience of concrete events, they also demarcate the scientific fields of study of the special sciences. Of course abstraction frequently occurs in normal, nonscientific, daily life. Identifying a human being, a car, a tree, and so forth, presupposes prior general abstract concepts; otherwise no one would be able to place this man or that car within the category of human beings or automobiles. Abstractions like these are not concerned with specific aspects or func-

tions of entities apart from the entities experienced. In nontheoretical experience, number will always be related to some
entity or things counted; spatial configurations are always
experienced in relation to things observed, and so forth. But to
abstract a certain modality we have to detach ourselves from
the concreteness of nonscientific experience and direct our
attention toward the uniqueness of the specific mode of being
we are considering.

The function of social intercourse is one of the many facets
of reality. Its indissoluble coherence with all the other aspects
of reality poses one of the most fundamental philosophical
problems for sociology as a special science. No sociologist can
bypass this foundational problem of the mutual coherence and
diversity of aspects in created reality. Must we, as O. Spann
claimed, completely disregard all terms referring to the physical aspect of reality as useless in analyzing real social phenomena? Must we view the term "motion" as being reserved for the
science of mechanics alone? Or may we follow Parsons and
MacIver in their sociological imitation of Galileo's law of iner-
tia? If we wish to speak of social endurance, social causality, or
social growth, will we not subject social phenomena to kinematical, physical, or biotical laws? If not, in what sense can we
differentiate social endurance and kinematical motion, social
causality and physical causality, or social growth and biotical
growth?

We can even broaden our perspective and look at concepts
like economic causality, juridical causality, and the like, or
economic growth, aesthetic growth, and so on. These concepts
clearly reveal the equivocal nature of terms like causality and
growth. If special science sociology uses these terms, it must
specify their modal context. The same requirement applies to
other sociological concepts, such as social consciousness, social
order, social solidarity, social differentiation and integration,
social consensus and conflict, social interpretation, social strati-
fication, social mobility, and so forth.

It is clear that sociology cannot, as a special science, account for the way in which these terms are used sociologically
without the aid of a foundational philosophical view, simply
because these terms refer to fields of special scientific investigation outside the limits of sociology.

A transcendental-empirical method

The central biblical revelation that God created everything underlies the theoretical idea that God's law-Word is the fundamental (transcendental) condition of all structured creatureliness, however diverse and variable that creatureliness might be in our concrete (empirical) experience of things, events, and relationships. If creation did not display a social aspect, it would have been impossible throughout to speak of the multifarious forms of social intercourse as they have been found in the history of humankind. This way of addressing the issues already shows the basic traits of the transcendental-empirical method of analysis developed within Reformed philosophy (among others, by Dooyeweerd, Stafleu, and Hommes). This method and its results are directed by the biblical appeal to reform our scientific endeavors (among other things). But it remains provisional, fallible, and improvable. Therefore it is fundamentally and dynamically open. Only in Christ are we, in principle, freed from the apostate inclination of our sinful heart to elevate something (or some aspect) relative in creation to the rank of the absolute.

Orientated to the integral structure of creation, the transcendental-empirical method cannot accept any methodological dualism, such as is present in the prevalent method-dispute in sociology.[46] Facets typical of human activities do not exist in isolation from the so-called natural sides of reality, although the natural scientific methodologies that study these nonnatural aspects normally reduce them to natural ones.

As a rule, methodological considerations do not account for the relation between our prescientific experience of the diversity (and qualitative differences between the aspects) in reality and our scientific disclosure and articulation of this diversity by (modally abstracting) analysis. Before special scientists can develop a method to investigate any givens from their special scientific viewpoint, they must have some prior idea of the internal nature of what they aim to research. The method of inquiry cannot provide this knowledge because it is itself totally dependent on the foundational knowledge of the qualitative character of the matter under consideration. The Frankfurt School was clearly aware of this problem:

To be sure, even the most rigorous methods can lead to

false or meaningless results, if they are applied to problems for which they are not adequate or which they deal
with in a distorting way.[47]

In view of this requirement of the scientific endeavor, we
must acknowledge that even the Reformed theory of modal
aspects simply reflects a given diversity experienced in nonscientific practical life. Nevertheless, theoretical research must
analyze this given diversity in its indissoluble coherence. To
accomplish this every special science is compelled, explicitly or
implicitly, to operate with some theoretical view of reality or
other. Among other things this imperative implies that special
scientists who do not want to be victims of some (philosophi-
cally founded) theoretical view of reality must be critically
aware of their philosophical starting point. They must examine
the special way in which they handle the fundamental basic
concepts of their scientific discipline.

Notes
1. Consulting the following two works of Pitirim A. Sorokin is enough to
convince anyone of the truth of this statement: *Contemporary Sociological
Theories* (New York: Harper & Row, 1928), and *Sociological Theories of Today*
(New York: Harper and Row, 1966).
2. Robert M. MacIver, *Community: A Sociological Study* (New York: Macmillan,
1917), 12.
3. Robert M. MacIver, *Social Causation* (Boston: Ginn, 1942), 273.
4. Pitirim A. Sorokin, *Society, Culture, and Personality: Their Structures and
Dynamics* (New York: Cooper Square, 1962), 3.
5. Robert M. MacIver and Charles H. Page, *Society: An Introductory Analysis*
(London: Macmillan, 1961), 498ff.
6. Robert M. MacIver, *The Challenge of the Passing Years, My Encounter with Time*
(New York: Simon & Schuster, 1962), 91.
7. R. Bierstedt, "The Means-End Schema in Sociological Theory (1938)," in
Power and Progress; Essays on Sociological Theory (New York and London:
McGraw-Hill, 1974), 37.
8. Bierstedt, "Means-End Schema," 38,39.
9. Bierstedt, "Means-End Schema," 5.
10. Bierstedt, "Means-End Schema," 7,8.
11. Bierstedt, "Means-End Schema," 133-49.
12. Bierstedt, "Means-End Schema," 141.
13. See Bierstedt, "Means-End Schema," 135 n. 3:

> Epistemology did not, of course, begin with Kant, but so profound was
> the influence of the Kantian philosophy upon subsequent intellectual
> history, an influence which incidentally persists in the German socio-

logical tradition, that no contemporary contribution to any of the sciences can afford to ignore altogether the Kantian philosophy.

14. Max Weber, *Basic Concepts in Sociology* (London: P. Owen, 1962), 29. In German:
Soziologie...soll heissen: eine Wissenschaft, welche soziale handeln deutend verstehen und dadurch in seinem Ablauf und seinen Wirkungen ursachlich erklaren will.

15. Otto Spann, *Kämpfende Wissenschaft* (Jena: G. Fischer, 1934), 130-31. Spann also pinpoints the tautologous character of Weber's formulation when Weber writes: "the social relations exists... (therein), that, ...social acts are performed" (132).
16. Spann, 131.
17. Spann, 131 n.b.
18. See Otto Neurath's "Empirical Sociology," trans. Paul Foulkes and Otto Neurath in *Empiricism and Sociology*, ed. Otto Neurath and R. S. Cohen (Dordrecht: Reidel, 1973), 358ff.
19. Neurath, 357.
20. See Herman Dooyeweerd, *A New Critique of Theoretical Thought*, 4 vols. (Philadelphia: Presbyterian & Reformed, 1969), I:188ff, and Herman Dooyeweerd, *Vernieuwing en bezinning om het reformatorisch grondmotief* (Zutphen: J. B. van den Brink, 1963), 143ff.
21. See the penetrating analysis of Jurgen Habermas in his *Theorie und Praxis: Sozialphilosophische Studien*, 4th ed., (Frankfurt am Main: Suhrkamp, 1971), 67ff. On page 88 Habermas remarks: "Hobbes wanted to rebuild classical political science after the model of modern science and in doing so to give social philosophy a foundation in the contemporary physics."
22. See H. Klages, *Geschichte der Soziologie* (Munich: Juventa, 1969), 38.
23. See *Lettres d'Auguste Comte a Monsieur Valat* (Paris, 1870), quoted in John Viertel, trans. "The Frankfurt Institute for Social Research," in *Aspects of Sociology* (London: Heinemann, 1973), 11-12.
24. Auguste Comte, *Cours de Philosophie Positive*, vol. 4, *La Partie Dogmatique de la Philosophie Sociale* (Paris: Muton, 1908), 132 n. 1, quoted in Viertel, "Frankfurt Institute", 12.
25. See H. Maus, "Geschichte der Soziologie," in *Handbuch der Soziologie*, ed. W. Ziegenfuss (Stuttgart: Enke, 1956), 7.
26. D. Martindale, *The Nature and Types of Sociological Theory* (Boston: Houghton Mifflin, 1960), 53.
27. Martindale, 4.
28. See W. Dilthey, *Der Aufbau der geschichtliche Welt in den Geisteswissenschaften* (Leipzig: B. G. Teutner, 1927), 86.
29. See H. Rickert, *Die Grenzen der naturwissenschaftlichen Begriffsbildung* (1902; Tubingen: J. C. B. Mohr, 1913), 224; and W. Windelband's rectoral oration of 1894, "Geschichte und Naturwissenschaft," repr. *Präludien*, vol. 2 (Tubingen: J. C. B. Mohr, 1924), 145, where he introduces the terms "nomothetic" and "idiographic."
30. H. Rickert, *Science and History, A Critique of Positivist Epistemology* (Prince-

ton, N.J.: Van Nostrand, 1962), 112.

31. R. Bierstedt, *The Social Order* (New York and London: McGraw-Hill, 1970), 7.

32. J. B. McKee, *Introduction to Sociology* (New York: Holt, Rinehart, Winston, 1969), 7.

33. Sorokin, (cited in note 4 above) 7.

34. Sorokin, 14.

35. Dooyeweerd, *New Critique*, 3:264 (cited in note 15 above). Also see Herman Dooyeweerd, *Verkenningen in de wijsbegeerte, de sociologie en de rechtsgeschiedenis* (Amsterdam: Buijten & Schipperheijn, 1962), 96.

36. Leopold von Wiese, *Soziologie, Geschichte und Hauptprobleme* (Berlin: W. De Gruyter, 1926), 85.

37. See the remark of A. Gaugler in "Graphologische Analyse," in *Buch des Dankes an Georg Simmel*, ed. Karl Gassen and M. Landmann (Berlin: Duncker & Humblot, 1958), 41-42.

38. Georg Simmel "The Problem of Sociology," in *Georg Simmel: On Individuality and Social Forms*, ed. D. N. Levine (Chicago and London: University of Chicago Press, 1971), 25.

39. Simmel, 24.

40. H. Kelsen, *Hauptprobleme der Staatsrechtslehre: Entwickelt aus der Lehre vom Rechssatze* (1923, reprint; Aalen: Scientia, 1960), 93.

41. The "connective will" is the external regulation and therefore, the "form of the concept 'Gesellschaft.'" See R. Stammler, "Wesen des Rechts und der Rechtswissenschaft" in *Systematische Rechtswissenschaft* (Leipzig and Berlin: n.p., 1913), 19. Law is a necessary tool for the establishment of the regularities (i.e., the form) of social life. See R. Stammler, *Lehrbuch der Rechtsphilosophie* (1928, reprint; Berlin: De Gruyter, 1970), 78.

42. Dooyeweerd, *New Critique*, 2:209 (cited in note 15 above).

43. Florijan Znaniecki, *Cultural Sciences, Their Origin and Development* (Urbana: University of Illinois Press, 1963), 393.

44. See H. Haferkamp, *Soziologie als Handlungstheorie* (Dusseldorf: Bertelsmann Universitätverlag, 1972).

45. Bierstedt, *The Social Order*, ix (cited in note 26 above).

46. See Th. W. Adorno et al., *Der Positivismusstreit in der deutschen Soziologie* (Berlin: Luchterhand, 1970).

47. Viertel, "Frankfurt Institute," 122, italics mine (cited in note 18 above). See the sensible remarks of Maarten Vrieze in his *Nadenken over de Samenleving* (Amsterdam: Buijten & Schipperheijn, 1977), 12ff. and 22ff.

Secularization: processes and interpretations

David Lyon

Prologue: Secularization and Christian believing

To propose that secularization is religious decline is to show evidence of religious faith. This paradox is central to the following discussion. It is my contention that those who hold theories of general religious decline or secularization exhibit religious commitment by that very act. Their belief in secularization can be used as evidence against the notion that religion is dying. This paradox is not the substantive focus of my argument, though it illustrates it well. Lest there be any misunderstanding, this is an attempt to discuss in a Christian way what sociologists mean when they talk about secularization. I will narrow the focus below, but I must say here that we are thus entering an extremely complex, controversial, and reef-ridden area. From the outset we must challenge those who hold to relatively simple views of secularization and see little that is controversial in the concept. If for no other reason, these views are complex and controversial because they hinge on certain understandings of religion and science at several levels. Both data (processes) and theories (interpretations) involve religion and science.

My topic has an obvious importance for both Christian commitment and for sociology, though its importance for the latter might require more demonstration than the former. On the one hand, Christians need a social understanding of our current situation. What is the context for our full-orbed witness to Jesus Christ? Authentic Christian commitment, to use Wolterstorff's phrase[1] is relative to persons and times. Since Christians can engage in inappropriate witness to our generation, it is imperative that we understand our milieu. Whether or not we live in a secular society and, more particularly, what we mean when we assert such a thing are important for the orientation and impact of our witness to the truth in Jesus Christ.

If secularization (whatever it is) is the context for contemporary Christian commitment, it is also the context for sociologizing. This is not always recognized. Given the preoccupation of sociology's founding fathers with both the context and theme of sociology, it is astonishing that contemporary sociologists, while ostensibly revering their founding fathers and their work, should have so systematically ignored this aspect of their contribution.[2] There are many sociologists of secularization (or religious change), but it is a measure of the very process they are discussing that they almost unilaterally overlook the relevance and relationship of secularization to other studies of industrial capitalism, state socialism, and so forth.

There is another way in which the study of secularization is important both for sociology and Christian commitment, and that is the way in which sociology is done. The study of secularization raises acutely certain crucial issues for sociological methodology in its broadest sense. Attacks on positivism have been mounted on numerous fronts in recent years, with a resulting proliferation of orientations and perspectives in sociology. The idea of secularization was quite acceptable to some positivists and, indeed, they sometimes saw a causal relationship between the two. This is amply illustrated, for example, by Kingsley Davis's notorious phrase about religion withering like a leaf before the flame of science.[3] But in the current flux of approaches, what is the status of secularization as a sociological concept?

Is there a Christian attitude that could guide acceptance or rejection of sociological approaches to secularization? Does Christian believing offer anything distinctive and constructive to the debate over secularization, clarifying the issues and advancing the quest for truth? This discussion of secularization provokes such questions.

What is meant, then, by the idea of *Christian* reflection on secularization? I believe that Christians ought to think Christianly and this intention ought also to be implicit and sometimes explicit in scholarly work. I am indebted to Nicholas Wolterstorff's lucid and brief exposition of what is entailed in Christian scholarship.[4] He has made a good case for a specific kind of Christian understanding that meets the objections and copes with the predilections of current philosophies of science. I will refer to other aspects of his work below (especially his rejection of foundationalism, which is important in discussing secularization), but here I will concentrate on his essential notion of control beliefs.

Because "everyone who weighs a theory has certain beliefs as to what constitutes an acceptable *sort* of theory," Wolterstorff holds that the Christian scholar "ought to allow the belief-content of his authentic Christian commitment to function as control within his devising and weighing of theories."[5] The Christian will want to find theories that comport well with Christian believing. We discover such theories through the weighing and possible rejection of certain given theories and through the devising of new ones. Wolterstorff's approach obviates the exclusivism of the ghetto ("we alone are left who know the truth"), yet it retains the distinctiveness of a Christian perspective.

Tom Bottomore has been skeptical of a "distinctive theory of society...conceived as being strictly dependent on the worldview—upon its ontology, theory of knowledge, and ethics."[6] He is wary of a Marxist or a Christian sociology. But his objection is that "...it is not the case at all that the construction and development of sociological theories has depended upon, or does depend upon, the prior elaboration of, and continual reference to, a total world view."[7] While it might be true that sociologists' control beliefs might not add up to a total worldview, this in no way permits sociologists to imagine they have no worldview. As we will see, worldviews can be comprised of a ragbag of components, but none are exempt from the demise of foundationalism. Worldviews are beliefs. The construction and development of sociological theories might not *depend* upon a coherent worldview, but this in no way precludes such dependence, either as a possibility or, from a Christian (or Marxist) point of view, as a necessity.

I think that it worries Bottomore that theories might take on the status of control-beliefs, making sociologists unwilling to modify their theories in the light of fresh evidence. Wolterstorff explicitly allows for, even expects, the qualification and refinement of theories accepted by the Christian scholar. Indeed, not only theories but even authentic commitment might change as a result of research. So Christian thinking in sociology (or any discipline) is far from closed to evidence or other theories. Sometimes the Christian and non-Christian will accept the same theory. Having said that, however, Wolterstorff still pleads that "authentic Christian commitment...function *internally* to scholarship, in the search for and the weighing of theories."[8]

To leave the matter here, however, would be to fall into the very trap that, according to Wolterstorff, has caught other Christian scholars as they substituted rhetoric and metaphor for close analysis. What control beliefs might we reasonably expect to play a part in evaluating the concept of secularization? For present purposes I will concentrate on three beliefs, though this by no means exhausts the possibilities! Secularization, by definition, must refer to a historical process: how something becomes something else. Secondly, the concept of secularization implies an analytical distinction between the secular and the previous unsecular state. This unsecular society, presumably, was a religious society. Lastly, secularization logically involves the study of the religious and/or secular activity of persons in a sociohistorical setting. So our control beliefs must relate (at least) to history, religion, and personhood. This is not the place to argue the derivation and elaboration of the control beliefs in detail. Rather, I simply state them as a prelude to trying to apply them.

Secularization refers to a fundamentally historical process. Historical change is assumed in the very word. Christianity, being a profoundly historical religion, yields control beliefs for historical understanding. One important word has already been used: process. History is seen biblically as a process, moving from the beginning to a definite end — the eschaton. Though some things improve through time (Jesus' revelation is superior to that of Moses, for example [Hebrews 1]), the notion of general human progress is alien to the Scriptures. The last times are characterized as both rife with evil and as the triumph of righteousness (Micah 4; Thessalonians 2). So the Christian scholar will be wary of any general evolutionary view of history where a single theme dominates and grows in intensity with time.

Authentic Christian commitment also believes in the universality of history. Old ethnic barriers were decisively broken in Christ (Galatians 3:28), and Christ explicitly said that the Christian mission was worldwide (Matthew 28:19). The gospel and Kingdom message is nothing less than global. Hence there is a need to suspect ethnocentric ideas of history. God's dealing with Israel (or anywhere else) is not paradigmatic for all people and all times. Of course, we could find other control beliefs that relate to historical analysis, but these will suffice here.

The process of secularization is also logically connected to religion. Here again, authentic Christian commitment has distinctive ideas on religion, germane to our discussion. Simply put, the biblical testimony asserts that all life is a religious activity. All things owe their origin and continued existence to God (Revelation 4:11), nothing makes sense or has coherence without Christ (Colossians 1:17), and people's lives are inevitably directed toward or away from the Creator (Romans 1:25). Those who do not orient their existence toward God are consistently described as pursuing some other religious end (Exodus 20:3, 4; Romans 1:25). Heart belief, from which come the springs of life, is decisive (Proverbs 4:23; Romans 10:10). Ritual and institution have a part, but right hearts are the fundamental requirement of the biblical God (Psalm 51:16,17; Amos 5:21). Religion, then, is no institutional phenomenon (though it takes institutional forms, for example, in the church); it is universal, finds its locus in heart commitment, and can be directed either toward the Creator or toward any other creaturely or transcendent object. But no one is not religious.

Following from this, thirdly, is the matter of personhood. Whenever we consider the activity of persons in a sociohistorical setting, control beliefs are inevitably involved.[9] The human sciences always assume some anthropology since people are variously seen as "agents," "actors," or "reactors." But what does it mean for people to be the "image of God" (Genesis 1:27)? Notions of freedom and responsibility, of consciousness and historicity, are highly significant. The Christian would want to see people as makers of culture, creating history as well as being shaped by it. Persons are also searchers for meaning (see, for example, the book of Ecclesiastes), which is either found in the Creator-Redeemer or in some alternative life pattern or institution.

Thus the Christian sociologist may never be content with a superficial understanding of persons that depends on some nominal definition. The biblical account suggests that there is far more to persons than they themselves can know ("man looks at the outward appearance, but the Lord looks at the heart," 1 Samuel 16:7). Yet consciousness of inner intentions and motives is a Christian virtue (e.g., Matthew 5:28), and this might imply that some kind of normative *verstehende* (sympathetic understanding) is called for. A realism that is not content with simple phenomena but probes deeper to the "essence of personhood" seems appropriate to authentic Christian commitment.[10]

Enough has been said, then, to indicate some of the Christian control beliefs that might be used to study secularization. Control beliefs, we recall, help us weigh and devise theories. The task before us is to consider the concept of secularization, as it has been used in sociology (by one theorist in particular) and to evaluate it in terms of these control beliefs.

Bryan Wilson and the process of secularization

Once upon a time the church dominated society....The church presented a massive, articulated, overarching system of belief which defined the horizon of hope, here and hereafter, just as it cast the shadows of fear....Then men gradually recovered the spirit of free inquiry and personal choice. The single perspective on the world was first broken in two by the Reformation and then almost immediately fragmented into innumerable fragments as a growingly differentiated society spawned a comparable differentiation of viewpoint. Nowadays it is everyman his own theologian: and if Everyman seeks legitimacy for his social arrangements or his revolutions he is more likely to appeal to the will of the people then to the will of God.[11]

So runs David Martin's characterization of the obvious view of secularization. Obvious or not, it certainly seems to be the received view, as we will see.

Though crudely put, it represents the view of Bryan Wilson, who has been writing on the topic for well over a decade. In *Religion in Secular Society* he assumed that "religious thinking, religious practice, and religious institutions were once at the very centre of the life of western society, as indeed of all societies." But now, he says:

It is simply taken as a fact that religion—seen as a way of

thinking, as the performance of particular practices, and as the institutionalization and organization of those patterns of thought and action—has lost influence.[12]

Simply defined, secularization is "the process whereby religious thinking, practice, and institutions lose social significance." In his book, *Contemporary Transformations of Religion*, Wilson declares his belief that this process "can be shown to be a broad, if albeit uneven evolutionary process."[13]

In the three sections of this book Wilson first gives evidence for his belief in secularization, secondly, contrasts new sects and cults in the Western and third worlds, and lastly, asks whether the growth of any new religious movements might indicate a significant "counter-culture," an effective desecularizing force.[14]

The world, for Wilson, has become an increasingly rationally constructed environment. Above all, modern society plans change in terms of present and future. The past-oriented character of religion as a repository of customs and an agent of social control makes religion inappropriate for today's impersonal world of the conveyor belt and bureaucracy. Over a long period there has been an observable trend toward a matter-of-fact orientation to the world. The rational, empirical orientation toward the world (made possible by Calvinism and Puritanism) has widened the gulf, so that now there is an irreconcilability between

suppositions of faith in the supernatural and its arbitrary unexplained authority, and the suppositions that underlie all other activities and operations in which modern men engage in their everyday lives.[15]

There existed not one age of faith, but several, perhaps better called "ages of the institutional church." As such, their decline is measurable, and the statistics indicate that people are now "disposed to give less credence to the supernatural...and are strongly convinced that religion has diminishing importance in the social order."[16] There are agencies of social control today, but they are essentially impersonal and amoral—such as traffic lights, identity pictures, and watches. Technical regulation has superseded moral regulation.

Moreover, the structure of the institutional church has been affected by the decline of faith. The church's authority is denied, tacitly, by being widely ignored. Church people turn to social science rather than to the Scriptures for answers to social questions. Attendance at church is steadily declining, as is the amount of financial support given. Wilson tentatively suggests that an index of secularization might be people's use of money:

> ...the more developed the economic techniques of a society, and the more affluent its circumstances, the lower the proportion of its productive wealth which will be devoted to the supernatural.[17]

Church activities have come to be reinterpreted, along with the role of the clergy and the nature of salvation. With some, political activity has replaced prayerful activity, while others have embraced ecumenism as a solution to the secularizing trend. But none of these changes has made any difference in the general decline of religion. For many, the charismatic movement is the one "growth sector" in today's church. Yet even this, argues Wilson, only reflects the general spontaneity and subjectivism of contemporary culture. The charismatic movement too can be interpreted against the pervasive background of secularization.

In the second part of his book, Wilson readily admits that there has been a recent proliferation of cults and sects, both in the West and the Third World. But he prefaces his cautious examination of these sects with the reminder that

> the most powerful trend is secularization, which occurs as our social organization becomes increasingly dominated by technical procedures and rational planning.[18]

There has been a huge migration of religious ideas (from the West to the Third World and from East to West) and a widening range of choices among them. Wilson notes the influence of forms of Western religion in the Third World, as Western forms are incorporated into more indigenous movements. But while these movements emphasize personal integrity and consciousness transformation, which might be an appropriate part of an ideology for development, they are subject to the same secularizing influences as their Western forms. Wilson remarks that the contemporary cults in the West, from encounter groups to Hare Krishna, emphasize the redemption of the self. This emphasis suggests external systems have lost their attractiveness (and it suggests a concentration on the here and now), which means that the cultural impact of external systems will always be limited.

There once was a time when religion offered a coming-to-terms with circumstances, especially death. But, according to Wilson, the new cults and sects offer no reconciliation. They are hedonistic and antimoral, and they certainly have no means of socializing a second generation or providing a plausible basis for morality in a world of impersonal interaction between role performers who play a segmented part in the whole. The powerful cultural constraint has gone. If from now on religion is to be as ephemeral as a generation, civilization might have lost something irreplaceable.

In the final part of the book, Wilson moves inexorably toward the conclusion that in the "evolutionary process, religions are always dying. In the modern world it is not clear that they have any prospect of rebirth."[19] Despite the rise of ecumenism, charismatic revivals, destructuration, rationalization, and eclecticism, secularization continues. None adds up to a religious revival because

> they have no real consequence for other social institutions, for political power structures, for technological controls and constraints. They add nothing to any prospective reintegration of society, and contribute nothing to the culture by which society might live.[20]

The old society has passed away, and capitalism has hastened its departure: "Laissez-faire economics inevitably led to laissez-faire morality, and the underpinnings of culture—a socially diffused and shared moral sense—are thus eroded."[21] There is no longer any value consensus; technique is all that holds things together.

> Permissiveness and pluralism indicate the social insignificance and systemic insulation of culture—and religion, which was the chief carrier of the cultural inheritance.[22]

Toward a critique

I have detailed Wilson's position at some length not to knock him down (for in many ways his is a sensitive and insightful analysis) but because his view is popular. It has been accepted by sociologists far less sympathetic to religion than Wilson (they would see this as the "triumph of the secular") and by biblical theologians.[23] While the theologians would not hold what follows, this current view is associated with a cultural myth described by Susan Budd as follows:

> People...believe in the superior powers of science in part because of a myth in our culture about the power of science...and part of the myth is about the clash between religion and science which was resolved in favour of science.[24]

It is worth examining Wilson's views because they elaborate a very common understanding of secularization, often shared by believer and unbeliever alike.

Peter Glasner has described as "mythification" the process whereby some concepts such as modernization and secularization become taken for granted in sociology. Myths like these represent rather than reflect reality, and the representations are rooted in a popular idea. They are relatively simple, all-purpose world-pictures that do not really describe, so that the originally popular idea gains credibility from science and is returned as fact. Thus a great variety of (often contradictory) analyses are used under the general banner of the secularization myth, thereby receiving a spurious validity. Glasner, along with several contemporary sociologists, would argue that the difficulties of mythification begin with the definition of religion. If there is a secularization process, then what is it that becomes secular?[25]

Defining religion

Wilson's definition of religion is an essentially institutional one. The institution, in his opinion, defines what passes as the "religious." He admits a variety of religious orientations, but he denies that there might be something religious about all of life. Religion is something that cannot only decline and diminish in social significance but, in principle at least, disappear altogether from the human scene. He narrows his definition greatly when he insists that to be religious there must be explicit reference to a supernatural source of values.

This institutional definition of religion underpins Wilson's analysis. Although he confesses that statistics are not a route to definitive truth, he depends on changes in church attendance, for example, to make his case. And while he rightly indicates the different meanings attached to church attendance in Britain and the U.S.A., nowhere does he indulge in a wider comparative analysis of how other voluntary organizations have fared over the decades since the nineteenth century. Stephen Yeo's work, for example, suggests that the churches have shown amazing resilience to social change during a period of general decline of voluntary organizations in England.[26] Though Wilson's analysis is in some ways sophisticated, it nevertheless retains a simplicity characteristic of concepts that have the status of social myth.

Wilson opposes other definitions of religion. He is skeptical of the notion of "a fund of religiosity" in people, which he attributes to Luckmann (and, by implication, Durkheim). As Wilson defines it, religion is virtually bound to die in modern society—indeed, it is difficult to imagine what could possibly prevent its death. But Luckmann (who, by the way, would not subscribe to the view that there is a "fund of religiosity" in people) wishes to consider other possibilities:

> The contemporary marginality of church religion and its "inner secularization" appear as one aspect of a complex process in which the long range consequences of institutional specialization of religion and the global transformations of the social order play a decisive role. What are usually taken as symptoms of the decline of traditional Christianity may be symptoms of a more revolutionary change: the replacement of the institutional specialization of religion by a new social form of religion.[27]

As Robert Towler suggests, Luckmann simply asks that we accept in principle that not every social process is one of decay and decline; some processes might be emerging and evolving.[28] Luckmann moves away from the nominal definition of religion, which uses substantive and institutional terms, to a realist definition that assumes that to be human is, ipso facto, to be religious. Religions are

> socially objectivated systems of meaning that refer, on the one hand, to the world of everyday life and point, on the other hand, to a world that is experienced as transcending everyday life.[29]

Everything depends on our definition of "religion." Berger, for example, would not go so far as Luckmann in perceiving an invisible religion in all human social life.[30] The humanly meaningful world might not necessarily be sacred. But Berger's definition of religion leads him to see the overriding effects of pluralism in religion where all views are relativized by competition.

David Martin, on yet another tack and speaking from the British context, questions the pluralism thesis:

> Enclaves of Hindus and Muslims and enclaves of middle class humanists do not in themselves necessarily make Britain a religiously pluralistic society. In fact, the religion of modern Britain is a deistic moralistic religion-in-general,which combines a fairly high practice of personal prayer with a considerable degree of superstition.[31]

This unofficial religion has been described by Towler as "common religion." One could not even discuss it if Wilson's definition were retained.

Our Christian control beliefs certainly do not restrict us to a narrow, institutional, and nominal definition of religion. Indeed, biblical Christians might well expect to find many kinds of alternatives to belief in God and to the worship pattern of the church. Idolatry (the making and worshiping of false gods who bestow meaning and salvation) takes multiple forms even in the biblical account.

Luckmann agrees with Wilson that today's religious movements tend to be more privatized, but he gives them far more weight (social significance) than does Wilson.

> The social form of religion emerging in modern industrial societies is characterized by the direct accessibility of an

assortment of religious representations to potential consumers. The sacred cosmos is mediated neither through a
specialized domain of religious institutions nor through
other primary public institutions. It is the direct accessibil-
ity of the sacred cosmos...which makes religion today
essentially a phenomenon of the private order.[32]

The new sacred themes, which give meaning to the lives of
modern people (and which are affirmed by several of Wilson's
sects) are individual autonomy, self-expression, self-realization, mobility, sexuality, family centeredness, and economic
growth and progress. This kind of religion is what Durkheim
saw that "each man will freely perform within himself." It is
differentiated from the structure of society, but this does not
mean that it will die. If this privatized religion provides an
escape from the bureaucratic cage, it might even grow in
strength.

Defining secularization
Does a broader definition of religion allow us to say anything
meaningful about secularization? The process of secularization
intrigued Max Weber. He saw the Western world as becoming
increasingly disenchanted. Rationalization increased along
with the displacement of magic and the growth in systematic
coherence and naturalistic consistency of ideas. Though it was
not his intention, Weber gave the impression of restricted
ideological space: science displacing religion in the cultural
bathtub. Or, as Martin succinctly puts it, "more science means
less non-science." Such an impression is part of the myth of
secularization, as is any extension of local, observable declines
in reference to the supernatural to universal proportions. But
Weber gave another impression, too. He pessimistically imag-
ined that modern people were permanently doomed to the
claustrophobic rational vision that would increasingly dominate all of life.
      Ernest Gellner, approaching the issue from a different
angle, has made some perceptive comments on the basis of
Weber's thesis.[33] He is concerned with the legitimation of belief,
cognition, and the modern world's transition to effective
knowledge. Having rejected the notion that cognitive certainty
can be found in an external Other, Western people have sought

certainty in what is accessible to human sight. But human sight, in a time of flux, cannot provide a starting point ("foundation" in Wolterstorff's terms) because our identity is also in question. How can we know that our starting point is not merely our custom or desire? Popper and Kuhn, argues Gellner, have done much to highlight the complexities and vagaries of the political economy of science, but even they assume science themselves. Popper might tell us about trial and error in science, but this does not allow him to say anything about the inception of science itself. And Kuhn might speak of qualitative leaps from paradigm to paradigm, but he never answers what a preparadigmatic state might have been like. In fact, argues Gellner, there is too much of Thomas Hobbes in Kuhn, for Kuhn seems to hold that before the order of paradigms there was a free-for-all. On the contrary, says Gellner, the savage mind had a different paradigm that did not separate cognitive functions and that generated a cozy and meaningful world (unlike modern paradigms that are cold, mechanical, and knowable and provide only an inhuman, icy climate, unfit as a living environment).

Gellner is in no doubt that some massive change has taken place:

> The world of regular, morally neutral, magically manipulable fact, which some of us are in danger now of taking too much for granted, and which is presupposed by science, is in fact not at all self-evident. Far from representing some kind of normality, a natural starting point, historically it is a great oddity.[34]

According to Gellner, the rationality of the modern world can neither replace the old paradigm nor provide a charter for social arrangements.

> Reason does not produce another, and a rival, total and closed picture, as gratifying for man as the old theological ones (or more so), only upside-down. It produces none at all. On the contrary, it merely erodes the old one.[35]

Both Marx and Weber (who saw alienation and rationalization as similar) mistakenly assumed that nineteenth century changes were typical of all changes and trends in industrial society. And Bryan Wilson has no more warrant than they to argue for an evolutionary universal of secularization. The new productive, organization, and cognitive bases of society need to be analyzed and understood, but it is not necessary to see them as pushing religions into a corner or out of the door of human experience.

Weber's partial error, according to Gellner, was to overdo the disenchantment thesis. Weber did not, like Kant or Wilson, imagine that disenchantment was part of the human condition per se, but he did seem to see religion as a declining phenomenon. Gellner argues that the very society associated with rationalization has the augmentation of leisure, diminution of economic pressures, decreasing authoritarianism in education, and greater general permissiveness, which allow for the growth of "escape religions." They might be superficial religions, in the sense that society really continues to rest on a productive, administrative, and order enforcing scientific technology, but they will continue to exist. "Thus in most of our life," concludes Gellner, "there is a complex symbiosis of diverse conceptual styles."[36] This he calls an "ironic culture." Serious and effective social convictions become increasingly separated from a growing luxuriant culture where thought is apparently serious but has no deep connection with the real (scientific) world.

I have argued that the definition of religion is crucial for understanding secularization, and that sociology must transcend the merely institutional definition. Further, we have seen that to assume that more science (and more social relationships based on rationality) means less nonscience is to follow Weber's overdone disenchantment thesis. Our technological society might throw up more, not less, religions. Wilson is in trouble on both counts. For even if the cults and sects of modern society are short-lived, this still does not amount to the decline of religion. And if modern society continues to throw up cults and sects, then they are not socially insignificant. They must be accounted for, even if they do not provide what Wilson thinks of as the value-base consensus of society.

Luckmann, of course, would see more religion in contemporary society than Gellner, though he would agree that religion operates in a different sphere from the rational.

Overarching subjective structures of meaning are almost
completely detached from the functionally rational norms
of these (public) institutions.[37]

As we have noted, Luckmann believes that the modern
social form of religion is found in the private sphere of autonomy, sexuality, family life, and so on. Moreover, he would
point to the increasing legitimation of institutional norms
(especially with regard to economics and politics) by functional
rationality. But, contra Wilson, Luckmann does not believe that
traditional sacred values simply faded away. Rather, the
"autonomous institutional 'ideologies' replaced, within their
own domain, an overarching and transcendent universe of
norms."[38] But Luckmann would argue with Gellner that no one
could live within such a scheme (even communism seems to
have failed to produce a "new man"). Hence the retreat to the
private.

However, having helpfully suggested where some contemporary religious orientations might lie, Luckmann tells us
little about the "overarching and transcendent universe of
norms" in different institutional areas. But it might be that
these, too, are part of modern religious belief in the wider sense.
Though such norms might have lost traditional, overtly religious legitimation, might they not have received some invisible
religious legitimation? Science, for example, might be understood in a religious way, since people now believe in science
"without understanding in the same way as they might once
have assumed that 'religion can explain it.'"[39] Likewise, sociologists might analyze nationalism or even the welfare state as
religious phenomena.[40]

Religious persons
Enough has been said, I think, to indicate that there are problems with Wilson's understanding of the secularization process on at least two counts. However, using his nominalist
definition, one thing is very clear: an increasing number of
people think that religion is unimportant to life. Narrowly
defined, religious institutions, thinking, and practice are losing
social significance. But this assumes too much. Above all, it
assumes that persons and their religion can be understood only
by external appearance and explicit reference. But the fact that

God, or even the supernatural, are invoked less often does not spell a decline of religion—if we adopt a realist definition.

Even without agreeing on the definition of religion, Martin, Gellner, and Luckmann as well as Towler, Greeley, and even Berger would question Wilson's conclusion. They would say that people still do exhibit religious commitment, whether in private religion, common religion, ideologies, or sects. Moreover, Luckmann and Greeley in particular would say that people are choosing their religious orientations deliberately and freely, and they are not simply subjected to the inevitable erosion of their beliefs by rationalization.

How "subterranean theologies" (Martin) or "homelessness" (Berger, et al.) are to be understood and evaluated is another question, but I am simply concerned here with how persons are studied. The control beliefs of the Christian sociologist would say that to examine the activity of persons in a merely external and quasi-objective manner is to miss what is distinctive about their activity. Therefore Christian sociologists would wish to go beyond Wilson. Within his frame of reference, as I have conceded, Wilson makes some important points, but Christian control belief denies the adequacy of his framework and must transcend it.

Theoretical and research implications
So far I have only outlined Wilson's argument for secularization and suggested that the work of Gellner and Luckmann (for example) can be used against it. I have tried to bring Christian control beliefs to bear on the issue. But Wilson's, Gellner's, and Luckmann's work merely illustrates the wider debate over the meaning of secularization. And other aspects of the debate also deserve discussion. Christian control beliefs then might help sort out the priorities here. But even the limited scope of my comments thus far allows one or two tentative theoretical suggestions. That is my first task. Finally, I will ask, where do we go from here?

A secularization paradigm and an alternating paradigm
Given that the definition of religion and the complexity of historical analysis are two of the crucial issues, what theoretical tools might we use in a framework compatible with our control beliefs? We will glance at the suggestions of Peter Glasner and

Robin Gill that are directed toward clarifying these issues.[41]

Glasner has argued that empiricist and nominal definitions of religion without adequate theoretical base have nurtured the social myth of secularization. For him the definition
of religion is crucial to a sociological understanding of secularization. He begins by distinguishing religion and the religious
and the different levels of analysis (interpersonal, organization, and cultural).

> At the organizational level, religions need not be continu-
> ously supported by the notion of the religious. Similarly
> the notion of the religious may be present in those institu-
> tional and organizational areas which are not specifically
> described as religious. This obviates the necessity of iden-
> tifying the "really religious" as the basepoint for the proc-
> ess of secularization.[42]

The religious, Glasner continues, is available at all levels,
but because of its nature it cannot become secularized. For his
understanding of the religious, Glasner looks to Simmel who
sees forms of social relationships as religious, based on faith
and expressed as dependence and unity. Any objects, then,
might become objects of faith. Because his purpose is theoretical, Glasner does not indicate how, with this kind of inclusive
and realist definition, something like a football supporters'
club might be so analyzed. One suspects that Simmel's (or
Durkheim's) ideas might be little more than suggestive here.
Nevertheless Glasner's distinction between religion and the religious is central.

Glasner continues his argument by suggesting that secularization (referring only, of course, to exclusively defined
religion) is best seen as a generic term. Within it a variety of
particular processes at varying levels, times, and places can be
discerned. Thus, if there is high correlation between secularization profiles at both organizational and cultural levels, then
secularization might be a good term to describe religious
change at the societal level.

But is it enough simply to distinguish between religion
and the religious? While he rightly argues that organizational
secularization of an exclusively defined religion cannot be
taken as evidence of religious decline, Glasner neglects to find

a place for any connection between religion and the religious. From a Christian point of view, it is desirable to know about both the state of Christian (or other institutional) commitment (insofar as it is measurable) and its relationship to its religious alternatives. But Glasner denies that this is possible:

> ...it should be remembered that nothing is said, nor indeed can be, about the religious, which may or may not be present at either the organizational or institutional levels.[43]

The complexities and ambiguities of secularization, which should make sociologists very cautious, have driven Glasner beyond caution. He refuses to admit that we can talk of religion and the religious at the same time.

Robin Gill responds to the complexity cautiously, but he accepts the ambiguity. Writing from the historical, process view of actual studies of secularization, desecularization, and the persistence of religion, he argues for an alternating model that embraces the ambiguities in one scheme. In so doing Gill rejects any general historical sweep that might be called secularization, and he invites concentration on smaller entities, leaving open the question of the overall social status of religion.[44]

Indeed, the control beliefs with which I began did not lead us to expect either more or less religious activity, or more or less institutional religion. Gill's alternating model is one that approaches evidence as complementary. His reason?

> The evidence of religiosity available in the west suggests, not simply that there are some phenomena which are most adequately interpreted in terms of secularization and other phenomena which are not, but that the same phenomena can equally be interpreted in terms of secularization or desecularization.[45]

For example, Wilson's data regarding the decline in certainty of people's belief in Christian doctrines might be interpreted by someone like Greeley as desecularization. He would argue that religious pluralism ensures that those who do believe in Christian doctrine do so out of choice and with conviction.

But with regard to other phenomena, it should be possible

within strictly limited boundaries to study decline in overt institutional religiosity and the rise of sects, belief in horoscopes and astrology, or the persistence of common religion. Possibly not Gill's model itself but the spirit behind it—an emphasis on small-scale studies that incorporate ambiguous evidence—might be fruitful for the sociology of secularization.

Orientations

A term that is ambiguous might give rise to ambivalent attitudes toward it. Because it has been used as an ideological weapon, David Martin once suggested that "secularization" be eliminated from the sociological dictionary.[46] But he continues to discuss secularization. This kind of ambivalence seems inevitable. However, the lessons can be learned—of the logical, semantic,[47] theoretical, and ideological pitfalls associated with "secularization." And a cautious use of the term may still be justified. In particular, from a Christian viewpoint, it is desirable to trace the dechristianization of institutions and cultural forms, though this must be done with care.[48] (This might also be extended to the religious social analysis of institutions [such as the welfare state] that was mentioned above.)

Perhaps there are three other areas that require special attention from those working with Christian control beliefs. First, there is the concept of secularization itself, how it came to be used,[49] and what connotations it has. It is vital to understand the ideological uses to which it might be put before we use the concept.[50] But in its popular usage the concept of secularization is important as a description of the perceived process in which many societies find themselves. The term is believed to be about the context of modern life. Christians and non-Christians alike believe this, which is why the term "secularization" cries out for conceptual clarification and, above all, limitation.

Secondly, there is the matter, only alluded to, of ages of faith that are often tacitly assumed as the baseline from which secularization began. Christians have been guilty of rather uncritically assuming such periods of Christian influence (or whatever). Francis Schaeffer's "Reformationalism" is a case in point, but there are other examples.[51] The baselines are as difficult to substantiate empirically as their alleged decline. But there might be another reason why the concept of an age of faith is not consistent with Christian control beliefs. At no point does the biblical testimony refer back to a past golden age as the exemplar for human society. True, the creation life-patterns are central to understanding how human life ought to be lived, but the biblical testimony never suggests that we ignore our contemporary context. Indeed, revelation is thought of as progressive, as God's life-patterns are applied in a fashion appropriate to the historical moment. By thinking of secularization as a general trend away from an assumed age of faith, we might divert attention from what is more important in the Scriptures: the coming Kingdom. It is in the light of the coming Kingdom that human life is lived. That is the age of faith that is at once exemplar and hope. Moreover, it is in the Kingdom that religion and the religious will become one, when all acknowledge the legitimate reign of the King over human social life.

Last, irreligion and revivalism might also be legitimate subjects of study in relation to the secularization thesis. I mean that, from a strategic Christian viewpoint, it is important to isolate and analyze social movements that deliberately or unintentionally hasten or delay the perceived process of secularization. Sociologists have given little attention to either until recently. [52] Such movements are worthy of far more attention.

The import of all this is that evaluation inevitably takes place in the study of secularization as in any other area. Luckmann claims neutrality, but he finally reveals his horror at the dehumanizing prospect associated with the increase of private religion. [53] Gellner stoically resigns himself to a world of meaninglessness by building a raft of assorted beliefs with which to float on the sea of relativism and uncertainty. Wilson, lastly, sinks more and more into pessimism at the demise of an orderly culture in which religion once played a vital part. He seems to believe in an immanent fate that mysteriously superintends the loss of faith and order. This is the religious faith that was mentioned at the beginning. A faith commitment lies behind Wilson's understanding of history and religion.

Every sociological framework, however patchy, assumes certain guiding control beliefs that can only be described as religious. Christians admit this and allows their control beliefs to guide their selection of problems and their weighing and devising of theories. But in the last analysis, the Christian's control beliefs must be traced to their source: authentic Christian commitment; not to "planks for a raft," but to Jesus Christ.

It is he who calls us to "mind-renewal," an activity which may lead not only to better theorizing of secularization but maybe to reversals of secularization in areas where this is appropriate and possible as well.

Notes

1. We need to distinguish here what Wolterstorff would call "authentic Christian commitment" and what actually makes one a Christian. The Christian gospel of salvation in Jesus Christ can be effectively proclaimed with a minimum of contextualization. Authentic Christian commitment, by definition, requires contextualization. See Nicholas Wolterstorff, *Reason within the Bounds of Religion* (Grand Rapids: Eerdmans, 1976), 67-71.

2. It seems to have become an unspoken assumption that we are in a secular civilization, leaving us with nothing left to discuss. See David Lyon, "Secularization and Sociology: The History of an Idea," *Fides et Historia* 13 (1981): 2.

3. C. T. McIntire, *The Ongoing Task of Christian Historiography* (Toronto: Institute for Christian Studies, 1975) is suggestive here.

4. See Wolterstorff (cited in note 1 above).

5. Wolterstorff, 63, 72.

6. Tom Bottomore, *Marxist Sociology* (London: Macmillan, 1975), 65.

7. Bottomore, 66.

8. Wolterstorff, 77.

9. See, for example, Peter Roche de Coppens, *Ideal Man in Classical Sociology* (Philadelphia: Penn State University Press, 1976). See also David Lyon, *Sociology and the Human Image* (Downer's Grove: InterVarsity Press, 1983).

10. See C. Stephen Evans, *Preserving the Person* (Downers Grove: InterVarsity Press, 1977) and David Lyon, "Images of the Person in Theology and Sociology," *Crux* 14, (1978, no. 2).

11. David Martin, "Towards Eliminating the Concept of Secularization," in *Penguin Survey of the Social Sciences*, ed. Julius Gould (Harmondsworth: Penguin, 1965), 81-82.

12. Bryan R. Wilson, *Religion in a Secular Society* (London: Watts, 1966), ix, xi.

13. Bryan R. Wilson, *Contemporary Transformations of Religion* (London: Oxford University Press, 1976), vii.

14. These were three Riddell Lectures that he gave at the University of Newcastle, England, in 1974.

15. Wilson, *Contemporary*, 13.

16. Wilson, *Contemporary*, 25.

17. Wilson, *Contemporary*, 25.

18. Wilson, *Contemporary*, 39.

19. Wilson, *Contemporary*, 116.

20. Wilson, *Contemporary*, 96.

21. Wilson, *Contemporary*, 113.

22. Wilson, *Contemporary*, 113.

23. See, for example, J. I. Packer, *For Man's Sake!* (Exeter: Paternoster, 1978).

24. Susan Budd, *Sociologists and Religion* (London: Macmillan, 1973), 143.

25. Peter Glasner, *The Sociology of Secularization: A Critique of a Concept* (London

and Boston: Routledge & Kegan Paul, 1977), 8.
26. Stephen Yeo, *Religion and Voluntary Organizations in Crisis* (London: Croom Helm, 1976).
27. Thomas Luckmann, *Invisible Religion: The Problem of Religion in Modern Society* (New York: Macmillan, 1967), 90.
28. Robert Towler, *Homo Religiosus: Sociological Problems in the Study of Religion* (London: Constable, 1974), 138-39.
29. Luckmann, 17.
30. Peter L. Berger, *The Social Reality of Religion* (Harmondsworth: Penguin, 1969), 178.
31. David Martin, *Tracts against the Times* (Guildford: Lutterworth Press, 1973), 86.
32. Luckmann, 103.
33. Ernest Gellner, Legitimation of Belief (London: Cambridge University Press, 1974).
34. Gellner, 180.
35. Gellner, 154.
36. Gellner, 193.
37. Luckmann, 105.
38. Luckmann, 101.
39. Budd, 142 (cited in note 24 above).
40. I would argue that the welfare state is an institutional expression of the belief in progress in the Comtist sense—the application of science to human welfare. This belief might otherwise have been shattered by two world wars, but the welfare state kept it alive. The very bureaucracy involved can be trusted religiously.
41. See Glasner (cited in note 25 above); see also Robin Gill, *The Social Context of Theology: A Methodological Inquiry* (London: Mowbrays, 1975).
42. Glasner, 109.
43. Glasner, 113.
44. Gill, 127.
45. Gill, 130.
46. Martin, "Towards Eliminating" (cited in note 11 above).
47. See Larry Shiner, "The Concept of Secularization in Empirical Research," *Journal for the Scientific Study of Religion* 6 (no. 2): 207-20.
48. See, for example, Herman Dooyeweerd, "The Secularization of Science," *International Reformed Bulletin* 9 (no. 26): 2-17, which involves a number of conceptual problems with the term "secularization." See also David Martin, *Tracts against the Times* 83 (cited in note 31 above), on the secularization of art. There are similar difficulties with Dooyeweerd.
49. See Owen Chadwick, *The Secularization of the European Mind in the Nineteenth Century* (Cambridge, Eng.: Cambridge University Press, 1975).
50. See Martin, "Towards Eliminating" (cited in note 11 above); see also Glasner (cited in note 25 above) and David Lyon, "Secularization and Reflexivity: A Case Study in Commitment and Theory-choice" (paper presented at the International Sociological Association World Congress, Mexico City, August 1982).
51. See Francis Schaeffer, *How Then Should We Live?* (Old Tappen, N.J.: Revell, 1977). Packer (see note 23 above) takes Victorian Britain as a baseline.

52. See Colin Campbell, Towards a Sociology of Irreligion (London: Macmillan, 1978); see also David Lyon, "A Utopian Wasteland," *Third Way* 2 (no. 6): 3-5.
53. Luckmann, p. 117 (cited in note 27 above).

The fiasco of the sociology of knowledge
Maarten Vrieze

Introduction

First impressions are often misleading. This is especially true of sociology. Even the more intelligent introductions still portray sociology as a mature, generally stable science that is rightfully respected and does not lose itself in empty speculation or fanciful guesswork, a science that follows strictly scientific strategies and grounds its conclusions in responsibly selected, irrefutable evidence. Not a word about confusion or uncertainty, and not a hint of crisis.

Sociology is not unlike the girl in the Virginia Slims commercial; it has come a long way. In the 1950s—its shady past momentarily forgotten—it became one of the most popular disciplines on campus. The exuberant self-confidence of its most sophisticated practitioners drew attention away from the hesitant few who, although they were sociologists, were not quite sure what sociology was. Publishers, understandably, were delighted; almost overnight they created an impressive "professional literature" that removed any remaining doubts as to sociology's academic respectability.

By the 1960s, however, the past was already coming back to haunt sociologists. The legitimacy of sociology was seriously challenged and its role in society was exposed as ideological. Indeed its very identity was questioned. There was the sociology of knowledge which intended, by following the path of theoretical abstraction, to turn sociology into a problem. However, it rendered sociology problematic.[1] Suddenly it was obvious: sociology's medicine cabinet contained no remedies to carry sociology through its crisis. Could this be because the sociological crisis was not just intrasociological or even intrascientific but cultural?

This much is obvious in the present crisis: the doubts, tensions, and challenges in sociology all revolve around the issue of knowledge. What, really, is the status of sociological knowledge? Is such knowledge anchored in some "objective reality" at which one arrives only after curious antics of abstraction? Is it anchored in some sort of *Lebenswelt* at which one arrives by way of different, but equally curious, abstractions? Is such knowledge conditioned by the same societal forces that condition the "world" the sociologist seeks to understand? Can the sociologist find—or construct—a criterion that would distinguish what counts as knowledge and what does not? In that case, what is the status of that which does not count as sociological knowledge? And how do the *sociologists* come to know that which does not count as knowledge? Is not that which does not count as knowledge still part of the reality they seek to understand? What does—and does not—belong to that reality? And what is the nature of that reality? Is it Durkheim's world of social facts? Is it Dilthey's *Geist*? Schutz's *Lebenswelt*? Berger's social construction? Goffman's stage? Laszlo's system? And what are we to think when Bottomore declares that he knows? When Merton says it? Or Zijderveld? Or Habermas, Touraine, or Gouldner? And what about the *meaning* of sociological knowledge? Is it a tool of reification or an instrument for consciousness-raising? Is it Blumer's conversation between Mead's I and me, or is it Gadamer's dialectic-linguistic event?

Many a sociologist fears the sociology of knowledge that raises these questions as if it were Pandora's box—and with good reason. The sociology of knowledge is most embarrassing. It exposes conventional sociology as a *fiasco*. That things backfire, that the sociology of knowledge, precisely because it is a *sociology* of knowledge, shares in the fiasco—all of this intensifies the embarrassment.

As in any crisis, many don't know quite what to do. It is only human that sociologists whose professional careers are bound up with sociology as a credible, respectable, academic discipline are less than eager to admit that the sociology of knowledge has exposed a fiasco and argue that "meta-sociological speculation" has little relevance for what they do in education, government, business, or industry.

Some turn to a different field; others stay in sociology and become cynical. Among the latter we find those whom I like to label "alternative sociologists." They are still sociologists, but they propose to break radically with whatever until now went by the name "sociology." They readily accept the fiasco of conventional sociology; in fact, they accept the fiasco of any sociology—including their own. The fiasco becomes their point of departure. It is an ambiguous point of departure, but this very ambiguity reveals that their alternative sociology is more than a new way of doing sociology. It is an increasingly cynical determination to come to terms with a *cultural* fiasco, the radical failure of humanism.

In what follows I focus briefly upon four representative versions of alternative sociology: the sociology of the absurd, ethnomethodology, the dramaturgical approach, and the work of Berger and Luckmann. My aim is not to describe these departures in creative sociology or to analyze them in some detail, but rather to emphasize that as long as sociology accepts its self-interpretation and structuration from modern humanism as the cultural driving force of the Western world, such novel approaches cannot but fail to help sociology break out of the impasse in which it has found itself ever since it began to question itself in the sociology of knowledge.

Sociology of the absurd

The "sociology of the absurd" developed by Lyman and Scott is undoubtedly one of the most outspoken examples of creative sociology.[2] Since Lyman and Scott try to integrate some of the major themes of the various practitioners of this sociology, their work is important.

Lyman and Scott make it clear from the start that they reject conventional sociology. They find it downright dangerous. Conventional sociology imagines a social reality but immediately forgets that that reality is a figment of its imagination, an arbitrary illusion. It is no longer puzzled by the "mystery of the social order"; instead it is convinced it can come up with answers. Its major concern, therefore, is to influence the policymakers of this world.

The conventional sociologist is a social engineer who looks for a "rhetoric calculated to convince those in power that one has both the appropriate ideas and the techniques with which to make the studies that are convincing to policy-makers."[3] Consequently, he is likely to be inclined to "low-level theorizing, quantification, axiomatic system building, and whatever other rhetorical stratagems are likely to be persuasive."[4]

The sociologist of the absurd, on the other hand, realizes the world is essentially without meaning. Grand theories, systems of belief, perspectives are all arbitrary. Social situations, interaction, and actors, including the sociologist, are intrinsically problematic. Conventional sociology dangerously deceives us with respect to the ultimate meaning of life.

Meaning is not given; it must be created in response to the meaninglessness of reality. It is not easy to posit meaning in the void of this world, for we have nothing to hold on to. A void is a void. Besides, meaninglessness represents a constant threat. Machiavelli, the father of the sociology of the absurd, was already aware that the inherently unpredictable, *fortuna*, could effectively neutralize any human *virtu*.[5] To act, therefore, is to take enormous risks. Things may turn out to be hopeless after all.

Human nature is like that of the animal—aggressive, searching for sexual gratification, constantly struggling for domination. But people, unlike animals, are insatiable. Therefore people are set over against people, enemy against enemy, lover against lover. Conflict is fundamental.[6] We are even in conflict with ourselves. We are like the players in a game, out to win and dominate others. But there are no prearranged rules. We design both the game and the rules *while playing*.[7] This is possible because of a certain human feature that still remains to be mentioned—the ability to communicate. We can talk and understand what is being said; we give impressions as well as interpret them. We engage in *impression management*; we project images of ourselves that manipulate others into subjecting themselves to us. Communication as manipulation—that's our nature.

Manipulation is never complete, and the search for domination goes on and on. After all, each victory becomes problematic at the very moment the actuality of the present recedes into the past. We live in the ever-actual now.[8] Time is episodic. Our "world," which is the only reality there is, is an episodic world, continuously recreated. We have no completed world, no security, no rest, for the game is never won. Each game gives way to yet another game in which not only the rules are new but also the players! The players may, episodically, change the rules and the game, but the game and the rules determine who the players are and how they function. In other words, our situation is not some neutral territory that we use as the scene of our endeavors; rather, that situation uses *us*, manages *us*, constructs *us*.[9]

Fortuna, communication as manipulation, episodic situatedness—these, no doubt, are the more discouraging features of what Lyman and Scott have in mind when they declare that the meaning of life can only be *created* by accepting the challenge of the meaninglessness, the absurdity of this world.[10] Does it make sense, from their point of view, to keep speaking of *meaning*? Is this undeniably metaphorical use of "meaning" anything more than unintended impression management by the sociology of the absurd? However we might choose to answer these questions, it seems clear that Lyman and Scott have abandoned conventional sociology. Yet, if communication is manipulation and if even the sociologist is episodically situated, why bother to develop a sociology of the absurd? Nevertheless, Lyman and Scott speak of strategic research sites and even suggest a specific sociological research technique.[11]

Apparently, the sociology of the absurd has difficulty with the spectator attitude that conventional sociology urges upon its practitioners. It may be so that taking distance is unavoidable. "Like the painter who can look up from the valley to perceive the mountain or down into the plain from a high peak to see the valley, the social theoriest must have an *optimum distance* from his subject in order to see it accurately."[12] More important, however, is the recognition that there is no such thing as a reality "out there" whose nature the sociologist discovers by the methods of natural science.[13] It is essential, therefore, that the sociologist's "marginality" be relativized to suit "that method appropriate to the Sociology of the Absurd—participant observation."[14]

Lyman and Scott sense that there is something unacceptably wrong with the spectator attitude of conventional sociology. Their proposal, however, to employ instead the method of participant observation is hardly helpful. The spectator attitude indeed assumes the existence of a (social) reality, the coherence and consistency of which is independent of any human perspective but capable of adequate logical reconstruction and rational identification and interpretation by an uninvolved observer. The sociology of the absurd must rebel against that assumption. It has no room for a reality, social or otherwise, "out there" that could become an object of observation. The only reality it recognizes is the one social actors pose episodically, that is, from disappearing moment to disappearing moment, in their encounter. That reality can be understood only from within the encounter, from within the episodic moment, and from within the actor's perspective. "One can study the social world from the point of view of the superior or the subordinate; of the lover or his mistress; of the bourgeoisie or the proletariat; of management or labor; of the deviant or the person who labels him deviant, and so on. What is important is that one should have a perspective, but the particular perspective employed is irrelevant to the rectitude of theorizing."[15] Contrary to what Lyman and Scott suggest, this requires of the sociologist more than "empathic identification" with actors in their encounter and even more than participant observation. The only way to gain access to a meaningful social reality, after all, is in the encounter to establish it. Sociologists must themselves become participants, not observers but the creators of meaning and social reality! That, however, means the end of any meaningful sociological theory.

The sociology of the absurd is caught in its own conviction that the world is created anew in each new encounter. The social reality to which the sociologist-turned-participant has access has no existence beyond the encounter in which it was established or beyond the perspectives of the participants in that encounter. For the sociologists this means that they are forever unable to report about the reality they once established. Together with the episodic encounter and with their perspective at the time that reality disappeared, yielding to different realities, different perspectives, and different episodes. Any account that the sociologists produce is an account from within such a new perspective, a new episode, and a new reality.

Lyman and Scott must have sensed that unless they retreated at a number of critical points, their sociology of the absurd would lead them into a dead-end street, and they must have realized that unless they conformed there where it really counts to the central tenets of twentieth-century mainline sociology, they would place themselves outside of the sociological discourse.[16] Their "radical departure from the conventional," therefore, is not so radical after all. They consistently relativize their critique of conventional sociology by reintroducing notions such as human nature, continuity, history, and thus structure.[17] They are not about to become disloyal to twentieth-century sociology as it understands and structures itself. In fact, their loyalty goes farther than that of many others. Their narrowing of the focus of sociology to what goes on in the *individual* encounter can be legitimately interpreted as an ideological affirmation of the societal status quo under which the sociologists of the absurd do their work!

Ethnomethodology

It's an awkward name, but it helps us to get oriented. The first part of the word ("ethno") refers to "Dick and Jane," that is, to everyday people in everyday life. The second part ("method") refers to the methods everyday people use to create for themselves a sense of reality, a sense of meaning, a sense of what is normal. The third part ("ology") expresses the surprise of those who wonder how there can be order in what Dick and Jane create as their "world."[18]

Garfinkel, who is ethnomethodology's major representative, apparently *assumes* the overall perspective of Lyman and Scott. He does not spell out his assumptions the way the sociologists of the absurd do—he simply follows them. And he has good reason to do so. His assumptions instruct him never to take *any* assumption quite seriously! Ethnomethodologists take it that any account given by any actor—including the account of ethnomethodologists themselves—is a way of negotiating and renegotiating reality. This involves a radical relativizing not only of conventional sociology but of ethnomethodology itself. Apparently the ethnomethodologist can accept that. What is it, then, that makes Garfinkel, Cicourel, Pollner, Schegloff, Sacks, and others write?

It has struck Garfinkel that everyday people in everyday life takes a great deal for granted. Though they do not talk about what they expect and usually are not even *aware* of what they expect, their "world," that is, reality-for-them, rests on *background expectancies*. It is easy to bring these expectancies to the fore. Simply do or say something that no one "in their right mind" expects, do something insane but with a straight face, and the "world" of everyday people will crumble! The possibilities for "garfinkeling" others into exposing their dependence on background expectancies are endless. If you use this method intensively on people, you can make them "lose their sanity," for it will then be impossible for them to "make sense of things." Fortunately, the only people who engage in "garfinkeling" are ethnomethodologists and practical jokers. Most of the time our "reality" stays intact, though it constantly changes.

This reality is not the "objective reality" of a detached observer (that figment of the conventional sociologist's imagination). The "detached observer" does not share everyman's world and does not participate in the continuous negotiation in which that world is accomplished. My "reality" is describable —but only if you participate in it. And it certainly does not lend itself to generalizations or to other such practices dear to the heart of conventional sociology.

In his reports about everyday people, Garfinkel pays close attention to *rules*. It is refreshing to note that he recognizes rules as *norms* and does not interpret them as regularities. Rules require positivization. Positivizing is always situational and intersubjective. Positivizing is twofold: there is positivizing that concerns societal structures (*constitutive* rules) and positivizing of conduct-orienting directives (*preferential* rules). Significantly, Garfinkel recognizes that norm-positivizing implies interpretation and, therefore, disclosure. The positing of norms affects the situation and makes it unfold or disclose itself.[19]

It should not surprise us that Garfinkel subjectivizes rules and the situational and intersubjective negotiation of their concrete-historic normativity. His constitutive rules (the ones that seem to point to structures of societal individuality) and his preferential rules (the ones that seem to refer to functional directives) have no transsubjective ground. Constitutive and preferential rules lack consistency. They seem to be up for grabs in the intrinsically arbitrary negotiation and renegotiation of what is to be reality. The "et cetera" character of rules inevitably makes every rule accidental.[20]

Cicourel, who relies heavily on Wittgenstein, Austin, and especially Chomsky and Schutz, tries to get out of the impasse of this all too vigorous relativism by assuming a "deep structure" of procedures acquired early in life—procedures of interpretation acquired along with language. These procedures constitute the possibility of a "world" that makes sense to both you *and* me. Via the reciprocity of perspectives or via the compilation of a stock of knowledge within a particular lingual community, these ways of interpretation enable us to act "normally," to react "rationally," to say what "makes sense," and even (after erratic behavior) to restore things to "normal" through the "right" kind of account.[21]

What Cicourel and other ethnomethodologists are trying to do is clear. They concentrate on what they take to be universal characteristics of lingual interaction, hoping thereby to account for what they call social order. This leaves us, however, with at least three crucial questions. First of all, what does it mean to the ethnomethodologist to *account for* the social order? Can such an account escape Garfinkel's relativizing of any theoretical method? In the second place, is it possible, given the standpoint of ethnomethodology, to reconcile its phenomenological reduction of the social order, or everyday life, with its rejection of theoretical detachment or nonparticipant observation? In the third place, given the standpoint of ethnomethodology and its critique of conventional sociology, how can it justifiably assume that the societal context—the existential condition for any lingual interaction—is itself produced by that lingual interaction?

The third question is especially important. Ethnomethodology is unable to answer it. But the ethnomethodologists realize this, and they declare that they have abandoned all attempts at "grand theory." They accept the verdict that their work is internally contradictory and intrinsically absurd.[22] In a way, ethnomethodology goes *beyond* the sociology of the absurd—but only because it has gone *through* it. We find a similar development in the work of a man who comes from a quite different sociological direction—Goffman, to whom we now turn.

The dramaturgical approach

Goffman began within the tradition of symbolic interactionism. Somewhat to the astonishment of the conventional sociologist, however, he came to disdain much of what symbolic interactionism tried to accomplish. The embarrassing fact is that Goffman, in his cynicism, remains a faithful symbolic interactionist and—by the same token—a conventional sociologist of sorts. An intriguing ambiguity.[23]

Goffman needs little introduction. Several of his books are best-sellers. His metaphor of human activity as stage performance has considerable popular appeal. Besides, his basic tenet is quite similar to both ethnomethodology and the sociology of the absurd, namely, that social reality is reality-for-the-actors, that reality is how the actors experience what, when, and where they experience, perceive, organize, intend, act. There simply is no social reality in and by itself, self-contained, and independent of perspective to provide the detached observer with an objectivity that can be reconstructed in publicly verifiable, logically clear propositions. To catch a glimpse of social reality the theorist must look through the eyes of the actors who are both the producers and the products of that reality. Therefore, meanings must be central in any theoretical account of the actors and their world.

Such meanings, however, are not simply individual creations of individual minds. They are social products emerging in social settings. Human behavior illustrates this. Behavior is motivated by the desire to project a certain image of oneself and one's actions, an image that will bring others to do certain things that will advance one's cause. In other words, in our behavior we "put on a show," we "play a part," we "perform a role" before an "audience." Like actors on a stage, we make use of "routines," "props," "special effects equipment," "programs," "scripts," and even a "backstage." Behavior, in short, creates a world of *make-believe.*

This very fact, however, illustrates that social reality is intersubjectively constructed. To construct a world of make-believe, actors need one another and together they need a captive audience. Their world of make-believe is precarious, easily shattered by a performance that does not come off as convincing, by an audience that is easily bored, by an incoherent script, by an unexpected interruption, or by any one of a thousand other things that could go wrong. Actors will often have to improvise, change routines, or cover up inconsistencies. There can be no world of make-believe, that is, no social reality, unless actors and audience cooperate, share meanings, and "internalize" the world of make-believe.

Goffman's metaphor is more than a hermeneutic device. Actors, to him, *are* actors. Yet, he wants to emphasize that they are *more* than actors. They are fellow actors and, of course, the audience as well. Though there are established routines (rituals, ceremonies, and the like), these routines have to be fitted into the creation of a world of make-believe. And the script for that unfolding world of make-believe is written, from episode to episode, by no one in particular. Yet that script imposes itself on actor, audience, and social setting alike in the arbitrary and unpredictable dialectic of performance, improvisation, interpretation, information, expectation, and situation.[24]

It appears that Goffman, in the tradition of symbolic interactionism, holds conventional sociology to its word. In his own cynical way he draws out the implications of the sociological enterprise. These he exposes in their bizarre consequences —and then accepts.

Conventional sociology assumes that social reality can be constructed and reconstructed by people; Goffman states that social reality *is* what human behavior produces. Conventional sociology assumes that people can be understood adequately in terms of their functioning within social reality; Goffman states that people are what that reality produces. Conventional sociology assumes we can adequately know social reality without metaphysical speculation, by proceeding from the social reality as it presents itself to anyone's observation; Goffman accepts this and states that social reality *is* what is being seen, perceived, and experienced. Conventional sociology assumes that the final meaning of our knowledge of social reality is our free control of that reality; Goffman agrees and applauds when he sees everyone getting away with advancing his own cause through opportunistic impression management procedures.

This is not quite the self-image that conventional sociologists intend to project. Could it be because their performance is not quite convincing? Or is the audience perhaps bored? Goffman's dramaturgical approach upstages them, in any event. Legitimately? Effectively? Before attempting to answer such questions, we should turn our attention briefly to the work of Berger and Luckmann.

The social construction of reality
Berger and Luckmann need even less of an introduction than Goffman. Their study, *The Social Construction of Reality*, is recognized (somewhat unfortunately) as the classic statement of a phenomenologically informed sociology of knowledge.[25]

The picture of human existence in Berger and Luckmann is even gloomier than the pictures painted by the sociology of the absurd, ethnomethodology, and Goffman. It is a picture of radical imprisonment and unmitigated determinism. True, Berger and Luckmann promise the imprisoned human a liberation of sorts, but it is hardly a liberation worth celebrating. It is a liberation from any illusion of liberation.

The picture is simple. Human existence, especially during the first years of life, is grossly underdeveloped. Becoming human takes place not only within a particular natural environment but also within "a specific cultural and social order, which is mediated to him by the significant others who have charge of him."[26] Our organismic development is socially determined, but this social determination, in turn, is itself socially determined! Organismic development goes hand in hand with the development of the self. "The same social processes that determine the completion of the organism produce the self in its particular, culturally relative form."[27]

> The character of the self as a social product is not limited to the particular configuration the individual identifies as himself (for instance, as "a man," in the particular way in which this identity is defined and formed in the culture in question), but the comprehensive psychological equipment that serves as an appendage to the particular configuration (for instance, "manly" emotions, attitudes and even somatic reaction).[28]

"Human existence, if it were thrown back on its organismic resources by themselves, would be existence in some sort of chaos."[29] However, human existence takes place in a context of order. How does that order come about? It is a human product—or better, it is an ongoing human production. Berger and Luckmann reject the tenets of conventional sociology: "Social order is not part of the nature of things, and it cannot be derived from 'the laws of nature.' Social order exists *only* as a product of human activity. No other ontological status may be ascribed to it."[30] Yet, the social world confronts people in the same way that the natural world confronts them, namely, as a force that determines their very existence.

Berger and Luckmann feel it is legitimate to speak of a

social construction of reality because human behavior is characterized universally by three processes: institutionalization, legitimation, and internalization.[31] The institutional world has the ontological status of objectivated human activity. Because it is historical, this institutional world requires legitimation; that is to say, it must be explained, interpreted, and thus made accessible to new generations to maintain the unity of history and personal biography. Legitimation informs individuals why things *are* what they are before telling them what to do and what not to do: knowledge precedes norms. A symbolic universe, for example, *interprets* people and things, but even this highest level of legitimation—interpretation—is itself socially constructed and, therefore, forever relative to a social reality it tries to interpret. Internalization, finally, makes social reality part of a person's psychic makeup by internalizing externalized meanings and making objective reality subjective reality-for-people.

These universal processes leave little room for human knowledge. If externalization is automatically followed by the internalization of what was first externalized, we are left with a hermetically closed circle. But how do Berger and Luckmann *know* that this *is* a circle? If they appeal to empirical evidence, we must remind them that such evidence is itself enclosed by the circle. Have they found a secret way out of the circle, so that they can transcend it? Is their sociology of knowledge perhaps an *exceptional* kind of behavior that avoids these universal processes?

Berger and Luckmann admit their enthusiasm for the present state of sociological theory is "markedly restrained."[32] They suspect a new movement toward the reification of social phenomena. Still, they see themselves as loyal to the sociological tradition. They even confirm their faith in the traditional dogmas of conventional sociology.[33] Are they convinced that if sociology remains faithful to its mission, it must of necessity lead to determinism and to the relativizing of *all* knowledge, including its own?

The Social Construction of Reality studies "knowledge that guides conduct in everyday life."[34] Even so, Berger and Luckmann also discuss sociological knowledge, that is, the possibility of sociology. In the attempt to overcome Husserl's unresolved problem of the relationship of the transcendental ego to concrete historic consciousness, they let the transcendental ego, ordinary self-consciousness in everyday life, and the theoretical zeroing in on his object of study of the sociologist coincide. The "consciousness" that emerges thus is a consciousness of "a world of multiple realities."[35] These realities are "finite provinces of meaning." At the same time these realities are "enclaves" within one of those provinces, a province which forms the "paramount reality," the true home of consciousness.

The geography is confusing. Consciousness makes "excursions" to the various provinces of meaning. In the process it leaves the province of paramount reality to which it will eventually have to return—and yet it never really leaves it, for paramount reality comprises all the other provinces.[36] What happens when the sociologists leave the province of everyday life to make their excursions to the province of theoretical reflection? Do they ever really leave the paramount reality?

These questions become more urgent when we hear that the meaning province of everyday life includes a "social stock of knowledge." Central to this stock of knowledge is what Berger and Luckmann call "recipe knowledge," that is, competence in routine performances.[37] As long as nothing upsets the normal course of everyday life, recipe knowledge is all that is needed. As a social stock of knowledge, it is available to every member of the (lingually interacting!) everyday life community. Even so, this stock of knowledge is socially distributed; it is possessed differently by different individuals and types of individuals.[38]

Where does sociological knowledge fit in? Is it recipe knowledge distributed to that "type of individual" we call a sociologist? Is it the kind of knowledge the everyday life community requires when the normal course of events is disturbed? Or is it a peculiar province of meaning to which one makes excursions and then always comes back from in a "return to reality"?

Berger and Luckmann are forced to answer these questions. Yet, given their standpoint, they do not easily come by a satisfactory answer. As Hamilton correctly observes, for Berger and Luckmann knowledge of social reality is coextensive with social reality itself. "What is taken for granted as knowledge in a society is identical with the knowledge itself, providing the framework on which future knowledge is to be ordered.

Knowledge of social order, we must assume, functions as the legitimation of social order."[39] There is no escaping the dilemma: either sociology leaves the province of everyday life and is, therefore, of the same order as aesthetic ecstasy, religious experience, and dreaming or it is ideological.[40] In either case, Berger and Luckmann are forced to interpret sociological knowledge as a social construction and, for that reason, as intrinsically relative. This accords with the determinism we noticed earlier.

Berger has tried to take the gloom off his relativism. He introduces the idea of "relativizing the relativizers."[41] He seems encouraged by a radicalization of relativizing, a pushing of relativism to its limits, since it liberates us from illusions. He comes close to the views of Zijderveld who links relativism (he prefers the term relationism) and human dignity.[42] Zijderveld accepts the fiasco of sociology, that is, its unavoidable self-relativization. He will not return to what he regards as dogmatism and fanaticism of those who claim to have found an Archimedean point outside our socially constructed everyday world. He opts for the stoical (!) attitude of an Archimedes who countered the absurdity of this world with a final demonstration of intellectual ascesis: *noli turbare ciculos meos* (don't disturb my circles).[43]

What about the structure of sociology?
The practitioners of conventional sociology are less than jubilant about the phenomenon of creative sociology. Their reaction is somewhat ambiguous and with good reason. Even though creative sociologists say things that conventional sociologists find hard to accept, their questions are not easily dismissed. The most obvious and certainly the most urgent of these questions is the question about the nature of sociology. What is it, precisely, that sociologists are doing when they do sociology?

The question is about the *structure* of sociology, not the *intention* of the one who does it or the *function* someone assigns to it. But what are we to think of when that term structure comes up?

Earlier we saw that the sociology of the absurd has difficulty with the idea of structure as conventional sociology uses it. It objects to the emphasis upon consistency, coherence, stability, and continuity as essential features of the social reality that sociologists investigate. It wants to instill a "sense of astonishment" into conventional sociology and make it wonder how, given the inherent meaninglessness of (social) reality, (social) order is possible after all.[44] Obviously, the difficulty is that both conventional sociology and the sociology of the absurd are reluctant to offer an account of the idea of structure. That it is possible to identify a particular societal phenomenon, to name it, to recognize it in different contexts, to differentiate it from other societal phenomena as being of a different kind, and even to make it a topic of discussion in the sociological discourse remains largely undiscussed.

One of the consequences of this failure to acccount for the idea of structure is that social theorists ignore vitally important distinctions, such as between structure and function or between structure as structural principle and structure as structuredness. With respect to the question of what sociology actually is, failure to distinguish between structure and function means an inability to differentiate between what sociologists happen to be doing and the different angles under which one could look at what they are doing or the different ways in which one might make use of it. And failure to distinguish between structural principle and structuredness means to be unable to differentiate between sociological praxis and the criterion with which such praxis ought to be measured.

It is not difficult to guess the reason for the reluctance to give an account of the idea of structure. Even to consider the possibility of an account already implies recognition that there *is* such a thing as structure and reality is *not* self-contained or self-sufficient. To concede the subjectivity of reality, however, is to revolt against the central thrust of Western humanism, the driving force that ever since the beginning of the modern age has dictated the course of Western culture. Twentieth-century sociology does not seem to be particularly eager to engage in any such revolt. In fact, it appears to be quite content with the general direction set for it by the claims of Western humanism, even though that means that it has to remain in the dark about its very structure.

We get a clear picture of the prevailing uncertainty about the structure of sociology when we note that there are at least three distinct attitudes that modern sociology asks its practitio-

ners to assume all at once. The first is the attitude of philosophers with their posing of ultimate questions and with their
totality focus. Like philosophers, sociologists seek to push
through to the existential conditions of the (in this case societal)
phenomena of human existence and like philosophers they
seek to identify the phenomena as they appear in a totality
focus in terms of such existential cconditions.[45] The second is
the attitude of the special scientists with their modal focus. Like
the special scientists, sociologists seek to account for a particular side of human existence and of the reality to which that
existence belongs.[46] And the third is the attitude of the concerned member of society not involved in theoretic but in
action-linked concrete reflection about what society should be
like and what should be done to bring it about.[47]

The sociologists are expected to integrate the three distinct
postures into one. The difficulty is that that cannot be done
without seriously distorting each one of them. One reflects
either theoretically *or* nontheoretically, and in theoretical reflection one has either a totality focus or a modal focus. It all seems
rather obvious, but we should not forget that such is the case
within a particular perspective. Change the perspective and it
is no longer possible to differentiate the three attitudes the way
it has been done here. In fact, within the perspective of modern
Western humanism a differentiation of this kind is quite illegitimate. Given the character of humanism, that is understandable.

Historically, there is a close connection between sociology
and humanism. It is essential that we have a clear pciture of the
nature of that connection.

Sociology and humanism
Auguste Comte coined the term sociology and it stuck. His
views illustrate the magnetism of an ideal that is itself
prompted by a radical motive such as humanism. Drastically
simplifying his account of what inspired him, we could say that
Comte was driven by the conviction that it was time to
(re)organize and to (re)arrange the intricate network of connec-
tions and relationships that links people and integrates their
many different activities. Besides, Comte was convinced that
he knew the direction into which that (re)organization and
(re)arrangement would have to take people.[48] What was now
needed, first of all, was a workable plan, a detailed road map,

a carefully designed *blueprint*. Only that would make it possible
to avoid at least some of the arbitrary effects of human behavior. Comte felt confident that he was the man of the hour and
that his science, sociology, was the tool of the hour.

To understand Comte's conviction and the sociologizing
that he helped develop we must place it against the backdrop
of Western culture and its increasing willingness to accomo-
date the all-embracing claims of a radical humanism.
Humanism is not simply what humanists believe; for example,
their conviction that reality is self-contained and self-sufficient,
that people are or will become independent, autonomous in
their rationality.[49] Humanism is what makes humanists believe
what they believe, what makes them interpret themselves as
they do. It is *what lies behind* the humanist faith and the humanist life and what gives them direction. It is, therefore, a radical,
that is *root*-directing, driving force.

Historically, humanism emerges in the confrontation with
and as the rejection of the driving force of the *basileia* (kingdom)
of which the New Testament speaks. It is the refusal to be set
free by that *basileia* and the claim to be able to be free without it.
Throughout its life that remains its distinctive character. It is in
this confrontation with the *basileia* of Christ's message that
humanism receives its messianic color and assumes its anti-
basileia and, therefore, *basileia*like posture.

I use the term *basileia* here in its New Testament connotation of what the *basileus* does, the ruler's rule or regime.[50] One
of the gospels tells us that Christ interpreted himself and his
presence in this world as the bringing of the good news of the
basileia of God.[51] In spite of the deep hesitation and the repeated
fumbling of the Christian community, that "word of the *basileia*" paved its way through the Western world. In the post-
medieval situation, we suddenly face the radical confrontation
with its claims. Humanism can be understood only in terms of
that confrontation.

To be sure, humanism is a radical motive that cannot be
accounted for theoretically. That does not mean, however, that
its thrust and claims are irrelevant for our theorizing. Two
historical dimensions of humanism need emphasis here. In the
first place, humanism must persistently legitimatize itself as
alternative basileia in a culturally relevant manner. It has to
provide orientation; it has to devise direction; it has to deliver

the goods that its *basileia* character implies, namely, freedom, peace, meaning, life, perspective. And it must do these things not just in one area of human existence, or even in all of them, but in the integral totality of our existence. But as it tries to live up to its promises, humanism falls victim to what Dooyeweerd has explicated as its inner dialectic.[52] It is not able to provide orientation because whatever might conceivably serve as "point of orientation" is itself in need of orientation. Besides, interpretation is impossible because every criterion for interpretation itself requires interpretation. Meaning cannot be found in humanism's "reality" because even that which might try to assign meaning itself needs to have meaning assigned to it.

In the second place, humanism's character as a *basileia* forces it to "rule" in every remote corner of "reality," but the very structure of reality resists the humanism that tries to negate it. Therefore, humanism is forever struggling with new obstacles, not the least important of which is its own relativity. These tensions characterize humanism's historical development and form the background to Comte's effort to "do sociology."

Sociology as it was developed by Comte, though certainly not by him alone, was new to the Western world. Still, it was product of the West's increasing susceptibility to the claims of humanism. To legitimatize itself as alternative *basileia*, humanism, once it had achieved a measure of control over the "natural world," had to draft an ever more encompassing blueprint and contrive new strategies for controlling the "social world." Sociology is the drafting of just such a blueprint.

Comte's attempts at making a blueprint has failed to hold the interest of later generations of sociologists, but *what* he attempted to do became a model for conventional sociology. The conglomeration of activities that today we call sociology has its own peculiar structure. We discover that structure when we examine the *pattern* into which the activities that make up sociology have been intertwined. Dominating the pattern is the making of a blueprint for human life and human society.

There is a sharp difference between a blueprint and a plan of action. A plan of action concludes in the light of normative structures and directives what is to be done in a given situation. A blueprint, on the other hand, does not accept structures or directives as given, but it designs and fabricates them! Humanism cannot avoid the notion of blueprint. Precisely because it rejects even the slightest suggestion of heteronomy, it has to *contrive* normative structures and it has to *create* directives. When it does that, however, it levels the boundaries between the various mutually irreducible meaning-unique areas of human responsiblity and it eradicates at the same time the rootedness that is structurally existential to all our knowledge and praxis and to their unity. It has to come up with its own organization of human existence and with its own ideas of the possibility and the unity of knowledge and praxis in the various areas of human enterprise. That is what makes the composition of a blueprint for humanism of such critical importance. No wonder that it enlisted the sciences, and particularly sociology, into its services to draft its blueprint.

Is sociology a science?
From the beginning sociology has allied itself with the scientific enterprise. It viewed itself as a science; in fact, at times even as the science par excellence. Such hybris merely illustrated how uneasy the alliance often was.

Sociology claimed scientific status at a time when there was a great deal of confusion and anxiety in the world of science.[53] Sociologists became stubborn participants in the *Methodenstreit* (conflict over methodology) in its various phases.[54] But there were questions about that. Whose side were they on? Were the issues in *Methodenstreit* really relevant to sociology's task of blueprint-making? Max Weber seemed to think so, and he dominated the sociological scene. But what kind of people are the "technologists" of society? Are they the exceptional kind of actors who spy on fellow actors as they try to make sense of life? What sense is being made? And if making sense is a vocation, who does the calling?

Durkheim did not make things easier. He pulled the rug out from under the sociologists' feet just when they appeared to have contrived a blueprint that established a rationally perspicuous order and, by the same token, a perspective of a controllable society. Our society, he suggested, is thoroughly Western. Even the categories of our thinking are products of—and relative to—a characteristically Western development.

Dilthey looked on, not really surprised. Although he was

not a sociologist, the sociological acrobatics of those who were trying to make sense of society and of sociology itself did not amuse him. He had troubles of his own. Soon enough these became the troubles of sociology.

What is the reason that sociology's practitioners repeatedly find themselves in the dilemmas and quandaries that frustrate nonsociologists such as Dilthey? One gets the impression that once sociology gets underway as both blueprint making and science, it loses control of its development. To see this more clearly, we now turn to some of the implications of the structure of sociology as it traditionally understood itself.

Implications of the structure of traditional sociology for its focus
Sociology has traditionally been interpreted as the complex of activities that results in the drafting of blueprints and in the contriving of strategies for their translation into concrete societal configurations and conditions. It was thereby understood that the making of blueprints included the invention and introduction of a new fundamental order for society, and that the criteria that sociologists needed to draft their blueprints would have to be derived from the observation of society itself.

Three kinds of requirements with which sociologists should comply should have our attention. First, the requirement that sociologists are sensitive to the historical dimension of societal reality. Second, the requirement that they are fully aware of the structuring of society by those who in their various societal bonds compose that society. And third, the requirement that they take into account the role of the *Weltanschauung* (world-and-life view) in the construction and forming of the "social world."

Both conventional and alternative sociology are aware of the historical dimension of societal reality. Both view the "social world" under the angle of possible change: a historical world is a changeable world. To recognize the historical dimension, however, means to introduce a measure of uncertainty into the very reality from which sociologists are to derive the criteria for the making of their blueprints. That relativizes not only their criteria, but also any blueprint they might make with the help of these criteria. That means: it relativizes sociology itself.

Sociologists now face an impossible dilemma. On the one hand, they *must* gain clarity about the transhistorical structuring of reality that makes both human society and its historical dimension possible. Without that clarity their sociologizing loses its meaning. On the other hand, unless they want to be out of step with Western culture, they *must* give in to the claim of Western humanism. Humanism asserts that it provides an alternative to the *basileia* of which the biblical message speaks. That assertion entails the conviction that all of "social reality" is fundamentally constructible and that, therefore, any notion of an order or structure that transcends either society or history ought to be abandoned.

There are two other dilemmas that frustrate sociologists who are trying to be sensitive to the historical dimension of societal reality. One concerns the relation between the sociological blueprint and the nonsociological plans and projects at work in society. The other concerns the relation between individual and communal. I'll discuss them briefly.

Sociologists are not the only ones concerned with the construction and reconstruction of society. Every member of society participates in it. Most people, however, are not familiar with the blueprints sociologists make for their society. They follow their own perspectives and directives. What are sociologists to make of that? On the one hand, as makers of a blueprint for society they simply have to assume that there is a need for such a blueprint: what the (sociologically uninformed) members of society do when they follow their nonsociological perspectives and orientations pushes society into the wrong direction and is for that reason *historically unacceptable*. Society should be reorganized, its course corrected, and its members reeducated. If there would be no need for that, sociological blueprint making would not only be irrelevant but also meaningless. Sociological theory would merely be one view among many, possibly even an incorrect view. From the standpoint of humanism, however, society is out of control and its course haphazard, a situation that calls for the blueprint making of sociology. On the other hand, however, sociologists who design a blueprint for society have to assume that what the (sociologically uninformed) members of society do makes good sense. That society after all is the only source from which they will be able to derive the criteria that they need to design their blueprint. To assume that historic society lacks sense until its course has been corrected by sociology's blueprint simply means to cut oneself off from one's only source of criteria. The dilemma is frustrating. Either sociologists assume that society needs their blueprint (but that means having to design such a blueprint without the necessary criteria) or they assume that society is such that it can provide these criteria (but that means having to concede that no sociological blueprint is necessary).

Sociologists who try to be sensitive to the historical dimension of societal reality face still another dilemma. Modern sociology, we saw earlier, rejects the idea of a transcendent structuring of human society. Implied in that rejection is that sociologists can legitimately identify societal phenomena only in terms of other societal phenomena. That means, however, that they are caught in the dilemma of "individual" versus "collective."

To make clear what a human community is, it is not enough to say that it is composed of individual human beings, for that leaves unanswered the question of what an individual human being is. Similarly, to make clear what an individual human being is, it is not enough to say that to be an individual human being is to be a member of a human community, for that leaves unanswered the question of what a human community is. It appears that we are caught in a vicious circle when we try to identify individual human beings in terms of the communities to which they belong or human communities in terms of the individual human beings who belong to them. Individualism and collectivism are attempts to break through that circle. Individualism accounts for societal phenomena in terms of the (illegitimate) abstraction of the "individual" as the basic unit in societal reality. Collectivism accounts for these phenomena in terms of the (equally illegitimate) abstraction of the "collectivity" within which one distinguishes "subunits." Both positions reduce societal reality. They ignore the significance of the diversity of human activities and their societal context. They have to, for that diversity reflects the transcendent structuring in which it is grounded, a structuring both of the kind of human activities and of the structural invariance of the communities that form the context of those activities. One consequence of that ignoring is that sociologists now find themselves unable to account adequately for the changes societies go through in the course of their history. Their account remains limited to one in terms of a few (arbitrarily chosen) modal notions such as continuity, change, and (degree of) coherence. What does not fit into such categories now has to be identified as the unpredictable, irrational, and uncontrollable.[56] The making of a sociological blueprint appears to be a strictly personal—one sociologists opts for an individualist psychological reduction, another for a collectivistic organicistic reduction, and so forth—and, therefore, a historically relative attempt to guess the unpredictable course of a societal reality fraught with irrationality. The course of societal reality cannot be controlled even though the *basileia* focus of traditional sociology demands it. The frustration is that even the blueprint making itself appears to be historically conditioned.

The second requirement I mentioned is that social theorists recognize the significance of the forming and shaping of society that goes on from day to day in the actions and interactions of its members. There is nothing unusual about the requirement, but it appears to be difficult to comply with if sociology is to be understood as the making of a blueprint for society.

People shape society not only through actions that are specifically aimed at that, but also through activities that are not so aimed. When members of a government design a social policy, they engage specifically in the shaping of society. When, on the other hand, the directors of a business firm decide to market a new product, it may not be their specific aim to (re)shape society, but what they do does affect their society: perhaps it reinforces its overall pattern, perhaps it subtly changes its course. Whatever the nature of these activities, however, they all share two intriguing features. Every human activity is of a particular kind, and every activity occurs in a context of interaction which also is of a particular kind. Economic activity differs in kind from political activity; a business transaction is different in kind from a mayoral election. Also, economic activity in a faith context differs in character from that same kind of activity in an economic, or in an ethical, context: a church's budget is characteristically different from the budget of a fast-food restaurant or from that of a hospital. There is double structuring here to which we need to pay attention when we focus on the shaping of society. That shaping is *a structured activity.*

What now does that mean for sociology? Earlier we saw that the definition of sociology as the making of a blueprint for society is a direct implication of humanism's ideal (also) to gain control of societal reality. To bring that ideal closer to its realization, it is essential that the blueprint making is done from a position which is free from interference and not affected by the interaction that is characteristic of society. That, however, conflicts with the structuring I just mentioned.

Present-day sociology, understandably, finds it impossible to account for that structuring in terms of an *order for* (societal) *reality* which does not coincide with that reality but transcends it. The very notion of blueprint forbids it. It now has two options. Either it avoids at any price giving an account of the fact of the structuring of its blueprint making, that is, it refuses to be questioned about its very nature, or it falls back on a modern version of Comte's "law of the three stages" and assumes that the structuring of the acts through which people shape society originates not with some transcendent order for society but with the observable *order of* society itself.

The first option surrenders sociology to anyone's arbitrary definition. The second also relativizes sociology, for to assume that developments in society itself lead to, and so structure, the blueprint making activity of sociology does not remove the fact that the structuring itself of that activity necessarily falls beyond any blueprint that sociologists could compose. Their designs remain unavoidably incomplete. As a result, their attempts to gain control of societal reality end in failure. Add to this that for the contents of their blueprints sociologists remain exclusively dependent on what they observe of society, and it becomes even more obvious that their blueprint making activity is unable to provide the control humanism is looking for. Their blueprints, moreover, are never more than a historically conditioned reaction to what they observe and, therefore, strictly relative and without any guarantee that they present an improvement over the current state of affairs.

The third requirement that should have our attention briefly is that sociologists have to be aware of the role of the *Weltanschauung,* or world-and-life view, in the ongoing construction and reconstruction of society.

A *Weltanschauung* is a normative direction of life. It is not

actually a "view" in the sense of subjective opinion and conviction, but rather a normative orientation that enables a community to form its opinions and convictions and to take its distinctive stand in concrete situations. The place of the world-and-life
view is on the law side, not on the subject side, of reality. One
should not confuse world-and-life view with religious perspective. The religious perspective is that which makes the world-
and-life view possible and, so to speak, calls it into existence.
Also, one should not confuse world-and-life view with ideology. Ideology is a complex of directives, usually limited in
scope, that has been adjusted so that specific interests of a given
(segment of a) population are safeguarded or served.

The *Weltanschauung* provides sociologists with important
clues when they try to understand the patterns of interaction in
a given society. A world-and-life view does not just affect how
the members of a society think or feel, but it also gets crystal-
lized in particular forms of association and communication in
a society, in mutual expectations and in "tracks" that members
of a society habitually follow.

One feature especially intrigues sociologists: every world-
and-life view reflects its (past and present) confrontation with
a particular culture and with particular cultural and societal
conditions. Sociologists will want to know where a world-and-
life view comes from, how it came about, and whether, perhaps, it is necessarily linked with a particular society or with
particular conditions in that society. That, however, raises the
even more intriguing question of how sociologists will be able
to understand a world-and-life view which is not their own.
There is something about one's world-and-life view that remains a mystery to anyone who does not share one's fundamental, religious commitment. Does that mean that one can
understand a world-and-life view only from within?

Clearly, when I encounter a world-and-life view it forces
me to take a position myself and to stand by my own world-
and-life view. Traditionally, sociology has had difficulties with
that. It intended to design a blueprint of a society for all
regardless of faith or *Weltanschauung*, and it believed that its
designing of that blueprint would be neutral and able to transcend conflicting world-and-life views. The belief was unfounded. The conviction that sociology was able to come up
with something better than the various world-and-life views

offered was consistently rejected by those world-and-life views themselves and brought sociology into an often open conflict with them. The claim of neutrality, though ideologically quite effective, was clearly illegitimate.

Sociologists have become more and more hesitant when it comes to the phenomenon of world-and-life view. That is understandable, for whenever it receives serious attention the conclusion seems unavoidable that already sociology's traditional self-interpretation betrays its embeddedness in a world-and-life view—one inspired by the religious perspective of modern Western humanism—and that the claim of neutrality and objectivity is an ideological ploy.

This review of requirements with which social theorists have to comply has brought out some of the implications which the structure of sociology in its traditional interpretation has for its focus. There is a paradox: whenever sociologists, by complying with the various requirements, try to sharpen their focus, the relativizing consequences of what they are trying to do forces them to leave their focus hazy and indefinite! No wonder that today many sociologists have grown tired of sociological self-reflection.

Conventional sociology, nowadays, seems less inclined to grand claims, more modest and especially more realistic about what sociology can—and should—do. Many sociologists are absorbed in what goes on in concrete situations, in urbanization, industrialization, discrimination, communication, manipulation, and whatever else may be characteristic of present-day society. There is little interest in what is often experienced as useless theoretic speculation. It is, it is felt, not the time for grand theory; theories of "the middle range" will do. The new modesty may have brought about a significant adjustment of the earlier claims of sociology, but it has not in any fundamental way changed the nature of sociology as it has traditionally been interpreted.

It is, therefore, certainly not surprising that much of the "world" of sociology has, so to speak, been taken over by the "worlds" of business, industry, government, social work, and education. By now the story of the subjection of sociology, through funding and other forms of coercion, is a familiar one.[57] It would not upset many people to hear that a large number of sociologists are employed specifically to justify, confirm, and advance certain existing societal structurations and configurations and to project and introduce new ones. At the same time, the ease with which many of the even more intelligent introductions to sociology brush aside critically important questions of the nature, focus, and scope of sociology is strikingly obvious.[58] They call attention to the agenda of sociology, not to its structure. They suggest that we *do* sociology, not *question* it. The legitimacy of the discipline is simply taken for granted.

That does not mean that there are not a good number of sociologists who feel ill at ease about their discipline. Some try to withdraw into the world of *academia*. Others may try to "quiet their conscience" by placing their sociological skills into the service of the Church, the poor, or the non-Western world. Again others accept sociological relativism, perhaps the relativism of "creative sociology" or of the "sociology of everyday life," or perhaps the relativism of a more Marxist, or neoMarxist, color. Mainly in these last two categories, here and there, one finds a renewed interest in the truly fundamental questions of sociology. Intriguingly, that interest is coupled with a new fascination with convictions that were at the root of the Enlightenment, and from that one may expect a renewed readiness to ground any "study of society" in humanism as alternative *basileia*. That, obviously, has implications for the agenda of sociology. Still, it really does not change that agenda as dictated by the structure of traditional sociology.

The sociological agenda
Sociology's traditional self-interpretation, directed by the driving force of modern humanism towards the control of "social reality," asks for an agenda which is all-encompassing. That has led to considerable tension between sociology and the sciences. The sciences have their own division of labor, one in which philosophy stands apart from the special sciences and every special science stands apart from the others. The structure of traditional sociology prevents it from accepting any one of the "available locations" in the house of science. It certainly does not want to share a room with philosophy. Being in the business of making blueprints, it must insist on establishing its own foundations; it cannot leave that to philosophy. In fact, sociology transcends philosophy; it sees its task also to deter-

mine the place and role of philosophy and of the other sciences. It cannot be satisfied with being one discipline among others. By its very nature, it breaks through any disciplinary boundary.

Tension between sociology and science seems unavoidable. On the one hand, sociology regards itself as science. Virtually every critical issue in the scientific discourse can become an item on the sociological agenda. On the other hand, sociology demands for itself an exceptional position. That, understandably, leads to critical reflection on, and even serious questioning of, its legitimacy. It is, therefore, no wonder that one after the other a sociology of knowledge, a sociology of science, and a sociology of sociology have been added to sociology's agenda.

Naturally, the sociological agenda includes other items than the ones that follow from sociology's entanglement with science. Even after the far-reaching modification of the customary interpretation of traditional sociology, blueprint and strategy remain the central sociological concerns. The standard textbooks still illustrate the power of the key conviction of traditional sociology: societal reality is constructible. The conviction has implications. The world that the sociologist projects is not just any world that *can* be constructed, but the world that is to replace this world, that is, the world that others who hold different ideals and who use different approaches have been, and still are, constructing. That means that the sociological blueprint, precisely because the sociologist designs it in a reaction against existing societal reality, remains forever tentative. The sociological agenda keeps changing with society and with the mood in the sociological community itself! One needs little imagination to picture what such matters as runaway inflation, women's liberation, nuclear threat, and increasing public manipulation can do to the sociological blueprint!

Two stumbling blocks
Wilhelm Dilthey placed two stumbling blocks on the path that modern sociology seeks to follow. He insisted—the first of his stumbling blocks—that we demonstrate that human interaction is indeed possible. He also insisted—the second stumbling block—that we demonstrate that our concept of knowledge is adequate.[59] The stumbling blocks are formidable. When traditional sociology attempts to remove them, it is hampered by its

positivist origins.

Positivism, to reassure itself of the certainty of what it regards as knowledge, assumes that for something to be counted as knowledge it will have to be established that it is "universally valid." Its methodology, therefore, prohibits interference by anyone or anything unique. As much as possible it strips the knower of his or her individuality, leaving only a small, and supposedly suprasocietal and suprahistorical, slice of human functioning, namely, the mechanical recording of (arbitrarily selected) sense impressions. At the same time it strips the knowable of whatever makes it what and how it is, leaving only that what can be registered and classified.

Dilthey had difficulty with a concept of knowledge that required such a method. But, himself steeped in the positivist tradition, he agreed that nothing could be accepted as valid that was not fully anchored in human experience. And there was to be no reference to anything transcending the horizon of that experience. Dilthey objected to positivism not so much for its procedure—he felt that it was quite appropriate for arriving at universally valid statements concerning the "natural world"— but for its use in our attempts to grasp the human world. *Naturwissenschaft* (natural science) addresses a different world than *Geisteswissenschaft* (human science). The former deals with an empirically perceivable, and rationally controllable, given world; the latter deals with *das Leben* (life).[60] *Leben* can only be *erlebt* (lived). *Erlebnis*, the living of *Leben*, differs from what positivism refers to as experience or knowledge. It provides its own certainty, directly and immediately, for it does not permit that which is essential to the procedures of natural science, namely, the separation between those who experience and that which they experience.

Dilthey was convinced that knowledge is certain provided it is grounded in the prereflexive stream of psychic experience in which subject and object have not yet parted company. In the *Erlebnis* there is no "I" positioning itself over against something which that "I" experiences. There is a coincidence, a not-having-been-taken-apart of *erleben* and *das Erlebte*. *Naturwissenschaftliche* investigation calls for causality-oriented knowledge; I know something because I see the causal connection between what is and what was. *Geisteswissenschaftliches* work requires *verstehen* (understanding).[61] How else would one come into contact, immediately and directly, with *Lebensäusserunge* (actions, concepts, etc.) and even *Erlebnisausdrücke* (the expressions of lived experience)? *Leben* can only be understood from within. Positivism's concept of knowledge, therefore, fails to do justice to the human world. It is empty, meager, and uncertain, for it fails to recognize the immediacy, indisputable certainty, and incomprehensible fullness of what is to count as knowledge in the *Geisteswissenschaften*. The positivist concept of knowledge forgets to take into account that human *Erlebnis* unites the whole range of feeling, knowing, hoping, imagining, and willing.

Dilthey also insisted it be shown how human interaction is possible. From the beginning, humanism has taken human interaction for granted. It did not wonder how such interaction was possible now that it had rejected any idea of a transcendent structuring of societal organization. Traditional sociology merely followed that example. Dilthey, however, raised questions. What makes human interaction possible? What are the conditions on which the formation of patterns of interaction and communication is founded? Is interaction more than the sum of the acts of interacting people? And, is it possible to find an answer to such questions?

Dilthey tried to avoid the frustrations of positivism by borrowing heavily from *Lebensphilosophie*. *Erleben* (experiencing, living) is *innewerden* (becoming aware) of *Erlebnisse* (experience, life). The *Erlebnis*, in which *erleben* and *das Erlebte* coincide, can itself be *erlebt* after the fact. *Lebensäusserungen* (issues of life) and *Erlebnisausdrücke* (expression of experience) are open to a kind of *nacherleben* (reliving) in which I experience from within the *Erlebnisse* of others or even of myself. I do not take distance from *Erlebnisausdrücke*. I transport myself, as it were, into *das Leben* itself as it comes to a kind of objectification in the *Ausdrücke*. *Leben* recognizes *Leben*. It is this reliving that forms the basis, for Dilthey, for human interaction and is its existential condition.

It should not escape us that this existential condition is itself historic in nature and, therefore, not at all invariant. That again undermines that interaction and challenges the very idea of *certain* knowledge. Intriguingly, repercussions of this *Geschichtlichkeit* (historicity) of the ground on which human interaction is to rest, according to Dilthey, are felt also in one of the latest alternative sociologies, namely, hermeneutic sociology.[62]

Max Weber was aware of the fundamental weakness in Dilthey's attempts to remove the stumbling blocks he himself had put up. Dilthey tried to interpret *Leben* from *Leben*. That was impossible, for if *Leben* is to interpret *Leben* it does not make sense to look for the meaning of *Leben*. Dilthey, Weber felt, was unable to differentiate between *Leben* and *Sinn* (meaning) because for him *Sinn* was not subjectively *zugerechnet* (assigned) to *Leben*, but it was implicit in it and, therefore, it shared its *geschichtliches* (historical) character.[63]

Weber realized that relativism was unavoidable unless *Leben* was interpreted in terms of something that does not emerge from *Leben*. To disentangle sociology from both positivism and *Lebensphilosophie*, he concentrated on constructing a rational, analytic order that, as it were, accentuated and exposed the irrationality and absurdity of reality. For Weber, it was obvious that reality is irrational.[64] People orient themselves to directives or values that are arbitrary, historically relative, and in principle absurd. The fate of our time, with the rationalizing and intellectualizing that characterizes it, is first and foremost the disenchantment (*Entzauberung*) of the world, which means that the ultimate, most sublime values retreat from public view. We should meet this fate head-on, courageously, and with dignity. Knowledge—not the "objectively valid knowledge" of the positivist or the experiential knowledge of Dilthey but strictly logical knowledge—is the dignity of humankind:

> Anyone who cannot face this fate of our time in a manly way must be told that he could much better return— silently, simply, straightforwardly, without the usual publicity accorded a renegade—to the merciful, wide-open arms of the ancient church....Somehow, in one way or another, he will have to make the "sacrifice of the intellect" —this is unavoidable. But we will not denounce him for this if he really manages to do it, for such a sacrifice of the intellect for the sake of an unconditional religious surrender is still something different in ethical terms than an avoidance of the simple duty to be intellectually honest, the kind of avoidance we see when someone does not have the courage to seek clarity about the ultimate position he is

taking but waters this duty down with feeble relativizing.[65]

How can we create an analytic order that is a concept of reality, though it is only theoretically valid and makes sense only within the theoretical enterprise? In other words, in the face of an irrational reality, how can we acquire rational knowledge of that reality? Weber believed the sociologist, through analytic reflection, could separate the irrational from the rational. A neo-Kantian, he tried to retain his faith in the suprahistorical, suprasocietal, a priori validity of the rules of formal logic.[66] At the same time, he relativized all possible knowledge when he introduced action orientation to historically relative, groundless, arbitrary values which, for no rational reason, direct the human world toward nowhere.[67]

There is no need to follow Weber on his sociological journey. Suffice it to say that he tripped over one of Dilthey's stumbling blocks and then sat down. He never really asked how society is possible. He concentrated on the one stumbling block—the concept of knowledge. In a way Weber demonstrated the fiasco of (traditional) sociology. He reached the unavoidable conclusion that the *Werturteil* (value judgment) underlying the decision to take up the *Beruf* (calling) of sociologist, as well as the *Werturteil* that makes the sociologist travel by the compass of rationality, are themselves irrational, historically and societally relative, and unable to provide a normative blueprint for a social world.[68] It is intriguing that he arrived at such conclusions as a sociologist and, to be precise, as a sociologist of knowledge.

Talcott Parsons's work was, at least for a number of years, the most influential version of Weberian thought in American sociology.[69] At first Parsons did not share Weber's relativism, but in later work he was no longer able to avoid it. He turned to the irrationalism of von Bertalanffy, who looked for support all the way back in Cusanus, and of Laszlo, whose pseudo-Simple Simon approach to matters appeared to appeal especially to some of the younger American sociologists.[70] Less sophisticated, but equally relativistic, the systems approach in sociology, with a cynically straight face, takes the fiasco of sociology for granted, only to continue as if nothing at all had happened.[71]

Positivism went through a self-confrontation of sorts in

Dilthey and that did something to the self-image of traditional sociology. Weber's thinking also affected that image—particularly his relativizing of the sociological enterprise has left some lasting scars. But sociology was not about to give up the convictions it had held ever since its positivistic beginnings. That positivism reasserted itself with great force in the work of the Vienna Circle, and even more effectively in the work done in various concentric and eccentric circles around it, meant a strong boost for traditional sociology. The stumbling blocks were not forgotten, but it suddenly looked as if there were new ways of getting around them.[72]

One "solution" especially became popular.[73] In it sociologists stand apart from the "decision makers." They assume the role of the neutral advisor who provides unbiased, "objective" information. They are being hired not only for their predictive skills, that is, for their ability to tell the decision makers how to go about implementing their decisions, but also for the role they can play in the actual decision-making process. To make decisions, decision makers need information that enables them to choose from different options concerning each of which they are told the possible outcome, the means required to realize such outcome, the risks involved, and even the unintended consequences. Because they have no stake in the outcome, sociologists—so the reasoning goes—are able to be dispassionate scientists, their "objectivity" and "value neutrality" safe from becoming compromised in this contact with values and interests. The "solution" is very popular. That it is unable to solve anything should, however, be clear even from the point of view of the positivist.

The reason for its appeal is not difficult to find. Making a decision, the positivist feels, is a value-controlled process. Per definition, there are no rational grounds for something to be a value; neither is there a rational ground for one's being controlled by this rather than by that value. Which decision one makes depends on the (irrational) values that one (irrationally) allows to control one's thought and actions. Also per definition, science is a purely rational activity and its main feature is that it stays free from value interference. To expect of scientists that they make decisions means to force them to go against the very nature of science. The "solution" appeals because it seems to make it possible for scientists to be at once practically useful *and* fully scientific.

One reason why the "solution" fails is the manner in which it differentiates between two kinds of knowledge. Implied in the "solution" is that decision makers need the services of sociologists precisely because their own knowledge, controlled by values and interests, is irrational and, therefore, unsound and distorted. The contrast between the two kinds of knowledge is sharp: irrational versus rational. That contrast, however, makes communication between decision makers and sociologists impossible. How are the sociologists to understand the decision makers if the considerations that led to the decision do not make sense to them? And how, in turn, are the decision makers to understand the sociologists' proposed strategies for which they have to assume responsibility, if they are incapable of rational knowledge, the very reason why they needed the services of the sociologists? A translation from irrational into rational knowledge is not possible either because precisely that which makes the decision what it is, the irrational, would get lost in the translation! In brief, the contrast implied in the "solution" makes that "solution" itself impossible because it prevents the decision makers and the sociologists from communicating with each other.

Understandably, some positivists have tried to "soften" the contrast between the two kinds of knowledge. The knowledge of the decision maker, they suggest, is not quite as precise and dependable as that of the scientist, but it should not be opposed to it as radically different. In fact, scientific knowledge serves as a model for all knowledge, and everyone, including the decision maker, should strive for that kind of knowledge. This attempt to save the "solution" fails. If it is not legitimate to oppose the decision maker's knowledge to the knowledge of the scientist, it is not legitimate either to oppose, as the "solution" suggests, decision making and sociology.

There is more. The arrangement which keeps decision making and sociology apart so that both retain their independence does not quite do what it claims it does. Sociologists are said merely to provide options from which the decision makers can choose and strategies with which they can implement their decisions. The options and strategies are, however, of a particular kind, namely, *rational* options and *rational* strategies. That now severely restricts the decision makers. They have no other options and no other strategies. The sociologists have their way after all: the *only* options and strategies are the ones *that belong to the sociological blueprint*! The "solution" is not so innocent as it looks; it is, in fact, a very effective piece of ideology.

Lately positivism has fallen on hard times. Even its proponents prefer a different label. It has become somewhat embarrassing to be referred to as a positivist. In the world of sociology, many feel that by now the positivist position has been at the center of attention long enough and that it is time for the discussion to move on to different matters. It is important to be very careful with such a first impression.

No doubt, the most fascinating dimension of the sociological discussion about the positivist position was that it led to confrontation at a fundamental level. Those who participated in the discussions often quite unintentionally forced each other to come out with the presuppositions, hidden loyalties, and deepest commitments underlying their position. That now brought about an increasingly clear awareness of the nature and importance of foundational decisions and of the need to choose between radically different directions. Not surprisingly, traditional sociologists did not particularly care for the turn things took in the sociological discussions. Traditional sociology succeeds or fails with the success or failure of its positivism. Seeing that the discussions exposed many of positivism's most central commitments and presuppositions and that that constituted a serious challenge of traditional sociology's claims, one could expect diversionary tactics. We should regard the suggestion that positivism is passé and that discussion of, and confrontation with, its principles and commitments are things of the past, as just a diversionary maneuver.

Traditional sociology received its structure from humanism's drive for control of societal reality. Positivism provided the foundations this kind of sociology needed. Its structure, the making of a blueprint for society, forced it also to take a close look at itself because *it had also to assign itself a place in its blueprint*. In the process, something happened to it. Its certainties were put into question and they suddenly became problematic. The questions of the sociology of knowledge and the answers of alternative sociologies illustrate and emphasize the pervasive uncertainty in sociology today. It is essential that the discussion continue at the level at which the foundational questions could be, and indeed were, raised. Specifically the questions concerning human knowledge, its nature, its possibility, and its limits. It is in the struggle for answers to those questions that not only humanism but also the *basileia* show what is at their very core. And it is in their encounter and confrontation that the significance is seen of the perspectives within which the theoretical reflection on human society occurs.

Perspective, communication, and confrontation

The cynicism of alternative sociologies with regard to possible answers to questions about human knowledge is understandable. There appears to be uncertainty on all sides. Mannheim's relationism and his "vision" of a *"freischwebende Intelligenz"* (freefloating intelligence) both implied capitulation to relativism.[74] When Schutz tried to clarify the nature of knowledge with the help of Husserl's notion of the *Lebenswelt* (life-world) —the historicity of which Husserl had indeed recognized—he robbed sociology of its privileged position, but at the same time he relativized both his own system of thought and the criteria he used to design it.[75] Ideology-critical sociology appeared to have an eye for the uniqueness of various kinds of human knowledge, but it proved to be unable adequately to differentiate between them and it too ended up in relativizing ambiguities.[76]

The issue of human knowledge is indeed of central importance. One can responsibly deal with it only at the level at which foundational decisions are made, the level of ultimate commitments and of the driving forces that set the course not only of individual human existence but also of the life of the human community, its society and its culture. At that level one confronts humanism in its true nature, that is, in its radical conflict with the *basileia*. At that level, we gain awareness of, and insight into, human knowledge as it is within the perspective of the *basileia* and as it is within the perspective of the alternative *basileia*, humanism.

The biblical message states that God knows. His knowing is the life of humankind.[77] When God knows Israel, Israel is secure—even in Egypt.[78] When God refuses to know, human existence perishes.[79] God's knowledge sets the foundational and all-encompassing communality between God and human-kind. Human knowing is first and foremost a knowing of the knowing God.[80] To be known by God, and because of that to know God, is life. Not to know God is radical alienation and disaster. It is the very nature of the work of Christ that he brings people back into the knowledge of God.[81]

Human knowing is not simply an exercise of one human faculty which enables people to experience and be in contact with others, with the world about them, and, in more or less the same manner, with God. Human knowing is *not* to be inter-preted as one particular human faculty, one human possibility, among several. People know because God knows them and wants them to know him in return. People know because the knowing God wants their response. Our knowing *is* response; it is the very structure of our existence.

Knowing, therefore, is never "individual" or "collective" but always both, and at once, personal *and* communal. In its being personal, knowing corresponds with human creation as *lebab*-being, as being-with-a-heart.[82] In its being communal, it corresponds with the creation of humankind as religious root-community, that is, as knowledge-and-response community *coram deo* (before the face of God).

In his knowing of humankind, God proves himself to be the *Emet*, the Rock that does not fail, the Ally who comes through, the Father who is there. In his being in and from God, Christ is the Truth.[84] Truth is not *adaequatio* (a copy). Knowing is not an activity to be measured by *adaequatio* as criterion. In knowing, what matters is truthfulness, that is, that one does not fail, that one comes through, that one does not run out.

It is possible to differentiate between modally and socie-tally diverse ways, or forms, of knowing. An illustration of modally diverse knowing is that *social* knowing ("John is a real gentleman; he knows his manners") is quite different from *ethical* knowing ("Mary is a born nurse; she knows what her patients need") or *economic* knowing ("Tom knows his busi-ness; he can smell a bargain"). An illustration of societally diverse knowing is that it makes a difference whether some-thing is a family secret or public opinion, or whether "Synod has learned that..." or "The whole neighborhood knows...." What matters in each of these different ways of knowing is that truth is brought out in the sense of a coming through, a not failing, a being dependable as a rock. In each of the diverse forms of knowing that means something unique. Not that there is a plurality of truths; truth is one, but multifaceted.

In theoretical knowing, too, truth has its own unique character. Science is a matter of accounting for, of distinguishing to identify and identifying to distinguish. In everyday life we identify something in terms of its use, or in terms of a function it has for us, or perhaps in terms of a relation in which we stand to it. For example, I identify a briefcase by saying that it is something to carry books in and I identify a piece of rock by saying that it is a souvenir from a trip to the mountains last year. When I do science I use different terms in which to identify things, namely, the existential conditions of the created reality to which I belong, that is, the conditions on which the existence of that reality depends and that make it this particular reality. I must be aware of and recognize those conditions if my scientific work is to be truthful. What matters is that my distinguishing and identifying, my participation in the composition of a theoretical account of reality, shows logical dependability and precision, logical awareness and correctness, logical accuracy and care, just to name a few features of the multicolored logical norm and of logically truthful action.

One critically important existential condition is the very structuration of human existence as personal-communal knowing-as-response existence. In it we find, and may learn to recognize, the possibilities and the limits of theoretical analysis as well as its norms and mandated direction. Thus we begin to recognize also that theoretic analysis is *structurally* set within a societally differentiated communality which makes it historically possible and asks for continued scientific communication and confrontation. One thing is obvious: recognition of such an existential condition is not an outcome of one's logical reflection but requires a particular religious commitment.

Humanism denies that state of affairs. It falls over the message of the knowledge of God. Humanism is not merely not wanting to be known by God and not wanting to know him, but it is wanting not to be known by him and wanting not to know him. Ever more consciously, modern humanism cuts the ties in order to design its own pseudodivine "knowing." The results are catastrophic. The new "knowing" vaguely imitates the knowing of God and then turns into the attempt to *posit* meaning and *construct* reality.

Historically, humanism first assumed a "reality" or "nature" that derived its meaning, supposedly evident in the "rationality" of "nature," from its being centered upon human "rationality." At a later stage, humanism enthusiastically accepted the irrationality of that same "nature" and set out to experience it as the dialectically necessary condition for, and challenge to, the act of freedom by which people carve out for themselves a semblance of "rational" control over, and in the face of, an absurd existence.

The *force majeure* of the structure of creation, however, compels humanism indefinitely to struggle to come to terms with such undeniable states of affairs, particularly with regard to the modal logical function which it absolutizes and, at the same time, forces it not to rest until it has solved the enigma of human communality.

Humanism has not been successful at all in its attempts to deal with human logical functioning. It has been unable to establish the criteria needed to recognize and account for the enormous diversity in which the logical mode of being appears in concrete historical individualizations.[86] It has been equally unable to come to terms with the fact of human communality in knowing. From the beginning, that communality threatened the unity of the autonomous subject of knowledge which humanism assumes as *arché*. At first, the major proponents simply ignored the problematics of the communality. Later they tried to account for it in terms of historic development (e.g., Mauss) logical constitution (e.g., Husserl), or even symbolic interaction (e.g., G.H. Mead). Such attempts were bound to fail. Any assumption of autonomous constitution of intersubjectivity contradicts the unavoidably simultaneous assumption that that intersubjectivity itself conditions a supposedly autonomous constitution! Humanism's account of communality, often presented from within the sociology of knowledge, exposed, be it unintentionally, the arbitrariness of its own presuppositions.

Here in our day is the challenge for those who, in science, want to work by the light of the *basileia*. In the uncertainties in and about sociology, particularly as they come to light in the work of the sociology of knowledge and in the various alternative sociologies, the community of science has begun, however implicitly and however cynically, in a most unique manner to question the legitimacy of the claims of humanism and, indeed, of the very idea of an alternative *basileia*.

If there is anything that should characterize the theorizing of thinkers who in their doing science want to be directed by the *basileia*, it is the recognition of, and the respect for, the transcendent structuring of science. I characterize science as the mandate directed, historically continuous, and communally undertaken composition of a systematic theoretic identification, or account, of created reality insofar as it presents itself within the horizon of historic human experience, in terms of the existential conditions of reality. To see this as the structuration of science has implications.

There is a place for sociology as a science provided we give up the idea of making a sociological blueprint for society or of treating sociology as a search for the solution of "social problems." It is time for the Christian academic constituency to recognize that. It is also time to realize that any reorientation with respect to the sociological focus is to be done in the communication, and undoubtedly also confrontation, within the wider community of science. Isolation on the part of the Christian scholar is irresponsible. Things happen in the discourse of that community. One simple illustration is the impatience with the curious intertwinement of what actually are modal sociology and philosophical societology.[87] Alternative sociologists have, perhaps unintentionally, provided some highly fascinating beginnings of a distinctively modal sociology.[88] Participation in the communication and confrontation in the community of science on issues as this one, however, is not simply a getting matters of sociological focus and scope straight. There is more at stake. Visible in the sociological discussion is the fundamental frustration of a humanism which finds itself at the end of its rope. In the community of science it is now up to the Christian scholar to demonstrate that by the light of the *basileia* there is a way out of that frustration.

Notes
1. It is possible to consider the sociology of knowledge as beginning with the work of Karl Marx and Emile Durkheim. Wilhelm Jerusalem seems to have been the first to use the term *Soziologie des Erkennens* in 1909. Max Scheler spoke of *Soziologie des Wissens* and Karl Mannheim of *Wissenssoziologie*. A useful

orientation is Gunter W. Remmling, *Towards the Sociology of Knowledge* (London: Routledge & Kegan Paul, 1973).

2. Stanford M. Lyman and Marvin B. Scott, *A Sociology of the Absurd* (New York: Appleton, Century, Crofts, 1970).
3. Lyman and Scott, 9.
4. Lyman and Scott, 10.
5. Lyman and Scott, 12ff.
6. Lyman and Scott, 5, 19.
7. Lyman and Scott, 30ff.
8. Lyman and Scott, 11, 23, 194.
9. Lyman and Scott, 66.
10. Lyman and Scott, 1, 11, 26.
11. Lyman and Scott, 8, 15, 27.
12. Lyman and Scott, 15.
13. Lyman and Scott, 8.
14. Lyman and Scott, 15.
15. Lyman and Scott, 16.
16. Lyman and Scott, 7.
17. Lyman and Scott, 217ff.
18. H. Garfinkel, *Studies in Ethnomethodology* (Englewood Cliffs: Prentice-Hall, 1967), 11.
19. Garfinkel, 104ff.
20. Garfinkel, 42ff.
21. A. V. Cicourel, *Method and Measurement in Sociology* (New York: Free Press, 1964) and A. V. Cicourel, *Cognitive Sociology* (Harmondsworth: Penguin, 1973).
22. See H. Mehan and H. Wood, *The Reality of Ethnomethodology* (New York: Wiley, 1975), 35ff and passim. An excellent survey is Ch. C. Lemert, *Sociology and the Twilight of Man: Homocentrism and Discourse in Sociological Theory* (Carbondale: Illinois University Press, 1979), 164-193.
23. Erving Goffman, *The Presentation of Self in Everyday Life* (New York: Doubleday, 1959).
24. Goffman, *Frame Analysis* (Cambridge: Harvard University Press, 1974), 1-3, 124.
25. Peter L. Berger and Thomas Luckmann, *The Social Construction of Reality* (New York: Doubleday, 1966); all subsequent citations are to the Penguin Books edition (1971).
26. Berger and Luckmann, 66.
27. Berger and Luckmann, 68.
28. Berger and Luckmann, 68.
29. Berger and Luckmann, 69.
30. Berger and Luckmann, 70.
31. Berger and Luckmann, 70ff.
32. Berger and Luckmann, 208.
33. Berger and Luckmann, 29.
34. Berger and Luckmann, 15.
35. Berger and Luckmann, 35.
36. Berger and Luckmann, 39ff.
37. Berger and Luckmann, 57.

38. Berger and Luckmann, 59.
39. Peter Hamilton, *Knowledge and Social Structure: An Introduction to the Classical Argument in the Sociology of Knowledge* (London and Boston: Routledge and Kegan Paul, 1974), 140.
40. Hamilton, 142.
41. Peter L. Berger, *A Rumor of Angels: Modern Society and the Rediscovery of the Supernatural* (New York: Doubleday, 1970), 28ff.
42. A. C. Zijderveld, *The Abstract Society: A Cultural Analysis of our Time* (New York: Doubleday, 1970).
43. Zijderveld, *De relativiteit* (Meppel: Boom, 1974), 215.
44. Lyman and Scott, 9 (cited in note 2 above).
45. M. Vrieze, "Sociologie en Kunst," *Philosophia reformata* 40 (1975), 102-140.
46. M. Vrieze, *Nadenken over de samenleving* (Amsterdam: Buijten and Schipperheijn, 1977), 124ff. Also see D. F. M. Strauss, *Inleiding tot die kosmologie* (Bloemfontein, 1978), 171ff.
47. Abraham Kuyper's famous commentary on the "Program of Principles" of the Antirevolutionary Party in the Netherlands, *Ons Program*, published in 1879, is an excellent example of such an engaged, nontheoretical discourse on society.
48. Not many sociologists read Comte. Two recent collections of writings of Comte are Stanislav Andreski, *The Essential Comte* (New York: Barnes and Noble, 1974) and Gertrud Lenzer, *Auguste Comte and Positivism: The Essential Writings* (New York: Harper and Row, 1975).
49. See Herman Dooyeweerd, *Roots of Western Culture: Pagan, Secular, and Christian Options* (Toronto: Wedge, 1979), passim.
50. See the articles by Kleinknecht, von Rad, Kuhn, and Karl Ludwig Schmidt on *basileus, basileia*, etc., in Gerhard Kittel, ed., trans. and ed. Geoffrey W. Bromiley, *Theological Dictionary of the New Testament*, 10 vols. (Grand Rapids: Eerdmans, 1964), 1:564ff. See also Herman Ridderbos, trans. H. de Jongste, ed. Raymond O. Zorn, *The Coming of the Kingdom* (Philadelphia: Presbyterian & Reformed, 1975).
51. Luke 4:43.
52. Dooyeweerd, 148ff.
53. An excellent orientation in J. M. M. de Valk, *De evolutie van het westbegrip in de sociologie* (Assen: Van Gorcum, 1970) and Johan Goudsblom, *Sociology in the Balance* (Oxford: Blackwell, 1977).
54. O. Stammer, ed., *Max Weber und die Soziologie heute: Verhandlungen des 15, deutschen Sociologentages* (Tübingen: J. C. B. Mohr, 1965); trans. under the title *Max Weber and Sociology Today* (New York: Harper & Row, 1971). Also see Th. Adorno et al., *Der Positivismusstreit in der deutschen Soziologie*.
55. A compact bibliography on Dilthey is given in the fascinating study by Rudolf A. Makkreel, *Dilthey: Philosopher of the Human Studies* (Princeton: Princeton University Press, 1975).
56. Goudsblom, 75ff. (cited in note 53 above).
57. Larry T. Reynolds and Janice M. Reynolds, *The Sociology of Sociology* (New York: McKay, 1970), 201ff. and passim. Also see Alvin W. Gouldner, *The Coming Crisis of Western Sociology* (New York: Basic Books, 1970) and Derek L. Phillips, *Abandoning Method* (San Francisco: Jossey-Bass, 1973).
58. Goudsblom, 153ff.

59. The most comprehensive summary of Dilthey's ideas is still Otto Friedrich Bollnow, *Dilthey: Eine Einführung in seine Philosophie* (Stuttgart: Kohlhammer, 1936-55), esp. 101ff.
60. Bollnow, 167ff.
61. Bollnow, 192ff.
62. See Zygmunt Bauman, *Hermeneutics and Social Science* (New York: Columbia University Press, 1978) and Janet Wolff, *Hermeneutic Philosophy and the Sociology of Art* (London: Routledge & Kegan Paul, 1977).
63. For a complete bibliography of Max Weber, see Johannes Winckelmann, ed., *Max Weber: Soziologie. Universalgeschichtliche Analysen. Politik*, 5th ed. (Stuttgart: Kröner, 1973), 490ff.
64. For a charactaerization that is directly relevant to our discussion, see Zijderveld, *De relativiteit van kennis en werkelijkheid*, 120ff. (cited in note 42 above).
65. Weber, *Gesammelte Aufsätze*, 597.
66. Weber, 580ff.
67. Weber, 180ff.
68. Weber, 475ff.
69. For bibliography on Talcott Parsons, see *Talcott Parsons: Action Theory and the Human Condition* (New York: Free Press, 1978), 434ff. Parsons translated Weber's *Protestant Ethic and the Spirit of Capitalism* in 1930.
70. For an excellent survey of the systems theoretical approach in sociology, see Walter Buckley, *Sociology and Modern Systems Theory* (Englewood Cliffs, N.J.: Prentice-Hall, 1967) and *Modern Systems Research for the Behavioral Scientist: A Sourcebook* (Chicago: Aldine, 1968). In the latter, see particularly the article by Ludwig von Bertalanffy, "General Systems Theory: A Critical Review," 11-30.
71. Buckley, *Sociology and Modern Systems Theory*, 36ff.
72. Cf. Otto Neurath, *Foundations of the Social Sciences: International Encyclopaedia of Unified Science*, Vol. 2 (Chicago: University of Chicago Press, 1944); Anthony Giddens, "Positivism and Its Critics," in Tom Bottomore and Robert Nisbet, *A History of Sociological Analysis* (New York, 1978), 237ff.
73. Cf. here also Frederick Suppe, ed., *The Structure of Scientific Theories*, 2d ed. (Urbana: University of Illinois Press, 1977), Critical Introduction and Afterword.
74. Mention should be made here of only two works of Mannheim, namely, Karl Mannheim, *Ideology and Utopia* (London: Routledge & Kegan Paul, 1936) and *Essays on the Sociology of Knowledge*, ed. Paul Kecskemeti (London: Routledge & Kegan Paul, 1952).
75. Another publication of relevant writings is Karl Mannheim, *Structures of Thinking*, ed. David Kettler, Volker Meja, and Nico Stehr (London: Routledge & Kegan Paul, 1982). See here also Max Scheler, *Problems of a Sociology of Knowledge*, ed. Kenneth W. Stikkers (London: Routledge & Kegan Paul, 1980); Alfred Schutz and Thomas Luckmann, *The Structures of the Life-World* (London: Heinemann, 1973); and Alfred Schutz, *The Phenomenology of the Social World* (Evanston, Ill.: Northwestern University Press, 1967).
76. Relevant are especially Jürgen Habermas, *Legitimation Crisis* (Boston: Beacon Press, 1975); and Th. McCarthy, ed., *Communication and the Evolution of Society* (Boston: Beacon Press, 1979).

77. See, for example, Gen. 18:19, Exod. 33:12-17, Amos 3:2, Nahum 1:7; Ps. 139:1 & 23, and Jer. 1:5.

78. See Exod. 2:25.

79. See Hosea 8:4, Pss. 37:18-20 and 138:6, and Matt. 25:12. For a comprehensive survey of notions of truth and knowledge, see J. H. Vrielink, *Het waarheidsbegrip* (Nijkerk, 1956).

80. See Isa. 1:3 and 11:9, Jer. 22:16 and 31:34, Hosea 4:6, Luke 11:52, and Col. 3:10.

81. See John 17:3, 25.

82. F. H. Von Meyenfeldt, *Het Hart (Leb, Lebab) in het Oude Testament* (Leiden: E. J. Brill, 1950).

83. Cf. D. F. M. Strauss, "The Central Religious Community of Mankind in the Philosophy of the Cosmonomic Idea," *Philosophia reformata* 37 (1972), 58ff.

84. Vrielink, 82ff. (cited in note 79 above).

85. Vrielink, 13ff.

86. The logical function displays an immense diversity which we ought to carefully recognize and respect. Even if we limit the analysis to the individualization of the logical function in human acts, we confront a wide diversity. A first illustration of the diversity we find is the differentiation between logically qualified acts, as theoretical acts, and nonlogically qualified acts. In the group of theoretical (i.e., logically qualified) acts we differentiate further. For example, theoretic association, theoretical organization, theoretical combination, theoretical differentiation, etc. Each of these logical acts is an individualization of the logical function, but each act is qualified by one of the many distinct moments within that logical function, as the social analogy in the logical function, or the kinetic analogy, etc. Among the many different nonlogically qualified acts, we find those in which the logical function serves in the role of the foundational functions and those in which the same function, also focused upon a nonlogical functioning, serves in the role of the so-called superstratum functions. The complication here also is that there is an overwhelming multiplicity of analogical moments, both in the logical function itself and in the nonlogical functions. Think, for example, of acts as social discrimination, technical differentiation, medical diagnosis, etc.

87. Cf. Vrieze, *Nadenken over de samenleving*, passim (cited in note 46 above).

88. I am thinking here particularly of work done by thinkers such as Goffman.

In what sphere is economics sovereign?
A. B. Cramp

Introduction

What is the scope of economics? Or, posed differently: In what sphere is economics sovereign? The answer that will emerge from our reflections is that economics is sovereign in the economic sphere.

I will argue that chaos ensues not only when we grant economic ideas a general sovereignty in understanding human affairs but also when, in understanding the economic dimension of life, we yield sovereignty to key ideas from other disciplines in the field of human studies. Similar difficulties exist for each of these other disciplines: political thought, sociology, psychology, and so forth.

Until the issue of sovereignty is at least provisionally settled, we cannot escape the chaotic pluralism of the modern multiversity. Fearful that no solution exists, modern academicians are prone (as Dennis Robertson used to put it) to look the matter firmly in the face and pass quickly on. It is an important dimension of the Christian academic task to haul these problems back and enforce a longer and more searching contemplation of the intellectual bankruptcy of humanism, a bankruptcy resulting from its false presuppositions.

The problem

It has been claimed that, whether or not Marx was justified in arguing that economic arrangements (the relations of production) necessarily determine general social arrangements, our culture is obsessed with economic problems. This might seem paradoxical in an age that, at least in the developed nations, has witnessed unprecedented economic growth rates and widespread increases in living standards. But the claim is easily supported with impressionistic evidence. Who would deny, for example, that economic issues are the main stuff of contemporary political debate?

It is less widely observed perhaps, but just as easy to support at an undemanding level of argument, that a dominance of economic concepts in scholarly discourse often parallels the dominance of economics in the practical realm. For example, the late Professor Harry Johnson's inaugural lecture at the London School of Economics was entitled "The Economic Approach to Social Questions."[1] In his lecture Johnson argued that economic theory was far from having been rendered excessively abstract and inapplicable to real problems—as some had suggested was the outcome of the post-1945 "Formalist Revolution." Rather, it was perfectly capable of illuminating not only applied *economic* issues but also such apparently unrelated *social* issues as student unrest.

We do not have to reflect on such themes for long, however, before we realize that economists are by no means alone in claiming that their particular professional apparatus can yield insight and understanding into a wide range of human behavior. At various times and in various ways, as we will soon see, psychologists, biologists, and sociologists have all claimed that their disciplines furnish the main key to understanding human behavior.

This phenomenon has become widely known in intellectual quarters as "reductionism." The term has a critical connotation that becomes clearer in the more explanatory label "the scientific fallacy of nothing but." One of the most forceful and articulate opponents of the fallacy (if such it be) has been Viktor Frankl, founder of the psychiatric school known as logotherapy. Frankl's key idea is that human motivation is based primarily on the search for *meaning*. Frankl believes that the meaning of human life and its essential features often becomes lost in the abstractions of the social sciences, each of which examines humans from one angle. In his chapter in *Beyond Reductionism*, Frankl illustrates his point with a simple piece of imagery.[2] Consider a cylinder, viewed A ("end on") and B ("side on"):

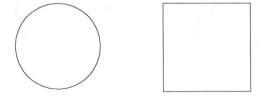

It is perfectly correct to say the object under consideration has a circular aspect; it is also correct to say it has a rectangular aspect. But even if we combine these two aspects, observed from different perspectives, we will not get a cylinder:

The reason for our failure is the "missing" dimension which the two partial perspectives cannot capture. But given that assumption, which perspective will prevail? The circle specialists are tempted to argue that the object is "nothing but" a circle. The rectangles described by colleagues observing from other perspectives are "imperfect circles" that are "essentially" circular. This reductionist approach avoids confusion and overt interdisciplinary squabbles by embracing a simplicity that apparently yields *some* valid insights and predictions. But in the Department of Rectangles, specialists speak of their colleagues in the same way. Teachers in each department might function happily, but it is awful being a student studying for a combined degree in the circular and rectangular sciences!

My parable suggests the problem is a bit broader than the term "reductionism" implies. There are, I think, usually three stages in the sciences, of which the first alone is valid. In the modern "social sciences" practitioners first *specialize*, unavoidably and quite properly, taking a partial view of human activity. They then *absolutize* their own "internal" viewpoint because an external one is absent. Finally (closely allied with absolutization and almost impossible to separate in practice), they *generalize* their own interpretation because they lack a framework that integrates work from conflicting standpoints. The shrinking of vision at stage two might be labeled reductionism. Its correlate at stage three, the improper expansion of vision, I prefer to call "imperialism."

It is important to emphasize that the threefold process belongs essentially to the present century—an era of fragmentation and specialization in social studies. Our nineteenth-century predecessors might not have known the answer to the sovereignty question, but they were aware of the problem. In Cambridge, England, at any rate, admittedly well-known for its cultural conservatism, economics undergraduates were weaned well into the twentieth century on a book by John Neville Keynes the father of John Maynard Keynes. The book was entitled *The Scope and Method of Political Economy* and it directed undergraduates' attention to the question of drawing boundaries between economics and other specialties.[3]

The question of sovereignty is certainly appreciated in Reformed circles. James Olthuis, for example, argues in his *Facts, Values, and Ethics* that "without...a [given] law-order there is in principle no barrier preventing the [specific] sciences from extending their borders as they see fit...."[4] He quotes Abraham Edel's *Method in Ethical Theory* to the effect that "there is a pie to be cut, but there is no injunction about the number and size of the slices."[5]

I will argue that it is precisely this overextension of boundaries, relating to the *framework* rather than to the *content* of humanist social science, that is responsible for much of the present chaos in human studies. My claim is specifically denied by some of our century's relatively few eminent specialists in the philosophy and methodology of science. Sir Karl Popper, for example, argues in his *Conjectures and Refutations* that

> subject matter, or kinds of things, do not constitute a basis for distinguishing disciplines. Disciplines are distinguished partly for historical reasons and reasons of administrative convenience...and partly because the theories which we construct to solve our problems have a tendency to grow into unified systems. But all this classification and distinction is a comparatively unimportant...affair. We are not students of some subject matter but students of problems. And problems may cut right across the borders of any subject matter or discipline.[6]

Popper explicitly denies our problem. But lest it be inferred that he represents modern secular methodologists in general, let us note the recent work by Martin Hollis (a philosopher) and Edward Nell (an economist) entitled *Rational Economic Man: A Philosophical Critique of Neoclassical Economics*.[7] In their attack of the positivism underlying neoclassical economics, they emphasize that positivism's program for testing hypotheses calls for a clear delineation of the economic sphere because economists are not so much interested in economic events as in the economic aspect of all events.[8] Economic theories, they claim, are not to be refuted by the intrusion of noneconomic factors into economic data; it is the function of the *ceteris paribus* clause, *inter alia*, to hold "exogenous" (or noneconomic) factors constant. For this purpose we need an interdisciplinary theory.[9] Such a theory or superscience needs to draw the borders between, say, economics and psychology authoritatively. Unless this is done, both economists and psychologists could protect their pet theories from refutation by blaming apparent exceptions on factors in the other subject's domain.[10]

How then do we build a superscience if (contrary to Popper) one is needed?

The framework
At this point we need to erect some sort of structure that protects our discussion from rambling. The elements of such a structure might be found in Boulding's classification of "social organizers" under the headings of threat/power, exchange/bargain, and love/integration systems.[11] These three organizers can, I believe, be usefully related to the three nonvoluntary social groupings, namely the state, the economy, and the family.

Without for the moment entering any formal judgments on the "right" answers, we can envisage the relation between organizers and groupings as either *defined* (by bedrock social realities) or *undefined* and shapeless. In the former case, the broad picture would be:

ORGANIZER   GROUPING
threat $\longleftrightarrow$ state
exchange $\longleftrightarrow$ economy
integration $\longleftrightarrow$ family

In the latter (Popperian?) case, we would have:

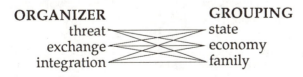

ORGANIZER   GROUPING
threat   state
exchange   economy
integration   family

I wish to claim that the *defined* picture points toward a valid

framework for human studies, and the *undefined* picture represents the existing chaotic and unsatisfactory situation of such
studies. Therefore, we should strive toward a political theory
based on an understanding of norms for power relationships
between people (individuals and groups); an economic theory
based on exchange relationships; and a theory of the family
based on love relationships. The nature of the interdependent
relationships between these major groupings obviously calls for
careful exploration, if only because so many major problems of
theory and practice occur at the interfaces when people, who
belong to all three groupings simultaneously, face conflicting
demands and loyalties. Nonetheless, my provisional hypothesis
will be that it is inherently invalid to seek a theoretical explanation (and related practical prescription) for any major grouping by referring to social organizers of another grouping or level.
That is, it is invalid to seek for a fundamentally political explanation, based on power relationships, of economic or familial
behavior; or a familial explanation, based on love relationships,
of the state or the economy; and so forth.

My approach is basically inductive. I will study examples,
which abound in human studies, of these "crossed-wire" cases
and exhibit their failure to illuminate the human situation.
Finally, I will point to constructive work being done toward
remedying the defects I will emphasize.

If we rearrange our triads of organizers and groupings, we
have this matrix:

	State	Economy	Family
threat	①	2	3
exchange	4	⑤	6
integration	7	8	⑨

The nine boxes represent nine possible types of theory, and our
hypothesis suggests that only three theories (the three num-
bered circles) are valid.

My framework is probably excessively simple in some respects. It omits explanations or theories given by disciplines that
are only indirectly relevant to these social groupings. For example, sociology, psychology, and biology have all claimed to
explain the existence and usefulness of the chief relationships
in these social groupings. I will single out biology to illustrate

the weaknesses of all such indirect explanations of the nature of social phenomena.

Sociobiology: The inadequacy of indirect social theories

In 1978 a new academic journal was launched, *The Journal of Social and Biological Structures: Studies in Human Sociobiology*. A pamphlet announcing the journal stated that it was launched because of the recently intensified search for general structural principles applicable for the entire spectrum of dynamic organizations from cells to social systems.

Edward O. Wilson, curator of entomology at Harvard Museum of Comparative Zoology, is a founder of this new synthesizing discipline and author of the popular book *Sociobiology*.[12] In the *New Scientist* (13 May 1976) he stated:

The role of sociobiology with reference to human beings...is to place the social sciences within a biological framework constructed from a synthesis of evolutionary studies, genetics, population biology, ecology, animal behavior, psychology and anthropology.[13]

Of this long list of synthesized disciplines, evolutionary studies and genetics are the most fundamental. Familiar Darwinian ideas are being linked to less familiar ideas of genetic survival. Humans (like animals) are (nothing but?) machines programmed to ensure the survival of genes.

In our discussion it is important to notice the comprehensive, imperialistic pretensions of sociobiology. It offers a biological explanation of the state, the economy, and the family. It seeks to explain not only all social groupings but also all social organizers.

The biological theory of the family

For sociobiology, the altruistic behavior that underlies Boulding's integration organizer is explicable without recourse to ideas of love, sacrifice, selflessness, and so forth. Altruistic behavior, in which animal A contributes to animal B's survival at its own expense, only occurs when B carries genes belonging to A. So a mother animal that shows apparently unselfish behavior toward its offspring is really safeguarding the payoff of her genetic investment.

But why does the mother, not the father, care for her off-spring? The father has made just as much of a genetic investment. Some sociobiologists suggest that the mother, having carried her young during gestation, has invested more energy in her off-spring and, therefore, she is more willing to ensure that her investment pays off. Others have stressed that the mother simply cannot desert her young until they are born. Since the mother cannot desert her young, by her courtship rituals with a male she forces the male to curb his greater freedom to desert the young. It is easier for him to care for the infants than to go of on an exhausting courtship elsewhere.[14]

By referring to a fundamental article of evolutionary faith, sociobiology then attributes these genetic reasons to humans.

The biological theory of the state

Some aspects of human social organization, however, find no parallel in the animal world. The state and our systems of justice are notable examples. Nevertheless, sociobiologists have little problem applying their fundamental ideas to these examples.

Robert Trivers, another Harvard biologist, has argued that individuals ensure the survival of their genes not only by selfless behavior toward close relatives; they also practice reciprocal altruism with members of larger social groups. Our system of justice simply restrains the inevitable tendency to cheat on such reciprocal relationships.[15]

The biological theory of economics

It was only a matter of time before these ideas were applied to economics. As a science of self-centered human choice, economics could hardly resist the idea that altruistic behavior is illusory and only represents genetic selfishness, especially since the natural sciences are its methodological mentors. Moreover, free market ideologists, hard pressed by today's growing collectivism, could be expected to accept that ineradicable hereditary factors, not pliable social and environmental ones, lie behind human selfishness. And these factors are insuperable obstacles to the enduring success of any collectivist measures.

Early in April 1978 *Business Week* reported:

> Bioeconomics says that government programmes that force individuals to be less competitive and selfish than they

are genetically programmed to be are pre-ordained to fail. And, according to bioeconomists, a Socialist society, predicated on selflessness and devotion to a collective ideal, simply will never last.[16]

Doesn't the sociobiological explanation of collectivism in politics give grounds, though, for extending collectivism into the economic sphere? Nevertheless, we must move on.

Political explanations

From "biologism" we turn to "politicism." It has not been very fashionable in the modern era to regard politics as the most fundamental of all human activities. The prevailing evolutionary philosophy, noting politics as an activity unique to human beings, tends to see politics as late in human development and, therefore, peripheral.

I am not much aware of political models applied to economics apart from the attempted neo-Keynesian resurrection of classical type of emphasis on income distribution as the central economic problem. To be sure, Marxist collectivists and liberal conservative individualists have applied economic models to politics. Politicism, then, has been mainly a political explanation of family relationships.

This form of politicism was found chiefly in ancient Greek philosophy, notably in Aristotle. Since Aristotle tried to understand human norms in human ends rather than in their beginnings, it was not a problem for Aristotle, as it is for modern evolutionists, that human beings are life's only "political animals." Human beings were political animals, not in the sense that they had a natural interest in political issues or a natural tendency to indulge in political activity, but in the sense that they could only realize their full human potential (or ends) within the state.

The state had justice as its norm or virtue. It was the perfect community, welding together rulers whose norm or virtue was wisdom, soldiers whose virtue was courage, and workers whose virtue was prudence. This all-embracing conception of the state could hardly be distinguished from society, and it was a framework for Aristotle's assumptions about the human nature rather than a conclusion based on reflection on the political process. Therefore, the reductionism—"man is a political animal"—

could scarcely avoid transformation into imperialism — "man is nothing but a political animal." The structure of Aristotle's thought necessarily implied that family relationships must be understood in political terms:

> [T]he polis is prior in the order of nature to the family and the individual...[because] the whole is necessarily prior to the part.[17]

> [The husband's] rule over his wife is like that of a states-man over fellow citizens; his rule over his children is like that of a monarch over subjects.[18]

Political rule and authority were for Aristotle the key concepts explaining all social relationships.

The sixteenth-century philosopher, Jean Bodin, set out a "familial" theory of the state in *De Republica*.[19] The theory is an illuminating contrast to Aristotle's political theory of the family, illustrating the infinite plasticity of conceptual frameworks once legitimacy is granted to what I have called crossedwire cases.

Bodin's theory was based on three fundamental propositions. First of all, the family is a given natural fact that we must simply accept. The head of the family has a natural right to own possessions and exercise authority over persons. Secondly, the family is the source and origin of the state. Thirdly, the authority of the head of the state has the same authority and the same natural title as that of the head of the family, inasmuch as the state is only a derivation and extension of the family.

Sir Robert Filmer advanced a similar patriarchal theory of politics in the following century. In his *Patriarcha* (1680) he traced the origin of family/political power to the divine commission of authority to the original patriarch, Adam.[20]

Economism

Economic explanations of family relationships (see 6 in our matrix) are especially abundant today, especially at the University of Chicago. The "Chicago view of the family" stems from that extreme atomistic liberalism enshrined in what I have elsewhere called the Western liberal orthodox tradition of economics. We can almost observe the reductionist-imperialist process at work in the following sequence of propositions, as they begin with a standard Western liberal orthodox tenet and then interpret the nature and role of marriage.

1. "Recontracting" improves welfare. That is, exchanges are beneficial. If I have clothes and want some books, and you have some books and want clothes, then we can benefit by getting together to arrange an exchange (provided our sartorial and cultural tastes are similar).

2. Marriage represents an institutional constraint on recontracting.

3. Since 1 above is true, the removal of constraints on free choice is good; therefore,

4. easier divorce facilities represent a welfare improvement.

Gary S. Becker has worked out these basic notions in more detail in his book, *The Economic Approach to Human Behavior*. Becker defines benefits in the broadest possible sense:

[A]t an abstract level, love and other emotional attachments, such as sexual activity or frequent close contact with a particular person, can be considered particular non-marketable household commodities.[21]

He then asserts that marriage will happen if the expected benefits exceed costs (in the sense of opportunities foregone), with benefits and costs measured in marginal, not average, terms, of course. Marriage will cease when this condition no longer holds. This basic proposition can then be modified and delicious intellectual games can be played, allowing for lack of information, risk, uncertainty, and so forth. Various factors are classified under the categories of substitutes and complements. Then elaborate mathematical methods are brought to bear on the information and numerous statistical correlations are reported, as is necessary and appropriate to scientific work!

Similar pseudosophistication characterizes Chicago treatment of parental motivation in raising children. Thus R. Blandy, in an article on "The Welfare Analysis of Fertility Reduction," delivers himself of the following insight:

> [I]f the net present value of a new human being treated as
> an investment good is negative, and children continue to
> be born into the society [when effective contraception is
> readily available], the inescapable conclusion is that
> children are not (entirely) investment goods, but rather
> consumer durables.[22]

Becker, Blandy, and their colleagues forget that false presuppositions and correct scientific techniques do not yield valid
conclusions. The conclusions of Chicago-style imperialist economic analysis are implicit in their presuppositions. They are not
results of the scientific techniques, whether or not those techniques are methodologically correct. As seen above, proposition
4 is implicit in proposition 1.

Therefore, we must be on the alert when demographers
such as Michael Anderson invite us to watch the trend toward
increasing divorce rates.[23] For them such a trend is not the result
of weakening social structures and the decline in the cohesion
of personal relationships. Rather it results from increased afflu-
ence and the reduction of material crises whcih gives greater
scope to various tastes and a new freedom in personal relationships. In effect they are inviting us to reverse the transformation
by renewal of our minds to which Paul exhorts us in Romans 12:2.
They are inviting us to be conformed to the worldview of fallen
humanity. In combating such false doctrines, Christians must
aim at the right target—the false presuppositions about the
human nature.

We should note that the Chicago school has, by its economist interpretation of the family, drifted into accepting the much
older, fundamental tenet of their Marxist ideological opponents,
namely that economic factors determine all social states and
relationships. Friedrich Engels, in *The Origin of the Family*,
argued that in the capitalist stage of society's development that

> [I]n the family, the husband is the bourgeois [owning the
> productive capital] and the wife represents the [property-
> less] proletariat.[24]

Finally, we should mention the economic interpretation of

politics (see 4 in our matrix). In recent times Dahl and others have made well-known attempts to apply the principles of market economics to the democratic political process. Edmund Burke defined a political party as a body of men united in promoting the national interest on some agreed common principle, and he saw political debate as a clash between differing ethical conceptions of the ideal order of society. But Dahl sees the political arena in somewhat the same way as the Chicago school sees the domestic arena. He sees the political arena as a marketplace in which politicians are entrepreneurs, offering the goods of political benefits in exchange for the circulating medium of votes. Unhappily, the synchronization of tax reductions and approaching elections in recent decades supports this interpretation.

But those who accept our current political situation as normative should remember Joseph Schumpeter's critique of Benthamite utilitarianism, a nineteenth-century economic theory of politics. Schumpeter wrote in his *History of Economic Analysis*:

> [I]ts application to political [as opposed to economic] fact spells unempirical and unscientific disregard of the essence —the very logic—of political structures and mechanisms, and cannot produce anything but wishful daydreams and not very inspiring ones at that. The freely voting rational citizen, conscious of his (long-run) interests, and the representative who acts in obedience to them, the government that expresses these volitions—is not this the perfect example of a nursery tale?[25]

We can agree that it is a nursery tale and then only be surprised that Schumpeter did not see that utilitarianism was just as harmful in the economic sphere as it was in the political. In the same passage Schumpeter said that utilitarianism's "'logic of stable and barn' may be considered as a tolerable expression of actual tendencies."[26]

Summary of our current chaos
The family and the state. Today's practitioners of human studies can hardly escape the current chaos of views. Nevertheless, we ignore its ramifications by busily occupying ourselves with a

more manageable, narrow specialism.

What is the family? A genetic survival mechanism, as the sociobiologists assert? A pocket state, as it was represented by Aristotle? A marketplace, as claimed by Chicago economists?

And how are we to understand politics? Is it an extension of family relationships into larger social groupings, as Bodin and Filmer believed? Or is it a subtle outworking of biological imperatives? Or is it a market-style area where hedonistic maximizers strive for maximum selfish benefit at minimum selfish cost?

The economy. In modern society, where the economic aspect exercises a staggering dominance, economics has been much more of an imperialist plunderer than a hapless victim of depredation. Yet I have mentioned an "indirect" interpretation of economics—the biological explanation of economic individualism. I suggested that the explanation was sufficiently pliable to be transformed into a biological defense of economic collectivism. Nevertheless, the explanation of economics would still be rooted in biology.

Let us round out our picture by observing some "direct" interpretations of economics. Beginning with essentially political explanations of economics (see 2 in our matrix), we might be tempted to include the Marxist belief that class conflict is the key element in the economic process. But it is arguable that Marxism represents an economic understanding of politics (and everything else), rather than a political understanding of economics.

However, since Marx's death, there have risen several types of non-Marxist economic theory based on power relationships. We can distinguish between theories that focus on production or on income distribution. Joseph Schumpeter has been one of the most prominent exponents of those political explanations focusing on economic production. Schumpeter has been strongly influenced by Continental traditions that reject the idea of social harmony, which is fundamental to the more Anglo-Saxon liberal paradigm. These Continental traditions accept the German Historical school's stress on induction from factual knowledge, experience, and observation, rather than deducing from rarefied, abstract principles. This stress on the actual, not the ideal, produces an emphasis on conflicts or interest and power struggles as the very essence of market relationships. In the Western liberal orthodox picture, these conflicts and struggles are only occasional monopolistic blemishes on market relationships. But production, for Schumpeter, is the sphere of "nature red in tooth and claw."

In the *Theory of Economic Development and Business Cycles,* Schumpeter gave the innovating entrepreneur a key role in the capitalist system.[27] He is the instrument of social advance, the forceful pioneer who applies the inventions of backroom technical geniuses to the market, introducing and distributing new productive processes and products and "educating" consumers if necessary. Writing in the 1930s, Schumpeter maintained that the innovating entrepreneur could effect nonmarginal changes in economic behavior — behavior that was supposedly unamenable to any analysis according to the static orthodoxy that was then prevalent. (It does not seem likely that subsequent attempts by Harrod, Marris, and others to explore orthodox presuppositions in a more mobile, dynamic context would have caused Schumpeter to modify his criticisms of those presuppositions). Schumpeter, then, views the economics of free market production as the economics of Darwinian natural selection. Social progress results from the competition of strong survivors while weaker individuals and groups suffer a good deal of transient, rough justice.

J. K. Galbraith paints a similar picture, except that the (semimonopolistic) competitors, facing an uncertain demand for products that involve large-scale initial development costs, wish to survive rather than dominate.[28] The power to influence consumer demand offers security in an uncertain and threatening world. Avoidance of disaster is a substantial achievement itself, regardless of "progress."

Neo-Keynesians focus on the economics of income distribution.[29] They argue that, in practice, power conflicts do more to determine factor incomes than do harmonious free market exchanges. The specificity and long life of capital (once equipment is installed) preclude the kind of free variablity of factor proportions that would, in principle, permit the competitive process to determine "equilibrium" factor rewards by reference to marginal productivity criteria.

In recent times there have been few attempts to understand economic relationships as extensions of family norms based on love motives and integration mechanisms (see 8 in our matrix).

As "privatization" has intensified and community sense declines, integration mechanisms have shifted to the political sphere where they can be backed by the force of law exercised against reluctant good neighbors and free riders. Mostly, we hear ephemeral, pious aspirations by pale-pink politicians seeking ways to hold down public expenditure, as in their rhetoric about the desirability of community care for the mentally ill.

I can only mention one substantial, well-argued explanation of this approach to economics. In *The Gift Relationship*, the late Richard Titmuss, former professor of social administration at the London School of Economics, directed a polemic against economists who had argued that blood transfusion services would be more efficiently handled through market mechanisms than through the charitable system of voluntary blood donations operated by the United Kingdom's National Blood Transfusion Service.[30] While avoiding explicitly demarcating "social integration" mechanisms from their "market exchange" counterparts, Titmuss argued powerfully that—at least in sensitive social services such as medicine—the spirit of altruism was in ineluctable conflict with market forces. Society would be gravely diminished if the latter expanded at the expense of the former.

An "is-ought" dimension
It is inevitable that some optimistic peacemakers would try to reconcile our long list of fundamental explanations of the economic aspect of social phenomena. They would explain the contradictions as only superficial and assert that each explanation can find a place in a rounded economic analysis. And they would probably resort to the "is-ought" distinction as their major synthesizing and reconciling principle.

Could we not say that Schumpeter primarily treats "what is" in the economic sphere while Titmuss treats "what ought to be" in an ideal world and what we might strive toward as the opportunity arises? The economics represented by 5 in our matrix is sometimes presented as a judicious blend of the "is" and actual and the "ought" and ideal, realistic and hardheaded, but having heart. D. H. Robertson spoke about how Alfred Marshall reluctantly recognized that economic progress called for reliance on the strongest rather than the highest of human motives, and in the meanwhile he held on to a vision of economics as a force moving toward a better world where eventually the highest and not the strongest of motives would rule.[31]

These are seductive ideas, but they will not do. They fail because the "is-ought" dualism is false. At bottom, our presuppositions are unified. We view the world through intellectual spectacles and we cannot cope with bifocals. We cannot see "what is" clearly because we observe and interpret the world with the aid of a conceptual framework that is inherently normative. For example, the sociobiological view of humankind derives from a supposedly scientific, evolutionary worldview. The presuppositions derived from our worldview constrict and confine our perception of "what ought to be" because they contain inherent beliefs about what humankind fundamentally is. Thus, our explicit or implicit answer to the foundational question of social studies—What is man?—guides our perceptions of the actual and the ideal in the human situation.

A way out of chaos?
These are larger themes than can be fully argued here. I have discussed them at greater length, still inadequately, in *Notes Towards a Christian Critique of Secular Economic Theory.*[32] My understanding of these issues has been derived from Dooyeweerdian Christian philosophy, a philosophy that holds facts and values to be inextricably intermingled. Moreover, that philosophy holds values and norms as fundamental because, as we have noted, they condition our perception of facts. So James Olthuis can write:

> Apart from normative structures, there is no way to acknowledge the institutions one confronts in reality, such as state, church and family. The relationship or correlation of fact and norm is obvious, e.g., when one talks of a good family. But it is just as obvious when one names a certain group of individuals a family. How does one know this particular group is a family? There is only one answer: it meets the norm for a family.[33]

The Dooyeweerdian schema proceeds from the unlimited sovereignty of God and the divine law—representing an externally given framework, through the notion of sphere sovereignty or limited, derived authorities in each aspect of the social structure, via a recognition that these spheres are intertwined, not independent, in mutual support and "the simultaneous realization of cultural mandates," to the conviction that no special science such as economics can be the key to understanding the whole of reality. Rather, economic norms are required to understand the economic aspect of reality.

These ideas delineating the economic sphere are clearly worked out by Peter C. Bos, and I feel justified in leaving the matter here.[34] I hope I have made a strong case for the central relevance of understanding economic norms that apply to the economic aspect of reality. The academic economic enterprise needs to begin and end with an economic norm that can only be derived from the will of him who is the Alpha and Omega.

Notes
1. Harry Johnson, *Economica* (February 1968): 1-21.
2. Viktor Frankl, "Reductionism and Nihilism," in *Beyond Reductionism*, ed. A. Koestler and J. R. Smythies (New York: Macmillan, 1970), 404-5.
3. John Neville Keynes, *The Scope and Method of Political Economy* (London: Macmillan, 1904).
4. James Olthuis, *Facts, Values, and Ethics* (Assen: Van Gorcum, 1968), 199.
5. Abraham Edel, *Method in Ethical Theory* (Indianapolis: Bobbs-Merrill, 1963), 335.
6. Karl Popper, *Conjectures and Refutations* (London: Routledge & Kegan Paul, 1963), 67.
7. Martin Hollis and Edward Nell, *Rational Economic Man: A Philosophical Critique of Neoclassical Economics* (London,Eng.: Cambridge University Press, 1975).
8. Hollis and Nell, 25.
9. Hollis and Nell, 27.
10. Hollis and Nell, 138.
11. Kenneth E. Boulding, *Beyond Economics* (Ann Arbor: University of Michigan Press, 1968), 98-111.
12. Edward O. Wilson, *Sociobiology* (Cambridge, Mass.: Harvard University Press, 1975).
13. Edward O. Wilson, "Sociobiology: A New Approach to Understanding the Basis of Human Nature," *New Scientist* 70, 1000 (May 1976): 342.
14. R. Dawkins and T. R. Carlisle, "Parental Investment, Mate Desertion, and a Fallacy," *Nature* 262 (July 1976): 131-32.
15. Robert Trivers, "The Evolution of Reciprocal Altruism," *The Quarterly Review of Biology* 46 (March 1971): 35-37.
16. "A Genetic Defense of the Free Market," *Business Week* (April 1978): 100.
17. Aristotle, *The Politics*, trans. and ed. Ernest Barker (Oxford: Clarendon press, 1948), 7.
18. Aristotle, 40.

19. Jean Bodin, *De Republica*, trans. and ed. M. J. Tooley, *The Six Books of the Commonwealth* (Oxford: Basil Blackwell, 1955).

20. Robert Filmer, *Patriarcha and Other Political Works*, ed. Peter Laslett (Oxford: Basil Blackwell, 1949).

21. Gary S. Becker, *The Economic Approach to Human Behavior* (Chicago: University of Chicago Press, 1976), 233.

22. R. Blandy, "The Welfare Analysis of Fertility Reduction," *The Economic Journal* 84 (March 1974): 112.

23. Michael Anderson, *Family Structure in Nineteenth-Century Lancashire* (Cambridge, Eng.: Cambridge University Press, 1971).

24. Friedrich Engels, *The Origin of the Family, Private Property, and the State*, trans. Lewis Morgan (New York: International Publishers, 1970), 65-66.

25. Joseph Schumpeter, *History of Economic Analysis*, ed. Elizabeth Boody Schumpeter (New York: Oxford University Press, 1954), 429.

26. Schumpeter, *History*.

27. Joseph Schumpeter, *Theory of Economic Development and Business Cycles*, trans. R. Opie (Cambridge, Mass.: Harvard University Press, 1934) and *Business Cycles*, abridged with introduction by R. Fels (New York: McGraw-Hill, 1964).

28. J. K. Galbraith, *Economics and the Public Purpose* (Boston: Houghton Mifflin, 1973), 215-324.

29. See Geoffrey C. Harcourt, *Some Cambridge Controversies in the Theory of Capital* (Cambridge, Eng.: Cambridge University Press, 1972), 1-13.

30. Richard Titmuss, *The Gift Relationship* (New York: Pantheon Books, 1971).

31. D. H. Robertson, *Utility and All That, and Other Essays* (London: Allen & Unwin, 1954), 45.

32. A. B. Cramp, *Notes Towards a Christian Critique of Secular Economic Theory* (Toronto: Institute for Christian Studies, 1975).

33. Olthuis, 186-187 (cited in note 4 above).

34. Peter C. Bos, *Money in Development* (Rotterdam: Rotterdam University Press, 1969), appendix, 161-77.

Man and methodology in economic science: about abstraction and obedience

Roelf L. Haan

Introduction

Man. The original title of this paper was "The Image of Man in Economics." I will try to deal with that topic, but let me change my title to "Man and Methodology in Economic Science: About Abstraction and Obedience" or, more briefly, "Man in Economics." Our task is not to present some image of man in economics as an interesting exercise for one who wants to study something more than economics or to discover some *petite histoire* —a by-product of the main trends in economic thinking. Rather, I will ask: How does economic methodology account for man? What is its basic orientation toward man? How does it relate to our *confession* of man?

To ask how economics relates to man is to probe the very foundations of its principles. Man precedes economics in a cosmological sense; he transcends it and stands at its very center. Since man transcends economic life, economic theory cannot make him an object of thinking by its concepts of him. We cannot derive our basic idea of man nor its economic implications from the theoretical work of a pretendedly autonomous reason. We cannot establish truth about man; we can only confess it and follow it. Thus we are really concerned with the image of economics in our basic thinking about man, not the image of man in our thinking about economics. Whether or not economics has human meaning depends on its confession of man.

Man, created in the image of God, must never be made into an object of scientific research; that would damage his honor and degrade his origin. Such a graven image would cause— and has caused—a radical loss of respect and love and inevitably leads to oppression, torture, and killing. Even an objectified image of man constitutes a relationship between men—a relationship in which man is made into an object and therefore violated. But what about the objectified man's personal life? And what picture would the one man draw of the other who had objectified him? Here the oppressiveness of definitions of man becomes clear. Such definitions, whatever their claim, never have universal validity. There are men—and there are men. There are 'developed' and 'underdeveloped' men; entrepreneurial men and men in the labor force; skilled and unskilled men; producers spenders; strong and weak men; white and black men; Christian men and unbelievers.

Segregationalism, racism, capitalism, and sectarianism apply universal definitions of man that, because human beings cannot objectify human beings, are necessarily relational, constitutive of an attitude toward other men. Graven images of men hurt and degrade because man was not created by social thinking but in the image of God. Just as God can only be known in a personal relation, his image too can only be known in such a relation. There is only one way to acquire knowledge about either God or our fellowmen, and that is to listen to their personal words, their revelation to us. As Reinhold Niebuhr said:

> Our approach to other human personalities offers an illuminating analogy of the necessity and character of 'revelation' in our relation to God. We have various evidence that, when dealing with persons, we are confronting a reality of greater depth than the mere organism of animal life. We have evidence that we are dealing with a "Thou" of such freedom and uniqueness that a mere external observation of its behavior will not only leave the final essence of that person obscure, but will actually falsify it, since such observation would debase what is really a free subject into a mere object. This person, this other "Thou," cannot be understood until he speaks to us; until his behavior is clarified by the "word" which comes out of the ultimate and transcendent unity of his spirit. Only such a word can give us the key by which we understand the complexities of his behavior. This word spoken from beyond us and to us is both a verification of our belief that we are dealing with a different dimension than animal existence; and also a revelation of the actual and precise character of the person with whom we are dealing.[1]

The basis of Christian anthropology can be stated in a clear and succinct way, showing there cannot be an economic way of thinking that reduces man to it. In the words of Herman Dooyeweerd:

> In the human ego, as the central seat of the *imago Dei*, God had concentrated the entire meaning of the temporal world into a radical religious unity. Man, created in the image of God, should direct all the temporal functions and powers of his existence and those of his whole temporal world unto the service of God. This he was to accomplish in the central unity of his ego by loving God above all.[2]

Economic functions are among these temporal functions of man. In economics, as in all the other functions, we meet with the great commandment of love in the all-embracing sense of the word. No economic problem is independent of that central issue of our whole existence. Human personality does not express itself solely in its moral functions, as Kant thought. The central commandment, the central Word about man's nature, embraces his whole existence. Therefore, Dooyeweerd continues:

> And, because, in the order of creation, every human ego in this central religious sense was united with every other human ego in a central communion of the service of God, the love for the neighbor was included in the love of God....We cannot understand the radical and central sense of this commmandment as long as we relate it only to the moral aspect of our temporal existence. Just as in the human ego all the aspects of our temporal experience and existence find their central reference point, so the commandment of love is the central unity of all God's different ordinances for the temporal world.[3]

This fundamental concept of human existence exposes the danger of the word "and" in such phrases as "man and economics," "economics and ethics," "economics and justice," "economics and politics," "economics and human rights," "economic objectivity and subjectivity," "positive and normative economics," "growth and distribution," and "economics and

ecology." In each of these, the very word "and," which sepa-
rates the various entities, presents a problem. In our Western
culture these distinctions are no longer coordinate but subordinate. "And" is more and more becoming "or." In this process
economic methodology itself is at stake as well as the entire organization of scientific specialization, that is, the method of
abstraction.

Economics. Just as we cannot define man, neither can we arrive
at economic knowledge by pure reason. Certainly, it is possible
to construct models of theory, but the more perfect they are, the
less they articulate the knowledge of others who did not draft
them and whose voices were not heard. When we understand
economics to be an aspect of meaning in human life and the
creation, we realize that the "economic problem" or the economic aspect of our experience cannot be man-made: it cannot
be originally constructed by the human mind, not even theoretically. There is always a remnant, a "kernel of meaning," that
resists human analytical activity, making further delineation
impossible. This reminds us of the respect we owe to him who
has created the basic conditions of economic life. Man can never
escape being in relation to the Other who judges him, questions
his ego, and asks for human self-reflection about himself or his
brother. God—as the Other—does not need man; but man
needs God.

   This dependency of man does not impede his true humanity; on the contrary, it reveals its very condition. "The way to
God leads ipso facto—and not as an additional possibility—to
man."[4] This is the heart of Calvinistic anthropology: the service
of God must realize itself in real life, in the here and now. It is
in this life that we meet our fellowman. In the words of the Latin
American theologian Miranda:

> If we perceive otherness as a defect, then we cannot see
> that only an absolutely irreducible Other—that of the
> word which speaks to me—is able to break through the
> solitude of my concepts and my ontological objectifica-
> tions.[5]

Miranda points, as Dooyeweerd has done, to the conflict between Western humanistic thought and biblical revelation.

Levinas says, in a way that reverberates through many Christian thinkers of Latin America, "Ontology, as the first philosophy that does not call into question the self, is a philosophy of injustice."[6] Miranda continues:

> If we are able to prescind from the cry of the poor who seek justice by objectifying God and believing that, because he is being, he is there as always, since being is objective and does not depend on any considerations of our minds nor on what we can or cannot do, at that very moment he is no longer God but an idol. And this is what happened to Christianity from the time it fell into the hands of Greek philosophy. When we demand the dehellenization of Christianity, what we are demanding is that idolatry not be imposed on us, for we do not wish to know any other god than the God of Jesus Christ.[7]

> In contrast, the God of the Bible must always be present as the Other. His exteriority and otherness cannot cease without his ceasing. The pluralism constituted by the self and the Other needs, in order to exist, the movement and the attitude of the self with regard to the Other. This movement and attitude is not a species of the genus called "relationship," that is, it cannot be converted into a "theme" for an objective understanding liberated from this confrontation with the Other. In other words this movement and attitude is impervious to "reflection." Levinas brilliantly observes, the famous "impossibility of total reflection must not be poised negatively as the finitude and imperfection of a knowing subject which prevent it from reaching complete truth, but rather as the surplus of the social relation, where the subjectivity remains in face of...."[8]

In the same way that "essentialist" philosophy and theology are to be rejected, so economics too has to account for the "movement and the attitude of the I before the Other." Economics cannot be dominated by and enclosed in our definitions. Such definitions would be reductionistic. Dooyeweerd has shown we cannot analyze the ultimate meaning of the economic aspect, the nucleus that accounts for its irreducibility. Something goes wrong in practice when we apply a theory that pretends to establish "pure knowledge" and confuses *Gegen-stand* and object. Such a theory cannot account for real states of affairs. Latin American theologians agree with these fundamental insights and hold that, where such a theory of the autonomy of theoretical thought exists, its practical consequences inevitably turn oppressive.

The human content of economics does not fit such a pretended pure and universally valid methodology since the ultimate irreducible meaning of the economic aspect of human life points to the presence of another Subjectivity. As soon as we try to construct a pure theory with absolutist pretentions, we lose sight of the Other and the other, of God and man. Economic science then becomes a tool of oppression. Instead of being pure knowledge to be "applied," it becomes the application of a will to dominate.

Concepts and theories themselves have a very accurate function in human relationships, notwithstanding their modern claim to be socially "neutral."[9] Relationships cannot be neutral, because man always acts before the Other. Hence we understand what E. F. Schumacher meant when he called the common criterion of success in economics—the growth of GNP —"utterly misleading" and leading of necessity "to phenomena which can only be described as neocolonialism." Schumacher tells of a manager of a textile mill who said: "Surely, my task is to eliminate the human factor." Our concepts and theories, then, lead us to adopt production and consumption methods that destroy the possibilities of self-help and self-reliance. "The results," says Schumacher, "are unintentional neocolonialism and hopelessness for the poor."[10]

Schumacher hesitates to use the term "neocolonialism" because it has a nasty sound and seems to imply deliberate intentions. "But this makes the problem greater instead of smaller. Unintentional neocolonialism is far more insidious and infinitely more difficult to combat than neocolonialism intentionally pursued."[11] How and to what extent are those unintentional results conditioned by an economic theory which, right from the start, accepts or rejects the human content? In other words, what do we mean when we say that economics studies an "aspect" of "human" behavior?

The problem is very clear in Latin America where in many cases the improvement of "economic indicators" goes hand in hand with the deterioration of human life. Economic policy concerns itself primarily with the preservation of the "functioning of the system." Economic life should operate well. But what does "well" mean if it appears to be compatible with dictatorship and hunger? In Chile, Argentina, and Uruguay the balance of payments—that ultimate sign of stability and the proper functioning of the system—has improved substantially, but the number of economic refugees and the increase of internal insecurity have assumed unprecedented proportions.

The economists, however, because of their model of thinking or their methodology, think this kind of criticism does not affect them. They treat the suffering as either an endogeneous variable—a kind of necessary evil to be overcome in the future by the same dynamics that causes it in the present—or as a exogeneous variable that "belongs to another field." In both cases the human character of economics is only a remote postulate. In both cases the problem is a method that (1) delimits the field of economics and (2) basically determines how to operate in this field.

It is my thesis that how economic theory internally, that is, methodologically, relates to man is of decisive importance for understanding the meaning of economics.

Adam Smith
Theory and social reality. How did economics produce today's impersonal, mechanistic scheme? How has economics assumed a life of its own that amounts to an empty operationalism?[12] That process began with the birth of economic science. Remarkably, the idea of an impersonal and mechanical economic system, driven by its own internal dynamics, is already found in Adam Smith, though Smith is usually considered the champion of economic liberty and individualism. Marx, then, did not bring anything new on that score![13] According to Smith, the regulating principle of economic life is the division of labor, made possible by the extent of the market and stemming from an inborn propensity to exchange. "It thus appears and grows as an entirely impersonal force, and since it is the great motor of progress, this progress too is depersonalized.[14]

However, Smith was a very keen observer of the human conditions of his day. But his chosen economic model would not let him account for human misery. Thus we find, on the one hand, a self-righteous theory based on conjectured individual propensities, originating in man's innate tendency to trade; on the other hand, we find a critique of the effects of the division of labor on factory workers, drawn from observation of the real social conditions. Robert Lamb concluded that these two methods—analysis and observation—lead to two conclusions. The former was "leading to an abstract theory of capitalism; the second to socialist criticism of existing society."[15]

Let us consider a notorious example of this conflict between theory and description in Smith. The theory speaks of the harmony of interests. "It is not from the benevolence of the butcher, the brewer or the baker that we expect our dinner, but from their regard to their own interest."[16] But the description points to the conflict of interests, for instance, between workmen and masters

> *whose interests are by no means the same.* The workmen desire to get as much, the masters to give as little as possible. The former is disposed to combine in order to raise, the latter in order to lower the wages of labour.

> It is not, however, difficult to foresee which of the two parties must, upon all ordinary occasions, have the advantage in the dispute, and force the other into a compliance with their terms. The masters, being fewer in number[17] can combine much more easily; and the law, besides, authorizes, or at least does not prohibit their combinations while it prohibits those of the workmen.[18]

Theoretically, Smith postulates a system of natural prices. But

> the price of labour, it must be observed, cannot be ascertained very accurately anywhere, different prices being often paid at the same place and for the same sort of labour, not only according to the different abilities of the workmen, but according to the easiness or hardness of the masters.[19]

Not only does Smith admit in his careful observations that there is a great deal of exploitation in the labor market. He also admits that the theoretical model supposing labor mobility does not, at least not always, apply (different prices being paid at the same place).

How could Adam Smith not incorporate his observations into his theoretical framework? This example is stranger still when we consider that Smith passed moral judgments, sometimes sharp ones.[20] Smith did not focus on the laboring class; nor was he writing for them. Rather, he was writing for "people of fashion"—the people who complained that "luxury extends itself even to the lowest ranks of the people."[21] Nevertheless, according to Smith,

> no society can surely be flourishing and happy, of which the far greater part of the members are poor and miserable. It is but equity, besides, that they who feed, clothe, and lodge the whole body of the people, should have such a share of the produce of their own labour as to be themselves tolerably well fed, clothed and lodged.[22]

He referred to the unreasonable and inhuman labor conditions that hurt the health of the laborer and to "the temptations of bad company, which in larger manufactories so frequently ruin the morals of the other."[23] And, of course, we must quote the famous "alienation passage"[24] in which Smith pointed to the negative effects of the progress of the division of labor as it becomes a danger to "the great body of the people":

> The man whose whole life is spent in performing a few simple operations of which the effects are perhaps always the same, or very nearly the same, has no occasion to exert his understanding or to exercise his invention in finding out expedients for removing difficulties which never occur. He naturally loses, therefore, the habit of such exertion, and generally becomes as stupid and ignorant as it is possible for a human creature to become. The torpor of his mind renders him not only incapable of relishing or bearing a part in any rational conversation, but of conceiving any generous, noble, or tender sentiment, and consequently of forming any just judgment concerning many even of the ordinary duties of private life. Of the great and

extensive interests of his country he is altogether incapable of judging, and unless very particular pains have been taken to render him otherwise, he is equally incapable of defending his country in war. The uniformity of his stationary life naturally corrupts the courage of his mind, and makes him regard with abhorrence the irregular, uncertain, and adventurous life of a soldier. It corrupts even the activity of his body, and renders him incapable of exerting his strength with vigour and perseverance *in any other employment than that to which he has been bred.* His dexterity at his own particular trade seems, in this manner, to be acquired at the expense of his intellectual, social, and martial virtues. But in every improved and civilized society this is the state into which the labouring poor, that is, the great body of the people, must necessarily fall, *unless government takes pains to prevent it.*[25]

Government thus has an educational task; it should stimulate and subsidize primary schools for the "common people." It might even impose on all an obligation to attend school.[26]

It is interesting to note that Smith did not have the dogmatic aversion to governmental intervention that characterizes so many of his followers. Nor did he hold the unrealistic view that the state must always be strictly impartial:

Whenever the legislature attempts to regulate the differences between masters and their workmen, *its counsellors are always the masters.* When the regulation, therefore, is in favour of the workmen, it is always just and equitable; but it is sometimes otherwise when in favour of the masters....Where there is an exclusive corporation, it may perhaps be proper to regulate the price of the first necessity of life.[27]

Smith was the man of natural liberty, but

those exertions of the natural liberty of a few individuals, which might endanger the security of the whole society, are, and ought to be, restrained by the laws of all governments, of the most free as well as of the most despotical.[28]

In Smith's defense we could say he was elucidating a theoretical model to be tested against a society of small entrepreneurs in which there were ranks and orders but which had not yet experienced the great capitalist class division of the years after the Industrial Revolution. Smith firmly believed in equality, but he supported his theoretical economic model which was supposed to protect and bring forth this equality.[29]

In general, the Scottish school believed with Miller[30] that every industrious man could hope to win a great fortune.[31] Smith and his contemporaries were impressed, not by the new submission of the worker to the capitalist, but by the worker's opportunity to convert himself into a small capitalist. Economic development, Smith felt, should lead to a situation like that of the Netherlands. Was the Netherlands not, "in proportion to the extent of its land and the number of its inhabitants, by far the richest country in Europe?"[32]

In a country which had acquired its full complement of riches, where in every particular branch of business there was the greatest quantity of stock that could be employed in it, [it would be] impossible for any but the very wealthiest people to live upon the interest of their money....It would be necessary that almost every man should be a man of business, or engage in some sort of trade. The province of Holland seems to be approaching near to this state. It is there unfashionable not to be a man of business.[33]

Similarly, in agriculture, according to Smith, extensive amounts of propertied land were unfavorable for crops.[34] Smith would have called Latin America's *latifundia* system a "barbarous institution."[35] Ideally, according to Smith, the worker should be proprietor of his land since tenants were not encouraged to make improvements except under very long leases. Unfortunately, the feudal proprietors of the land "were anciently the legislators of every part of Europe"; their avarice and injustice hurt the improvement of the lands; they were consumers and taxers rather than farmers.[36] "After small proprietors, however, rich and great farmers are, in every country, the principal improvers."[37] The "laws and customs so favourable to the yeomanry have perhaps contributed more to the present grandeur of England than all their boasted regulations of commerce taken together."[38]

It is clear that for Adam Smith the proletariat did not yet exist. Wages, for that matter, were rising. As a matter of fact, economic development, according to Smith's growth model, was to be to the advantage of the laborers, at least for as long as development lasted.[39]

In most of the cases to which Smith referred, the laborer was still the independent workman laboring for the master. The farmer, the master manufacturer, the wholesale merchant, and the retailer, on the other hand, were not pure capitalists since they were laboring as well.[40] To learn a technical trade "cannot well require more than the lessons of a few weeks."[41] Being a great merchant does not require great knowledge, but capital; and this is exactly what frugal men might be able to save. Besides, "in years of plenty, servants frequently leave their masters, and trust their subsistence to what they can make by their own industry."[42] "The women return to their parents, and commonly spin in order to make clothes for themselves and their families."[43]

It is obvious that Adam Smith was writing prior to the great social upheavals of the Industrial Revolution. His world was that of the relatively independent workman and the petty businessman living in relative harmony. That situation seemed to justify the theoretically constructed harmony of economics.[44]

The economic aspect: the classical "homo economicus." Smith did not use the technical term "economic man" (*homo economicus*), but the term could have been coined then, given what was understood to be economics at that time. Modern economics considers "economic man" to be a technical term derived by abstraction and resulting in an esoteric "pure theory." If we asked for the real basis of this "pure" methodology or, in other words, if we asked where we might meet this strange "economic man," we would be placed by Lord Robbins as one of "the ignorant or the perverse."[45]

As we know, classical political economy did not yet adhere to a "pure" concept of economics. The current, shadowy idea of economic man is a subjectified and emptied version of a type of man that classical economics believed was part of natural reality. However, Smith's concept of man is still important, not only because the more abstract idea of the *homo economicus* developed from it, but also because modern economic theory —think of development economics!—in spite of its pretended neutral character is highly production oriented, like Smith's own theory. Our special concern, however, is the relation of the economic method of abstraction to the concept of man and its inseparable correlate, the concept of God.

The prototype of economic man—which later subjectivistic economic theory generalized to include laborers, consumers, and those engaged in "unproductive" activity—was the capitalist or, in Smith's terms, the "owner of stock."[46] Smith described the function of the entrepreneur in the following way:

> As soon as stock has accumulated in the hands of particular persons, some of them will naturally employ it in setting to work industrious people, whom they will supply with materials and subsistence, in order to make profit by the sale of their work, or by what their labour adds to the value of the materials. In exchanging the complete manufacture either for money, for labour, or for other goods, over and above what may be sufficient to pay the price of the materials, and the wages of the workmen, something must be given for the profits of the undertaker of the work who hazards his stock in this adventure. The value which the workmen add to the materials, therefore, resolves itself in this case into two parts, of which the one pays their wages, the other the profits of their employer upon the whole stock of materials and wages which he advanced. He could have no interest to employ them, unless he expected from the sale of their work something more than sufficient to replace his stock to him; and he could have no interest to employ a great stock rather than a small one, unless his profits were to bear some proportion to the extent of his stock.[47]

It is stock, or capital, that sets labor and production into motion. The agents in this impersonal economic process work within it quite "naturally." Smith did not speak of the profits of the entrepreneur, although, of course, they are *his* profit. Rather, he spoke of the profits of stock.

A fundamental conflict is bound to rise between this

theory and Christian ethics. Economic man does not consider the content of his activities, only their profitability in monetary terms. Only the growth of production matters, not its composition or organization, for these are ultimately determined by the monetary incentive.

Smith understood this productive process to be impersonal, as revealed by his language on the formation of income. "The whole annual produce of the land and labour of every country...naturally divides itself...into three parts: the rent of the land, the wages of labour, and the profits of stock...."[48]

These three production factors are impersonal.[49] The person who has accumulated capital follows a natural economic law. He has no proper identity (note again the similarity with Marx) and only follows his capital.

> A merchant, it has been said very properly, is not necessarily the citizen of any particular country. It is in great measure indifferent to him from what place he carries on his trade; and a very trifling disgust will make him remove his capital, and together with all the industry which it supports, from one country to another.[50]

The merchant is a passive executor of the invisible hand. His link to the "natural course of things" is the profit motive, his own interest as a proprietor of capital. Thus it is silently introduced as an anthropological postulate that every person really conceives of his interest, or life goal, in these financial terms.

Here we are a long way from the traditional thinking of the Church, a discrepancy that Smith did not even bother to explain. Apparently, no one cared about that anymore![51] This is the profound materialism—not of Marxism, but of the capitalism that gave rise to Marxism.

This concept of man was generalized by Smith as he spoke of "every individual":

> The produce of industry is what it adds to the subject or materials upon which it is employed. In proportion as the value of this produce is great or small, so will likewise be the profits of the employer. But it is *only for the sake of profit* that *any man* employs a capital in the support of industry; and he will always, therefore, endeavour to employ it in

the support of that industry of which the produce is likely to be of the greatest value, or to exchange for the greatest quantity either of money or of other goods. But the annual revenue of every society is always precisely equal to the exchangeable value. As *every individual*, therefore, endeavours as much as he can both to employ his capital in the support of domestic industry, and so to direct that industry that its produce may be of the greatest value; *every individual* necessarily labours to render the annual revenue of the society as great as he can. He generally, indeed, neither intends to promote the public interest, nor knows how much he is promoting it. By preferring the support of domestic to that of foreign industry, he intends only his own security; and by directing that industry in such a manner as its produce may be of the greatest value, he intends only his own gain, and he is in this as in many other cases, led by an invisible hand to promote an end which was no part of his intention. Nor is it always the worse for the society that it was no part of it. By pursuing his own interest he frequently promotes that of the society more effectually than when he really intends to promote it. I never have known much good done by those who affected to trade for the public good. It is an affectation, indeed, not very common among merchants, and very few words need be employed in dissuading them from it.[52]

This concept of man is utterly incompatible with biblical anthropology and theology, except (if we might borrow the words of Robbins) for the "ignorant and the perverse."

Smith identified the public interest with the pursuit of a national product of the greatest monetary value. This product is the result of "industry," that is, the exertion of industrious and frugal men. For that reason, man's essential nature is that of the laborer or the producer.[53] Only in this way do things run their natural course, and only so will the "Process of Improvement," civilization itself, be furthered.[54]

The economic model based on this cosmology and anthropology, besides being speculative, does not provide much hope for the more remote future. The theory leads straight into a crisis, although Smith did not worry about eschatology and its organizational problems.[55] The theory reveals Smith's ideas about personal morality and demonstrates clearly the new breach between (personal) ethics and (depersonalized) economics. For example, the landlords, in their role as those who love "to reap where they never sowed,"[56] have an interest in the ultimate result of the "Process of Improvement."[57] A high national product brings great wealth to the proprietors of the land, who do not understand economics and who are indolent, ignorant,[58] ridiculous,[59] and prone to childish vanity. In short, the economy benefits those for whom Smith had little moral appreciation.

The laborer, however—the real author of wealth, the one who has sacrificed his whole life and personality[60]—reaches the end of his rising wages when the country acquires "that full employment of riches which the nature of its soil and climate, and its situation with respect to other countries, allows it to acquire." "When this real wealth of the society becomes stationary, his wages are soon reduced to what is barely enough to enable him to bring up a family or to fall even below this."[61]

Similarly, the capitalist, who sets people to work by the force of his own interest, is also threatened by the ultimate success of his endeavor. For in the final state of the economy, the stationary situation, the rate of profit is at its minimum: "it is naturally low in rich and high in poor countries."[62] In this situation the regulating principle of economic life, that is, the search for new investment opportunities, seems to fade away. Furthermore, businessmen are inclined to narrow the competition, "raising their profits above what they naturally would be, to levy, for their own benefit, an absurd tax upon the rest of their fellow-citizens."[63] Note how Smith considered this monopolistic practice to be a natural one, but he still could not call it "natural" in a theoretical sense! Once more a gap appears between his theory of harmony (natural profits) and his own description of social reality (excessive profits). Dealers, merchants, and master manufacturers are "an order of men whose interest is never exactly the same with that of the public, who have generally an interest to deceive and even to oppress the public, and who accordingly have, upon occasions, both deceived and oppressed it."[64]

These developments produce a paradox. Dealers (capitalists) have an interest in raising their profits above what is natural. Hence there is a general tendency to deviate from what is natural. This general tendency appears as unnatural for the order of dealers, but it is natural for "every individual." According to the atomistic pattern of Smith's theory, the invisible hand leads every private interest into harmony. But in the case of the agents of the whole economic process, the natural becomes perverse. For "to widen the market and *to narrow the competition* is *always* the interest of the dealers."[65] The dealers are not simply abstract individuals, but actual proponents of dangerous legislation—men whose "superiority is not so much in their knowledge of the public interest, as in their having a better knowledge of their own interest than [the country gentleman] has of his." The landlord would have promoted general welfare, if only he understood economics; the businessman injures the general interest precisely because of his shrewd knowledge of it.[66]

Smith's economic model is ethically perverse and self-contradictory. The passive and useless landlord will become lazy and rich. The producer of wealth, the laborer, works for his own final misery. The dealer, who understands economics and is the dynamic element, has no interest in the end of the process; therefore he damages the public interest by seeking his own advantage which, contrary to the general theoretical premises, is not converted to the good by any invisible hand.

Nevertheless, Smith maintained his theoretical scheme by making it "abstract" (in the sense of autonomously constructing it, i.e., without taking reality into account), even in the historical context in which it should have had most applicability. Smith absolutized his model and derived his ethics from his economic model. The scheme has no external reference, there is no "sphere sovereignty" whatsoever. Violence is, in the last analysis, violence against the economic model; it is anything that disturbs Smith's ideal theoretical order.[67] This answers our previous question: How could Adam Smith not incorporate his observations into his theoretical framework? Here theory becomes autonomous.

The situation is worse today. Now even the description is lacking in the economic textbooks. The Other—and so the human content—has disappeared because he had been left out from the theoretical model of economics from the start. In his impressive economic history of Latin America, Eduardo Galeano asks whatever happened to the other, Cain's slain brother, and observes: "the more liberty is granted to business, the more prisons are necessary to build for those who endure this business."[68] James F. Petras has pointed to the negative correlation in Latin America between the freedom for foreign capital and the extent of democracy and social participation.[69] It is clearly time to ask ourselves about the basic meaning of the economic aspect and to redefine our concept of economics accordingly. There can be no Christian economics—that is, economics methodologically oriented to the Christian faith—unless it is performed by those who are prepared precisely in their theory (which cannot endure long without practice) to seek for the other and the Other, for man and for God.

What I have called the "economic anthropology" of Adam Smith is intimately related to his economic model, especially his model of growth. Economic theory and anthropology are very much related. Since anthropology precedes economics, we must infer that Christian economic thinking is bound to differ radically from liberalism precisely because of their anthropologies. As Schumacher says, the theoretical iniquity of Adam Smith has been visited upon the third and fourth generations. The one who said, "a man must be perfectly crazy who, where there is tolerable security, does not employ all the stock which he commands," and the Other who said, "Consider the lilies of the field, how they grow," belong to radically different kingdoms.[70]

Christian thinking on economics

Calvinism, Sismondi, and human socialism. We have stressed that Christian economic thinking must concentrate on man confessed as created in the image of God. Adam Smith was a representative of the Scottish social thinkers of his time. He was an adherent of natural theology, a theology in which the God of the Scriptures was already dead. As a professor of moral philosophy, he not only taught "ethics," "justice," and "political institutions" but "natural theology" as well—"Natural Theology, in which he considered the proofs of the being and attributes of God, and those principles of the human mind upon which religion is founded."[71] We might describe this as "God as an attribute of Natural man" or "God theologically created in the image of man."

The economic man assumed by economic methodology,

the frugal laborer trying to accumulate capital, can be considered as the secularized version of the Puritan. Economic theory absolutized a human characteristic that, of course, had a real empirical counterpart. This counterpart was the man of abstinence and frugality, always looking for profit opportunities, whose traditional occupation was no longer sacrosanct or a custom to be kept.[72] On the contrary, he believed in geographical, social, and economic mobility. His own interest was given legitimacy by the great goal either of the glory of God or of the "Improvement of Society."

But there are differences between the Puritan and economic man. The Puritan acts by personal obligation. The economic man, largely a theoretical construction, acts through a natural inclination coordinated by the invisible social mechanism of harmony. For the Puritan, man is elected (or better, man can be elected) by Providence; for Adam Smith, Providence created man as an animal of exchange, who in the natural course of things would find his way into civilization. The Puritan thinks of life as a struggle; economic man sees it as an affair of rationalism and enlightenment. The Puritan does not view profit as his basic motive although he is led along via profit; the economic man acts only for the sake of profit. The Puritan, in his own way, worries about the common good; economic man does not intend it nor does he necessarily even refer to it. (In our days, however, he avails himself continuously of apologetic language concerning his responsibility for employment, economic development, and the like). Puritanism is pessimistic; liberalism is optimistic about man.

Despite the differences of motive and theological outlook, there is a practical similarity between the Puritan and economic man. The Puritans paved the way for the type of man who was the model for *homo economicus*. There is much truth in Max Weber's thesis that the road to capitalism was paved by the individualism and asceticism of the Puritans, Calvinists, Pietists, Methodists, Baptists, Quakers, and even the Moravian Brethren. His essays on the subject make fascinating reading.[73] His argument is far more sophisticated than the secondhand popular versions suggesting that Calvinism was the cause of capitalism. He pointed to the psychological influence of Puritan pastoral praxis, which coincided with the rise of capitalism as such. He made only slight reference to Calvinistic theology.

However, because of his pretended neutrality (*Wertfreiheit*) toward his subject and his methodology of the "ideal types," there are failings in Weber's analyses.[74] By means of his ideal types, Weber took account of certain elements and left out others in a totally arbitrary way. In addition, Weber never supposed that the elements he included in his "ideal types" were influenced by the ones left out.[75] Since neutrality is an anthropological (as well as a theological) impossibility, his interpretation of Calvinism turns out to be a caricature rather than an analysis. Certain elements are isolated and hence, necessarily, misinterpreted. Weber's whole idea of religion is —in the Dooyeweerdian sense—an immanent one, one in which God is the product of the genius of man. Hence, he speaks of Luther as a "religious genius."

Tawney's analysis is different.[76] His critique was motivated by his preoccupation with the message of the Church. Tawney pictures the Church dropping its resistance and finally capitulating to outside forces. Though it warned against extortion and oppression in general, the Church did not define it[77] (as Calvin had vigorously attempted to do). The Church left social thinking to the social philosophy "of a self-regulating mechanism, moved by the weights and pulleys of economic motives."[78] The influence of Bacon and Descartes—in general, the mathematical ideal of science—created this alienating impact on the Puritan mind,[79] rather than Calvinistic theology as suggested by Weber. The mere repetition of traditional views would not do; "the social teaching of the church had ceased to count, because the church itself had ceased to think."[80]

Granted that I should love my neighbour as myself, the questions which, under modern conditions of large-scale organization, remain for solution are, Who precisely *is* my neighbour? and, How exactly am I to make my love for him effective in practice? To these questions the conventional religious teaching supplied no answer, for it had not even realized that they could be put. It had tried to moralize economic relations, by treating every transaction as a case of personal conduct, involving personal responsibility. In an age of impersonal finance, world markets and a capitalist organization of industry, its traditional social doctrines had nothing specific to offer, and were merely repeated, when, in order to be effective, *they should have been thought out again from the beginning and formulated in new and living terms.* It had endeavoured to protect the peasant and the craftsman against the oppression of the moneylender and the monopolist. Faced with the problems of a wage earning proletariat, it could do no more than repeat, with meaningless iteration, its traditonal lore as to the duties of the master to servant and servant to master. It had insisted that all men were brethren. But it did not occur to it to point out that, as a result of the new economic imperialism which was beginning to develop in the seventeenth century, the brethren of the English merchant were the Africans whom he kidnapped for slavery in America, or the American Indians whom he stripped of their lands, or the Indian craftsmen from whom he bought muslins and silks at starvation prices. Religion had not yet learned to console itself for the practical difficulty of applying its moral principles, by clasping the comfortable formula that for the transactions of economic life no moral principles exist. But for the problems involved in the association of men for economic purposes on the grand scale which was to be increasingly the rule in the future, the social doctrines advanced from the pulpit offered, in their traditional form, little guidance. Their practical ineffectiveness prepared the way for their theoretical abandonment.[81]

Tawney also remarked, pointedly, that "an institution which possesses no philosophy of its own inevitably accepts that which happens to be fashionable."[82]

In a world of *Realpolitik,* colonialism, and materialism and of double morality and mechanistic social thinking, where man was more and more depersonalized, the new concept of man was not only applied to economic man—especially its prototype, the "business man"[83]—but to the *poor* as well and increasingly so. This change in the concept of man and in the corresponding economic philosophy has affected economic man's view of himself and his judgments of the other.

The other was being treated as from the point of view of economic man, and the contempt for the unsuccessful poor served as self-justification and self-confirmation. Ethically, this treatment of the other was required by the new economic system. Economic success was from now on a personal virtue; poverty was guilt. Hence there was to be a new medicine for poverty: moral discipline through (dependent) labor. The sixteenth century's acknowledgment of the social character of wealth and poverty was abandoned. Medieval almsgiving was gradually brought to an end. Man no longer had a dignity of his own, nor did he value the economic system or study it in the light of the Scriptures. The economic system, in which man played merely a mechanical part, determined the value of man. Wealth did not serve man; man became the slave of wealth.

Is all this merely hindsight? Certainly not. At least one Christian classical economist saw clearly that the loss of man in orthodox economics (he was the first to speak of "orthodox" economic theory!) called for a change in the methodology of economic thinking itself. Simonde de Sismondi[84] was "surprised and troubled" by the economic reality half a century after Adam Smith.

> The people of England are destitute of comfort now, and of security for the future. There are no longer yeomen [the world of Adam Smith very clearly had passed!], they have been obliged to become day-labourers. In the towns there are scarcely any longer artisans or independent heads of small business, but only manufacturers. The *operative*, to employ a word which the system has created, does not know what it is to have a station; he only gains wages, and as the wages cannot suffice for all seasons, he is almost every year reduced to ask alms from the poor-rates.[85]

Sismondi was moved by a Calvinistic passion for justice, truth, and liberty. As a political economist *and* historian he was as astute an observer as Adam Smith had been, but he could not tolerate to see that "men are confiscated for the advantage of things."[86] "Above all," wrote Sismondi, during the serious illness that would cause his death, "I have always considered wealth as a means, not as an end. I hope it will be acknowledged by my constant solicitude for the cultivator, for the artisan, for the poor who gain their bread by the sweat of their brow, that all my sympathies are with the labouring and suffering classes."[87] A contemporary commentator called him the only economist who pleaded for his fellow people, repeating that "man does not live by bread alone."[88]

This is not the time to dwell on the theoretical work of Sismondi. His analytical merits are recognized in every standard work on the history of economic science,[89] especially as a forerunner of Keynes who, like Sismondi, related macroeconomic consumption to income instead of production. I only mention this great classical economist who explicitly stressed the immediate link between concepts of man and methodology and who tried to start with man rather than with the economy, "constantly addressing himself to the best feeling of man for man,"[90] seeking another economy than the one in which production increases while enjoyment diminishes.[91] For Sismondi, wealth was not the only end of economic policy; distribution and security were also economic goals. This great Calvinist economist, generally considered one of the fathers of socialism, merits further study.[92]

Emmanuel Levinas. It is said that economics studies the allocation, utilization, and development of resources and that more production brings more enjoyment. However, few people are prepared to test these hypotheses. Liberalism brought more production—Sismondi said that the shops in the great towns of England displayed goods sufficient for the consumption of the world—but it left all classes of society in great fear for their security.[93] Rich men gathered their insecure wealth; poor men became more poor and destitute.

Economics, if it is not to enslave man, ought to reorient itself to the study of the economic aspect of human relations. In other words, economics should be the study of—as Marxism in its own way has well understood—economic relations between men. It should not merely ask how to increase production, regardless of the human relations that condition and are conditioned by the economic process.

It has been said that Adam Smith provided the solution to the new question of Western society: What can order this world of individualism, change, and competition? Smith's answer was liberalism, based theoretically in natural law in which the economic field of action is considered to be autonomous. Calvinism has never accepted this double sphere of morality (analogous to that of Machiavelli)—the personal one and the economic one ruled by its own laws. Therefore Smith's solution poses a new, far more serious problem. After Smith economic injustice is no longer a personal affair; economic ethics is confined to faithfulness to the system, and the system takes care of its own ethics.

This really means there is no ethics. Automatism always spells the end of responsibility; mechanistic economic action is no longer human action. Indeed, such mechanistic economic action loses its proper economic meaning. After this new economics came about, Christians had to ask: How do we fight for the glory of God in all spheres of life since the "pure spheres" of the modern "differentiation process" claim they have already put their own houses in definitive order on the basis of an anti-Christian concept of man? Must we renounce (in Míguez Bonino's phrase) the historical efficiency of the Christian faith? If neocolonialism and exploitation spell injustice and they are, as Schumacher says, in most cases, "unintentional," who is responsible?

Dooyeweerd has stressed that it is the Christian's historical task not only to obey the law but to form it as well, giving it positive shape in obedience to the underlying normative principle. The historical "opening process" is fulfilled under the guidance of faith, be it in God or in a modern idol like "the natural course of things." In the historical and posthistorical aspects—like the economic one—"the laws acquire a concrete sense through human positivizing of Divine normative principles. The human formative will is then to be conceived of as a *subjective moment* on the law-side of these law-spheres themselves."[94]

We are fully responsible for our organization of things that have no natural course beyond the human formative will. Hence liberalism clearly presents us with a problem of conscience. In fact, by pretending to be beyond the grasp of conscience, it attacks the very core of Christian conscience. Hence Levinas says liberalism is a stumbling block between man and God. He observes:

> In the fact that the relation to the divine passes through the relation to man and coincides with social justice, lies the spirit of the Jewish Bible.[95] Moses and the prophets don't worry about the immortality of the soul, but about the poor, the widow, the orphan and the foreigner. The rela-

tion to man, through which the contact with the divine realizes itself, is not a kind of *spiritual friendship*, but a friendship that expresses, proves and completes itself in a just economy and for which every man is fully responsible.[96]

Levinas remarks that it is the economy in which the problem of the relation between the I and the totality of being should be solved. Totality consists of many I's, each representing an absolute, irreducible being that finds its expression in the human face. This multitude of I's related to one another is a structure of creation, not the result of any human conception. Therefore, totality refers to a totality of beings—beings who themselves fall outside the totality. For them totality is, as Levinas says, exteriority. Their relation to this totality is essentially economic. If the totality is conceived of as a system of competition of freedoms, that leads to violence and guilt. Human responsibility should form an economic system that allows the presence of the many I's without their becoming guilty as economic subjects. Hence, working for economic justice is not a substratum of spiritual life but its kernel expression.

God is the absolute who breaks through the intimate love bond between two partners. He is not only Thou; above all he is He, watching our mutual privacy, asking and questioning us about the third person, who is outside our mutual relationship but who undergoes its violent influence. God reminds us of the totality. We cannot isolate ourselves in an intimate love bond with God,[97] for He is to be worshiped with a view to the inevitable needs of society which contains the third person. In economic language Levinas means that the economic problem persists as long as there are external effects that harm third persons (external diseconomies), which we do not take account of. Hence, a just society surpasses love for man is also responsible for the effects of actions that transcend his intentions.[98] We must seek out those who stand beyond our private love-concerns. In this sense law surpasses the command to love one's neighbor.[99]

Liberalism challenges our conscience because it does not recognize any responsibility for external effects.[100] Liberalism says: thou shalt not obey thy conscience—that is, thy Jewish or

Christian conscience—but only the system. The market system is the mediator between man and man to which economic ethics must be relegated.

The Christian conscience cannot be satisfied with this liberalism since it does not believe in such a mediator (no more than it believes in an equally mechanistic Marxist morality). It continues to feel guilty when it sees the economic suffering of the third person revealed to it by economic analysis (though not analysis of the liberal sort).

Violating the third person is a serious religious problem because, as Levinas observes, we do not stand with the other in a community of love that permits forgiveness by him. Our relation to the totality that embraces the third person who has been violated in his freedom is necessarily one of injustice.

> If the mistake is too big to investigate our conscience, man as interiority is not of importance anymore....Nobody is able any more to find the law that governs his deeds in the depth of his heart. The impasse of liberalism lies in this exteriority of my awareness and conscience towards myself. The subject of the mistake expects the sense of his being from outside; it is not any more a man who confesses his sins, but one who admits the accusations.[101]

Levinas does not believe in a mathematical ideal of the equality of man. Such an ideal suggests we can form a general concept embracing all the I's, of which the individual would be an element. There is, however, no such concept corresponding to the I. We have seen that Smith's liberal individual destroyed himself. Smith began with a depersonalized view of man, and he concluded with the mechanism of economic man—man as the passive executor of market forces. To Levinas, men are not equal; therefore he tries to avoid even the word "neighbor." Because the other stands higher, as the Other, I am not equal to my neighbor. *Totality consists of relations of singularities that cannot be brought under one denomination of being.*

The biblical concept of man and the concepts of liberalism are irreconcilable. Levinas compares war and the liberalist economy's violation of labor. In both the other is seen only from a logistical point of view. I do not seek his face. Levinas often quotes from Charles V in Victor Hugo's play *Hernani*: "I am a going force" (*"Je suis un force qui va"*).[102] This is the blind force of violence. Machiavelli's pure power corresponds to pure economics which eventually ends in the pure nihilism of efficiency, the "praxiological" interpretation of utility. "It is not the quality of the goal that is of importance; what matters is that a given aim of economic activity can be achieved in different degrees."[103]

Is man's relation to totality bound to be violent? Can he not relate to his exteriority without infringing on the freedom of the other? According to Levinas, "The exteriority without violence is the exteriority of dialogue (*discours*)." The absolute that is the basis of justice is the absolute of my interlocutor. His way of being and of manifesting himself consists in his turning his face to me. The absolute is a person and the demand of justice is absolute, coming to me from beyond history.

The word is a relation between freedoms that neither restrict nor deny each other but confirm each other. It is communication between men whose faces express their being beyond totality. It is not the slogan of commercial propaganda or indoctrination by military regimes.

To be rooted outside history and totality, though working within them, does not imply resistance against totality. Rather, it is putting oneself in its service, that is, struggling for justice. The objective is economic justice. We must introduce equality, not based on an anthropological concept of equality but on the absoluteness and highness of the other, in a world given over to a deadly fight between individual freedoms. Justice comes from outside, as the command of the Other. It cannot exist in the unreal realm of "pure respect" but must be realized in economic relations.

We cannot use more profound language to stress the inner relation between democracy and economics. More and more we understand that economic underdevelopment is basically political underdevelopment.[104] The freedom of the word—which, as Levinas observes in line with Hebrew tradition and language, is essentially command—is the most fundamental condition lacking for Latin America's economic development.[105]

Methodological conclusions
The irreducibility and universality of the economic aspect as a condi-

tion of human freedom to be respected by economic theory. In an impressive address Abraham Kuyper once pointed out that the Otherness of God—God being different from the world—is the basic truth that both logic and the methodology of social sciences must obey.[106] Therefore he sharply rejected Hegelian logic and ideas of totality three quarters of a century before the Latin American critique of the philosophy of oppression would do the same. Kuyper was aware that the political consequences of denying God as the Other and the Sovereign would lead straight to totalitarianism. The fact that totality does not mean totalitarianism and that the worship of God and societal freedom cannot be separated found its concise expression in the watchword of "sovereignty within its own sphere"—the basis of true Calvinist social philosophy. God's sovereignty in all spheres of life implies man's obedience in whatever he does.

Calvinistic philosophy has thoroughly elaborated the principle of sphere sovereignty, even in the very methodology of the special sciences. This philosophy criticizes the place man gives theoretical thought in his investigations. The struggle is against violence and corruption that arise from the fictions and antinomies that prevent genuine theoretical insight into the empirical world. Indeed, anytime man does violence to his fellow-man by the theories he falsely develops, it is the Word of God that is violated.

Christians cannot recognize the face of economic man as a human countenance because it is expressionless. Those who propagate such a man have long forgotten that the I must express itself and "live into" the economic aspect of life while not coinciding with it; economics remains exterior to the I. Marx saw clearly that Smith's contradiction of this fact of nonidentity amounted to a revolution of anthropological perspectives.[107]

A fundamental awareness of the highness of the Other should govern our understanding of the economic aspect (which precedes the question of how to theoretically abstract the "economic problem"). In the introduction I pointed out that such an attitude of respect takes on a methodological significance because the meaning center or "nuclear moment" of the economic aspect is an irreducible category, not accessible to further analysis. The "economic," rather, is a modal aspect of temporal reality.

The economic aspect does not coincide with reality nor is it a "part" of reality. However, it is a real aspect of the world we live in and not a logical construction. It is not a being per se, but a way of being for specific entities. Hence, economics does not refer to a special "sector" of society, such as "production" because production, like every real phenomenon, functions in all modal aspects. It has a social aspect (in the Dooyeweerdian sense of the social intercourse of the partners who meet in productive activities), juridical and ethical aspects, and so forth. In turn, these aspects are present, as meaning moments, within the structure of the economic aspect itself. This is what is meant by the sphere universality of the economic way of being in the world.[108]

This means that we cannot submit the economic aspect because of its many-sided interwovenness with all the modalities of being to which it refers, to a totalitarian, self-enclosed, autonomous interpretation. Such an interpretation is not the meaning of "sovereignty within its own sphere." Rather, it is its most wrong and frequent misinterpretation. The economic aspect is just one meaning-side of experience. If economics could deal with "production" and "consumption" exhaustively, as though they were "purely economic" affairs, then we would lose the coherence of meaning of reality and consequently, the kernel meaning of the economic aspect itself.

When we do not acknowledge the coherence of meaning, then we destroy the meaning of the economic aspect itself because the economic aspect cannot be conceived in isolation from the rest. Similarly, the "isolated abstraction" of *homo economicus* destroys the liberty of man. Many Calvinists have forgotten the profound difference in origin between the "Puritan" and the *homo economicus*. Hence, wanting to be "Puritans," they end up portraying *homo economicus*, often using theological language. "Private initiative" means quite different things for each. For the capitalist it means the initiative of the *homo economicus* who has no private initiative at all when it comes to ethically shaping economic action toward justice. For the Christian initiative means human action flowing, like all the springs of life, from the heart which must be "kept with all vigilance" (Prov. 4:23).

The total accomodation of ethics to liberalist economics appears in the well-known letter from the Amsterdam-Rotterdam Bank to the World Council of Churches concerning "investments in" South African apartheid.[109] The letter asserts that banking has its own "inherent objective." This statement implies that business has an "automatic pilot" represented by managers fully adapted to their role. These managers, as true economic men, raise vigorous formal protests when a church points to the relation that exists between the hearts of these men and their economic functions and asks for true "private initiative." The Reformation discovered the real individuality of man (which is different from the self-destroying individualism of liberalism) in his indivisible responsibility.[110] By dividing economics and ethics, by assigning each of them to its own "sector," we inevitably distort the economic aspect itself, the economic concepts based on it, and the direction of economic theory.

Economic science can never acquire absolute competence in the real matters of production. Man surpasses the economic concepts of the economist as they, of necessity, remain external to him. By leaving out the noneconomic aspects of reality, as expressed in analogies in the economic aspect itself, we are left with only a formal and nihilistic concept of economics. Thus economics itself becomes meaningless and, thereby, oppressive, destroying the other man.

Knight is very explicit about the correlation between the "practical" *homo economicus* and his theoretical counterpart, the "pure" economist. Both emanate from the same "profession of man" and both are equally violent. "Everybody who dedicates himself to the study of social science should first of all accustom himself to recognizing the fact that 'man' (not in our culture, but in a universal way), including he himself and his colleague-scientists, is an animal with a propensity to competition, to quarreling and fighting, who likes to increase his power and is inclined to justify all means leading to this end."[111] In the modern world, especially in impersonal, "scientific" language, communication turns into dogmatism and dogmatism into propaganda. The Word—the basis of every society—has disappeared. The economic interpretation of things must be a dialogue not only between economists but also between the economist and the other with whom economic theory deals.

Hence João da Veiga Coutinho calls "theory" the "theoretical context": "The 'theory' or 'theoretical context' of problemization is dialogue, that is, the examination and appropriation of mediating reality by conscious actors who stand in a subject-to-subject relationship to each other. This theoretical context may, however, degenerate into ideology, which is the opposite of dialogue."[112] Unless we want to give up empirical and theoretical truth for the sake of ideology, we cannot expel the other from the field of scientific investigation. To put it another way, we cannot convert the image of God into an element[113] that fits our image of an ideal type needed by an autonomous economic methodology asking for *"exakt bestimmbare Bedingungskonstellationen."*[114] Economic methodology is unavoidably based on a concept of man,[115] which is an attitude toward the other and the Other.

Levinas says that the Other constitutes the order of freedom. Hence freedom is heteronomy. The relation to the Other precedes our division of human behavior into "theory" and "practice." In fact, *our recognition of heteronomy, evidenced in the face of the other, is the beginning of philosophy.* It is, as Dooyeweerd would say, a religious ground motive. This basic attitude towards the Other always exists, even when it is denied and concealed behind a pretense of scientific neutralism.

We need to remember that while modern economic methodology pretends to be neutral as to its ends, in practice it completely serves the growth of production irrespective of what really ought to be called economic growth, namely, growth (opening, deepening, and development) of economic relations. Levinas's analysis applies both to the world of Adam Smith and to modern economic theory and practice. In any civilization that is reflected by the philosophy of the Same (and thus of the Self: the "egology" of Western philosophy), "freedom realizes itself as wealth."[116] The rise of classical economic man as the main product of modern paganism was no accident. It is the result of a pretended and idolized "natural course of things" that shuns any questioning of the self by true religion—religion which is "to visit orphans and widows in their affliction, and to keep oneself unstained from the world" (James 1:27).

The pretended autonomy of theoretical thought seeks to delimit sectors on which the "pure" principles of a special social science can be "applied." In doing so it denies the presence of the Other and the normative structures of creation to which man must respond—not in domination, but in service. This pretension began when modern thought assigned God to his own sector, namely, the hereafter. To Descartes, theology was the special science that would "teach how to earn heaven":

> I respected [says Descartes] our theology and strived at earning heaven as everybody else; but having discovered, as a thing which is very sure, that the way is not less open to the most ignorant as it is to the most learned and that the revealed truths which conduce to it are beyond our intelligence, I have not dared to submit them to the weakness of my arguments and have considered that to set oneself to examine them and with success would require an extraordinary assistance and to be more than man.[117]

Hence Descartes decided "not to seek another science than could be found in myself or in the great book of the world."[118] In other words, Descartes's theoretical thought was no longer watched by the face of the other. A theology that withdraws God from the world is correlative to autonomous "profane" science. Social science did not need the "supposition" of a living God as a continuous interlocutor with man. This is the dualism between heaven and earth that Calvinism radically rejects, a dualism of which Tawney said, "as its implications were developed, emptied religion of its social content, and society of its soul."[119]

Final remarks. When we no longer think of production and consumption as the exclusive preserve of economics, but consider them as concerns of biology, psychology, technology, medicine, and law as well, then "conscious actors" should be able to communicate concerning the different aspects of these same real phenomenon and speak about the direction in which productive activity is to go. Economists do not have exclusive competence to speak about production, for others study different aspects of it. The way in which these various scientists make their model abstractions will, in turn, influence the possibility of communication between the specialized disciplines.

Those who claim an absoluteness or purity for economics are the same ones who hold that the economic abstraction is in itself insufficient. It is generally accepted that economics is not the only "aspect" of things. Its method proceeds through "isolating abstraction." Therefore, it is said, any analysis of policy must naturally be confronted with other points of view, such as the ethical. But who, and what, decides the conflict between points of view? In practice conflicts are really between the powerful interests within the economic aspect and within the ethical aspect. But this practice is disguised (in our theories) as a conflict between economics and ethics. A Christian cannot believe in this pretended conflict between normativities, for he knows that each is based in the creation of the Lord who is one Lord (Deut. 6:4).[120]

The religious direction of human life expresses itself in all the modal aspects; it is the guiding principle of faith that governs the entire historical opening process through which modal normativities are positivized.[121] Economics has its ethical implications just as ethics has its economic implications. Ethical development is possible only on the basis of economic development just as economic development anticipates ethical development and already implies it through the direction in which the economic modality of life is historically developed. This direction depends on the faith that leads the development process. This is the ontological and historical coherence of "modal universality." The economic aspect has its ethical moment (Dooyeweerd also says "analogies") within its own structure; the ethical aspect has its economic ones.[122]

Therefore the economic abstraction is, in itself, not necessarily defective or insufficient. When the economic aspect of concrete phenomena is made really transparent, we gain insight into our real experience. This scientific truth needs neither correction nor complementing by "interdisciplinary cooperation." The methodologies of modern economics and modern sociology[123] are so similar that they cannot alter the basic directions of each other's analyses. Each discipline presents its particular point of view as universally valid, but they share the same philosophical base. It would be far more fruitful to have discussions between economists who do not share the same basic philosophical views. It is not wrong to abstract a particular modal aspect of reality, but unsound, isolating abstraction goes awry.

Social science must direct itself to justice as the only creational condition in which the Other can be respected. Justice not only relates itself to what has been called "normative econom-

ics" but to the structure of positive economics itself. Positive
economics depends on our idea of the structure of the economic
modal aspect. This, in turn, depends on the religious ground
motive at work in our thinking. When there is no obedience in
our work of abstraction, that is, when we do not listen but only
issue dogmatic propaganda, then the whole of creation suffers
injustice and violence. Charles Birch refers to Hosea: "When
there is no fidelity, no tenderness, *no knowledge of God in the
country*, only perjury and lies, slaughter, theft, adultery and
violence, murder after murder, all who live in it pine away,
even the wild animals and birds of heaven; the fish of the seas
themselves are perishing."[124] This is a graphic picture of the
devastating ecological effect of our violent economic development and methodology.[125]

There is nothing wrong with economics as such, or with
the economic aspect itself. Historical development is not a
question of more or less economics or weighing the economic
against another point of view (such as the ethical). I once heard
a Dutch business leader, in a discussion with a church delega-
tion about justice and investments in South Africa, say: "But we
are   here to take care of economics. You could not blame a
businessman for that. There has to be economics (he meant production, which he claimed to be socially neutral) in any societal order." Unfortunately, the word "economics" has assumed
a meaning fully shaped by capitalist practice and theory. *It has
ascribed universal and ontological meaning to what in fact is a subjective, human, culturally determined objective.* The goal of this
absolutized economic meaning is growth of production. But
this growth is presented as universally important, independent
of any concept of man.

This practical and theoretical identification of the economic aspect with the goal of production growth is a fundamental problem. Economic theory cannot prescribe goals and
thus encroach on religious liberty. The phrases "economic
motive" and "scarcity," when presented as ontological and anthropological claims, are bound to have totalitarian effects. In
the debate between the Dutch church community and (Christian) business circles about foreign investment in South Africa,
one should not have tried to establish a kind of quantitative
equilibrium between economics and ethics or between economics and politics. Rather, the issue at stake was economic. It

is not that some are speaking for economics and others are presenting subjective political views. Rather, all of us are discussing real economics. Real economics does not need additional normative qualification by some interfering ethical designs.

No norm of growth in production has absolute validity. Christian economics must share the Christian objective of justice. How can we achieve respect for the oppressed other in economic relations themselves? Will we seek the basic idea of the economic aspect in obedience or apostasy? This is the only perspective in which we can put the question of obedient or apostate economic behavior.

Current economic science *presupposes* and *produces* the *identification of man and methodology*, methodology losing its exteriority to man and man being scientifically ordered to obey an ontologically determined built-in objective, that of the generally surviving economic man of classical economics. *A particular way in which the economic mode of being has been historically realized is presented as the fundamental economic normativity*, thus denying the possibility of any further opening process or the historical opening of economics in another *direction*. Man's freedom of religion, however, never is compatible with any such reduction of man to an element of a totalitarian (theoretical or practical) economic system. In the meantime, to use the phrase of Sismondi, economic language is made up of "words which the system has created."

Current economic language does relate to some existing reality. Capitalism has produced scarcity, and now the capitalist apology claims this is universally existent because capitalism considers itself to be universal. Therefore scarcity, instead of being analyzed as a concrete, historical situation,[126] is transformed into an anthropological postulate that is a new ontological basis for the idea of, and the practical propagation of, economic man. The economic man *does* exist—as alienated man.[127] In this sense traditional economic theory does have an empirical base. Similarly, Marxist economic determinism does lay down an account of the real states of affairs and the real processes that are essentially the outcome of the liberal economic practice and theory. Our denial of class society cannot do away with the problems itself; so our theory must take that fact into account. The question is: How should our theory take that fact into account and on the basis of what concept of man and society?

Here, again, we cannot separate our scientific and practical tasks. They both refer to our stand in life, that is, to our religion. Knight was correct to point out that life is a struggle; but we may not accept his ontological and anthropological foundation of it. We do not accept an anarchical power play of economic and political forces nor a love of war and gain. We accept

> another war, affording a grander scope for human effort; another object, demanding as much activity, prudence, and reflection as the love of gain; the war against moral and spiritual evil, conquering the kingdoms of this world, to become the kingdoms of God and of Christ; that combat which was begun by him and has been carried on by his followers, with varying numbers, and varying success, to the present time.[128]

If man cannot live by bread alone, we must end the economic system that proclaims that struggle for material gain is the basis of all society. This society is a real, concrete fact, but Christian economic methodology must not succumb to it by accommodating and confirming traditional materialist thinking. We must have our own profession of man if we are not to lose our belief in the real meaning and effects of the Christian faith.

Christians can share the view that man is a laborer, but Christians view labor in a way radically different from the capitalists.[129] A stable economy, characterized by security, can help man perform his cultural and spiritual tasks. That economy must be based on a solution to the traditionally materialist economic problem of scarcity that is, in the first place, *scarcity for the poor.* This solution might be disadvantageous to the growth of production not only in capitalist organizations but everywhere.

But economic growth is not merely growth in production. This general use of the term "economic" mystifies what is really happening. Our methodology must clarify our language, say what is meant, and not conceal interests and unexamined worldviews. The growth that merits our theoretical and practical interest is the growth, development, and opening up of the economic aspect of our concrete production and consumption. Production, in turn, should no longer be called simply economic because production functions in all modal aspects. We have always to unmask the concrete meaning of the word "economic," be it "individual," "financial," "capitalist," "quantitative," "relating to production," "production growth," "domination," or "geopolitical." In this sense Christian economic theory must start virtually from zero.

This means primarily two things. First, we must draft an economic theory that is essentially institutionalist, largely along the lines of the great example of Gunnar Myrdal. Myrdal, in *Asian Drama* and elsewhere, has pointed out that attitudes and institutions are an economic problem of their own that cannot be left to the automatic effects of the market mechanism or to Western development recipes. The general disdain for "institutionalism" in economics ("a closed chapter in economic thought today")[130] shows only that pure economics does not realize that it is itself excessively institutionalist in a universalist way, particularly in its absolutization of the concept of function on the basis of "the illegitimate introduction of a specific structure concept of individuality as a functional one."[131] How could such a pure theory deal with multinational corporations that decide the success or failure of entire political systems in Latin American and shape the prevailing economic order instead of obeying it? Or, let us take a concrete example from the showpiece of traditional economic theory, the theory of international trade. While theory proclaims the principle of comparative cost differences, the multinational firm—the decisive factor in the "new international division of labor"—acts on comparison of absolute costs. The adjustment mechanism of the dependent economy has no "invisible hand" at its service to prove the validity of the traditional economic theory.

In the second place, Christian respect for the other must debunk any personification and, therefore, mystification of the category of capital. Here Adam Smith's impersonal way of speaking about the function of stock, rather than the role of the owner of stock, should be of help. The ownership of stock should itself be open to economic development. Ownership of stock should not govern economic relations; economic relations should govern the way capital itself is used. Capital is no ontological category. Money does not breed; it has no productivity of its own. It only functions according to the prevailing order, whose development is the field of investigation of economic theory. Our theory and our practice converge in the meeting with the other and the Other. We may not theorize in an abstract, empirically unjustified, theoretically autonomous way, in which we do not take into account the expression shown in the face of the other. Christians should appreciate that the Other comes to them through the other. Should not the central meaning of the Word of Christ, who referred to "the least of his brethren" (Matt. 25:40) be of methodological relevance?

Notes

1. Reinhold Niebuhr, *The Nature and Destiny of Man: A Christian Interpretation* (New York: Charles Scribner's Sons, 1955), 1:130.
2. Herman Dooyeweerd, *In the Twilight of Western Thought: Studies in the Pretended Autonomy of Philosophical Thought* (Philadelphia: Presbyterian & Reformed, 1960), 123.
3. Dooyeweerd, *In the Twilight*. These words can be easily misunderstood to refer to practical Protestantism's exclusive emphasis on the center of the personality as corresponding to the rise of the individualistic bourgeois ideal of personality. Dooyeweerd has always stressed the community of man in sin as well as redemption. But we must distinguish sharply between what Tillich has called "the Protestant principle" and the actual behavior of Protestants who have often "replaced the great wealth of symbols appearing in the Christian tradition by rational concepts, moral and subjective emotions, rightly protesting against the magical use of the sacramental element in Roman Catholicism but destroying the spiritual use which is essential for religious life as well" Paul Tillich, *The Protestant Era*, 3d ed. (Chicago: University of Chicago Press, 1948) xxiii.
4. Emmanuel Levinas, *Het Menselijk Gelaat*, ed. Ad Peperzak, 3d ed. (Bilthoven: Basisboeken, 1975), 44.
5. Jose Porfirio Miranda, *Marx and the Bible: A Critique of the Philosophy of Oppression*, trans. John Eagleson (Maryknoll, N.Y.: Orbis Books, 1974), 48-49.
6. Emmanuel Levinas, *Totalité et Infini, Essais sur l'extériorité*, 2d ed. (The Hague: Martinus Nijhoff, 1965), 14. The English translator puts it as "a fundamental philosophy" instead of "the first philosophy." Levinas's idea is for the *first time* in history.
　　　Theo. de Boer explores some fundamental resemblances between Levinas and Calvinistic philosophy (in this case, the writings of Professor Vollenhoven) in "Beyond Being: Ontology and Eschatology in the Philosophy of Emmanuel Levinas," *Philosophia reformata*, 38 (1973): 17-29.
7. Miranda, 58.
8. Miranda, 65. Miranda is quoting Levinas, *Totalité et Infini*, 196.
9. Ignacy Sachs, ed., *Main Trends in Economics* (London: Allen & Unwin, 1973), 21:

Another characteristic feature (of modern economic thought) has been the progressive elimination of social and meta-sociological questions. To the past belong not only the great tradition of analyzing economic and social problems in their organic unity, with which such names as Karl Marx, Wener Sombart, Max Weber and Rosa Luxemburg are associated, but also the far less ambitious approach of studying economic problems at least in a limited socio-historical context (Alfred Marshall). The very questions which made economic science a social discipline are now increasingly left to newspaper pundits and mass media experts.

10. E. F. Schumacher, *Small Is Beautiful: Economics As If People Mattered* (New York: Harper & Row, 1973), 182-84.
11. Schumacher, 182-83.
12. On the operationalist character of modern science, see Herbert Marcuse, *One Dimensional Man*, 2d ed. (London: Abacus, 1974), 24-25.
13. Smith also had a clearly materialist view of the economic structure determining the legal superstructure. In his introduction to Adam Smith's *Theory of Moral Sentiments* (London: H. G. Bohn, 1861), Dugald Stewart said:

Upon this subject he followed the plan that seems to be suggested by Montesquieu; endeavouring to trace the gradual progress of jurisprudence, both public and private, from the rudest to the most refined ages, and to point out the effects of those arts which contribute to subsistence, and to the accumulation of property, in producing correspondent improvements or alterations in law and government.(xviii)

This was the way in which Adam Smith, a professor of moral philosophy, taught the subject matter of "justice."

In *Economía e Ideología y otros ensayos* (Barcelona: Ariel, 1972), Ronald L. Meek says that the classical political economy "developed in close relation with a more general system of ideas concerning the structure and the development of society, a system we could call 'classical sociology'" (57, translation mine; original English edition published under the title *Economics and Ideology and Other Essays* [London: Chapman & Hall, 1967]).

This "classical sociology," especially under the influence of the Scottish universities in the eighteenth century, was remarkably similar to the later Marxist sociology in its general outlook. Meek mentions Smith, Adam Ferguson, William Robertson, John Millar, and others as undergoing the influence of Montesquieu's view of man as a social being and of the evolution of law in relation to the environment.
14. J. A. Schumpeter, *History of Economic Analysis* ed. E. B. Schumpeter, 6th ed. (London: Allen & Unwin, 1954), 187-188.
15. Robert Lamb, "Adam Smith's Concept of Alienation," *Oxford Economic Papers* 25 (1973): 279.
16. Adam Smith, *An Inquiry into the Nature and Causes of the Wealth of Nations* 2 vols. (London: Everyman's Library, 1964), 1:13. I apologize for all the quotes from Smith, but his flavor is in the words and details.
17. Note the conflict between capitalism and democracy, so apparent in Latin America today.

18. Smith, *An Inquiry*, 1:58-59 (italics mine).
19. Smith, *An Inquiry*, 1:69.
20. Smith, *An Inquiry*, 1:61, 63, 65.
21. Smith, *An Inquiry*, 1:70.
22. Smith, *An Inquiry*, 1:73-74.
23. Smith, *An Inquiry*, 1:75.
24. Smith does not use the term "alienation" except in the meaning of "sale." His reference to "common humanity" and to human dignity seems to imply the concept, though not exactly in the later Marxian sense.
25. Smith, *An Inquiry*, 2:264 (italics mine).
26. Smith, *An Inquiry*, 1:267.
27. Smith, *An Inquiry*, 1:129 (italics mine).
28. Smith, *An Inquiry*, 1:289.
29. Regulations disturb the natural equality of commerce (see Smith, *An Inquiry*, 1:113). Law should therefore protect the freedom of commerce. Essentially it protects private property. Private property is the origin of the state. With the appearance of property there arose the need for the law to protect it. Smith recognized that the system of property did not offer the same advantages for all. That "order of people" who, for instance, simply occupy the land, "with all the liberty and security which law can give, must always improve under great disadvantages" (Smith, *An Inquiry*, 1:350). However, Smith maintains his optimistic view of improvement lying in the natural course of things, even with respect to those who have to cope with disadvantages. Here we can see the conflict between empirical observations and the prefabricated theory of improvement.
30. Meek, 73 (cited in note 13 above).
31. Daniel R. Fusfield calls this "the folklore of individualism." See the chapter entitled "The Philosphy of Individualism" in his book, *The Age of the Economist* (Glenview, Ill.: Scott, Foresman, 1966).
32. Smith, *An Inquiry*, 1:334.
33. Smith, *An Inquiry*, 1:86.
34. Smith, *An Inquiry*, 1:344. Also:

> A small proprietor however, who knows every part of his little territory, who views it with all the affection which property, especially small property, inspires, and who upon that account takes pleasure not only in cultivating but in adorning it, is generally of all improvers the most industrious, the most intelligent, and the most successful. (Smith, *An Inquiry*, 1:370)

35. Smith, *An Inquiry*, 1:343.
36. Smith, *An Inquiry*, 1:349.
37. Smith, *An Inquiry*, 1:351.
38. Smith, *An Inquiry*, 1:348.
39. Smith, *An Inquiry*, 1:228ff.
40. Smith, *An Inquiry*, 1:100-101, 323.
41. Smith, *An Inquiry*, 1:111.
42. Smith, *An Inquiry*, 1:74.
43. Smith, *An Inquiry*, 1:76.

44. Situated in the year 1793, Anthony Burton's gripping novel, *The Navigators* (London: Futura Books, 1977), is interesting reading about the rapid change of British society through extensive canal building.
45. Lord Robbins, *An Essay on the Nature and Significance of Economic Science* 2d ed. rev. and extended (London: Macmillan, 1969), 1. Also:

> The efforts of economists during the last hundred and fifty years have resulted in the establishment of a body of generalizations whose substantial accuracy and importance are open to question only by the ignorant or the perverse. But they have achieved no unanimity concerning the ultimate nature of the common subject-matter of these generalizations. The central chapters of the standard works on economics retail, with only minor variations, the main principles of the science. But the chapters in which the object of the work is explained still present wide divergences. We all talk about the same thing, but we have not yet agreed what it is we are talking about. (Robbins, 1)

One wonders who are the "ignorant and the perverse"—those who believe in "accuracy and importance" without understanding their meaning or those who ask questions? This kind of unfounded pragmatism and operationalism is always—understandably—defended in a very emotional way.

See also the controversy between Frank H. Knight and Melvill J. Herskovits, included as an appendix to Melvill J. Herskovits, *Economic Anthropology: A Study in Comparative Economics*, 2d ed., rev., enlarged, and rewritten (New York:Knopf, 1952). To Herskovits's observation that he never had met a creature similar to the *homo economicus*, Knight points to his opponent's ignorance and perversion. Knight claims that if Herskovits had been a true economist, he would have known that "economic man" does not exist. The concept "refers to an analytical expedient, essentially only of a terminological nature, indicating the aspect of economic behaviour, which is proper to all behaviour according to a conscious end."

This modern idea of an economic aspect, apart from not being able to delimit economics, cannot even stand an immanent critique, as I have shown in my *Economie in Principe en Praktijk: Een Methodologische Verkenning* (Groningen: Jan Haan, 1975).
46. The term "capitalist" was not used before the 1860s.
47. Smith, *An Inquiry*, 1:42.
48. Smith, *An Inquiry*, 1:230.
49. Smith did not consider stock to be a productive force in itself (as does today's dominant economic ideology) because stock generates profit. For Smith, stock generates profit as an implication of economic organization. The national product, that is, "the annual product of the land and the labour," originates from natural resources and labor. In this respect Smith is a forerunner of Marxist theory and he can be given a socialist interpretation.
50. Smith, *An Inquiry*, 1:373.
51. Richard H. Tawney's *Religion and the Rise of Capitalism* (Gloucester, Mass.: P. Smith, 1962) is obligatory reading for Christian economists.
52. Smith, *An Inquiry*, 1:400 (italics mine).
53. The common Christian reproach that Marx introduced the concept of man

as essentially a laborer is not accurate. Marx was well aware that it was Smith who had fundamentally changed Western anthropology. Marx followed Engels in noting that Adam Smith had been "the Luther of economics."
54. Smith, *An Inquiry*, 1:6ff., 184, 201, 211, 223, 298, 358 ("the improved and civilised part of the world"), 363, 368, 371, etc. "[G]ain is the end of all improvement, and nothing could deserve that name of which loss was to be the necessary consequence" (1:209).
55. Note again the parallel with Marx.
56. Smith, *An Inquiry*, 1:44.
57. Smith, *An Inquiry*, 1:228ff.
58. Smith, *An Inquiry*, 1:230.
59. Smith, *An Inquiry*, 1:369.
60. On the other hand, it is the landlords who "are the only one of the three orders whose revenue costs them neither labour nor care, but comes to them as it were, of its own accord, and independent of any plan or project of their own" (Smith, *An Inquiry* 1:230). Nor could the profits of stock be considered a renumeration for the

> labor of inspection and direction. They are, however, altogether different, regulated by quite sufficient principles and bear no proportion to the quantity, the hardship, or the ingenuity of this supposed labour of inspection and direction. They are regulated altogether by the value of the stock employed, and are greater or smaller in proportion to the extent of this stock. (Smith, *An Inquiry* 1:43)

Rates of profits are more equal than wages (Smith, *An Inquiry* 1:100). The only class that really exerts and sacrifices itself is laborers. Landlords have a passive, if not negative, role, and capitalists have a functional, impersonal role.

> But though the interest of the labourer is strictly connected with that of society, he is incapable either of comprehending that interest or of understanding its connection with his own. His condition leaves him no time to receive the necessary information, and his education and habits are commonly such as to render him unfit to judge even though he was fully informed. In the public deliberations therefore, his voice is little heard and less regarded, except upon some particular occasions, when his clamour is animated, set on, and supported by his employers, not for his, but their own particular purposes (Smith, *An Inquiry* 1:230-31).

61. Smith, *An Inquiry*, 1:84, 230.
62. Smith, *An Inquiry*, 1:231.
63. Smith, *An Inquiry*, 1:232.
64. Smith, *An Inquiry*, 1:232. His description of the role of the three classes is surprisingly relevant to Latin America today. He thoroughly understood certain implications and characteristics of a system that operated in his time and still operates in many dependent capitalist countries.
65. Smith, An Inquiry, 1:231-32 (italics mine).
66. It was for that reason that the mercantilist practices existed, which Smith

severely and convincingly attacked. "The merchants knew perfectly in what manner [foreign trade] enriched themselves. It was their business to know it. But to know in what manner it enriched the country was no part of their business" (Smith, *An Inquiry* 1:380).

67. See, for instance, Smith on the violence of feudalism (1:249-50, 366), on the violence of benevolence (1:369), as well as on the violence of laws preventing dissipation of family property, and so forth.

68. Eduardo Galeano, *Las venas abiertas de America Latine*, 2d ed. (Mexico: Siglo Veintiuno Editores S. A., 1975), 3.

69. James F. Petras, "La Mort du Capitalisme Démocratique: L'Amerique latine, banc d'essai d'un Nouveau Totalitarisme," *Le Monde Diplomatique* (April 1977).

70. Smith, *An Inquiry*, 1:249; Matt. 6:28. The idea of economic man is explicitly dealt with:

> [T]he principle which prompts us to save is the desire of bettering our condition, a desire which, though generally calm and dispassionate, comes with us from the womb, and never leaves us till we go into the grave. In the whole interval which separates those two moments, there is scarce perhaps a single instant in which any man is so perfectly and completely satisfied with his situation as to be without any wish of alteration or improvement of any kind. (Smith, *An Inquiry* 1:305)

71. Smith, *Theory*, xvii (cited in note 13 above).

72. See the text that Max Weber said played such a decisive role, through Luther's translation, in both Lutheranism and Puritanism (through the inclusion of Luther's concept in the northern European languages): "Stand by your covenant [Luther: *Beruf*] and attend to it, and grow old in your work" (Sirach 11:20).

For the Puritan it was not just a matter of faithfulness in one's *Beruf* (profession as "calling") within a static God-given world order. Labor was the dynamic element of that order itself.

73. See *Die protestantische Ethik und der Geist des Kapitalismus* (Tübingen and Leipzig: J. C. B. Mohr, 1904 and 1905), especially part 1, section 3, about Luther's concept of *Beruf*; and *Die protestantischen Sekten und der Geist des Kapitalismus* (1906), reprinted in *Gesämmelte Aufsätze zur Religionssoziologie*, 3 vols. (Tübingen: J. C. B. Mohr, 1920-21).

74. Weber influenced economics not only by his own economic writings (see note 73 above), but also through his influence on specialized methodological studies. For example, see W. Eucken, *Die Grundlagen der Nationalokonomie*, 7th ed. (Berlin: Springer, 1959). I have criticized Eucken's methodology in my *Economie*, 15-30 (cited in note 45 above).

75. This critique also fundamentally invalidates the *ceteris paribus* method in economic theory.

76. See Tawney (cited in note 51 above).

77. Tawney, 161.

78. Tawney, 161. The common term "economic motive" means financial (or, at least, material) self-interest. This use of "economic" in all popular and scientific economic language is the result of existing economic methodology.

79. Note the great advance and influence of the natural sciences in Scotland. See also Adam Smith, *Essay on the History of Astronomy* (London: A. Murray, 1969).
80. Tawney, 157.
81. Tawney, 156-57 (italics mine).
82. Tawney, 160.
83. Tawney, 221:

> Few tricks of the unsophisticated intellect are more curious than the naive psychology of the business man, who ascribes his achievements to his own unaided efforts, in bland unconsciousness of a social order without whose continuous support and vigilant protection he would be as a lamb bleating in the desert.

84. Jean-Charles Leonard Simonde de Sismondi (1773-1842) was the son of a Calvinist minister in Geneva. His ancestors, the "illustrious family of the Sismondi" of Pisa, fled to France in 1524 after the subjugation of their country. The Sismondis, whose name was eventually transformed into Simonde, lived in France until the revocation of the Edict of Nantes. Having embraced Calvinism, they sought asylum in Geneva.

In 1793 Geneva sympathized with the ideas of the French Revolution, while the Sismondis did not. Hence they took refuge in England. In the following year they settled in Val-Chiusa, Italy, where Sismondi prepared his study, *Tableau de l'agriculture Toscane* (Geneva: J. J. Paschoud, 1801). He was continuously bothered by the Austrian police, who considered him a sympathizer of revolutionary ideas, so he fled back to Geneva in 1800. The family's fate—persecution for the sake of conviction—undoubtedly deepened the independence and the religious foundation of Sismondi's thought.

Apart from the number of articles on economics, Sismondi published the following larger works: *De la Richesse Commerciale ou Principes de l'économie Politique: Appliqués à la Legislation du Commerce* (Geneva: J. J. Paschoud, 1803), a fully "Smithsonian" account of economics; "Political Economy," an article written in 1815 for the *Edinburgh Encyclopedia* in which he began to reorient himself away from the classical economists who followed Smith (see *Political Economy and the Philosophy of Government: A Series of Essays from the Selected Writing of J.C.L. Simonde de Sismondi* [1847; reprint, New York: A. M. Kelley, 1966]); *Nouveaux Principes d'économie Politique ou de la Richesse dans ses Rapports avec la Population*, 2d ed. (1819; Paris: Delaunay, 1827), a full development of his "new principles"; and *Études sur l'économie Politique*, 2 vols. (Paris: Treuttel and Wurtz, 1837-38) which was an elaboration and historical illustration of his theories.
85. Sismondi, *Political Economy*, 116-117.
86. Sismondi, *Political Economy*, 51.
87. Sismondi, *Political Economy*, 49.
88. Sismondi, *Political Economy*, 27.
89. Though recognized, Sismondi is always evaluated only according to the methodological criteria of the author. Thus the meaning Schumpeter ascribes to the contributions of past economic thinkers in his monumental *History of Economic Analysis* (cited in note 14 above) always depends on what he, in line

with the current tradition, considers to be true economic analysis.

90. Sismondi, *Political Economy*, 42.

91. Sismondi, *Political Economy*, 115.

92. *Political Economy* (publishing information cited in note 84 above) is probably the best introduction to Sismondi, dedicated to Madame de Sismondi as an "attempt to make the character and opinions of her justly revered husband better known to the English reader."

93. See Sismondi's preface to the 1826 edition of *Nouveaux Principes*, reproduced in English in *Political Economy*, 113ff. (cited in note 84 above).

94. Herman Dooyeweerd, *A New Critique of Theoretical Thought*, 4 vols. (Philadelphia: Presbyterian & Reformed, 1955), 2:239.

95. It is the thesis of Miranda's admirable Bible study (see note 5 above) that in this respect there is no difference between the Old and the New Testaments. Everyone who does right is born of God (1 John 2:29). Whoever does not do right is not of God (1 John 3:10).

96. Levinas, *Het Menselijk Gelaat*, 45 (cited in note 4 above). When the Catholic bishop of San Juis in Argentina says,

> I pray to the Lord that all families might have the means of life according to their necessities and that wages would really be in line with the obligations which the maintenance of a home and the education of the children imply (*La Razon*, 3 November 1977),

he reverses things, asking for something prohibited by the actual economic policies against which he does not seem to protest at all. Levinas would say that God conceals himself from such a prayer. There cannot be any positive answers to prayers made to God as long as injustice prevails—injustice for which all the leaders of Argentina's society, not in the least the Catholic church, are responsible. To my knowledge the Bible does not know prayer without repentance.

97. There is a great resemblance between Jewish and authentic Calvinist thinking in this respect, as illustrated in the words of the sixteenth-century Dutch national hymn: "Dat ik toch vroom mag blijven, Uw dienaar 't allen stond; de tyrannie verdrijven die mij mijn hert doorwondt" (That I might remain faithful, your servant at all times; and drive out the tyranny that wounds my heart). The words *vroomheid* ("piety") and *gerechtigheid* ("justice"), with which the anthem ends, are used in the Bible to point to the same thing that Miranda observes: the pious ones are the ones who are upright and who do not break justice.

98. He is even responsible for the trespasses of his neighbor. Levinas refers to Ezekiel 3:16-21; 33:1-9.

99. One should not conclude from my short presentation of Levinas that his thought does not parallel the Calvinistic philosophy of Vollenhoven and Dooyeweerd. There might be terminological and theological differences, but I believe that basically they are very much related (as can also be said about Judaism and Calvinism).

Love, in Levinas, resembles Dooyeweerd's "love in temporal relationships" rather than love in its full religious sense (*agape*) which is not different from the biblical "righteousness." And the basic societal (and philosophical) meaning that Levinas attaches to the word "economic" does not necessarily interfere with Dooyeweerd's modal interpretation. There might again be a terminological difference, but, after all, the two philosophers have created their own languages. We could say that in Dooyeweerdian terms Levinas points to the human calling to open the anticipatory structure of the economic aspect in the direction of justice.

100. Though we live in a world that still adheres to the liberalistic methodology of economics, it can no longer find empirical justification for its adherences since Adam Smith's empirical observations no longer apply. Smith could still say: "Some..., perhaps, may sometimes decoy a weak customer to buy what he has not occasion for. This evil, however, is of too little importance to deserve the public attention" (Smith, *An Inquiry*, 1:323).

101. Levinas, *Het Menselijk Gelaat*, 119 (cited in note 4 above). My presentation in this section is based on the chapter, "Het ik en de Totaliteit," a translation of "Le Moi et la Totalité," *Revue de Metaphysique et de Morale* 59 (1954): 353-73. Also see "La Philosophie et l'idee de l'Infini," *Revue de Metaphysique et de Morale* 62 (1957): 2241-53, which is chapter 14 in *Het Menselijk Gelaat*, 136-51.

102. Levinas, *Het Menselijk Gelaat*, 216.

103. Sachs, 17 (cited in note 9 above).

104. See Carlos Rangel, *Del Buen Salvaje al Buen Revolutionario: Mitos y Realidades de America Latina* (Caracas: Monte Avila, 1976), who historically elaborates this thesis on Latin America.

105. See Levinas's essay on the state, "Liberte et Commandement," *Revue de Metaphysique et de Morale* 58 (1953): 264-72, which is chapter 12 in Levinas, *Het Menselijk Gelaat*, 96-107. The military does not recognize the absoluteness of the I. It only recognizes the absoluteness of the totality embracing the I and this inevitably means violence. The military, then, of necessity loses sight of the meaning of the Word as a command from beyond. Political expression is not a *discours* or a speaking but opposition and threat. By not recognizing politics, the military conceives of any opposition as absolute opposition to be destroyed in the name of totality. The essence of the state itself, its leading mode of being then is war. The army, as the bearer of force, is hence ontologically destined to represent the state (while the people have no independence as a separate category).

106. Abraham Kuyper, *De Verflauwing der Grenzen* (Amsterdam: J. A. Wormser, 1892).

107. See note 54 above.

108. Albert M. Wolters's excellent Glossary of Terms of Dooyeweerdian philosophy in L. Kalsbeek, *Contours of a Christian Philosophy: An Introduction to Herman Dooyeweerd's Thought*, ed. Bernard and Josina Zylstra (Toronto: Wedge, 1975), 353, describes "sphere universality" as

[t]he counterpart of modal sphere sovereignty. It is the principle that all the modalities are intimately connected with each other in an unbreakable coherence. Just as sphere sovereignty stresses the unique distinctiveness and irreducibility of the modal aspects, so sphere universality emphasizes that every one depends for its meaning on all the others, especially as evidenced by the analogies in the modal structure of each.

On the universality of the economic aspect see chapter 8 of my *Economie,* 58-67 (cited in note 45 above). For an earlier and shorter English version, see my *Special Drawing Rights and Development* (Leiden: Stenfert Kroese, 1971), 157-64.

109. See Roelf L. Haan, "Christelijk Ondernemerschap als Baanbreker voor het Geweten in een Kapitalistische Wereld en het Alibi van de Amro-bank," *Antirevolutionaire Staatskunde* 47 (1977): 71-95.

110. Niebuhr, 1:60 (cited in note 1 above).

111. See Herskowits, 455 (cited in note 45 above), translation mine. I apologize for translating from a book already translated.

112. Paulo Freire, *Cultural Action for Freedom* (London: Penguin Books, 1972), 10.

113. See the (anonymous) preliminary essay in Sismondi, *Political Economy* (cited in note 84 above) and 104-5: "...the labour market! Alas! by this term are we not too often reminded of the slave market?...The commodity which the working man brings is life; he must sell it or die." The same essay continues:

> Men must be taught (say the political economists) not to produce so much of a commodity as materially depreciates its value. Is it possible to make this abstract proposition intelligible to the minds of working men, and if it were, would it not be more impossible to make them act upon it? Was any man, high or low, ever deterred from marrying by the idea that he might rescue the value of the labour market? (105)

114. Eucken, 124 (cited in note 74 above).

115. Although Christian philosophy does not, in fact, permit us to do so, I have used the term "concept of man" because it is widely accepted. We could better say "idea," "vision," "view," even "belief," or "confession" of man.

116. Levinas, *Het Menselijk Gelaat,* 140 (cited in note 4 above).

117. R. Descartes, *Discurso del metodo,* trans. J. Rovira Armengol, 7th ed. (Buenos Aires: Aquilar, 1971), 35. (translation mine).

118. Descartes, 36.

119. Tawney, 90 (cited in note 51 above).

120. See the text at reference to note 112.

121. To borrow again from the Glossary of Terms in Kalsbeek (cited in note 108 above), "positivize" is a word coined to translate Dooyeweerd's Dutch term *positiveren* which means "to make positive." In jurisprudence "positive" means "what is actually valid in a given time or place." Positive law is the legislation that is in force in a given country at a particular time; it is contrasted with the principles of justice that require "positivization." The same applies to the principles of economics, ethics, and so on. Instead of "principles of economics" I used the phrase "economic normativity."

122. "Moments" is a Hegelian word referring to realities that have no existence of their own; they are only real as composing entities that are integrated (*aufgehoben*) in a whole that embraces them. (See annotation of editor Ad Peperzak in Levinas, *Het Menselijk Gelaat,* 245, cited in note 4 above.)

123. See Andre G. Frank, *Sociology of Development and Underdevelopment of Sociology* (Andover, Mass.: Modular, 1967), 15-16:

Parsons, Hoselitz, and recent sociological theorists in general (in confining [their] attention to the arithmetic sense of social roles in general and...forgetting about the social, political and economic structure of a particular society under study) not only modify Marx but also depart from Weber. Parsons' structuralism and holism is confined to the analysis of a wholly abstract model of any and all real or imaginary societies and not with the study of any existing real society.

124. Charles Birch, "Creation, Technology and Human Survival: Called to Replenish the Earth," *The Ecumenical Review* 28 (1976): 76.
125. This is, of course, not a new problem at all. See Galeano about the ecological disaster of colonialism (cited in note 68 above).
126. On the logical untenability of an economic principle based on the scarcity hypothesis, see my *Economie*, 46-58 (cited in note 45 above).
127. The Marxist concept of alienation offers an important point of communication with Christians. It is, in the last analysis, sustainable only on the basis of the Word Revelation.
128. Sismondi, *Political Economy*, 110 (cited in note 84 above).
129. In its view of the Other, racism is similar to capitalism. When whites refer to a "negro woman" or "an Indian" instead of to a woman or a man, they treat the individual as one of a kind, just as if speaking about a cat or a horse. But the other always has an absolutely unique face which is, in the terms of Levinas, the expression of his absolute being.
130. Sachs, 11 (cited in note 9 above).
131. Dooyeweerd, *A New Critique*, 1:555 (cited in note 94 above).

The capital debate and the economic aspect of reality
Bas Kee

Introduction

The science of economics studies reality from the economic point of view. In other words, the science of economics sets apart the economic aspect of reality and disregards other aspects in the process. Historically, this separation, which we call "abstraction," occurred not automatically but through a long period of struggle. In fact, economics has existed as an independent science for no more than two hundred years. The continued existence of economics in its own right has never been a matter of course, and economists have constantly been forced to cultivate the abstraction of an economic point of view.

Within the science of economics a precarious balance exists between two tendencies. There exists, on the one hand, the risk and the temptation to abandon the economic point of view. This is the case with authors who deny the independence of economics and allow it to merge with sciences like sociology, psychology, and mathematics. This step often is taken after one of these sciences is given an ancillary function within economic thought.

On the other hand, there exists the risk and temptation to *isolate* the point of view that has been set apart, that is, to exaggerate the abstraction until it becomes a viewpoint turned in upon itself. The abstraction causes an isolation of the economic aspect that sharply severs it from the other aspects of reality. The result is a formal theory drained of content that must then be filled with noneconomic data. Although this procedure aims at preserving economics as a science, it surreptitiously reduces the economic point of view to another point of view.

These introductory thoughts are a variation on the philosophy of Herman Dooyeweerd and, in particular, on his theory of the modalities. According to Dooyeweerd it is possible to distinguish a series of irreducible aspects or modalities of reality, including the economic aspect. That these aspects can be distinguished is not a theoretical a priori but a fundamental hypothesis for theoretical work.

In this analysis I will accept this hypothesis. Proceeding from it, I intend to discuss a thorny problem in economics. My discussion will produce two results: in the first place, it will cast light on the situation of economics today (the diagnosis); and in the second place, it will provide the inspiration and point of departure required to change this situation (the therapy).

The economic problem I have in mind is the "Capital Debate," also referred to as the "Cambridge-Cambridge Controversy." To both parties I pose this question: To what extent do you analyze production, exchange, and distribution from the economic point of view? By "economic point of view" or "economic aspect" I shall mean the economic value dimension of phenomena as expressed in prices.

I shall demonstrate that both parties isolate the economic point of view and that, consequently, they must revert to extraneous "physical" entities to explain the economic value dimension. This reduction not only causes tensions within the economic theories but even leads to a crisis within economic thought.

I will first outline what is at stake in the Capital Debate and indicate my analyses of this debate. Secondly, I will discuss the neoclassical theory as it has been criticized. At the end of the exposition I will evaluate this criticism. Thirdly, I will critically discuss the nature of the Cambridge (England) theory. Finally, I intend to delineate the situation of economics today and to indicate to what extent that situation can be resolved.

The capital debate

In his interesting book, *The Cambridge Revolution: Success or Failure?* Mark Blaug indicates what is at stake in the confrontation between the schools of Cambridge, England (or the post-Keynesians) and Cambridge, Massachusetts (or the neoclassicists). He points out that the post-Keynesians (the followers of Piero Sraffa) defend the proposition that "the wage-profit relationship in an economy can be whatever we would like it to be: economic forces do not limit the possibilities of an income policy."[1] The neoclassical theory of distributive shares opposes this thesis; according to the theory of marginal productivity, the operation of the market regulates income distribution, given the production techniques and the supply of production factors.

According to the post-Keynesians, the neoclassical theory leaves property relations out of the picture. The neoclassical theory admits this criticism; it does not consider social classes as explanatory variables. Introducing such variables would mean succumbing to the temptation to find simple theoretical answers to sociologically motivated questions.[2] According to the post-Keynesians, the fatal mistake of the neoclassicists is that they regard payments on the factor market (wages, profit, interest) as exchange, just like payments on the commodity market. Against this, neoclassicists claim that they still have their hands full with the task of "exposing the fallacy that the pricing of inputs is somehow a quite different economic problem from the pricing of output."[3] In this controversy the post-Keynesians level immanent criticism at the neoclassicists, asking them to capitulate. So far, however, they have not succeeded in spite of the fact that the neoclassicists have conceded the criticism in part.

What is the origin of this rivalry? And why has no conclusion been reached that is definitive and satisfactory to both parties? The episode threatens to become another sterile quarrel in economics, serving to reinforce the aversion of economists toward methodology and philosophy and toward reflection on their own activities. But just as in the case of earlier debates on method, economics in all its facets is at stake. There is therefore every reason within economics for philosophical reflection on, say, the relation between macroeconomics and microeconomics, the status of an economic law, causality, the position of time in the analysis, the relation between the special sciences, and the question of whether or not economic theory is normative in character. I shall limit our inquiry to the manner in which each party treats the economic aspect. Instead of a clash of methods, I would rather speak of a "battle for the scope of the economic aspect." By "scope of the aspect" I mean that which is regarded as determinable within the economic system. What does the economic system encompass? The controversy focuses on how the production of goods and services should be seen within the economic system.

Neoclassical theory

Characteristics. The fundamental category of the neoclassical view is the notion of scarcity. Price is regarded as the index of the scarcity of a commodity. That scarcity is basic is clearly revealed in the simple case of the original exchange (or the two-sided exchange). In original exchange, individual preferences and amounts of objects desired are *given*. The relation between preferences and stocks determines the marginal utilities awarded to the various goods by individuals, and the price in the exchange is explained by these marginal utilities. In my opinion this means that price, as a part of the economic value dimension, is identified with the relation between marginal utilities, which is to say that scarcity is the relation between preferences and the available amounts. But if the production of goods is included in the analysis, we can no longer speak of given amounts of the objects desired. Production tends to eliminate the scarcity of commodities. This tendency can only be prevented by placing the construction of scarce, original pro-duction factors behind consumptive goods. Price can then be maintained as an index of the scarcity of the available produc-tion factors in relation to individual preferences.

But the introduction of the production of goods leads to a pair of problems. First, individual preferences are concerned with consumption goods. An indirect relationship between consumption goods and production factors can now be con-structed by regarding consumption goods as the embodiment of productive services supplied by production factors. This link requires that we deduce the value of productive services from the value of the consumption goods—a value that itself is an expression of preferences. This is the problem of "imputa-tion," which we will not consider further.

Second, since the value of productive services is deduced, it follows that production itself can have no influence on the value of consumption goods. Production must be neutral with respect to value. This thesis leads to an important question: How is this neutrality of production with respect to value formulated in theory since, theoretically, production should have an economic significance?

To find its economic significance, the neoclassical school turns to production as a mechanism for allocating the intertem-poral stream of consumption goods. In other words, it conceives of production as the means by which utilities may be preserved up to the time of consumption. The neutrality of production with regard to the aim—that is, production's neutrality with respect to value—is then attained by identifying economic significance with the technical significance of production—that is, with the purely material transformation of given amounts of scarce resources into consumption goods.[4]

Now, this identification results in two further identifications: capital in the sense of postponed consumption becomes identical to capital in the sense of "produced means of production"; and the rate of profit represents both the relative scarcity of capital (as the possibility of postponing consumption) and the technical productivity of the capital factor. These deduced identifications are most clearly expressed in the so-called neoclassical parable, a one-commodity model in which identifications become tangible in physical entities. In this model capital in the sense of postponed consumption corresponds directly to the "produced means of production," and the rate of profit corresponds to the marginal product of capital.

The post-Keynesian criticism. On the basis of the neoclassical parable, Geoffrey Harcourt establishes four relations that have given rise to the capital debate.[5] The post-Keynesians aim the arrows of their immanent criticism at the deduction of these four relations. The relations are: first, an association between lower rates of profit and higher values of capital per person employed; second, an association between lower rates of profit and higher capital output ratios; third, an association between lower rates of profit and higher sustainable steady states of consumption per head. This leads to the conclusion (and fourth relation) that under competitive conditions the distribution of income between profit receivers and wage earners can be explained by a knowledge of marginal products and factor supplies.[6]

Post-Keynesians attack the neoclassical assumption of the homogeneity of capital in the sense of the produced means of production. Cambridge, England, claims that capital in that sense must be heterogeneous. If it is made homogeneous, two difficulties arise: first, the heterogeneous composition of capital can only be made homogeneous by means of prices. But this procedure presupposes the use of the rate of profit, which, in turn, must be explained by means of the production function. This is a circular argument that undermines the first-mentioned relationship. But the ratio of capital to labor cannot be regarded as a necessarily inverse function of the profit rate. The second problem is that of the Wicksell effect, namely, capital reversal and reswitching of techniques, whereby techniques cannot be uniquely ordered according to the rate of profit. The neoclassical production function is based on the assumption that such a unique ordering exists. This problem implies the fall of the second and third relations.

The neoclassicists have been forced to admit that no unique relation exists between the wage-profit relationship and the capital-labor ratio in production. The post-Keynesians have concluded that the theory of income distribution based on marginal productivity cannot be maintained and, furthermore, that distribution within the "exchange system" cannot be determined. The neoclassicists, however, refuse to concur with this conclusion.[7]

It strikes me that the debate has arrived at an impasse at this point. This is regrettable because the discussion involves all the important problems of economic philosophy.

The insufficiency of the Cambridge criticism. Can we make any progress in our analysis of the confrontation if we ask why the criticism leveled by the post-Keynesians has not been as compelling as was expected?

If no more than the heterogeneity of capital goods were involved, the resistance of the neoclassicists would be understandable. After all, could the purely numerical difference between one or more capital goods have such far-reaching consequences? Furthermore, Blaug, among others, objects that the same problem of heterogeneity exists in the cases of labor and output, so that the more obvious procedure would be to abandon the aggregate, macroeconomic approach rather than join the ranks of the post-Keynesians who treat labor as homogeneous.[8]

It could be said that the post-Keynesian criticism does not strike the neoclassical theory at the core. It approaches the heart of the matter insofar as it aims to undermine scarcity as the fundamental economic category.[9] But the criticism fails because the post-Keynesians' own fundamental category—pro-

duction—severely limits the effectiveness of the post-Keynesian criticism of the one-commodity model.

I shall elucidate the insufficiency of the post-Keynesian
criticism. In the course of his discussion, Edward Nell formu-
lates the fundamental trait of neoclassical thought precisely:
"that a simple monotonic relationship can be found, which
holds *independently of prices*, between the value of a set of capital
goods and the general rate of return."[10] But Nell does not
mention the essential difficulty. The independence of prices
seems possible in the one-commodity model. However, the
model is misleading for it appears that the absence of differences between capital goods (and thus also the absence of
relative differences in price) leaves us with nothing but the net
productivity of capital, physically defined. As a result, we seem
to have moved out of the value dimension as such. The productivity of this "physically defined" capital is then identified with
the productivity of capital seen from the economic point of
view. This shifting identification confronts us with the essential
difficulty of the model.

If we acknowledge an economic aspect in reality, then we
must distinguish it from the other aspects *within the one-commodity model*, as with any other model. The coincidence of the
price of the capital good and currency (the *numeraire*) in the
one-commodity model creates the illusion that the economic
aspect is eclipsed, reappearing only in the presence of more
capital goods. In fact, however, the economic aspect is eclipsed
by the postulation of a one-to-one relationship between the
economic sphere and the production sphere as seen from the
technical point of view.[11] The post-Keynesian criticism demonstrates that this one-to-one relationship cannot be maintained
in view of the above-mentioned problems. Interest and profit,
for example, cannot be linked to something like "physical
capital" because they are indigenous to the original economic
dimension.

The purpose of the criticism by Cambridge, England, as we
shall see, is to grant the problem of distribution a new place in
economic theory. But the criticism can also be understood as
criticism against the attempt to reduce the economic aspect. We
might even say that the post-Keynesian criticism supports the
hypothesis that reality exhibits an irreducible economic aspect
—an aspect that can be damaged by attempts at reduction. In

fact, it seems that the contradictions arising from such attempts so greatly disturb the precarious balance existing within the economic aspect today, that we could speak of a crisis in economic thought. Ontological necessity will not resolve this crisis; economists themselves are responsible for abstracting the economic aspect.

The post-Keynesian theory
Characteristics. What the post-Keynesian school of thought advocates can be determined better by its intentions than by its results. Its results are not as yet canonized like those of the neoclassical theory, especially as far as the theory of distribution is concerned. Nevertheless, we can clearly discern a new direction in economics; we hear the ring of a new alternative paradigm.[12] The novelty emerges most clearly from the often repeated statement that the problem of distribution should occupy a central position in economic theory. If we were to establish a succession of central problems in the history of economic thought, the post-Keynesian emphasis on distribution forms a new element in the series, next to the problem of the accumulation of capital in classical thought, the problem of allocation in neoclassical thought, and the problem of employment in John Maynard Keynes. True, the argument for the central significance of distribution is supported by an appeal to classical thinkers, Ricardo in particular; for this reason there is an inclination to speak of "political economy" instead of "economics."[13]   But this appeal is no more than relative. The post-Keynesian desire to award the problem of distribution a central position has elicited a reaction against neoclassical theory. The thrust of the reaction is that the problem of distribution must first be disengaged from the context in which neoclassical theory has placed it. Ultimately, however, it seems that the intention is to consider the problem of distribution, in all its aspects, within the science of political economy alone.

The significance of Sraffa's analysis. Neoclassical theory links distribution—as part of the process of exchange—to production in the technical sense, via the pricing of production services. Sraffa's analysis destroys this link by coupling production with the pricing of commodities to be reproduced.[14] In his theory, prices are primarily determined by conditions of production. In the case of production without surplus, the determining factor is the necessity of reproduction, given the technical circumstances:

> There is a unique set of exchange-values which if adopted by the market restores the original distribution of the products [i.e., among the industries], and makes it possible for the process to be repeated; such values spring directly from the methods of production.[15]

Only when a production system generates more than is necessary for reproduction does the problem of distribution arise in connection with surplus. The social problem of distribution emerges when wage goods are no longer regarded as part of the "basic goods" (that is, goods involved in the process of reproduction). Prices are then determined by the necessity of reproduction and the (given) distribution.

Clearly, in this view distribution cannot be regarded as a process of pricing. After all, pricing here concerns both produced and reproducible goods. Distribution and pricing have become distinct but not separate from one another since a change in distribution leads to a change in prices.

The link forged between production and exchange in Sraffa's analysis "liberates" distribution from exchange relations. However, two questions immediately arise. First, can production and exchange be so closely linked? Or, to pose this differently, is the economic aspect kept sufficiently distinct from the technical aspect? Second, since distribution exerts an influence on prices, distribution must be related to exchange. Is it possible to relate these without affecting the previously constructed relation between production and exchange? In discussing these two questions we shall make use of Edward Nell's thoughts on the matter.

Production and exchange. According to Nell, production or "reproduction" is the fundamental category of economic thought.

> The material conditions for the continued existence of a social system provide necessary criteria of application for economic terms...the concept of "production" is to occur

essentially in any analysis of our economic system, in that no theory is an economic theory unless it involves production.[16]

This is then related to the concept of exchange:

[T]he Ricardian concept of exchange is irrevocably tied to the technological characteristics of the good involved; there is no exchange unless both items traded have a production equation.[17]

To Nell it is essential that production and exchange be interconnected because only in this way can distribution be kept apart from exchange relations. If exchange is linked to production in the technical sense, payments on the factor market (profit, interest, wages) cannot be regarded as prices in an exchange. Nell attempts to prove the necessity of the link between exchange and production by demonstrating that the use of the one-commodity model is impossible given the world in which we live. For him there are always at least two distinguishable activities:

[1] supporting and replacing a working population, or family life, and [2] producing food, each of which depends on the other. An exchange rate is defined between them.... In short: labour and food are exchanged; the price in the exchange is the "real wage."[18]

But it remains to be seen whether this kind of defense against the one-commodity model is tenable. In the first place, we can note that the distinction between the two production actitivies, whereby the idea of production at the same time implies the idea of exchange, is in fact nothing but a description of the relation between a person and nature. This description conceives of a person's *cultivation* of nature (that is, production) to also be an act of *exchange* between person and nature. Production and exchange are identified. This is a postulate, not an unavoidable deduction about the relationship between production and exchange.

In the second place, it may be said that the identification of production and exchange actually contradicts Nell's intention.

The link that Nell forges between production and exchange is acceptable only if a production equation is awarded to the labor force, that is, the labor force as the product of food. And the consequence of this, as Nell admits in so many words, is that wage reveals itself as price (exchange rate), so that it becomes part of the process of exchange. Nell claims that distribution is not a process of exchange; however, then, wage is not included in distribution which runs counter to Nell's intention.

To recapitulate: post-Keynesian economics has entangled itself in a problem. With respect to relations between production, exchange, and distribution, distribution is made independent by linking production to exchange. But there is now a dilemma: if the point of departure is production (with which exchange is necessarily connected), wage is not an element in the distribution problem. Therefore, it is only possible to "liberate" one part of the distribution problem. If, however, the point of departure is the distribution problem, as in Sraffa's analysis, one arrives at a one-commodity world in which the necessary link between production and exchange is absent.[19] Consequently, an "orderly relation" between production and exchange must be postulated, much as in neoclassical economic thought.

In my discussion of the neoclassical position I have already pointed out that Nell does not mention the essential difficulty of the one-commodity model. The reason now becomes clear. His criticisms are preoccupied with denying the existence of the one-commodity world. In its stead he places another extremely simplified situation. His difficulties flow from the same source as those of the neoclassicists. The economic aspect cannot be based on and characterized by a *situation*. When this is attempted, the economic aspect is reduced and subverted.

Distribution and exchange. For the post-Keynesians, one of their most important criticisms against neoclassical theory is that, next to conditions of production, distribution is the factor determining the prices of commodities. Thus, distribution occurs via the market, although distribution is not a process of exchange.[20] How is this expressed theoretically? Is it possible to link the relation between production and exchange to the relation between distribution and exchange?

At this point the post-Keynesians become embarrassed, to

put it mildly. Of the Sraffa analysis (that is, of the link between production and exchange by which distribution is assumed as given), D. M. Nuti makes the following remark: "Unfortunately, however, there is no simple way of closing his system, i.e., of determining which point of the wage-profit relation is actually reached and how in any economy."[21]

This difficulty can be sketched further. Taking distribution as the point of departure implies a struggle for surplus, which means that the market will display features typical of this struggle. Nell, in fact, remarks that "the marketplace is the arena for the exercise of economic power, the battlefield in which the division of spoils...is settled."[22] But when production is the point of departure, then the analysis proceeds as follows: given the production equations and the demand for reproduction, and given the wage share and the necessity of a uniform rate of profit, prices and the rate of profit are determined simultaneously. Prices and the rate of profit are the result of a mathematical calculation. Nell adds that he places the accent on "the interlocking possibilities and necessities rather than on motives, plans, and information."[23] In this analysis the struggle for distribution is not discernible.

The analysis continually moves on two levels: (1) real prices and (2) nominal prices. Post-Keynesians regard progress in this matter as a concern for the future.[24] But it is doubtful whether this attitude can be maintained because—as in the case of neoclassical thought—the question concerns the relationship between a world lying behind the economic value dimension and the dimension itself.

Conclusion

Diagnosis and therapy on the basis of the philosophy of Dooyeweerd. In his treatise on the law spheres Dooyeweerd makes the following remark: "The special theoretical antinomy must consequently be due to a subjective violation of the modal sovereignty of the different law-spheres by theoretical thought."[25] My intention in the argument above was to demonstrate that both the neoclassicists and the post-Keynesians are guilty of such a "subjective violation." Both schools of thought entangle themselves in difficulties at the point where production is conceived in a technical rather than economic sense. These difficulties touch the internal unity of economic theory, namely, the unity of production, exchange, and distribution. This is the case with economists who wish to maintain economics as an independent science. But the internal unity of economic theory exists only by virtue of the economic aspect or the economic point of view. When due consideration is not given to the modal sovereignty of the economic aspect, internal unity is violated.

The background to this inability (rather than unwillingness) to maintain the economic point of view in economic theory is the absence of a clear distinction between the law side and subject side of reality. When this distinction is not made, the law obtaining for the subject is found in the subject itself. In the case under discussion this shift is possible only when phenomena of a noneconomic nature are regarded as determining the economic function of facts and events. The shift is unavoidable, because "generally speaking, knowledge of the subject is never separate from knowledge of the law and [because] in the case of science and philosophy the subject can only be known through the law obtaining for it."[26]

In both neoclassical and post-Keynesian theories the lawfulness of economic phenomena originates from phenomena of a noneconomic nature. The meaning of economics as such is therefore also found elsewhere. For the neoclassicists it is found in consumption; for the post-Keynesians in production. Thus, psychological and physiological preferences on the one hand and technical production on the other supply the basis for exchange as an economic phenomenon. Both neoclassical and post-Keynesian economic thought upset the already precarious balance characterizing the treatment of the economic point of view. Each school searches for the law of the economic modality in a subject that lacks economic qualification. Although the patterns of thought of both schools are very similar, I shall now proceed to indicate a difference between them by using the philosophical distinction between *subject* and *object*.

Neoclassical theory takes the active subject as the point of departure of its analysis. It assumes that this subject possesses a rationality enabling it to investigate the world around it with a view to the structural possibilities within which the rational subject might act, that is, with a view to how it might achieve an optimal adaption to the given world: the allocation of scarce means.

A number of neoclassical authors claim that their theory explains and predicts economic events. So far, however, the results have not been impressive. This is because neoclassical theory assumes the rationality of the subject. Because subjects often do not act in accordance with rationality, neoclassical theory has a normative, not an explanatory, character. Or, if the term "normative" is too heavily charged, we can at least say that it is primarily a theory of procedures. This formulation reveals the continued presence of the normative character of the economic aspect, which even a reduction cannot eliminate.

Post-Keynesian analysis departs from the object or from the world as it lies at the disposal, direction, and control of the subject. Nell says of the new paradigm that its purpose—contrary to that of the neoclassical theory—is not

> the decision making, the prediction of the behaviour of what will occur. The new vision concerns itself with an analysis of what keeps the economy going, what is thought to happen in the economy, and hence: what the reason is for its downfall, and what causes it to develop into an economic system of a different nature.[27]

Here, too, normativity is in play. Now, however, it stands not within the economic process but over against it. "The new paradigm is intended precisely as political economy, as indicating the way for criticism of the capitalistic socio-economic system."[28] In both of the economic theories discussed above, we miss exactly that element that could have rendered them explanatory—the theoretical consideration of the normativity that binds acting subjects. From this diagnosis, this must clearly be our therapy: we must realize that economics is a science of an aspect and put this realization into practice.

For example, in elaborating the diagnosis, we could point out to economists that the necessity of delimiting their field of study should not force them to assume a nonreciprocal relation between factors when considering the influence of noneconomic factors on economic factors. An essential part of their task is to analyze the influence exerted by economic factors on noneconomic factors. When the term "data" is used in economic theory, it refers to the explanatory factors in a given economic problem. However, data must never function as a criteria for delimiting economic phenomena. The economic point of view requires the economists to ask repeatedly about the economic significance of each phenomenon that confronts them.

The relevance of Christian studies. What is the relevance of this diagnosis and the therapy provisionally indicated? Without underestimating the significance of Dooyeweerd's philosophy, I must conclude it contains no clear consequences for economics. In the tradition of Reformed philosophy that has taken shape after Dooyeweerd, economics has received due attention and much criticism. Yet I can hardly say that these results have penetrated the daily work of the economists. Not that Reformed philosophy has no cultural force; but day-to-day work has only been affected to a limited degree.

Perhaps I apply philosophy to the day-to-day work of economists too hastily. After all, philosophical reflection is stimulated by scientific imagination and intuition, and this process can be made theoretically explicit only in part. Should we not be content to appeal to the economists from within the sphere of philosophy, bringing the appeal as close to them as possible by means of economic philosophy?

To me this would be a very disappointing conclusion, especially in light of the hopes that have been raised by our studies. By following antinomies as I have done, the theoretical thought of immanence philosophy can be caught violating boundaries. This study of antinomies raises hopes for a new and different philosophical beginning. However, this kind of diagnosis so severely condemns current economics that it cuts us off from the tradition of economic thought, thereby crippling, rather than inspiring, scientific activity. In other words, the criticism as it is formulated in terms of Dooyeweerd's philosophy draws too heavily on the existence of economics as such.

But after realizing fully that the day-to-day work of the economists has as yet been insufficiently affected, I now wish to answer a possible denial of the significance of economic philosophy. Some would say that this Dooyeweerdian diagnosis threatens to turn against the philosophy of economics in two ways. In the first place, there is the possibility that when the method of antinomy is applied consistently the philosophy of economics may be forced to condemn and reject all economic theory on the grounds of its failure to recognize the irreducibility of the economic aspect. It thus leaves the economists with empty hands and, if this is the result, then the whole undertaking of economic philosophy is superfluous. Could we not have predicted from the outset that economic theory in Western culture would meet with such a condemnation?

It seems to me that this conclusion should be rejected. Is it not preferable to understand an analysis of antinomies as the discovery of historical disclosures and petrifications of the economic aspect? What nuances of economic meaning have been revealed in the course of history? What references derived from economic meaning have been examined theoretically? Is it possible to discover new nuances of economic meaning, or should we reappropriate them from the past? If we accept this understanding of a Dooyeweerdian diagnosis of antinomies, there is no reason to condemn the history of economic thought exclusively on the grounds of its compromising background in immanence philosophy, the mistakes of the past notwithstanding.

In the second place, it seems to me that recent Reformed philosophy and Dooyeweerdian diagnosis suggests that the economic aspect will, regardless of economic philosophy, automatically assert itself, especially in guaranteeing the possibility and the existence of economics in a process of disclosure. We need not immediately deny this suggestion. But it is equally important to point out that the meaning of the economic aspect is vulnerable and that it can be deformed and suppressed by people. The philosophy of economics can reveal a glimpse of this truth, demonstrating thereby the primary responsibility of the economists for cultivating the economic point of view. For in their theoretical labor they are personally responsible for unfolding the economic aspect of reality.

Notes
1. Mark Blaug, *The Cambridge Revolution: Success or Failure?* (London: Institute of Economic Affairs, 1975), 30.
2. Blaug, 59-60.
3. Blaug, 59.
4. This identification is given its theoretical formulation in the form of the "production formula." To the neoclassicists this is an essential concept. In "Rejoinder: Agreements, Disagreements, Doubts, and the Case of Induced Harrod- Neutral Technical Change," *Review of Economics and Statistics* (No-

vember 1966): 444-45, Paul Samuelson so strikingly says: "Until the laws of thermodynamics are   repealed, I shall continue to relate output to input — i.e., to believe in production functions." In his *On the Theory and Measurement of Technological Change* (Cambridge, Eng.: Cambridge University Press, 1966), 9, 10, Murray Brown then says:

> As such, the production function ideally embodies no economic magnitudes such as prices or interest rates....Who is responsible for constructing a firm production function as we have defined it? ...[I]t is the economist who makes the transformation from the physical-technical properties of production to the production function he requires in his analysis.

5. Geoffrey Harcourt, *Some Cambridge Controversies in the Theory of Capital* (Cambridge, Eng.: Cambridge University Press, 1972), 122.
6. Charles Ferguson outlines the matter in a similar fashion as Harcourt in *The Neoclassical Theory of Production and Distribution* (Cambridge, Eng.: Cambridge University Press, 1969), 250:

> The essential features of the neoclassical model developed above are the assumptions of continuous, linearly homogeneous production functions and of a single homogeneous capital good. This model, and certain more realistic ones involving heterogeneous capital goods, yield, when applied to capital theory, the following conclusion: there is an inverse relation between the rate of interest and the wage rate; graphically, the relation usually exhibits concavity from above. A further generalization can be stated: if the capital-labor ratio varies directly with the wage rate of interest ratio, the wage rate, net national product per worker, and the permanently sustainable consumption stream will all vary inversely with the rate of interest.

7. See, for example, Yew-Kwang Ng in his article, "The Neoclassical and the Neo-Marxist-Keynesian Theory of Income Distribution: A Non-Cambridge Contribution to the Cambridge Controversy in Capital," *Australian Economic Papers* 13 (June 1974): 127. He says:

> The neo-Marxist-Keynesians have made a significant contribution in revealing the negative Wicksell effects which eliminate the logical necessity of the said inverse monotonic relationship. But I think that they claim too much in trying to condemn the marginal productivity theory....The fact remains that, if profit maximization and competition are assumed, factor price must equal its marginal productivity, irrespective of whether we have an inverse monotonic relationship between the value or capital and its marginal productivity."

Another example is Robert Solo in "On the Rate of Return: Reply to Pasinetti," *Economic Journal* 80 (June 1970): 427-28, who says:

> I have some good news and some bad news for Professor Pasinetti. The

bad news is that he will have to reconcile himself to the equality of the interest rate and the rate of return, because it is so. This does mean that there is an important relation between the competitive equilibrium interest rate and the technical possibilities of the economy. The good news is that this is only part of an explanation and no part of a "justification" of the rate of profit. And nobody is trying to slip over on him a theory according to which the rate of profit "is higher or lower according to whether the existing quantity of capital is lower or higher, and as such represents a general technical property of the existing quantity of capital." That is just what neoclassical capital theory in its full generality can do without.

8. Blaug, 8,10 (cited in note 1 above).
9. It seems to us that both parties unduly accent either the homogeneity or heterogeneity of capital. The neoclassicists regard the matter as a problem of aggregation, and in this respect they defend themselves by pointing out to the post- Keynesians that they, too, are still confronted with the problem. In their article entitled "The Wicksell Effects in Wicksell and in Modern Capital Theory," *History of Political Economy* 3 (Fall 1971): 367, Charles Ferguson and Donald Hooks state that "the assumption of homogeneous labor is as heroic as the assumption of homogeneous capital. Perhaps the Cambridge Critics have not mentioned this point because their 'alternative theory' would then collapse."
      In the eyes of the post-Keynesians the matter involves more than a problem of aggregation alone. Thus J. A. Kregel writes in *The Reconstruction of Political Economy* (New York: Wiley, 1973), 93:

> One must also be careful to note that this problem concerning the quantity of capital is not unique to capital goods, but applies to all produced output in the system....[T]he result not only challenges the neoclassical analysis of capital, but the entire theory of prices, in terms of supply and demand, utilized in the neoclassical economic theory.

But precisely at this point the discussion arrives at an impasse because the problem of aggregation was chosen as the access to the problem.
10. Charles Ferguson and Edward Nell, "Two Review Articles on Two Books on the Theory of Income Distribution," *Journal of Economic Literature* 10 (June 1972): 448.
Harry Gordon Johnson emerges as another fervent defender of the neoclassical theory. In *The Theory of Income Distribution* (London: Gray-Mills, 1973), 127, he   discusses the phenomenon of reswitching and also arrives at a dimension extraneous to and independent of prices:

> We would like to be able to assume a monotonically declining relationship between the rate of return on capital and its values, parallel to the assumption of a declining marginal product of capital as its physical quantity increases relative to the quantity of original factors of production, because we view accumulation of capital as involving foregoing the consumption of current goods and services.

11. See Ferguson, *Neoclassical Theory*, 257 (cited in note 6 above). He says that the neoclassical theory establishes an orderly relation between the physical realm of production and the commodity and factor markets. "In particular, we can say that the lower the ratio of interest, the greater the capital intensity of production. All other neoclassical results follow immediately from this simple relation."

12. See J. A. Kregel and Alfred Eichner, "An Essay on Post-Keynesian Theory," *Journal of Economic Literature* 13 (December 1975): 257: "[I]mplicit...is the view that post-Keynesian theory has the potential for becoming a comprehensive, positive alternative to the prevailing neoclassical paradigm."

13. Kregel, *Reconstruction* xv (cited in note 9 above):

> "It would seem more appropriate to link Keynes' own theory with the long-period theory of the classical political economists...a Reconstruction of Political Economy in the sense of the Classics....The relation of post-Keynesian theory to the classical is quickly seen from the emphasis that this theory places on social relations, the distribution of income and the analysis of an economy that changes and grows over time.

14. In connection with the value of Sraffa's analysis, Joan Robinson and John Eatwell remark in *An Introduction to Modern Economics* (Maidenhead, Berkshire: McGraw-Hill, 1973), 184,187:

> The point of Sraffa's argument was to show that the "value of a stock of capital," in general, has no meaning independently of the distribution of net product between wages and profits; so that there is no meaning in the idea that the rate of profit is determined by the "marginal product of capital." ...Sraffa's analysis of the distribution of the product of industry between wages and profits...provides the indispensable framework for an understanding of the problem of distribution in a private-enterprise economy.

15. Piero Sraffa, *Production of Commodities by Means of Commodities* (Cambridge, Eng.: Cambridge University Press, 1960), 3.

16. Edward Nell and Martin Hollis, *Rational Economic Man* (New York: Cambridge University Press, 1975), 189, 254.

17. Edward Nell, "Theories of Growth and Theories of Value," in *Capital and Growth*, ed. Geoffrey Harcourt and N. F. Laing (Hammondsworth: Penguin Books, 1971), 207.

18. Nell and Hollis, 248.

19. Blaug, 38 (cited in note 1 above).

20. Nell and Hollis, 254.

21. D. M. Nuti, "'Vulgar Economy' in the Theory of Income Distribution," in *A Critique of Economic Theory*, ed. E. K. Hunt and Jesse Schwartz (Baltimore: Penguin Books, 1972), 226.

22. Nell and Hollis, 210.

23. Nell and Hollis, 208.

24. In *Theories of Value and Distribution since Adam Smith* (Cambridge, Eng.: Cambridge University Press, 1973), 272, Maurice Dobb states:

One can only conclude, at the time of writing, that such alternative explanations of distribution in our twentieth-century world are *sub judice* in current economic discussion, and that discussion (or even elaboration) of them has proceeded insufficiently far as yet to make final judgment possible, still less to speak of a consensus. Unsatisfactory this may be as a concluding note; nonetheless it would appear unavoidable.

25. Herman Dooyeweerd, *A New Critique of Theoretical Thought*, 4 vols., (Philadelphia: Presbyterian & Reformed, 1953-58), 2:45.
26. Hendrik van Riessen, "Over de Betekenis van de Wetsidee in de Wijsbegeerte," *Philosophia reformata* 39 (1965): 163.
27. Edward Nell, "De Herleving van de Politieke Economie," in *De Armoede van de Ekonomiese Wetenschap* (Nijmegen: Bundel, 1975), 97.
28. Nell, "De Herleving," 106.

A Christian critique of neoclassical welfare economics
George N. Monsma, Jr.

Introduction

This paper deals with "neoclassical welfare economics." I use this term to signify the avowedly normative or prescriptive branch of modern economic theory as practiced by mainstream economists in the West (particularly by English-speaking economists). This main or "orthodox" stream of economic thinking is often called "neoclassical." I am using the term in a broad sense, including in it, for example, both Keynesians and Monetarists but excluding such critics of basic neoclassical presuppositions as the Marxists. And in the term "neoclassical welfare economics," I include not only the highly theoretical and abstract welfare economics but also its applications to actual situations, that is, its use in evaluating particular economic institutions and actions.

A common key element in this broad range of welfare economics is the acceptance of the standard of "Pareto optimality" (often called "economic efficiency") as a major, if not the only, standard for evaluating various situations and actions. A Pareto optimum or economically efficient situation is "a position from which it is not possible...to make anyone better off, without making at least one person worse off."[1] This is not a situation unique to any one economy; rather there are many such positions or situations, each differing in their distributions of welfare. This standard for an "optimum" is generally extended to changes between "nonoptimal" positions by saying that position A is better than position B if at least one person is better off in A than in B and no one is worse off. What I am calling neoclassical welfare economics thus includes the highly abstract Hicks/Kaldor/Scitovsky "new welfare economics" and the Bergson/Samuelson "social welfare function" approach (insofar as the social welfare function is assumed to be a positive function of each individual's utility—a common assumption) as well as most economists' applied work in areas such as cost-benefit analysis, "optimal" taxes, tariffs, regulated-utility prices, "efficient" treatment of external effects (such as pollution), and evaluations of various types of market structure (e.g., competitive or monopolistic).

This is a very broad area to cover in a single paper, but the fact that these analyses have certain key common features, such as the acceptance of the Pareto criterion, makes a general critique possible. Of course, within this wide spectrum of work some studies show more awareness of the limitations of the analysis than others. The highly abstract and theoretical writings make references to the limitations of the analysis that often seem to be forgotten in the applied work.[2]

Major faults in neoclassical welfare economics
Desire for objectivity. From a Christian point of view there are a number of major faults in neoclassical welfare economics. Many of these faults are problems from other points of view as well. In the first place, neoclassical welfare economics was originally developed to obtain an "objective," "value free," or "scientific" normative economics. As Samuelson has said, "it is not uncommon for expositors of the 'new' set of doctrines to imagine that their results have significance even if one is unwilling to make any ethical assumptions."[3] Although Samuelson and others have pointed out the impossibility of a value free normative economics and have even made explicit some of the ethical judgments implicit in the neoclassical welfare economics,[4] many economists continue to treat efficiency as an objective goal for the economy or, at the very least, do not make explicit in their writings (textbooks, journals, and popular writings) the ethical presuppositions on which their advice is based.[5] They continue to desire a purely objective economics, devoid of any ethical or value judgments and at the same time to be able to give scientific or professional advice concerning economic actions. Of course, since normative statements tell people how they *ought* to behave, they must, by their very nature, be based on some ethical principles. Thus any statement that purports to be an ethically neutral normative statement is obviously false, and normative arguments devoid of support for their underlying ethical principles are incomplete at best.[6]

Some economists attempt to get around this problem by stating that although economists qua economists may not allow their own values to influence their work, they may use ethical judgments that are commonly accepted or use the ethical values of the person or persons for whom they are performing the analysis. But these statements are themselves ethical judgments, and false from a Christian point of view. Economists are morally irresponsible when recommending a certain act if that act is contrary to correct ethical principles, even if that act is in line with either commonly accepted (but false) ethical principles or the principle of the particular person to whom they are giving advice.[7] In fact, the ethical principles underlying the goal of Pareto optimality are not consistent with the Christian faith, and it is very doubtful that they are as commonly accepted as economists assume.

False individualistic ethical assumptions. The goal of Pareto optimality is based on, among other things, two individualistic ethical assumptions that are unacceptable from a Christian point of view. To see this let us restate the definition of Pareto optimality as follows: Pareto optimal (or economically efficient) situation is one in which it is not possible to make anyone better off *according to his or her own reckoning* without making at least one person worse off *according to that person's own reckoning*. The underlined phrases make it clear that individuals are to be the judge of their own welfare. Although such phrases are not commonly included in the definition, I know of no economist using the concept of Pareto optimality who does not, at least inplicity, make that assumption. This is the first invalid individualistic ethical assumption: that individuals are always the proper judge of what is best for themselves.

In the development and application of neoclassical welfare economics it is also assumed that individuals choose what is best for themselves, given their situation (wealth, income, knowledge, the prices they face, etc.). As Christians we know this is not true. All of us are sinful, and our sin distorts both our evaluations of what is best for ourselves and our actions. Sin limits our knowledge of the true effects of actions on our lives and the lives of others (e.g., of the true effects of consuming or producing a particular good), and in this way sin leads to actions that are not truly best for ourselves, that do not contribute to our true welfare.[8] Sin also causes us to desire things contrary to God's law and to act on these desires; it distorts our evaluations of what is best for ourselves and then leads us to actions that are not best for ourselves. For example, many willingly use their income and wealth to seek welfare from false gods (material goods, economic security, power, prestige, etc.) rather than trusting in God for their welfare and seeking to act in accordance with his will. And even when we know what we should do and want to do it, sin often causes us to do something else. Paul's statement, "I do not do the good I want, but the evil I do not want is what I do" (Rom. 7:19, RSV), is true for all of us in the economic sphere as well as in other spheres of life. We may have concern for the poor and a desire to adjust our behavior to help those with less than ourselves, but we may continue to spend too much on ourselves or our families and friends instead of giving to those in need. Or we may know that it is best for us to lose weight, stop smoking, or stop drinking, and we may wish to do this; nonetheless, we continue to overeat, smoke, or drink. Because of human sinfulness, therefore, Christians cannot accept the ethical assumption that individuals are the proper judge of what is best for themselves and that they will act in such a way as to maximize their welfare given the options open to them.[9]

A second basic individualistic assumption implicit in the Pareto optimality criterion is that *individuals'* valuations of how actions affect them fully constitute the *social* value of that action. For example, if individuals changed their consumption in such a way that they believe they have a higher level of welfare and if no one else's self-perceived welfare is diminished by this action, the Pareto criterion would say that *society's* welfare has increased. But this is not acceptable from a Christian point of view, for if people's perceptions of their welfare are distorted by sin, their perceptions should not be taken as determining true social welfare.[10] Indeed, despite the objections of some economists, this assumption is not completely accepted for purposes of social policy, even in highly individualistic societies such as the United States where we find laws against the use of certain drugs and against pornography, though it is not clear that individual, private use of these things harms others (beyond the misuse of scarce resources). Laws requiring the use of seat belts by motorists and helmets by motorcyclists are also motivated by more than concerns for the possible costs to others if these devices were not used.[11]

False materialistic ethical assumption. In addition to these unacceptable individualistic assumptions, neoclassical welfare economics, as it is normally developed, makes a false materialistic assumption. It assumes that individuals' welfare necessarily increases if they can fulfill to a greater degree their insatiable desire for goods by means of a higher level of consumption, other things being equal. This is certainly far from the spirit of Proverbs 30:8, 9: "give me neither poverty nor riches; feed me with the food that is needful for me, lest I be full, and deny thee, and say, 'Who is the Lord?' or lest I be poor, and steal, and profane the name of my God." And it is far from the spirit of the Bible as a whole with regard to material goods. The Bible teaches that people are stewards of resources God has entrusted to them and that they should use these resources according to God's law—a law that involves as much concern for the needs of others as for one's own needs. While it may be true that sin causes most people to perceive themselves as better off when they have more goods (other things being equal, including the amount that other people have), it seems clear from the Bible that people can have too many goods for their own welfare as well as too few, and that they should attempt to restrain their desires, rather than continually attempt to fulfill them with ever-higher levels of consumption (1 Tim. 6:6-10).

Neglect of the relationship between the economic sphere and other spheres. The above quotation from Proverbs is relevant to another weakness of neoclassical welfare economics — it invalidly treats economic welfare as a completely separable part of overall welfare and assumes that actions in the economic sphere or changes in economic welfare will not affect other aspects of welfare.[12] But people are not mechanisms that you can change one part of them without affecting the other part; nor is society mechanistic in that sense.[13] As the proverb indicates, our material situation may affect the degree of our trust in God. Economic systems and actions may influence our attitudes towards our fellow humans.

Some economists have argued that a competitive economic system advantageously economizes on people's benevolences, a very scarce resource. But people do not have a fixed quantity of benevolence; rather, if benevolence is not practiced, it atrophies; but if it is practiced, in many instances it grows. If this is true, the constant practice and social justification of individualistic economic activity may well lead to less and less benevolence and bring less, not more, welfare to society. Furthermore, to constantly strive for the economic goal of efficiency, many resources (including human labor) would be constantly changing use as economic demands changed. Prices would be very flexible, constantly rising and falling according to shifting demands and supplies. But this would hinder the achievement of other social goals such as the stability and financial security of the family.[14] A welfare economics that neglects such deleterious effects of economic institutions and actions on "noneconomic" aspects of welfare is skating on thin ice when it makes recommendations, even if it carefully includes a *ceteris paribus* phrase in its theoretical formulation.

False assumption of fixed preferences. The individualistic and materialistic ethical assumptions underlying neoclassical welfare economics, which cause it to evaluate an economy on the basis of how well it satisfies individuals' preferences and desires for goods and which prevent it from questioning and evaluating these preferences and desires, also create a serious technical problem for analysis if economic systems and actions can influence the desires and preferences of people for goods (commonly called their "tastes" by economists). If an economic action changes the very standard by which that action was to be evaluated (i.e., the degree of fulfillment of individuals' desires), there is no longer a consistent way of judging economic situations. This could only be remedied if the economist had a welfare (utility) measure for each individual that took into account changes in tastes as well as changes in consumption, wealth, and so forth, but few, if any, economists would be so bold as to claim that such a measure is feasible. And even if such a measure could be obtained, the fact that economic actions caused changes in tastes would make the conditions required for Pareto optimality much different and more complex than the standard ones and would thus render void most, if not all, of the policy conclusions presently derived from neoclassical welfare economics. (There are also major dynamic problems if changes in tastes are not always reversible.)[15]

It seems quite clear that tastes are influenced by economic actions. As Scitovsky has stated, "Even the most ardent believers in consumer sovereignty must realize that most tastes are acquired."[16] Desires for consumption are created by the level and type of consumption of others, by advertising, and by other promotion of goods.[17] Perhaps, as Veblen stated, "invention is the mother of necessity"[18] more often than the reverse. As the level of production and consumption of goods rises, people may well perceive themselves to be worse off than they were before, if their own consumption remains constant. In such cases even perfectly competitive markets will fail to give Pareto optimality, and it is possible that an increase in production and consumption by all people will leave none better off in their own perception or even leave everyone worse off, a result that is certainly at odds with the normal conclusions of neoclassical welfare economics.[19]

Hirsch, in a recent significant book, gives cogent reasons why such external effects of consumption become more and more important for both physical and psychological reasons as production and consumption rise in a society.[20] Easterlin examined data from thirty surveys of happiness (at various times in the United States and across countries with different levels of income per capita) and found that, although in all societies at a given time people with higher incomes reported higher average levels of happiness than did lower income people, the average happiness level of a society as a whole was not correlated with its average level of income or with changes in that average level. He explains this apparent paradox with the hypothesis that individuals' perceived happiness is dependent on the relation between their *perceived* needs and their income (among other things), and in general individuals' perceived needs (desires) rise with the average standard of living in their society.[21]

It appears that negative external effects of consumption are general and significant. Thus even if one accepts the ethical judgment that social welfare is determined by individuals' perceptions of their own welfare, the overall level of production and consumption becomes less important and the *distribu-*

tion of that production becomes important. But neoclassical welfare economists neglect questions of distribution because they wish to avoid the obviously ethical principles involved in distribution.

Lack of distributional criteria. There is in neoclassical welfare economics an absence of criteria for judging the implications of changes in the distribution of individual welfare on social welfare. Thus in almost every instance it is impossible for neoclassical welfare economics to indicate whether or not a particular economic action improves social welfare because almost every action will make at least one person worse off (in his or her own perception) even if that action makes many others better off (in their perception). In such a case the Pareto criterion cannot determine if the new situation is better or worse than the old. If one had a fully specified social welfare function and knew all the effects of an economic action, one could then evaluate it on that basis, but neoclassical welfare economists are not generally willing to make the ethical judgments necessary to define such a fully specified social welfare function, especially since it has become clear that such a function cannot be obtained from some combination of individual preferences.[22] There have been attempts to get around this problem; for example, by suggesting tests of the hypothetical possibility of compensation to those made worse off by the action. No matter how rigorous the test, though, the possibility of hypothetical (as opposed to actual) compensation cannot eliminate the ethical significance of redistributions of welfare. In any case, "perfectly efficient" compensation or redistribution devices that would not upset the efficiency conditions are just not available.[23] Thus the refusal to make ethical judgments concerning distributions of welfare (or income or wealth) even makes neoclassical welfare economics impotent when it comes to making statements about the economic desirability of particular economic actions. (Of course, economists do make statements about the economic desirability of actions, based implicitly or explicitly on the Pareto criterion, but such statements are invalid when they ignore the distributional implications of the actions as they usually do.)

No adequate second best conditions. Neoclassical welfare economics has an additional problem when evaluating practical economic actions. It has been discovered that meeting one or more previously unmet necessary conditions for a Pareto optimum is not a sufficient condition for improving social welfare (by the Pareto criterion) if one or more of the conditions necessary for the Pareto optimum still remains unmet. As long as one or more of the necessary conditions cannot be met, the "second best" solution may violate most or even all of the necessary conditions for a "first best" Pareto optimum.[24] This is a serious problem because most of the work in neoclassical welfare economics has dealt with the necessary conditions for an optimum rather than with the sufficient conditions for an improvement in welfare, and it is clear that the empirical data needed to calculate a set of "second best" conditions for any practical situation are enormous and generally unattainable. Unfortunately these problems are all too often neglected in applied welfare economics.

Neglect of dynamic effects. Furthermore neoclassical welfare economics is basically a static theory that neglects many dynamic effects of economic institutions and actions, such as effects on the rate and types of technological innovation and depletion of scarce natural resources.[25] But these dynamic effects are very important determinants of social welfare now and in the future, and they should not be neglected.

Profit maximization assumption. Additional technical problems with neoclassical economics could be mentioned, but one more will suffice. It is assumed in much of theoretical and applied neoclassical welfare economics that the goal of each firm is to maximize its profits. However, it is not at all clear that this is indeed the goal of all firms, especially large oligopolistic firms, and if these firms do have goals other than profit maximization, conclusions based on this profit-maximization assumption may be seriously in error.[26]

Neglect of biblical principles. Concluding this section on the faults of neoclassical welfare economics from a Christian perspective, we should make explicit a basic flaw that has been implicit in much of the above. Neoclassical welfare economics does not develop the implications of biblical principles (particularly ethical standards) for the economic aspects of the determinants of social welfare (or more formally the specification of the social welfare function). It does not consider the necessary or sufficient conditions for improving social welfare from a Christian point of view. Hence it cannot give a proper Christian evaluation of economic institutions or action. Rather, as we have seen, in an attempt to be value free it has grounded itself on false ethical principles, and thus it will give erroneous evaluations and recommendations.

Some limited uses for neoclassical welfare economics
Then is neoclassical welfare economics of any use to Christians? In spite of the above faults it has some limited uses. If used with due recognition of its limitations and complexity, it can be used to attack the still commonly held idea (in the United States, at least) that the capitalist system, if left to itself (or left almost to itself), will maximize social welfare in individualistic, materialistic terms. This capitalist idea is often based (at least implicitly) on an incorrect application of neoclassical welfare economics, one which neglects the limitations discussed above and the complexities of the social and economic systems. Many are still slaves to the notions of the "invisible hand" or its more technical counterpart—the efficiency of perfect competition.

In addition, if individual preferences are to be accorded an important role in an economic system,[27] and if neoclassical welfare economics is used with due recognition of its limitations and complexities, then it will probably result in recommendations regarding government policies that are somewhat better than the most prominent alternatives in government policy making today (at least in the United States): either laissez faire or policy making in response to special interest groups. Sometimes these two are the same. An interest group that thinks it can achieve its goals through the market will often argue for laissez faire in a particular area, even if it is pressing for government involvement in another.[28]

Of course, there are great dangers in using neoclassical welfare economics in these ways. If its limitations are not kept clearly in mind and made explicit often, it can and frequently does result in economic recommendations that are harmful to true social welfare. In fact, neoclassical welfare economics and the underlying neoclassical "positive" economics have often served to maintain the power and position of various powerful interest groups by "legitimizing" their activities in the minds of many people.[29]

The task that lies ahead

Where should Christian economists go from here? They can, as indicated above, find some uses for neoclassical welfare economics, although they should use it with great care, and when they use it they should try to modify and develop it in ways that will overcome its limitations. But Christian economists should also make a major effort to develop an alternative welfare economics based on biblical principles. I know of no such well-developed Christian welfare economics today, but I will briefly state some of the characteristics I think it should have.

Among the important biblical principles that must be used to build such a Christian welfare economics are the following:

1. People are creatures responsible to God, their Creator, for all of their actions.

2. People are not the owners of resources but stewards of resources that God has entrusted to them, and God has given guidance in his Word regarding the proper use of these resources. The biblical evidence indicates that those who have been entrusted with material goods have a duty to help those who are in need. Furthermore, it indicates that the economic institutions of a society should if possible: a) assure all families access to the basic necessities of life at all times; b) provide all families the opportunity to develop and use their God-given talents and resources in such a way that they can provide for their own needs (at least in the long run); c) provide all families with economic and political freedom that enables them to exercise responsible economic stewardship of their resources. (This includes being responsible economic decision makers in production as well as consumption and in the control of enterprises.)[30]

3. People's response to God is distorted by sin.

4. People can find true welfare only by placing their trust

in God, accepting his gift of salvation, and attempting to live in accordance with his law for their lives.

5. People are not made up of separable parts. In particular, their economic lives are influenced by and influence the rest of their lives (e.g., the spiritual, social, and biological aspects). Economic institutions and actions must not impair other God-ordained institutions (such as the family and church).

A welfare economics built on such principles would evaluate economic institutions and actions on the basis of how well they provided justice for all, allowed (or even encouraged) proper development of other spheres, and encouraged loving behavior. It would be concerned with efficiency and economic growth only to the extent that they contributed to such things, not as goals in their own right.

The development and applications of such a welfare economics will require extensive theoretical and empirical work. It will be able to make use of some of the empirical and theoretical work of neoclassical and other economists. But such a welfare economics and its accompanying descriptive economics will have to take into account many things ignored by neoclassical welfare economics (as discussed above), including the effects of various economic institutions and actions on the distribution of income, wealth, and power, as well as on tastes and things outside of the economic sphere over time. It will also have to be concerned about ways to improve welfare in a far-from-optimal system. It must recognize that both economic institutions and personal behavior within those institutions as well as both changes of heart and technical changes in institutions are important for achieving welfare.[31]

I doubt that the development of such a Christian welfare economics would result in a fully specified, mathematical, social welfare function and certainly not one that would be universally applicable or accepted by all Christians or even all Christian economists. If a Christian social welfare function could be developed, however, it would certainly not be just a function of the self-perceived utility of the individuals in the society, as the neoclassical social welfare functions are. But I do believe that by the grace of God such a Christian welfare economics could become a useful instrument for the evaluation of economic institutions and actions by Christians seeking to establish the kingdom of God more fully in their societies.

Notes

1. E. J. Mishan, *Welfare Economics*, 2d ed. (New York: Random House, 1969), 22. Chapter 1, to which the citations in this paper refer, is a reprinting of Mishan's "Survey of Welfare Economics, 1939-1959," *Economic Journal* 70 (June 1960): 197-256.

2. For critical surveys of neoclassical welfare economics, see Mishan, especially chapter 1; J. de V. Graaff, *Theoretical Welfare Economics* (Cambridge, Eng.: Cambridge University Press, 1957); P. A. Samuelson, *Foundations of Economic Analysis*, (Cambridge, Mass.: Harvard University Press, 1947), chapter 8; and W. J. Baumol, *Welfare Economics and the Theory of the State*, 2d ed. (Cambridge, Mass.: Harvard University Press, 1967), introduction to the second edition. Many basic articles, especially about applied welfare economics, are contained in K. J. Arrow and T. Scitovsky, eds., *Readings in Welfare Economics* (Homewood, Ill.: Richard D. Irwin [for the American Economic Association], 1969).

3. Samuelson, 247.

4. See Lester W. Thurow, *Generating Inequality* (New York: Basic Books, 1975), 24-25; and Mishan, 13-14.

5. Consider two especially egregious (but at least explicit) examples from recent economic journals. In "Three Basic Postulates for Applied Welfare Economics: An Interpretive Essay," *Journal of Economic Literature* 9, no. 3 (1971): 785-97, A. C. Harberger argues that economists should reach a "professional" consensus concerning the sum of costs and benefits of a given action and then limit their "professional" evaluation to that, disregarding distributional and other aspects of the action (which might be important, but which are beyond the economists' "professional" pronouncements). In "Bayesian Decision Theory and Utilitarian Ethics," *American Economic Review* 68, no. 2 (1968): 223-28, J. C. Harsanyi argues that "Bayesian rationality postulates are absolutely inescapable criteria of rationality for policy decisions; and...that these Bayesian rationality postulates, together with a hardly controversial Pareto Optimality requirement, entail *utilitarian ethics* as a matter of mathematical necessity." Examples of normative statements based (correctly and incorrectly) on the "economic efficiency" criterion without any ethical justification of this standard are frequently found in textbooks and journals.

6. Even economic statements or models that only describe or predict effects of economic institutions or actions ("positive" economics) cannot be value free or objective. A discussion of this point is beyond the scope of this paper, but we can note that the initial steps in abstracting data and building models will be influenced by such things as the investigator's view of people and society and his or her epistemological assumptions. Moreover, testing of models can never eliminate the differences in the models that arise from different faith perspectives. Thus the quest for an objective or purely scientific economics is doomed to failure, whether or not the economics is "positive" or "normative."

7. For example, even if the social Darwinist position—that the fittest should

have the best (or only) chance of survival and reproduction in a society — were commonly accepted, economists would not be morally responsible in recommending policies to achieve such an end. Or if a person stated that her goal in life was to amass the greatest possible wealth for herself, economists would not be morally responsible in recommending actions that would achieve that end, just as a physician would not be morally responsible in recommending ways to die to a patient who wanted to commit murder or suicide. (See S. K. Nath, "Are Formal Welfare Criteria Required?" *Economic Journal* 74 [September 1964]: sec. 2, a.) This does not mean that economists should not investigate the implications of various ethical standards (even some false ones) for economic institutions and actions. But I believe that, in general, economists should concentrate on the implications of those ethical standards they believe to be true. They would not be morally responsible if they were just hired analysts helping clients achieve their ethical ends, whatever they might be.

8. Some economic theories, including some in neoclassical welfare economics, do consider problems caused by incomplete knowledge concerning goods; but sin's role in this is not considered and very often the problems of limited knowledge are ignored.

9. Problems such as overeating are so well recognized that economists cannot easily claim that it is commonly accepted that individuals, given their available options, always act to maximize their welfare. One could not prove this even in a society that commonly (though falsely) considered individuals as the proper judge of what is best for themselves. (And many, if not most, people would even have some exceptions to this principle.)

10. There are conflicts between what many individuals perceive as best for themselves and what is best for society as a whole, such as when one person desires an inordinate proportion of wealth, income, or power. But I believe there is no conflict between individuals' true welfare and that of their society. The welfare of both individuals and society are increased to the extent that individuals trust in God for their salvation and live in closer harmony with God's will.

11. It is true, however, that in an individualistic society like the United States, individuals' judgments about the effects of various actions on their welfare are generally accepted as valid (with important exceptions). Likewise, individuals' judgments, in some sense, are thought to determine the social value of these various actions. However, though these ethical assumptions are usually made, they are not accepted as immutable principles. That distinction is important.

12. See Graaff (cited in note 2 above) and Nath, sec. 2, b (cited in note 7 above).

13. See the discussion of a mechanistic vs. an organic view of the economy in R. E. Kuenne, *Microeconomic Theory of the Market Mechanism* (New York: Macmillan, 1968), 5-11.

14. See M. Olson, Jr., "What Is Economics?" in *Modern Political Economy*, ed. James Weaver (Boston: Allyn & Bacon, 1973).

15. See J. Rothenberg, "Consumers' Sovereignty Revisited and the Hospitality of Freedom of Choice," *American Economic Review* 52, no. 2 (1962): 269-83 and S. Wellisz, "Discussion," *American Economic Review* 52, no. 2 (1962): 286-88.

16. T. Scitovsky, "On the Principle of Consumers' Sovereignty," *American Economic Review* 52, no. 2 (1962): 267-68.

17. See Baumol, 128-130 (cited in note 2 above); J. K. Galbraith, *The Affluent Society* (Boston: Houghton Mifflin, 1958), chapter XI; and Graaff, 43-44 (cited in note 2 above).

18. Quoted by Graaff, 44.

19. Graaff, 51, refers to this as the case of "excessive" external effects of consumption.

20. See F. Hirsch, *Social Limits to Growth* (Cambridge, Mass.: Harvard University Press, 1976).

21. See R. A. Easterlin, "Does Money Buy Happiness?" *The Public Interest*, no. 30 (Winter 1973): 3-10. This article is a nontechnical summary of R. A. Easterlin, "Does Economic Growth Improve the Human Lot? Some Empirical Evidence," in *Nations and Households in Economic Growth: Essays in Honor of Moses Abramovitz*, ed. P. A. David and M. W. Reder (Palo Alto, Calif.: Stanford University Press, 1974).

22. See K. J. Arrow, *Social Choice and Individual Values* (New York: John Wiley & Sons, 1951) and Thurow, 33-43 (cited in note 4 above).

23. See Mishan, 37-63 (cited in note 1 above), and Graaff, 84-92 (cited in note 2 above), for a discussion of the compensation controversies.

24. See K. Lancaster and R. G. Lipsey, "The General Theory of the Second Best," *Review of Economic Studies* 24, no. 63 (1956): 11-32.

25. Neoclassical welfare economists have tried to encompass the future as well as the present. But these attempts are subject to some time horizon and there is no way to determine the proper time horizon as well as what should be left for later generations, without making ethical judgments of the type that such economics tries to avoid. However, the choice of a time horizon and the specification of the terminal conditions strongly influence the evaluation of competing economic options. See Graaff, chapter 6 (cited in note 2 above). And many important dynamic effects are left out of these neoclassical models. Of course, the effects of economic actions on tastes and on "noneconomic" aspects of welfare (discussed above) are also often dynamic rather than static.

26. See, for example, J. K. Galbraith, *The New Industrial State* (Boston: Houghton Mifflin, 1967) and J. K. Galbraith, *Economics and the Public Purpose* (Boston: Houghton Mifflin, 1973).

27. I believe individual preferences should be accorded an important role in many aspects of an economic system, though I have argued against making them absolute. People are decision-making creatures, responsible to God; thus they should have the opportunity to make responsible decisions, though they will often respond incorrectly. And the alternatives to individual decisions — collective or dictatorial decisions — are also subject to sin and thus should not be absolute.

28. Large U.S. oil companies are a prime example, demanding an end to government price controls but also pressing for special tax subsidies.

29. See Galbraith, *Economics*, especially chapter 1 (cited in note 26 above).

30. To achieve these conditions, we must limit concentrations of wealth, income, and economic power. This paper cannot discuss the derivation of these standards for justice from the biblical evidence. I believe the Mosaic economic laws were directed toward achieving these conditions, and I believe they are consistent with other biblical teachings regarding the proper use of resources.

See G. N. Monsma, Jr., "Economic Inequities in the United States," in *Papers for a Conference on the Inequitable Distribution of Wealth and Power* (Classis Lake Erie, Christian Reformed Church, 1977) 1-12 and G. N. Monsma, Jr., "Strategies for Improving the International Economic Order," in *Justice in the International Economic Order* (Proceedings of the Second International Conference of Reformed Institutions for Christian Higher Education, Calvin College, Grand Rapids, Mich., 1980). These papers briefly discuss the derivation of standards of justice from the biblical evidence and their application to the United States. These standards for equity, of course, also have important international and intertemporal implications.

31. See Monsma, "Strategies," sec. 1, 2, and 3.

Unity and diversity among states: A critique of assumptions in the study of international relations

James W. Skillen

Introduction

Within the contemporary and very broad discipline known as political science, there has emerged in the past thirty years a relatively new subdiscipline known as "international relations"—the study of international politics. This is not to say that the relations among states were not studied prior to World War II; rather, until World War II international affairs were examined largely from the standpoint of the diplomatic purposes and accomplishments of separate sovereign states, including their mutual formation of a considerable body of international law. James E. Dougherty and Robert L. Pfaltzgraff, Jr., describe the period before World War I this way:

> The period of European history from 1648 to 1914 was the golden age of diplomacy, the balance of power and international law. Nearly all political thought focussed upon the sovereign nation-state—the origins, functions and limitations of governmental powers, the rights of individuals within the state, the requirements of order, the imperatives of national self-determination and independence....Until 1914, international theorists almost uniformly assumed that the structure of international society was unalterable, and that the division of the world into sovereign states was necessary and natural. The study of international relations consisted almost entirely of diplomatic history, international law and political theory.[1]

It took the shocks of World War I, the world depression, and World War II, as well as the postwar decolonialization movement and the entrance of the United States into global entanglements to provoke new approaches to the general study of interstate relations. According to Stanley Hoffmann it also required the "democratization" of foreign policy, starting in the United States. Throughout the nineteenth century "international politics remained the sport of kings, or the preserve of cabinets—the last refuge of secrecy, the last domain of largely hereditary castes of diplomats."[2] In the United States, however, "foreign policy was put under domestic checks and balances, knew no career caste, and paid little respect to the rules and rituals of the initiated European happy few."[3]

Between World War I and the end of World War II several new streams of thought about international affairs were converging; the United States was putting isolationism aside, and the new "global village" was emerging. Several Marxist and socialist theories about "imperialism" were spreading, and the impact of "realist" arguments began to be felt, especially in the wealthy and powerful states. The realists were taking a hard, critical look at the utopian optimism of older liberalism which had dreamed of eventual world peace through the development of world law.[4]

Thus, what emerged as the discipline of international relations after World War II resulted from historical and political changes that forced political scientists to adopt new perspectives. If, however, one asks what characterizes this discipline today, one will fail to discover a coherent, integrated body of doctrine, uniform method, or shared organization of subject matter. Stanley Hoffmann remarks that of the work in the last thirty years he is

> more struck by the dead ends than by the breakthroughs; by the particular, often brilliant, occasionally elegant, but generally nonadditive contributions to specific parts of the field, than by its overall development; by the contradictions that have rent its community of scholars, than by its harmony.[5]

Martin Wight's question of almost twenty years ago, "Why is there no international theory?" still holds![6] Apparently, the best that can be done to get at the discipline of international relations is to summarize the "contending theories" as Dougherty and Pfaltzgraff have done or to edit broad and eclectic texts as Rosenau, Thompson, and Boyd have done.[7]

These brief, introductory remarks should sufficiently explain that our critique of assumptions in the study of international relations will not mean a general critique of the discipline, as if the discipline were homogeneous. At the same time we can argue that current international political realities force any scientist or theorist to make certain fundamental assumptions about the unity and diversity among states. Whether one accepts or rejects the legitimacy of the state, glamorizes or denounces war, argues for or against greater interdependence among states, attempts a "value free" or a "value laden" analysis of international politics, one will have to assume something about the unity that does or does not, that ought to or ought not to characterize the relations among diverse states in our world today. By uncovering the assumptions about this issue, we will be able to gain substantial insight into the contemporary science(s) of international politics and, thereby, be able to clarify the relevance of a specifically Christian contribution to this field.

In looking at the variety of approaches to the study of international relations, it strikes us almost immediately that all of the methodological and ideological influences in the general field of political science also operate in international relations studies. Liberal and socialist, elitist and democratic, and nationalist and transnationalist perspectives can all be found. Behavioralists, systems analysts, historical realists, functionalists, legalists, and others present explanations and accounts of what is (and in some cases, what ought to be) taking place internationally. Equally striking is the continuous critical tension between those who desire "hard" results from a methodologically rigorous scientific study of international relations and those who believe that history, philosophy, ethics, and even futurology[8] must play an important part in the study of international politics.

On the one hand, Karl W. Deutsch[9] repeatedly reaches for a physical or mathematical analogy and explanation in analyzing international relations, neglecting almost entirely the historical, philosophical, and ethical judgments that a Hans Morgenthau, Eric Voegelin, or John Herz would concentrate on.[10] On the other hand, Kenneth Waltz takes as his point of departure the interpretation of classical and modern philosophers,[11] and F. Parkinson goes so far as to warn against the danger of scientism in the field:

The greatest potential danger to the field of study of international relations comes from the uncritical rejection of traditional philosophy and history, resulting in the growing separation of the social sciences from the mainstream of the humanities.[12]

The question of the unity and diversity among states is especially important in this disciplinary tension because the problem of political unity and diversity is ancient, antedating both the rise of the modern state and the emergence of contemporary social science research methods. In the main body of this paper, we will examine closely three contemporary perspectives and approaches in the field of international relations— those of Hans Morgenthau, Karl Deutsch, and the joint effort of Robert Keohane and Joseph Nye. First, however, we will glance briefly at a few of the ancient traditions that continue to influence contemporary life and scholarship.

Ancient perspectives on the unity and diversity among states
Three main cultural streams lie at the root of modern Western political life—the Biblical Hebraic, the Classical Greek, and the Roman Stoic. These three streams were interrelated in various ways in the European Middle Ages. Each stream has a different emphasis but the Middle Ages is also unique, being more than the mere sum of the earlier three streams. Each tradition, however, and the Middle Ages had a very definite conception of the *unity* that should pervade or control the earthly *diversity* of "political" realms.

The Hebraic-Christian tradition proclaims that the only God, the Creator of all things, is the Ruler of the ends of the earth. The earth is a unity because it belongs, as the creation, to the only God. All kings and kingdoms, therefore, exist as servants of God, subject to his ultimate will and purpose.[13] Psalm 2 is a concentrated example of this:

> Why do the nations conspire, and the peoples plot in vain?
> The kings of the earth set themselves,
>   and the rulers take counsel together,
>   against the Lord and his anointed, saying,
> "Let us burst their bonds asunder, and cast their cords
>   from us."

He who sits in the heavens laughs;
    the Lord has them in derision.
Then he will speak to them in his wrath,
    and terrify them in his fury, saying,
"I have set my king on Zion, my holy hill."
I will tell of the decree of the Lord:
He said to me, "You are my son, today I have begotten you.
Ask of me, and I will make the nations your heritage,
    and the ends of the earth your possession.
You shall break them with a rod of iron,
    and dash them in pieces like a potter's vessel."
 Now therefore, O kings, be wise;
    be warned, O rulers of the earth.
Serve the Lord with fear,
    with trembling kiss his feet,
lest he be angry, and you perish in the way;
    for his wrath is quickly kindled.
Blessed are all who take refuge in him.

For the prophet Isaiah this could only mean that the diverse kings and kingdoms existed in order to reveal the glory of God's one Kingdom, God's unified rule over the whole earth. They were literally at God's disposal. "All the nations are as nothing before him, they are accounted by him as less than nothing and emptiness" (Isa. 40:17, RSV).

Have you not known? Have you not heard?
    Has it not been told you from the beginning?
    Have you not understood from the foundations of the
        earth?
It is he who sits above the circle of the earth,
    and its inhabitants are like grasshoppers;
who stretches out the heavens like a curtain,
    and spreads them like a tent to dwell in;
who brings princes to naught,
    and makes the rulers of the earth as nothing.
(Isa. 40:21-23, RSV)

With the coming of Jesus, the Old Testament revelation about God's universal Kingdom was attached to the historical person and work of Jesus, God's Son, the Christ. Jesus claimed that "All authority in heaven and on earth has been given to me" (Matt. 28:18, RSV). The New Testament letter to the Hebrews quotes Psalm 2 and other passages and argues that the Son, begotten by the Father, is Lord and King over all. Other New Testament passages elaborate this.

Not only did the biblical tradition insist that God ruled behind and above all earthly dominions, but it pointed ahead, through history, to the eschatological and visible fulfillment of his reign over all. Kings and rulers, therefore, hold stewardly offices beneath God's rule, and they should use those offices for the sake of divine justice, lest God depose them now and bring them to judgment in the end.

In Classical Greek thought, particularly that of Plato and Aristotle, the unity of all earthly political orders was found, on the one hand, in the universal cosmic rhythms that controlled their birth, growth, and decay and, on the other hand, in the universal rational form or principle in which each order participated (or which informed each particular city-state).[14] The attempts at federation among Greek city-states came later;[15] Plato and Aristotle never considered that option seriously. Consequently, the main contribution of Classical Greek thought arises from its polis-centered movement in two directions: on the one hand, it sought to adequately account for the recurring patterns of change to which every city-state seemed to be subject; on the other hand, especially in Plato, it sought by philosophical ascent to discover the universal, changeless form of true political order, the paradigmatic norm for all particular and changing city-states. While Plato lacked the vision of a personal, transcendent God who revealed his sovereign will and historical purpose through kings, prophets, and eventually his own Son, he nevertheless believed that the philosophic (noetic) quest could lead to the discovery of the normative, transcendent "city-state of health and goodness" that was not of human origin. According to Eric Voegelin, the great theme of Plato's late work, the *Laws*,

> is the question, whether paradigmatic order will be created by "God or some man" (624a). Plato answers: "God is the measure of all things" rather than man (716c); paradigmatic order can be created only by "the God who is the true ruler of the men who have *nous*" (713a); the order created

by men who anthromorphically conceive themselves as the measure of all things will be a *stasioteia* rather than a *politeia*, a state of feuding rather than a state of order (715b).[16]

Plato comes closest to an apocalyptic eschatological vision, according to Voegelin, in his reinterpretation of the historical ages of Cronos and Zeus. During the age of Cronos people lived "under the direct guidance of the gods" and later, in the age of Zeus, they lived in man-made city-states (*poleis*). A new age must now appear.

> After the unhappy experiences with human government in the age of Zeus, the time has now come to imitate by all means life as it was under Cronos; and as we cannot return to the rule of daimons [gods], we must order our homes and poleis in obedience to the *diamonion*, to the immortal element within us. This something, "what of immortality is in us," is the *nous* [intelligent mind] and its ordering *nomos* [rational laws]. The new age, following the ages of Cronos and Zeus, will be the age of Nous.[17]

Whereas for Israel and later for Christians the political disorder and disunity of this age would be overcome by the fulfillment of God's Kingdom, for Plato the disorder would be overcome, if at all, by the full dawn of the age of Nous.

In Greece, soon after Aristotle but coming to fuller expression in the early Roman Republic and the later Roman Empire, was the ethical-juridical philosophy of Stoicism. "To the Stoics," Parkinson reminds us, "the world was a unit, irrespective of the manifold particularisms which it displayed, and an object from which to extract a set of laws."[18] Stoic thought was characterized by a rational quest for the unchanging order of the cosmos. Thus it was clearly Greek. But it developed after the city-state declined, when the great empires of Alexander and the later Romans were emerging. Thus it became increasingly oriented to the ecumenic universality of the world.

Chrysippus (280-207 B.C.), "who wrote a treatise *On Law* and was the greatest Athenian seminarist of his time," developed the idea of a metapositive order of world law that reduced the immanent social distinctions among various people to relative insignificance.[19] In fact, he believed that those distinctions should be reduced to a minimum.

This applied to all states as much as to individuals. Harmony between states was a Stoic ideal and could conceivably be attained if all states were linked together in a system of universal values based on principles of equality. In the Stoic mind, customs varied, but the element of reason which underpinned natural justice was uniform.[20]

The Stoic mode of thought came to have a tremendous influence in Roman law, especially in the development of the *jus gentium*. The Stoic conception of a natural law, *jus naturale*, controlled the reinterpretation of Roman law in its application to the peoples with their own customs and legal traditions being integrated into the Roman Empire. The resulting body of legal interpetation was called *jus gentium* — "the law common to all people making up the Roman Empire."[21]

Marcus Tullius Cicero (106-43 B.C.) summarized the Stoic philosophy of law, reason, nature, and God in this classic statement:

There is in fact a true law—namely, right reason—which is in accordance with nature, applies to all men, and is unchangeable and eternal. By its commands this law summons men to the performance of their duties; by its prohibitions it restrains them from doing wrong. Its commands and prohibitions always influence good men, but are without effect upon the bad. To invalidate this law by human legislation is never morally right, nor is it permissible ever to restrict its operation, and to annul it wholly is impossible....It will not lay down one rule at Rome and another at Athens, nor will it be one rule today and another tomorrow. But there will be one law, eternal and unchangeable, binding at all times upon all peoples; and there will be, as it were, one common master and ruler of men, namely God, who is the author of this law, its interpreter and its sponsor.[22]

As Eric Voegelin points out, the Ciceronian formulation has remained a constant in history "because it is the only elaborate doctrine of law produced by the ecumenic-imperial society."[23] It became the formative force in Roman law, and the early Latin Christian fathers adopted it instead of developing an independent philosophy of law out of the Hebraic-Christian tradition. "The background of Roman Law in the formation of the European lawyers' guilds, and the neo-Stoic movements since the Renaissance, have left us the heritage of a 'higher law' and of 'natural law.'"[24]

Parkinson points to an important tension that gradually emerged in Rome between the legal universalism of Ciceronian Stoicism and the conquering particularism of the successive imperial foreign policies. Emperor Marcus Aurelius (A.D. 121-80) manifested this tension. On the one hand, there is his famous Stoic dictum, "My city and country as Antonius is Rome—as a man it is the world." On the other hand, he believed in the autonomous voluntarism of individuals and states. Says Parkinson, "Here was the philosophical frame within which the tragic dilemma of international relations was to pose itself time and again, with the freedom of individual states pitted against the ideal of a preordained universe."[25] The rational, moral, legal universalism of Stoic philosophy did not sufficiently come to grips with the reality of diverse political powers. The idea of a cosmic legal unity that controlled Stoic thinking easily transcended the limits of the small Greek city-states, but it apparently did not reach very far outside the Roman Empire.

The Christian-Hebraic, Greek, and Roman cultural streams flowed together during the centuries after Christ. Parkinson summarizes this development compactly:

> Once Christianity had been adopted as the state religion of the Roman Empire at the end of the fourth century A.D., Stoic notions of universality, reinforced by the powerful memory of the Roman imperial structure, were to facilitate the eventual transition from *res publica romana* to *res publica christiana*. It also led to the transformation of Seneca's conception of a universal mankind held together by universally valid moral ties to the notion of an imperial theocracy imposing a universal dogma binding on rulers and their subjects alike.[26]

The transition from Roman Empire to Holy Roman Empire was not rapid, however. The process took centuries. The most important figure during the transition was Augustine (A.D. 354- 430), and the thinker who best represents its culmination is Thomas Aquinas (A.D. 1225-74).

Augustine took the Stoic idea of an eternal natural law and identified it with the eternal law of the biblical God.[27] The special revelation of God to the Jews and through Christ explicates the eternal natural law.

> Since natural law or the law of conscience is innate in man, it has existed since the creation of Adam. Therefore, it precedes the Fall and the introduction of sin into the world, and it antedates and is distinguished from the written law given directly by God to the Jews through Moses as well as the law of Christ in the Gospels. The Ten Commandments and the Gospel precepts do not contradict or annul the law of nature; rather, they make it more explicit and overt and give it the greater force of God's direct commandment to men.[28]

The crucial difference between Augustine and the Stoics, however, lay in Augustine's conviction that while *social* life is natural to humans, *political* and *legal* orders are not. The latter are divinely instituted remedial orders established because of human sin and designed to restrain sin in this age. They are not originally part of human nature. The very existence of diverse political entities, therefore, is evidence of the disunity and brokenness of natural society among humans. The recovery of true social life, of true justice, will occur only in the City of God —the eschatological community of God's new people that is being redeemed by Christ in this age but will only appear concretely and fully after he returns to judge the earth. The present age, therefore, can only be an age of relative order and justice maintained coercively in the midst of injustice, war, and disorder. The earthly political orders themselves can never achieve true justice, and an international order of justice in this world would be even more unthinkable.[29]

Augustine manifests a degree of Platonism in his notion that the relative justice and equity sometimes achieved on earth are due to "vestiges,""semblances," and "images" of true justice that can still be found in human life on earth. Although earthly peace is different from heavenly peace, it may be thought of as a "blurred image" of the heavenly.[30] But in the final analysis he does not view the City of God as a paradigm of earthly political order. The remedial earthly political orders are only temporary restraining devices that will finally succumb to the triumph of the City of God, a City that is much more than a polis or an empire.

Augustine's outlook led him along a different path than the one Plato or the Stoics had followed. He was not preoccupied with the philosophical attempt to define the eternal, universal, paradigmatic political order, nor was he preoccupied with the attempt to relativize all earthly political differences before the eternal natural law. Moreover, Augustine certainly did not try to justify the Roman Empire's claim to universality. He kept looking beyond the limited political orders, including Rome, toward the Church, which he saw as the earthly anticipation of the City of God. The only true unity and universality that Augustine would admit was God's reign in Christ.

In the end Augustine was bold enough to argue that "*it concerns Christian kings of this world to wish their mother the Church, of which they have been spiritually born, to have peace in their times.*"[31] Such a wish required action for its fulfillment and, therefore, Augustine argued "let the kings of the earth serve Christ by making laws for Him and for His cause."[32] The superior authority of the universal Church within this world was not something that Augustine worked out in any great detail as part of a systematic political theory. But the implications of his thought were worked out both doctrinally and politically in Europe during the next one thousand years. At the peak of the High Middle Ages, Thomas Aquinas articulated what Augustine had only anticipated and which in the meantime had become the reality of the Christian Roman Empire.

Thomas Aquinas elaborated a view of social, political, and religious life that recognized the universal superiority of the Church as it guided and integrated the diverse, limited political orders into one *corpus Christianum*, a unified *res publica Christiana*. While weaving together some Augustinian, Stoic, and Platonic themes, Aquinas made much more use of Aristotle in his political theory. This meant, among other things, that

Aquinas returned to the Greek idea of the naturalness of political life—political orders existed by nature, not first of all because of sin.

Although Aquinas extended the Aristotelian conception of the polis or city-state to the much larger political realms of his day, he nevertheless maintained that political order is a diversity of limited domains. "There is no open mention, in the whole of St. Thomas's work, of the idea of a universal empire," says A. P. D'Entreves:

> No doubt the idea of the fundamental unity of mankind is preserved in the general outlines of St. Thomas's conception of politics. It survives in the very notion of a natural law, common to all men, from which the several systems of positive laws derive their substance and value. It survives in the conception of the *unus populus Christianus,* which embraces all countries and nations, and which finds its highest expression in the *Corpus mysticum Ecclesiae.* But in the sphere of practical politics it is the particular State which carries the day.[33]

It is clear, then, that for Aquinas the unity of political realms or domains is not found in some form of political unity per se but in the Church's universal embrace of the different political orders. And the Church actually functioned at that time as an international legal order within Europe. Here is one of Aquinas's important statements on the relationships between the Church and earthly governments:

> We must note that government and dominion depend from human law, but the distinction between the faithful and infidels is from divine law. The divine law, however, which is a law of grace, does not abolish human law which is founded on natural reason. So the distinction between the faithful and the infidel, considered in itself, does not invalidate the government and dominion of infidels over the faithful. Such right to dominion or government may, however, with justice be abrogated by order of the Church in virtue of her divine authority; for the infidel, on account of their unbelief, deserve to lose their power over the faithful, who are become the sons of God. But the Church

sometimes does and sometimes does not take such steps.[34]

Whatever the authenticity and permanency of natural law, natural political life, and natural reason, it is clear that for Aquinas the final authority among nations resides in the Church as the divinely appointed channel of unity on earth. Aquinas was willing to recognize political diversity as natural because he saw the ultimate unity among peoples achieved and maintained by a suprapolitical legal authority—the Church.

The modern realism of Hans Morgenthau

With the decline of the Holy Roman Empire—unified as it was under the Roman Catholic Church—and the rise of the new states, a different kind of international order emerged in the West, an order that no longer reflected the theories of Aquinas, Augustine, Cicero, or Plato. Figures such as Hugo Grotius, Immanuel Kant, G. W. F. Hegel, and Napoleon Bonaparte were conscious of this difference and each tried in his own way to reconceive or rebuild world unity out of its new fragmentation —the modern world of supposedly self-determining, sovereign states. We will try to discover what three contemporary interpretations assume about the unity and diversity among modern states, and we will try to discover the significance of the ancient perspectives for understanding our contemporaries.

Hans J. Morgenthau is perhaps best known for the many editions of his text, *Politics among Nations*. But in 1970 he published a collection of essays, including some of his best philosophical ones, entitled *Truth and Power*.[35] One of the essays entitled "On Trying to be Just," first published in 1963, reveals Morgenthau's basically agnostic, secularized Augustinianism. Human nature is fundamentally faulty in a moral sense, according to Morgenthau, and for this reason anything like a just state or a just world order is simply out of the question.

> Justice, immortality, freedom, power, and love—those are the poles that attract and thereby shape the thoughts and actions of men. They have one quality in common that constitutes the distinction of men from beasts and gods alike: achievement falls short of aspiration....Man alone is, as it were, suspended between heaven and earth: an ambitious beast and a frustrated god. For he alone is

endowed with the faculty of rational imagination that
outpaces his ability to achieve.... His freedom is marred by
the power of others, as his power is by their freedom.[36]

But whereas Augustine's pessimism about sinful human nature was controlled by his faith in the ultimate will and purpose
of God in Christ, Morgenthau's pessimism is qualified only by
agnosticism. Even if we assume that justice is a reality, argues
Morgenthau, "we are incapable of realizing it" and incapable of
knowing what it demands:

> The position we are taking here has the advantage, at least
> for cognitive purposes, that it coincides with the one men
> have always taken because they could not do otherwise.
> Men have always thought and acted as though justice were
> real. We are proceeding here on the same assumption,
> trying to show that, even if justice is real, man cannot
> achieve it for reasons that are inherent in his nature. The
> reasons are three: Man is too ignorant, man is too selfish,
> and man is too poor.[37]

Morgenthau is working with a negative universality in his
conception of human nature and political reality. He puts forth
a thesis that few would attempt to deny, namely, that human
creatures manifest selfishness, ignorance, and poverty. But this
thesis comes to us as a self-evident truth only because of
modern relativistic cynicism and skepticism regarding norms
that ancient traditions believed could be known. If we did not
have firm roots in traditions that established norms of "unselfishness," "knowledge," and "richness" of human life, we
would not be so *certain* now about the negations of those norms.
Morgenthau's "agnosticism," in other words, has an eerie
sense of "certainty" about it; he knows with certainty much that
cannot be known with any certainty. Counting on the universality of his reader's skeptical, agnostic relativism, he can then
depend on their agreement with him that we can recognize
injustice without having a knowledge of justice, that we can
know selfishness without being sure of what unselfishness is:

> In sum, our knowledge of what justice demands is predi-
> cated upon our knowledge of what the world is like and

what it is for, of a hierarchy of values reflecting the objective order of the world. Of such knowledge, only theology
can be certain, and secular philosophies can but pretend to
have it. However, even theology can have that knowledge
only in the abstract and is as much at a loss as are secular
philosophies when it comes to applying abstract principles to concrete cases.[38]

Augustine located true justice in the City of God and for
that reason he never adequately accounted for its relationship
to earthly political life. In that sense his "theology" was too
abstract in Morgenthau's terms. But Morgenthau simply final-
izes the abstract Augustinian separation of justice from the real
world without accounting for his dismissal of the City of God.
With assured certainty that his modern readers will not try to
recover the ancient moral arguments, Morgenthau dispenses
with considerations of justice for all practical purposes, even if
he allows that justice might exist beyond our knowledge or our
ability to realize it. Then he confidently moves forward with the
primary thrust of his negation, namely, his belief that human
creatures are *universally* self-deceptive and selfish. Moreover,
he assumes that this universal condition of humans essentially
explains international political behavior.[39] Without any doubt
of the universality of his claims, Morgenthau argues that:

All of us look at the world and judge it from the vantage
point of our interests. We judge and act as though we were
at the center of the universe, as though what we see
everybody must see, and as though what we want is
legitimate in the eyes of justice....This propensity for self-
deception is mitigated by man's capacity for transcending
himself, for trying to see himself as he might look to others.
This capacity, however feeble and ephemeral it may be, is
grounded in man's rational nature, which enables him to
understand himself and the world around him with a
measure of objectivity. Yet where rational objective knowledge is precluded from the outset, as it is with justice, the
propensity for self-deception has free rein. As knowledge
restrains self-deception, so ignorance strengthens it. Since
man cannot help but judge and act in terms of justice and
since he cannot know what justice requires, but since he

knows for sure what he wants, he equates with a venge-
ance his vantage point and justice. Empirically we find,
then, as many conceptions of justice as there are vantage
points, and the absolute majesty of justice dissolves into
the relativity of so many interests and points of view.[40]

As a consequence of this argument, both the human quest
for a normative understanding of true justice as well as human
receptivity to God's revelation are excluded without exception
from the realm of politics, if not from life altogether. The only
reality in political life, as Morgenthau sees it, is the self-interested quest for power and that reality is truly universal, not as
a norm but as a natural fact.[41] Thus Morgenthau would resolve
the tension that existed between the normative Stoic universalism and Roman imperial expansionism by eliminating the
former from consideration. The autonomous voluntarism of
particular states is the *only* international reality. Consider how
Morgenthau responds to those who criticize as immoral and
unjust the post-World War II struggle between the United
States and Soviet Russia to secure "spheres of influence" in the
rest of the world.

> Spheres of influence, as Churchill and Stalin knew and
> Roosevelt recognized sporadically, have not been created
> by evil and benighted statesmen and, hence, cannot be
> abolished by an act of will on the part of good and enlight-
> ened ones. Like the balance of power, alliances, arms races,
> political and military rivalries and conflicts, and the rest of
> "power politics," spheres of influence are the ineluctable
> byproduct of the interplay of interests and power in a
> society of sovereign nations.[42]

The only way to stop the struggle for spheres of influence is to
change the world from a place of competing sovereign states to
a place where a single "sovereign government can set effective
limits to the expansionism of the nations composing it."[43] This
suggestion for global politics, though Morgenthau does not
argue for it morally at this point, is an enlarged version of
Hobbes's answer to the domestic power struggle among competing individuals. Only Leviathan, a superpower, can put an
end to the power struggle.[44]

Since international politics is essentially a power struggle, this explains why no predictive or normative theory of international relations is possible, according to Morgenthau.[45] The only unifying factor in interstate relations is the universality of the power struggle. But that struggle implies that unpredictable competitive diversities will rule the world until a single world organization of power is attained—something that cannot be predicted. The new post-war theorists of international relations are not really offering theories, says Morgenthau; they are simply putting forward their own new dogmas. "They do not so much try to reflect reality as it actually is as to superimpose upon a recalcitrant reality a theoretical scheme that satisfies the desire for thorough rationalization. Their practicality is specious, since it substitutes what is desirable for what is possible."[46] A new era of international relations theory does not exist in fact but only in rhetoric or hope. The distinctive quality of politics is the struggle for power, and just as this struggle is morally repellent to Christians, it is intellectually unsatisfactory to theorists because power, like love,

is a complex psychological relationship that cannot be completely dissolved into a rational theoretical scheme. The theoretician of international relations who approaches his subject matter with respect for its intrinsic nature will find himself frustrated morally, politically, and intellectually; for his aspiration for a pervasively rational theory is hemmed in by the insuperable resistance of the subject matter.

The new theories of international relations have yielded to the temptation to overcome this resistance of the subject matter by disregarding its intrinsic nature.[47]

Does this mean, then, that international relations cannot be studied in any fruitful theoretical manner? Does it mean that the contingent, unpredictable behavior of autonomous states will yield no theoretical generalizations? No, Morgenthau does not want to come to that conclusion. Instead, he proposes that the right kind of reflection on the actual history of international relations can help "to bring order and meaning into a mass of unconnected material and to increase knowledge through the logical development of certain propositions empirically established."[48] But how is this possible? Did not Morgenthau contend that the struggle for power is not amenable to "intellectual ordering?" Can one develop logical propositions on the basis of the empirical struggle for power? Morgenthau's answer is that while a final and complete predictive theory of international relations is impossible, a theoretical clarification of different practical political alternatives is possible, if we see political theory's practical function within a relatively limited political environment.[49]

> Edmund Burke is a typical example of how great and fruitful political theory develops from concrete practical concerns. It is not being created by a professor sitting in his ivory tower and, with his publisher, looking over a contract that stipulates the delivery of a manuscript on the "theory of International Relations" by a specified date. It is developed out of the concern of a politically alive and committed mind with the concrete political problems of the day. Thus, all the great political theory, from Plato and Aristotle and the Biblical prophets to our day, has been practical political theory that intervenes actively in a concrete political situation with the purpose of change through action.[50]

Clearly, then, Morgenthau's agnostic consideration of justice and modern scientific theories of social behavior is not *total*. His estimate of the ignorance, poverty, and selfishness of human creatures is not *completely* pessimistic. While giving up the Platonic and biblical convictions that universal justice can be known, he nevertheless hopes that some "practical wisdom" can be gained for life in this world. While rejecting the modern social scientific pseudohope of achieving a complete empirical theory, Morgenthau nevertheless believes that historical empirical evidence can yield some practical, relatively universal generalizations. Morgenthau's skepticism about human nature is not total; the practical wisdom of a few realistic people in this world can transcend the nearly universal ignorance, selfishness, and poverty of humankind.[51]

Thus Morgenthau does not live as a man without any knowledge or hope, but as one who is dismayed only by the normative moralist and by the pseudoscientific system builder.

If we could do away with those who believe they know what justice is and with those who hope to predict with certainty what will happen, then we could begin to have real confidence in the practical theory of the Hans Morgenthaus of this world. In fact, the ultimate task that his kind of theory can perform, argues the author, "is to prepare the ground for a new international order radically different from that which preceded it."[52]

How, we might ask, can a practical theory devoid of ultimate moral norms and predictive powers nevertheless prepare for a new world order? It does so, according to Morgenthau, because the rational powers of the practical theorist can "anticipate" the future on the basis of past experience. The political power struggle is sufficiently universal and repetitive that logical extrapolation from the past, which takes into account new technologies such as nuclear weapons, can foretell and lead us into the future even without prediction:

> It is a legitimate and vital task for a theory of politics to anticipate drastic changes in the structure of politics and in the institutions which must meet a new need. The great political utopians have based their theoretical anticipation of a new political order upon the realistic analysis of the empirical status quo in which they lived. Today, political theory and, more particularly, a theory of international relations, starting from the understanding of politics and international relations as they are, must attempt to illuminate the impact nuclear power is likely to exert upon the structure of international relations and upon the functions domestic government performs. Further, it must anticipate in a rational way the intellectual, political, and institutional changes that this unprecedented revolutionary force is likely to require.[53]

Karl W. Deutsch's analysis of international relations
While Morgenthau is skeptical of the moralist as well as the scientific system builder, he still hopes for a practical political theory that can guide real political leaders toward a new international order. Karl Deutsch, on the other hand, is the kind of scientist that Morgenthau would criticize for attempting the impossible—that is, attempting to rationalize or systematize in

an almost natural scientific fashion a reality that cannot be so reduced. Deutsch's assumptions are clear and simple in their reductionistic disregard of human political and moral reality in its integral complexity. He is much more than an agnostic when considerating "justice," "morality," and "truth." Deutsch views human nature and the world as a closed universe manifesting stimulus-response actions and reactions based on the struggle for satisfaction and survival against pain and death. True justice is not merely unknowable; it is irrelevant when scientifically examining the "facts."

Governments, says Deutsch, "pursue their goals in either a conscious or a machine-like fashion."[54] "Goal" should be defined as follows:

> A *goal* (*goal state* [condition]) for any acting system is that state of affairs, particularly in its relationship to the outside world, within which its inner disequilibrium—its drive—has been reduced to a relative minimum. If a state is in some sort of disequilibrium or tension—and most states, like most other acting systems, are in some disequilibrium of this kind—it will tend to change some aspects of its behavior until this disequilibrium is reduced.[55]

This quotation justifies our impression that Deutsch is working with abstract physical, mechanical, or psychological concepts and analyses that do not explain the full and integral reality of human political life. Deutsch makes use of a physical, mathematical, or mechanical illustration repeatedly. For example:

> The making of foreign policy thus resembles a pinball machine game. Each interest group, each agency, each important official, legislator, or national opinion leader, is in the position of a pin, while the emerging decision resembles the end-point of the path of a steel ball bouncing down the board from pin to pin. Clearly, some pins will be placed more strategically than others, and on the average they will thus have a somewhat greater influence on the outcome of the game. But no one pin will determine the outcome. Only the distribution of all the relevant pins on the board—for some or many pins may be so far out on the periphery as to be negligible—will determine the distribu-

tions of outcomes. This distribution often can be predicted with fair confidence for large numbers of runs, but for the single run—as for the single decision—even at best only some probability can be stated.[56]

One need not read too far into Deutsch, therefore, to discover that the unifying concept of the "system" that holds the field of disparate political facts together is an unqualified, highly abstract, general concept describing any complex set of interactions. For Deutsch, then, unity and diversity among states has nothing to do with divine sovereignty over our one world or with universal moral or political principles that can be discerned by a common rational quest. If there is any unity in the political world, Deutsch believes it is to be found in the universal mechanical necessity of interactions within a system where equilibrium is pursued and disequilibrium is avoided. It is a unity to be abstracted by the proper scientific tools of measurement that can "cut into" the vast array of facts.[57]

Interestingly, Deutsch's method and approach to international relations keep him from adequately answering three very important questions that he poses at the beginning of *The Analysis of International Relations*. Of the twelve fundamental questions he asks, the first two are concerned precisely with the unity and diversity among states:

1. *Nation and World*: What are the relations of a nation to the world around it? When, how, and how quickly are a people, a state, and a nation likely to arise, and when, how, and how quickly are they apt to disappear? While they last, how do they relate to other peoples, states, and nations? How do they deal with smaller groups within them, and with individuals, and how do they relate to international organizations and to the international political system?

2. *Transnational Processes and International Interdependence*: To what extent can the governments and peoples of any nation-state decide their own future, and to what extent does the outcome of their actions depend on conditions and events outside their national boundaries? Are the world's countries and nations becoming more "sovereign" and independent from each other, or are they be-

coming more interdependent in their actions and their fate? Or are they becoming both more independent and more interdependent, but in different sectors of activity? What will the world look like in, say 2010 A.D. in regard to these matters?[58]

His fifth question is perhaps the most important one for the scientist or theorist: "What is political in international relations, and what is not? What is the relation of international politics to the life of the society of nations?"[59]

Deutsch's questions are dogmatically confined to the "hows" that might possibly yield empirical descriptions and measurements. He does not ask about the "whys" and "oughts" or about the assumptions that guide his investigations of the "hows." Moreover, after raising the questions, he first adopts a concept of "system" that is too abstract and general to serve as a sufficient "tool" for selecting and collecting information about specifically *political* "facts." Only after he has defined a system in general does he begin to define politics, but by that point the full reality of political life can no longer be grasped or contained in his reductionistic concept of system. Thus his fifth question is never answered satisfactorily.

In his writings, Deutsch greatly depends on the work of Norbert Wiener, the mathematician and cybernetic theorist, and on Talcott Parsons, the sociological systems theorist.[60] From Parsons he obtains an idea of the social system, but unqualified in any way. Deutsch accepts Parsons' conclusion that "there are certain fundamental things that must be done in every social system, large or small (that is, in every group, every oganization, every country) if it is to endure."[61] A social system must 1) maintain itself, 2) adapt iself to change, 3) attain its goals, and 4) integrate its own internal and complex diversity. The scientific key to the functions of any social system, according to Deutsch, is to map the "flow" of the system's communication network which functions as a cybernetic web within the system and which also connects it with its external environment.

It should be clear to any social scientist that Deutsch, following Wiener and Parsons, has indeed abstracted certain dimensions, modes, or functions of universality that characterize any social entity. It is hard to object that *all* social entities seek to maintain their identities, adapt to change, maintain a flow of communication, and so forth. The fundamental problem, however, is that the study of any particular *mode* or *function* of a social system *presupposes* the system's *prior identity* as a social whole. Deutsch does not indicate an awareness of this and, consequently, he reduces the political (or any other) system to its communication patterns or its general functions without explaining what is functioning or processing information. Instead of first accounting for what is political and then carefully examining the abstracted communication flows, Deutsch works backward in a typical reductionistic fashion, first positing an abstract, general social or cybernetic system and then using that abstraction to identify political life and processes. In effect he reduces the integral reality of political life to one or two of its modes or functions.[62]

Furthermore, though Deutsch does not claim that his approach is normative, he nevertheless believes that a political system that suffers a communication breakdown, or disappears, or fails to adapt quickly to change, or fails to attain its goals, or remains disorganized, is not living up to the universal necessity of survival and development which, by definition, is incumbent on all systems. In other words, it is not doing what it *ought* to do if it wants to survive and grow. The conceptual tool of "system" thus enables theorists to do more than simply describe facts; it also helps them to judge successful and unsuccessful systems based on their predisposition to believe that things (including social things) *ought* to survive rather than perish.

Deutsch defines every social system by the above abstraction. What, then, distinguishes a political system from a nonpolitical system? Deutsch is not any more helpful than Morgenthau on this point. Both men more or less assume that common sense acquaints us with "laws" and "forces" that define states or "nation-states."[63] Morgenthau moves from that point to an assumed macrocosmic "person" or "actor" known as the state or political system that seeks (or should seek) to maintain and enhance its own self-interest. The nominalistic and behavioralistic Deutsch does not so readily acknowledge the existence of a structured social whole. Instead, his "political system" is a pattern of combined individual behavior patterns:

Politics consists inthe more or less incomplete control of human behavior through voluntary habits of *compliance* in combination with threats of probable *enforcement*. In its essence, politics is based on the interplay of habits of cooperation as modified by threats.[64]

Deutsch does not stop to address the possible objections to his assumptions. He does not ask whether the individual habits preceded and helped to shape the particular contours of the political system or, on the contrary, were created by the system. He does not ask why such systems came into existence in the shapes and sizes in which we find them. And the above definition no more defines a *political* system than it defines a family, a school, or a business enterprise since all social systems depend on voluntary compliance and the use of some kinds of enforceable threats. Deutsch goes on to talk about "law," but he does not distinguish state (political) law from church law, school rules, or business regulations for employees. In other words, he quickly passes over, with some statements about behavior patterns, the very thing that needs to be accounted for, namely, the identity of the political system. If this seems inadequate or peculiar, it is only so for the person looking for something more than measurements of, and probability predictions about, certain functions carried out by existing domestic and international habits of political behavior.

The concluding sections of Deutsch's *Analysis of International Relations*, which discusses international interdependence and interrelationships, contribute no additional insight into the unity and diversity among states. The *diversity* of states is simply assumed as a fact of modernity. The *unity* he looks for is the universality of shared system properties and the growing complexity of system interdependencies—interdependencies that seem to require change if the many separate state systems and the world as a whole are to survive.

Once again, however, without first accounting for the identity of interstate political relationships (as compared with the identity of a state), Deutsch simply assumes the validity and sufficiency of a general systems concept for analyzing international relations. He introduces chapter 15, "Integration: International and Supranational," in this way:

To *integrate* generally means to make a whole out of parts —that is, to turn previously separate units into components of a coherent system. The essential characteristic of any *system*, we may recall, is a significant degree of interdependence among its components, and *interdependence* between any two components or units consists in the probability that a change in one of them—or an operation performed upon one of them—will produce a predictable change in the other.

Integration, then, is a relationship among units in which they are mutually interdependent and jointly produce system properties which they would separately lack.[65]

When Deutsch discusses the United Nations, he explicitly refers to two themes that can be traced throughout the history of that organization: 1) "the search for centralizing power" and 2) "the search for pluralistic communication and accomodation."[66] In other words, the very identity of the United Nations implies the problem of *unity* and *diversity* in global politics. Deutsch judges that a true unification of the world by means of a great centralization of world political power in the United Nations is not likely in the near future. But he is sympathetic to the suggestion of a "second way" made by Senator Arthur Vandenberg in 1945:

It is to make the United Nations the town meeting of the world, where all issues can be brought out into the open, and where governments can learn how to manage differences of interest and ideology, and how to avoid head-on collisions....In these respects, the United Nations since 1945 has been remarkably successful.[67]

Almost apart from his "scientific" study of communication flows and system functions, and certainly without adequate historical evidence or argument, Deutsch voices his hope for the eventual attainment of world security and unity. His hope seems to be rooted in nothing more than his belief that human beings, when forced against the wall, will find a way to survive rather than perish. Deutsch believes that somehow a "fit" system will appear and survive.

An era of pluralism and, at best, of pluralistic security communities, may well characterize the near future. In the long term, however, the search for integrated political communities that command both peace and power, and that entail a good deal of amalgamation, is likely to continue until it succeeds. For such success, not only good will and sustained effort, but political creativity and inventiveness will be needed, together with a political culture of greater international openness, understanding, and compassion.

Without such a new political climate and new political efforts, humanity is unlikely to survive for long. But the fact that so many people in so many countries are becoming aware of the problem, and of the need for increasing efforts to deal with it, makes it likely that it will be solved.[68]

Unfortunately Deutsch contributes little or nothing to our understanding of how compassion, openness, understanding, inventiveness, and political creativity can be found and nurtured. He offers no explanation of why these ingredients will or should be desired and sought after by the same human beings that Hans Morgenthau believes are all too ignorant, selfish, and poor. One is even left wondering whether Deutsch and Morgenthau, who share so many characteristics of the same culture, language, and political culture, understand each other.[69]

Keohane and Nye: Complex interdependence
Robert O. Keohane and Joseph S. Nye are fully aware of both Morgenthau's realism and Deutsch's more general and abstract systemic analysis. The thesis of their book, *Power and Interdependence,* is that a more sophisticated approach is necessary for the study of world politics, one that will take into account the partial truthfulness of both realism and various forms of systems analysis. According to Keohane and Nye, neither "modernists" (a term that would characterize Deutsch in several respects)[70] nor "traditionalists" (like Morgenthau) have an adequate framework for understanding contemporary international politics.

Modernists point correctly to the fundamental changes now taking place, but they often assume without sufficient analysis that advances in technology and increases in social and economic transactions will lead to a new world in which states, and their control of force, will no longer be important. Traditionalists are adept at showing flaws in the modernist vision by pointing out how military interdependence continues, but find it very difficult accurately to interpret today's multidimensional economic, social, and ecological interdependence.[71]

In contrast to Morgenthau's traditionalism, Keohane and Nye argue that states are not persons with single wills confronting each other as military powers with a single overriding national interest.[72] States are interdependent, not merely as potential military allies or enemies but also as economic, social, and ecological entities. Moreover, many international relationships are nongovernmental, and these many "complex interdependencies" are not always organized within each state as parts of a fully integrated, hierarchically arranged, coherent plan of self-interested state action.

In the Canadian-American relationship, for example, the use or threat of force is virtually excluded from consideration by either side. The fact that Canada has less military strength than the United States is therefore not a major factor in the bargaining process.[73]

And if we consider United States-Canadian relations apart from military interdependence, we discover that there is not a single or uniform "national interest" on either side. The interdependence is more complex than the realist would imagine.

On the other hand, we cannot assume with the modernist that the complex interdependence of states within a shrinking global system can be taken for granted as a single-system fact that will yield empirical measurements of interactions within "the system." The concept of "system" must be used with more agility if we are to take into account the many kinds of systemic interdependencies in the world and the ways in which systems themselves can change.

In the main body of their book, Keohane and Nye examine two major issues and two interstate relationships: international monetary systems from World War I to 1976 and the international ocean regimes during that period, and American-Canadian and American-Australian relations over a significant period of time. They seek to demonstrate that there is no single model of a system that can be used to explain either the changes of "regimes" in money and oceans or the changes in bilateral relations between the United States and Canada and between the United States and Australia. In fact, in certain cases the older realist framework comes the closest to providing an adequate account. "Our conclusion is that the traditional tools need to be sharpened and supplemented with new tools, not discarded."[74]

We find in Keohane and Nye, then, a more systems-analytical, multidimensional, functionalistic, and prediction-oriented approach than in Morgenthau. At the same time the authors display a sensitivity to, and a concern for, the policy-oriented, practical, and historical sides of international politics that are the primary concern of the realists. Given this breadth and complexity, what do Keohane and Nye assume about the unity and diversity among states?

On the basis of *Power and Interdependence*, it is difficult to answer this question. In one respect Keohane and Nye only test a few limited hypotheses about the predictive power of certain methods and theoretical approaches. Therefore they end their book with a series of qualifying statements suggesting the need for further research rather than with a series of general conclusions that would reveal their standpoint more clearly. In another respect, however, they make a case for the severe limits of a scientific study of international politics, because the closer they come to an account of all the elements of complex interdependence, the farther they are from any clean predictive conclusions. This would seem to imply that Keohane and Nye would examine the assumptions of contemporary theorists rather carefully since they are calling into question contemporary methods and conclusions. Nevertheless, Keohane and Nye do not critically reflect on the basic assumptions of international theorists. Instead, they appear to merely call for greater empirical completeness within the framework of traditionalist and modernist assumptions. The authors conclude by sounding a note already made at the beginning, namely, that they want to synthesize and enlarge traditional and modernist contributions in the direction of greater empirical completeness. Traditional views, on the one hand,

> fail even to focus on much of the relevant foreign policy
> agenda—those areas that do not touch the security and
> autonomy of the state. Moreover, the policy maxims de-
> rived from such traditional wisdom will often be
> inappropriate.Yet the modernists who believe that social
> and economic interdependence have totally changed the
> world fail to take elements of continuity into account. As
> a result, their policy prescriptions often appear to be
> utopian. All four of our cases confirmed a significant role,
> under some conditions, for the overall military power
> structure. Appropriate policies must take into account
> both continuity and change; they must combine elements
> of the traditional wisdom with new insights about the
> politics of interdependence.[75]

We can gather that Keohane and Nye stand with Morgenthau and Deutsch in their basic assumptions about the unity
and diversity among states. For example, they simply accept
the existence of separate states as a fact of modernity without
attempting to define the state. Likewise, along with Morgenthau and Deutsch, they are looking to empirical theorists for an
adequate understanding of changing world conditions to help
states (and humanity) survive. They point out the growing
significance of the universal ecological, technological, economic interdependencies among states, functioning as limiting
global necessities that states must acknowledge. But Keohane
and Nye give no hint that they are interested in reopening the
older normative debates about what kind of justice, equity, or
unity ought to characterize the world in its diverse interdependence. They remain entirely agnostic about the normative
obligations that states, political leaders and international organizations have for one another and for the creation in which
we all live. Just as they want to see into the future with
Morgenthau and Deutsch, so they are skeptical with them
about all forms of foreknowledge other than scientific prediction.
   Keohane and Nye may be more exhaustive than Morgenthau in their empirical examinations, but they are still realists
at heart who want to provide nonutopian help to policymakers.

They may be less optimistic and less reductionistic than Deutsch, paying more careful attention to actual institutions, historical developments, and complex system changes, but they are still systems analysts who limit themselves to the study of the functional relationships among states—especially the developed Western states. They do not leave the positivistic terrain to reflect on and evaluate the assumptions that have guided modern states and political leaders. Thus they have no apparatus and no criteria for assessing the various normative visions that political leaders have worked with during the past several centuries of nationalism, imperialism, anticolonialism, and neocolonialism. They merely fall back on a simplistic distinction between realism and utopianism, hoping to avoid the latter at all costs.

Keohane and Nye come closest to recognizing international political norms when they conclude that political scientists must give greater attention than previously to international *organizations* and *leadership*:

> Our analysis implies that more attention should be paid to the effect of government policies on international regimes. A policy that adversely effects or destroys a beneficial international regime may be unwise, even if its immediate, tangible effects are positive. Concern with maintenance and development of international regimes leads us to pay more attention to problems of *leadership* in world politics. What types of international leadership can be expected, and how can sufficient leadership be supplied? And focus on contemporary world leadership stimulates increased attention to problems of *international organization*, broadly defined.[76]

But even here it is apparent that Keohane and Nye do not define either "adverse" or "positive" effects, nor do they explain what a "beneficial" international regime would be.[77] And their questions about leadership are the positivistic ones about "what might be expected" and what is "sufficient" without considering what leadership ought to be or even what "sufficiency" means.

Conclusion

The writings of Morgenthau, Deutsch, and Keohane and Nye should not be underestimated, nor should we dismiss their approaches and findings lightly because of their inadequacies. Global relations among states are so complex, so rapidly changing, and so resistant to scientific analysis and measurement that we should not be surprised or disappointed to find only limited insights and highly tentative conclusions. Instead, we ought to try to gather the contributions of these thinkers into a more encompassing and adequate philosophy and science of international politics developed by a "school" of Christian political scientists.

For example, in spite of his agnosticism, Morgenthau has an appreciation for at least two crucial things. First, his realism, for all of its shortcomings, is anchored in the important awareness of the *identity-structure of the state and the lack of a similar structural identity in interstate relations.* Morgenthau has not brought this awareness to the forefront for theoretical analysis, but his disdain for abstract system builders who ignore how states act as integral wholes reveals his keen historical insight into a fundamental feature of the modern global arena.

The *first task* of the political scientist, then, is to clarify the identity-structure of the modern state, illuminating the important similarities and differences between the newer and older states and between complex, highly developed and simpler, less integrated public entities. And he must distinguish interstate relations from intra-state activities. Morgenthau correctly insists that military power and potential power is crucial at this point, but Deutsch, Keohane and Nye also correctly point to the other complex dimensions of interstate relations.

Secondly, Morgenthau knows the importance of *practical political knowledge.* That is to say, he knows that international relations are shaped by real persons making concrete decisions in their political offices, making judgments about what ought to be done to secure peace or prosperity, to preserve or to end war, to advance justice or to promote certain interests. Keohane and Nye show their dependence on Morgenthau when they, too, indicate the importance of understanding leadership. An analysis of international relations that fails to explain and evaluate this moral, judgment-making, decision-making human dimension of international politics and only tries to measure quantities will not come closer to the status of an exact science but only distort more thoroughly the reality of politics.

The *second task* of political science, then, is to reconsider, through critical reflection, the assumptions necessary for a fully empirical examination of international politics—"fully empirical" referring to the full reality of relationships that are human, institutional, moral, juridical, and social in character. Natural scientific, cybernetic, mathematical, and other models simply abstract modes and functions from the integral totality of international politics and to continually refine those models is to continue a dogmatically blind effort rather than to advance empirical science.

Deutsch, in contrast to Morgenthau, is aware of some of the *universal modes or dimensions of social structural identities* that can be abstracted from real states and actual interstate relations. Deutsch specializes, of course, in the study of communications systems and networks. International relations are not simply the free and autonomous relations among separate states in an open field. Especially in the last one hundred years, advancing modern technologies, communications systems, and worldwide military and economic interdependencies are manifesting the rise and triumph of the West over an increasingly interrelated "global village." It is important, then, to consider the universal social modes and functions that characterize all states and interstate relations and limit the more individualistic quests for national self-interest. We should not simply ignore or reject quantification procedures that emphasize these universal characteristics because they are reductionistic. They should be carefully employed within a larger, more adequate, nonreductionistic science of politics. Deutsch has only abstracted one or more functional elements of social systems, ignoring moral, juridical, aesthetic, historical, and other modes of political existence, and he has almost obliterated the very identity-structure of state and interstate systems, but we should not entirely reject his information or methods.

The *third task* of political science, therefore, is to carefully analyze all the functional modes of existence that characterize state and interstate systems, clarifying the differences betweeen intrastate political, interstate political, and nonpolitical system functions. If we pursue this task along with the first two tasks, then we can mine the work of Deutsch and others with value, if only with minimal results.

In Keohane and Nye we recognize careful empirical research that is almost completely tentative about the massive complexity of factual international political relations. They consider less than a century of history. They only investigate money, oceans, and United States-Canadian and United States-Australian relations. This demonstrates the narrow focus necessary for scientists to do justice to the full complexity of international politics. Such humility and narrowness must be appreciated and imitated by those who wish to do science. Even a large team of scientists cannot simply study the international political system in general. First they must carefully analyze the several different models of investigation.

The *fourth task* of political science, then, is to test hypotheses and assumptions carefully against actual cases over time in order to see whether all the elements of the political reality are taken into account. Keohane and Nye do not lack carefulness, but their systems-analytical assumptions and methods of measurement circumscribe their project, obscuring the full integrality of political life for the scientist and politician.

Is it possible to bring together the theoretical efforts of Morgenthau, Deutsch, and Keohane and Nye into a larger political scientific project guided by a Christian view of the world? Clearly such a project will have to be much grander than a picky eclecticism or synthesis of existing contributions. Recalling the first half of this paper, we remember that the contemporary world of international relations and the general moral disposition of Western scientists is recent. Morgenthau, Deutsch, and Keohane and Nye—all essentially moral and religious agnostics or skeptics when it comes to human knowing and doing, each allowing "survival" as highest moral value —are sidestepping the biggest questions of political concern now and for the last few millenia. Supposedly knowing the most about the emerging "new world," they have left untouched the most fundamental question of all: What kind of *unity*, if any, ought to characterize international political diversity? The general tenor of their work, however, is not actually one of empty ignorance, as though they could really ignore this question and stick to a "purely scientific" description of the facts. They constantly try to fill the void with careful qualifications and negations. They refer frequently to the uselessness of moralists, the danger of utopian thinking, the need to avoid nuclear war, the value of cooperation for world economic growth, or the importance of system maintenance. They want a world unity sufficient to keep most (or enough) humans in a condition of greater pleasure than pain. They leave the means for attaining this end (which all hope for but none can predict) in the hands of the political decision makers—but with the undisguised hope that the decision makers will heed the scientists' analyses and not get caught in the grip of dangerous moralisms, utopianisms, and so on. With such Western sterility it is no wonder that Marxist, nationalist, and other ideologies enjoy such power and influence among political leaders and activists looking for meaning, purpose, and direction for political life.

A "school" of Christian political scientists ought to boldly demand that accurate and progressive scientific work call into question the sterile biases and confining dogmatic assumptions of realists, systems analysts, and functional model builders who stand in the tradition of Enlightenment secularism. They ought to sift carefully through the work of such secularists, just as they ought to sift through the works of Plato, the Stoics, Augustine, and Aquinas. But, for the sake of authentic political science, they must recover the vision of the prophets and of Christ himself which reveals a proper standpoint from which to ask the important questions about political integration and differentiation in our small, shrinking world. From that standpoint, as a team, they should recover ancient questions and hypotheses, investigate historical realities, and systematically analyze contemporary structural identities and functional universalities that define our political world. Critically, they should clarify the guiding presuppositions and assumptions necessary to full empirical investigation of political reality—including any human shaping of institutions and relationships that does justice or injustice to the image of God and to all other creatures who live in God's one world where Christ is King.

Notes
1. James E. Dougherty and Robert L. Pfaltzgraff, Jr., *Contending Theories of International Relations* (Philadelphia: J. D. Lippincott, 1971), 3. As the authors indicate, the major exceptions to this were the various branches of socialist thought.
2. Stanley Hoffmann, "An American Social Science: International Relations,"

Daedalus (Summer 1977): 42.
3. Hoffmann.
4. The Marxist influence came from people such as V. I. Lenin, *Imperialism: The Highest Stage of Capitalism* (New York: International, 1939) and Rosa Luxemburg and N. I. Bukarin, *Imperialism and the Accumulation of Capital* (London: Allen Lane, 1972). The critics of liberal optimism were E. H. Carr, *Twenty Years Crisis* (London: Macmillan, 1939), Hans J. Morgenthau, *Politics among Nations* (New York: A. Knopf, 1948; 4th ed., 1967), Reinhold Niebuhr, *Moral Man and Immoral Society* (New York: Charles Scribner's Sons, 1932), and others.
5. Hoffmann, 51.
6. "Why Is There No International Theory?" *International Relations* 2, no. 1 (April 1960): 35-46, 62.
7. James N. Rosenau, Kenneth W. Thompson, Gavin Boyd, *World Politics: An Introduction* (New York: Free Press, 1976).
8. On futurological concerns note the work of the "World Order Model Project" introduced in volumes such as Saul H. Mendlovitz, ed., *On the Creation of a Just World Order: Preferred Worlds for the 1990's* (New York: Free Press, 1975).
9. Karl W. Deutsch, *The Analysis of International Relations*, 2d ed. (Englewood Cliffs, N.J.: Prentice-Hall, 1978).
10. Morgenthau, (cited in note 4 above); Eric Voegelin, "World Empire and the Unity of Mankind," *International Affairs* 38 (1962): 176ff. and "Industrial Society in Search of Reason," in *World Technology and Human Destiny*, ed. Raymond Aron (Ann Arbor: University of Michigan Press, 1963), 31-46; and John Herz, *The Nation-State and the Crisis of World Politics* (New York: David McKay, 1976), especially chapter 9, "Relevancies and Irrelevancies in the Study of International Relations."
11. Kenneth Waltz, *Man, the State, and War* (New York: Columbia University Press, 1959).
12. F. Parkinson, *The Philosophy of International Relations* (Beverly Hills: Sage, 1977). A recent important contribution to the general problem of scientism in the study of politics is that of Gabriel A. Almond and Stephen J. Genco, "Clouds, Clocks, and the Study of Politics," *World Politics* 29 (July 1977): 489-522.
13. See Martin Buber, *The Kingship of God*, trans. Richard Scheimann (New York: Harper Torchbooks, 1967) and Eric Voegelin, *Order and History*, vol. 1, *Israel and Revelation* (Baton Rouge: Louisiana State University Press, 1956), 185-352.
14. See Eric Voegelin, *Order and History*, vol 3, *Plato and Aristotle* (Baton Rouge: Louisiana State University Press, 1957).
15. See Victor Ehrenberg, *The Greek State* (New York: Norton, 1960), 103-31.
16. Eric Voegelin, *Order and History*, vol. 4, *The Ecumenic Age* (Baton Rouge: Louisiana State University Press, 1974), 226.
17. Voegelin, *The Ecumenic Age*, 227.
18. Parkinson, 10 (cited in note 12 above).
19. Parkinson, 11.
20. Parkinson, 11.
21. Parkinson, 12.
22. Marcus Tullius Cicero, *On the Commonwealth*, trans. George H. Sabine and

Stanley B. Smith (Indianapolis: Bobbs-Merrill, 1976), 216 (3.22).
23. Voegelin, *The Ecumenic Age*, 47.
24. Voegelin, *The Ecumenic Age*, 47.
25. Parkinson, 12.
26. Parkinson, 13.
27. See Herbert A. Deane, *The Political and Social Ideas of St. Augustine* (New York: Columbia University Press, 1963), 78ff.
28. Deane, 86.
29. Deane, 116ff.
30. Deane, 97, 102.
31. Deane, 200 (italics mine).
32. Deane, 200.
33. A. P. D'Entreves, ed., *Aquinas: Selected Political Writings*, trans. J. G. Dawson (Oxford: Basil Blackwell, 1970), xxv.
34. D'Entreves, xxiii.
35. Hans J. Morgenthau, *Truth and Power* (New York: Praeger, 1970).
36. Morgenthau, *Truth and Power*, 61.
37. Morgenthau, *Truth and Power*, 62, 63.
38. Morgenthau, *Truth and Power*, 63-64.
39. As for the limits and problems of this assumption that the "depraved" condition of human nature explains international politics, see Waltz, 16-41 (cited in note 11 above) and James Skillen, "International Interdependence and the Demand for Global Justice," *International Reformed Bulletin*, 1st and 2d quarter (1977), 20-23.
40. Morgenthau, *Truth and Power*, 64-65.
41. Dougherty and Pfaltzgraff, (76, cited in note 1 above) comment that the concept of the power struggle "gives continuity and unity to the seemingly diverse foreign policies of the widely separated nation-states. Moreover, the concept 'interest defined as power' makes evaluating the actions of political leaders at different points in history possible." In other words, Morgenthau's attempt to define the universal uniformity of human nature provides him with the principle of universality and unity that is necessary because without it the diversity would have no meaning or common relationship.
42. Morgenthau, *Truth and Power*, 80.
43. Morgenthau, *Truth and Power*, 80.
44. Commenting on Hobbes, Eric Voegelin puts it beautifully, in *The New Science of Politics* (Chicago: University of Chicago Press, 1952), 184:

> The style of the construction is magnificent. If human nature is assumed to be nothing but passionate existence, devoid of ordering resources of the soul, the horror of annihilation will, indeed, be the overriding passion that compels submission to order. If pride cannot bow to *Dike*, or be redeemed through grace, it must be broken by the Leviathan who "is king of all the children of pride." If the souls cannot participate in the Logos, then the sovereign who strikes terror into the souls will be "the essence of the commonwealth." The "King of the Proud" must break the *amor sui* that cannot be relieved by the *amor Dei*.

For more on this theme of Morgenthau and Hobbes, see Cecil V. Crabb, Jr., and

June Savoy, "Hans J. Morgenthau's Version of Real Politik," *The Political Science Reviewer* 5 (Fall 1975): 201ff., 210ff.

45. Morgenthau, *Truth and Power*, 252.

46. Morgenthau, *Truth and Power*, 242-43. Morgenthau is criticizing the kind of theory that attempts to reduce politics to some functional interrelationship such as the economic, or the kind that try to reduce international relations to quantifiable units that can yield greater predictability.

47. Morgenthau, *Truth and Power*, 243.

48. Morgenthau, *Truth and Power*, 257.

49. Morgenthau, *Truth and Power*, 256-57. For more on Morgenthau's conception of political theory as rational hypothesis testing, see his *Politics among Nations*, 4th ed., 4ff. (cited in note 4 above).

50. Morgenthau, *Truth and Power*, 257.

51. See Crabb and Savoy (cited in note 44 above). They comment: "Why the intellectuals within a society escape involvement in the 'universal' power struggle—or why the moral-ethical professions of intellectuals do not also conceal an egocentric quest for power—are questions Morgenthau never clarifies" (202).

52. Morgenthau, *Truth and Power*, 259-60.

53. Morgenthau, *Truth and Power*, 260-61.

54. Karl Deutsch, *The Analysis of International Relations* (Englewood Cliffs, N.J.: Prentice Hall, 1968), 91.

55. Deutsch, *Analysis*, 91.

56. Deutsch, *Analysis*. 89-90. Deutsch also compares the political system with a telephone switchboard in *The Nerves of Government* (New York: Free Press, 1964), 76-98. In this book Deutsch develops his basic cybernetic-systems theory which underlies all of his political analysis.

57. Amazingly, *The Analysis of International Relations* (cited in note 5 above) lacks any historical account, even of its own assumptions. The following utterly nominalist statement introduces the second chapter, "Tools for Thinking," but Deutsch nowhere indicates that he is even aware of his nominalism.

> Since a concept is a symbol, and a symbol is, so to speak, a command to be mindful of those things to which it refers, it follows that a concept is a kind of command to remember a collection of things or memories. It is an order to select and collect certain items of information—these will refer to facts, if they should happen to exist. Hence a concept is a command to search, but it is no guarantee that we shall find. (14)

See the beginning of chapter 4 (45) for a similar comment.

58. Deutsch, *Analysis*, 9.

59. Deutsch, *Analysis*, 10.

60. See especially Deutsch, *The Nerves of Government* (cited in note 56 above). Also note Robert L. Pfaltzgraff, Jr., "Karl Deutsch and the Study of Political Science," *The Political Science Reviewer* 2 (Fall 1972): 90-111.

61. Deutsch, *Analysis*, 14.

62. Deutsch defines a "people" very abstractly, as in this quote from *Politics and Government: How People Decide Their Fate*, 2d ed. (Boston: Houghton Mifflin, 1974), 130:

> A people, then, is a group with complementary communication habits whose members usually share the same language, and always share a similar culture so that all members of the group attach the same meaning to words. In that sense a people is a community of shared meanings.

Also see Deutsch, *Analysis,* 76ff.

A state or political system for Deutsch presupposes one or more *peoples,* and it is then defined (also quite abstractly) as "an organization for the enforcement of decisions or commands, made practicable by the existing habits or compliance among the population....A state can be used to reinforce the communication habits, the cooperation, and the solidarity of a people" (Deutsch, *Analysis,* 79).

63. The term "nation-state," as Deutsch frequently uses it, is one manifestation of his inadequate definition of politics, or the state, or a political system. Note especially the criticism of Walker Connor, "Nation-building or Nation-destroying," *World Politics* 24 (April 1972): 319-55.

64. Deutsch, *Analysis,* 19.

65. Deutsch, *Analysis,* 198.

66. Deutsch, *Analysis,* 224.

67. Deutsch, *Analysis,* 224-25.

68. Deutsch, *Analysis,* 253.

69. Pfaltzgraff comments in "Karl Deutsch and the Study of Political Science," 107 (cited in note 60 above):

> Deutsch calls for unprecedented breakthroughs in the social sciences toward an understanding of international conflict. His assumption is that, having gained such understanding, peoples would forego war for peace. He thus calls for a transformation in human behavior as remarkable as the advances which he proposes in the social sciences. The political transformation for which Deutsch calls at the international level far exceeds both in scope and in rapidity those which he describes in the development historically of political communities at the national level. If the prospects for their realization in the international system of the next generation are minimal, the question remains as to whether Deutsch's assessment of the future is accurate.

This paper does not include a general discussion of the general framework of Deutsch's thought. For some background and criticism of the traditions in which Deutsch stands, see Floyd W. Matson, *The Broken Image* (Garden City: Doubleday, Anchor Books, 1964), 66-110; Alec Barbrook, *Patterns of Political Behaviour* (Itasca, Ill.: F. E. Peacock, 1975); Gabriel Almond, "Political Theory and Political Science," *American Political Science Review* 60 (December 1966): 869-79; Robert A. Dahl, "The Behavioral Approach in Political Science," in *Politics and Social Life,* ed. Nelson W. Polsby, Robert A. Dentler, and Paul A. Smith (Boston: Houghton Mifflin, 1963); and Peter Nettl, "Concept of System in Political Science," *Political Studies* (October 1966): 305-38.

70. On this point, however, Keohane and Nye are referring specifically to Robert Angell, *Peace on the March: Transnational Participation* (New York: Van Nostrand, 1969).

71. Robert O. Keohane and Joseph S. Nye, *Power and Interdependence* (Boston: Little, Brown and Co., 1977), 4.
72. In *Power and Interdependence*, 23-24, Keohane and Nye argue that three assumptions are integral to the realist vision:

> First, states as coherent units are the dominant actors in world politics....Second, realists assume that force is a usable and effective instrument of policy....Thirdly, partly because of their second assumption, realists assume a hierarchy of issues in world politics, headed by questions of military security: the "high politics" of military security dominates the "low politics" of economic and social affairs.

73. Keohane and Nye, 18-19.
74. Keohane and Nye, 162.
75. Keohane and Nye, 224.
76. Keohane and Nye, 221.
77. On this subject, as well as on some others, see the following works produced by Robert O. Keohane and Joseph S. Nye: "Transgovernmental Relations and International Organizations," *World Politics* 27 (October 1974): 39-62; "International Interdependence and Integration," in *Handbook of Political Science*, ed. Fred I. Greenstein and Nelson W. Polsby, vol. 8 (Reading, Mass.: Addison-Wesley, 1975), 363-414; and *Transnational Relations and World Politics*, (Cambridge, Mass.: Harvard University Press, 1972).

From systems analysis via systems design to systems control
Egbert Schuurman

Introduction

My title clearly indicates that to concentrate on my main point —systems control—I will need to discuss briefly systems analysis and systems theory. I want to draw your attention to the cultural consequences of systems theory in connection with modern technology, especially in connection with information technology or computer technology. Hence, I could have also called this essay "From Systems Analysis Via Information Systems to Computer Systems" or: "How Systems Theory Fulfills Itself in Cybernetics as the Science and Practice of Control." I intend to analyze the origin, development, and future possibilities of systems theory in connection with computer technology, a complex called cybernetics.[1]

I will show that the technicization of modern culture complements the scientization of modern culture. Systems theory has strengthened this tendency of scientization and technicization. Numerous philosophers have called our modern culture a technocracy. With the help of systems theory and computer technology, this technocracy might very well become a computerocracy. This prominent tendency in modern culture confronts us with many problems: How must we evaluate the recent cultural situation? Can we change this new, prominent tendency in modern technocracy? Finally, what conditions must be met to set modern culture in a more responsible direction?

I will restrict myself to how systems theory has shaped our culture, not to systems theory as a science. Moreover, I cannot devote much attention to details and subleties. For instance, I will not deal with the influence of cybernetics on fields such as sociology, economics, or politics. My concern is the spiritual background and the development of modern culture as a whole.

I will refer only to publications by prominent philosophers on cybernetics and related fields, Norbert Wiener, Karl Steinbuch, and the Marxist Georg Klaus, who orientate themselves to cybernetics as a part of modern technology. Ludwig von Bertalanffy is a biologist or a philosopher of biology; David Easton is a philosopher of politics; Kenneth Boulding is a philosopher of economics; and Russel Ackoff and Ervin Laszlo are sociologists. They are all inspired by systems analysis and cybernetics. From their different scientific backgrounds, they are interested in the new science of systems theory and the new technology of information.

Origin
Where did this development start? To make a long story short, we will find the historical origin of systems theory and cybernetics in the field of *modern technology*. Norbert Wiener is the father of this development. Before Wiener, von Bertalanffy had already demanded special attention to the organization of a living organism as a whole.[2] But he developed his systems theory[3] only after the pioneering work of Wiener in the field of cybernetics, that is, the field of control and communication in the animal and the machine.[4]

Because of Wiener, we no longer interpret systems as mechanisms or "clockworks." The concept of information has focused our attention on the whole system. Before Wiener a system was seen as the sum of all its parts, but after Wiener the system as a whole was more than the sum of its parts.

Some have thought that this development has sent us beyond the period of mechanistic thinking and returned us to the organistic thinking of Aristotle and the Middle Ages. Aristotelian and Medieval organistic thought, however, were inspired by biology, while modern organistic thinking is much more inspired by and oriented to technology. Today's interpretation of a given entity as a whole is a technical interpretation. The given entity is seen as a constructed, artificial, technical whole governed by the cybernetic principles of information, communication, feedback, equifinality, steady-state, and so on.

When some people say it is not possible to conceive all given entities as cybernetics systems, they are usually speaking of an unknown X within a system that is still interpreted in terms of cybernetics. This X might be "life," "growth," "play," "creativity," and so on. Such an approach, however, easily forgets this X when cybernetics is used to control the given system. Hence people might recognize the limitations of the cybernetic interpretation at first, but later on reduction still takes place. Here we find the origin of so many difficulties in the philosophical comparisons of humans and computers. In this case, instead of a new organicism, it is better to speak of cyberneticism.

Cybernetics describes or explains; it is the technology of (or better, a technique for) controlling a system. It is science and technique in one. This conception of cybernetics is already found in the pragmatic, neorationalistic work of Norbert Wiener. This progress in technology and especially the progress in the new branch of technology, information technology or cybernetics, has inspired many to use the new technological-scientific method, the method of cybernetics, for all sectors of modern culture and its future, resulting in systems analysis and systems designs. Cybernetics is now absolutized and imperialistic. Cybernetics has become a new philosophy.

Since the early sixties, several studies have appeared devoted to the subject of cybernetics and philosophy. In 1969 the book *Kybernetik, Brücke zwischen den Wissenschaften* was published.[5] In 1961 the Marxist Georg Klaus had already written *Kybernetik in philosophischer Sicht*.[6] And in 1973 he published *Kybernetik, eine neue Universalphilosophie der Gesellschaft*.[7] *Philosophie und Kybernetik* is a joint study by the professor of information theory at Karlsruhe, Karl Steinbuch, and the philosopher Simon Moser.[8]

Besides these studies several introductions to systems theory were published. In 1956 the economist Kenneth Boulding published "General Systems Theory: The Skeleton of Science."[9] In 1973 the sociologist Ervin Laszlo published his main work, *Introduction to Systems Philosophy: Toward a New Paradigm of Contemporary Thought*.[10] A critical survey of systems theory within the social sciences was given by R. Premo, J. Ritsert, and E. Strache in *Systemtheoretische Ansatze in der Soziologie*.[11] And Russell L. Ackoff published *Redesigning the Future: A Systems Approach to Societal Problems*.[12] All these studies develop a new scientific approach which at the same time results, via information theory, in a new technology, namely computer technology. In one of his studies, Ackhoff says:

I believe, and will try to show, that our society is now in the early stages of a change of age that results from a radical change in our point of view, our way of thinking, and the kind of technology we are producing. We are going through an intellectual revolution that is as fundamental as that which occurred in the Renaissance. The Renaissance ushered in the Machine Age which produced the Industrial Revolution. The currently emerging intellectual revolution is springing with it a new era that can be called the *Systems Age*, which is producing the *Postindustrial Revolution*. I believe these changes give rise to most of the crises we face and simultaneously offer whatever hope there is for dealing with them effectively.[13]

In the 1950s teleology (the study of goal-seeking and purposeful behaviour) was brought into science, and it began to dominate our conception of the world. Teleology's cultural effect was the automation, planning, and control of the future by cybernetics. Cybernetics became the content of redesigning the future. Through systems theory, systems design, and systems control all the disadvantages of the industrial age—focusing on parts rather than wholes, reductionism, the primacy of the analytic mode of thought, mechanism, determinism, and dehumanization—are being transformed into the advantages of the postindustrial age: holism, expansionism, a new synthetic mode of thought, teleology, information, and self-control.

We can tentatively conclude, therefore, that there is a strong tendency with these modern thinkers no longer to orient themselves to physics but to cybernetics. Physical parts are exchanged for technical wholes, that is, for artificial wholes. And as a result the computer has made its introduction in several fields in modern society. With the help of the computer, people try to control (and to direct) the fields of economics, politics, and management. The concept of information is the bridge between systems analysis and systems control and, with the help of a mathematical information-theory, it is possible to simulate the system being studied with the computer. It is even possible to simulate the consequences of certain decisions within a system, so that one can make an optimal decision.

A lot of publications that can be seen as fruits of systems

theory and information-theory have appeared in recent years. A few of the most important ones are: *Computers and the World of the Future* edited by M. Greenberger,[14] *Perspectives on the Computer Revolution* edited by Zenon W. Pylyshn,[15] the study of Joseph Weizenbaum entitled *Computer Power and Human Reason*,[16] and *Computer Models in the Social Sciences* by R. B. Coats and A. Parker.[17] All these studies make it very clear that the social sciences have become technologically oriented. The interest in systems design and systems control by computers has steadily grown since the activities of the Club of Rome, and the possibilities of cybernetics have become apparent to many social scientists.

Ervin Laszlo's thought
Laszlo's thinking illustrates the general trend I have outlined above. According to Laszlo his new systems theory and his systems philosophy will someday constitute the only science and philosophy about the future. He intends to unify science on the basis of a natural systems view of the world and restore the relation between philosophy and science. According to Laszlo science today is reductionistic; he intends to provide a holistic approach. He prefers a science of the entity, of the whole, not a science of a part or an aspect of reality. As a result Laszlo begins with the largest whole (the world system) and then descends to the smaller systems. Furthermore, he wants to effect a close relationship between the science of systems and politics.

To understand Laszlo's ideas we have his General System Theory (GST). What is a system? A system is a complex of interacting elements; or a system is the sum of the parts of an entity and their interrelations. These interrelations are characterized by feedback or a circular causality. Hence the entity is a cybernetic system. The relations between system and environment are expressed as input and output of matter, energy, and information which means that the relations between the system and the environment are also cybernetic.

In the preface of *The Introduction to Systems Philosophy* we read that this philosophy is founded on the natural scientific picture of the world, but it centers on people and society. It provides a basis for unifying science and scientific control. GST is apt to bridge the antithesis between the sciences and the humanities, between technology and history. Systems philosophy is concerned about the roots of our present cultural crisis, be it the dangers of modern technology, the disturbances in the ecosystem of nature, or even the innumerable psychological, social, economic, and political problems of the present situation.

Clearly, systems philosophy is not modest. It wants to bring philosophy back into the mainstream of present-day science, and it wants to involve philosophy in the many urgent problems confronting science and society. It is also clear that GST is not to be compared with a special science. GST tries to approach the whole of reality. The whole of reality is a hierarchy of systems. The smallest system is an atom, and the largest is the world system. GST is an integrated pluralism, proclaiming both the diversity and the unity of the world.

Each system is characterized by four invariants, and the form of the invariants is the same for all four systems while their content differs. The first invariant is that all systems can be analyzed in terms of cybernetic principles. The system as a whole does not have mystery anymore since everything can be explained by the sum of the parts and the cybernetic interrelations between the parts. The second invariant is the self-stabilization of the system in its environment by means of negative feedback. The third invariant is the self-organization of the system in its environment by means of positive feedback. And the fourth invariant is that each system is part of a hierarchy of all the systems.

These four invariants guarantee the isomorphism between the systems. It is also important to note that the four invariants can always be expressed in the categories of mathematical information theory. As a consequence each system can be simulated by the computer. In information theory we find the bridge between systems theory and computer technology. In other words, a systems approach, with the help of information theory, is the basis for applying computers to several sectors of our culture.

Society, in this way, becomes a computerized society. According to Laszlo the global (social, cultural, political, economical and ecological) system is the top of the hierarchy of all systems. Every other system has to adapt itself to this system. The world-system ought to be in optimal condition which it is not at present. And the optimal world-system will be obtained when every subsystem has adapted itself to the goal of the world-system which is survival. And this goal of survival has to form the framework for the ethos of the new age and a new world religion. The content of the new ethos ought to be reverence for all natural systems, and the content of the world religion ought to be "universal humanism." According to GST both the boundaries between the various disciplines and boundaries between geographic nations must disappear.

GST and systems philosophy have grand visions for politics and, via politics, for social-economic practice. GST believes in world politics as the highest form of politics, and it believes a world political order should determine the goals of a global society.

Criticism

Systems philosophy does not excel in subtlety and profundity; it is superficial. Though it is easy to criticize systems philosophy on immanent and transcendental grounds, it nevertheless has gained a tremendous influence in our modern culture. The reason for this is that this philosophy gives a very important, almost exclusive place, to objective cultural power. It is dominated by the passion to control the future completely, and many people wish for this control in the face of the menacing dangers and catastrophes of our day. I intend to direct my critique, above all, to the consequences of this cultural influence.

It is almost superfluous to say that the new systems philosophy is a new expression of autonomous, humanist philosophy. We are dealing with a revolution in scientism, not its conversion. As a revolution in scientism, it has strengthened and enlarged scientism because systems philosophy has extended scientism beyond the theoretical fields to the formation of our culture and our culture's direction. In short, the spiritual background of the new philosophy is the old religious worship of *ratio*, and in this case that worship is a magical devotion to the imperialism of an instrumental reason completed by the computer.

Because of their faith in abstract scientific thought and abstract cybernetic thought, people tend to humbly submit themselves to that thought. They forget that science is reductionistic, and they imply that the new science of cybernetics produces full and concrete knowledge of all reality. However, cybernetics does no such thing; rather it distorts reality and dislocates culture. Cyberneticism cannot but encumber us with new, more distressing problems than what we already have.

Cyberneticism reinforces the scientization of culture, as the characteristics of cybernetics become cultural characteristics. Characteristics of cybernetics—logical coherence, universiality, abstractness, and durability—are in tension with the uniqueness, coherence, and changeability of concrete reality and with the responsible creativity of people. When, for instance, systems goals and computer ethics prescribe ways to solve cultural problems, then there is no appreciation of people's historical situation in which they should be active and they should shape creatively. Cyberneticism regulates human cultural activity and hence robs people of their responsibility, freedom, and inventiveness. Of course, within the boundaries of the cybernetic system people are free, but if people do not accept those boundaries they will be oppressed and compelled into obedience.

Laszlo and Ackoff stress that the cybernetics of systems philosophy is not reductionistic because it draws attention, not to a function or an aspect but to the whole, right to the top of the hierarchy of all systems, the world-system. In reality, however, we have a new reductionism. For instance, we must distinguish a given entity as a whole and the system as an interpretation or an artificial construction of such a given entity. Moreover, when a computer simulates the artificial system with the help of information theory, then another reduction of the given original system takes place. Therefore, with the absolutized introduction of cybernetics, we can speak of new scientization and technicization.

Cybernetics is biased toward the large scale. The large scale especially comes to expression in its proposed world politics. Nevertheless, it is a reductionistic large scale. So in the cyberneticized culture, not only are people and human communities reduced but political systems as well since they will be controlled by computers. From this point of view we can say that technocracy reaches its fulfillment in cyberneticized culture or computer technocracy. The future of that culture is a cybernetically controlled future. Based not on the principle of linear causality but circular causality, such a future is more flexible yet more stable than a technocratic future. In the long run, however, a cybernetic future has bigger disadvantages than a technocratic future because of the large scale of cybernetics, the dynamics and the range of its decisions. That also implies that the cybernetic future is reduced since the cybernetic experts choose the goals to be realized. An elite of experts will direct the development of that culture, and that elite can be hidden. They have to make decisions, but they are wrong to choose cybernetics to control the future according to their ideas or the ideas of their authorities in economics and politics. The situation can even become so complex that the goal is hidden. In that case nobody knows the "wherefore" of a decision because all attention is given to solving a complex problem. In that case people will manipulate all the more. Though some people think that democracy will prevent such evil, they forget that democracy is incompatible with cybernetics because democracy has a very slow feedback, whereas cybernetics needs a dynamic and automated feedback. In politics we are confronted with a centralized, nearly autonomous cybernetic world culture or a worldwide computer technocracy. It is clear that there will be a growing regimentation of life in such a culture.

Management shows the same tendency. Abbe Mowshowitz, in his study *The Conquest of Will: Information Processing in Human Affairs*, says that a centralized management is facilitated by our technology in transportation, communication, and information-processing.[18]

George Grant has given a very instructive contribution about the cultural influence of the computer in "The Computer Does Not Impose on Us the Ways It Should Be Used."[19] He makes clear that computers do impose the ways they are used and that we are hiding from the problems of the computer age and people's responsibility in this age. All existing communication and information processes in computers are scientifically and technically controllable. This implies that such processes are reductionistic processes. With an information system we reduce reality so that it accords with our universal information system. Such information systems have characteristics opposite to the characteristics of reality, as we have already seen. The individual user or receiver of information becomes a standardized user or receiver of selected and formed universal, uniform information. So the computer does impose on us the ways it should be used, and people have to obey the structure of the computer.

The increasing use of the computer reinforces the notion that people are no longer in control of their culture. Rather, they seem controlled by this seemingly autonomous development. The computer works faster and more accurately than people, has nearly inexhaustible endurance, and works by itself. In this sense it is, indeed, relatively autonomous. Furthermore, it gives the appearance of becoming entirely independent of people, because while people set the conditions under which the computer must function, the functioning machine runs independently of its makers. People simply cannot oversee the functioning of the computer. The results therefore have, albeit within certain limits, the character of a surprise. In addition, a computer's user is not necessarily its programmer, which again widens the gap between people and the computer. Finally, the gap is widened even further as one user replaces another, so that the user no longer has a notion of the criteria by which the computer functions. The program has become incomprehensible. People must yield to it and trust it. This problem will grow in scope and seriousness in the future as we use machines that learn and reproduce themselves. Computer technocracy will perfect itself.

Evaluation
First, I would like to call attention to the reformational view of science from which we can assess the real meaning of systems analysis. Second, I will note the reformational view of the relation between theory and practice. And finally, I will point out the implications of the first and second point for the increasing use of the computer and its problematic results.

The reformational view of science recognizes that, historically and structurally, scientific knowledge is limited and based on a more fundamental, uncompartmentalized, and concrete knowledge. This prescientific knowledge, which consists of both actual and factual knowledge of changes brought about by human action, is in turn guided and kept on course by an original and irreducible, ultimate trust. This "trust-knowledge" constitutes people's point of reference for all their philosophical and scientific endeavors regardless of whether or not they realize it. But autonomous theoretical reflection, inspired since the beginning of the modern age by a religious faith in philosophical and scientific thought, perverts and falsifies this prescientific trust-knowledge. Meanwhile, scientific knowledge and its practical application are accorded superior status.

Reformational philosophy, however, rejects the autonomy of people, and therefore it rejects the autonomy of philosophical and special scientific thought. Divine revelation leads us to a knowledge whose content is open to understanding by faith. It is our most profound knowledge which our thinking cannot fathom. It is knowledge springing from the heart.

What does this mean for science? We need to relativize science and the scientific method by opening our hearts to full revelation. On the one hand, science is a very fascinating activity of people; on the other hand, scientific knowledge is only a conditioned, partial, restricted, abstract, and tentative knowledge. If we can accept this, then we can be open to science and to a pluralistic methodology, and we can then appreciate cybernetics as a new, valuable, scientific approach.

Scientific knowledge must be continually integrated into our full, direct, concrete human knowledge and experience which has fundamental trust-knowledge at its core. Systems theory, too, must be continually integrated into and corrected by prescientific knowledge so that the restrictions inherent in scientific knowledge are lifted. In this way, people's integral, pretheoretical knowledge is gradually enriched and their measure of responsibility is increased. Seen in this way, scientific activity can be carried out with faith as its starting point and a strengthened faith as its result. Then our scientific endeavors will serve the cause of wisdom and will lead to an increasingly comprehensive insight. It will buttress and enlarge our responsibility so that we will be better able to orientate ourselves toward the future.

My second point deals with the relation between theory and praxis. In the tradition of Western thought, the philosophers of systems theory try to span the bridge between systems theory and praxis only from the side of theory. For them autonomous thinking is the beginning and end of all activities. Therefore, systems theory leads to new scientization and technicization of culture, bringing old and new problems. Systems philosophers try to overcome these problems with the help of politics which is an advantage over the solutions of other thinkers. But in the long run their problems will be larger, as we have already seen.

From a Christian philosophical point of view, we ought to bridge the distance between theory and praxis from a deep sense of responsibility that has its root in faith. We cannot accept any science as the guiding principle for chartering the future. Philosophy and science must not conquer the future according to their own models of the future. As we have seen, systems theory sometimes tries to create a new ethic and a new religion. But people have to disclose the creation in faithful responsibility under the guidance of the given revealed, normative principles. Science has its useful function in forming culture, and we can use systems theory in several fields of our modern culture. But science and systems theory must strengthen our insight in complex matters so that we can make ethical, responsible decisions. The central point in all such decisions is the meaning of creation—the kingdom of God.

But how is it possible to make such decisions in our secular culture? I want to stress again that the problems, dangers, and catastrophes of our culture arouse reactionary spirits that try and sometimes do propose good ideas and alternatives, although such ideas and alternatives are just as secular as the culture. Christians can learn from these ideas and alternatives, but they must also redirect and deepen them. At the same time we should not underestimate the problems that confront the Christian. These problems are not only cultural problems; they also pertain to a religious and biblical background. In short we are to be concerned about the kingdom of God. We believe that this kingdom is absent because of the fall into sin but that the kingdom is present in Jesus Christ. At the same time, however, this kingdom will not be fully present till the second coming of Christ. We cannot be optimistic about our efforts to redirect the future.

Nevertheless I will end with a few suggestions. As we consider the idea of an inner reformation of sciences, so we have to consider what we have erroneously called "the applied sciences" which includes the field of computer technology. We have seen that computer technology gives the appearance of being almost totally autonomous. Computers have accumulated so much information relevant to decision making that no one making a decision can grasp all of this information. Moreover, there is a strong tendency to centralize. Thus the information system becomes autonomous in the selection of relevant information, the interpretation of information, and the decisions grounded in it. Theorists have given little attention to this development because the centralization is not quantifiable in the first place but spiritual. We must, therefore, acquaint ourselves with and analyze the views of those who use computer technology, giving special attention to their hidden but pervasive views on people, communities, society, politics, and the future.

Where and how should we use computers? Sometimes, as in space travel, we have to use them. We also have to use computers where the norm of efficiency is most important, and also with work done under very dangerous conditions. But in most cases we use the computer even though the computer is not necessary. In such cases we must make the incomprehensible programs comprehensible. The users have to bear their responsibility and they are accountable to those affected by the consequences of their decisions. In short, we have to integrate computer systems with the faithful responsibility of the users of computers. Only that kind of responsibility can prevent a constraining of the creation and promote the disclosure of creation.

Centralization is not a necessary consequence or an autonomous development of information technology. Computer technology, if kept within its normative limits, can make a powerful contribution to people's cultural task. It can promote a pluriform, stable, wholesome, and enriched culture. But to realize our cultural task, we have a lot of work to do.

Notes
1. This essay is a sequel to my article "The Scientialization of Modern Culture," *Philosophia reformata* 74 (June 1978): 34-38.
2. Ludwig von Bertalanffy, *Organismic Psychology and Systems Theory* (Worcester, Mass.: Clark University Press, 1968).
3. Ludwig von Bertalanffy, *General Systems Theory* (New York: Brazillon, 1968).
4. Norbert Wiener, 8th ed., *Cybernetics; or Control and Communication in the Animal and the Machine* (New York: Wiley, 1950).
5. Helmar Frank, *Kybernetik, Brücke, zwischen den Wissenschaften*, 5th ed.

(Frankfurt am Main: Umschau Verlag, 1965).

6. Georg Klaus, *Kybernetik in philosophischer Sicht* (Berlin: Dietz, 1961).

7. *Kybernetik, eine neue Universaphilosophie der Gesellschaft* (Frankfurt am Main: Verlag Marxistische Blatter, 1972).

8. Karl Steinbuch and Simon Moser, *Philosophie und Kybernetik* (Munich: Nymphenburger Verlagshandlung, 1970).

9. Kenneth Boulding, "General Systems Theory: The Skeleton of Science," *Management Science 2*, no. 3 (April 1956): 197-208.

10. Ervin Laszlo, *The Introduction to Systems Philosphy: Toward a New Paradigm of Contemporary Thought* (New York: Gordon & Breach, 1972).

11. R. Premo, J. Ritsert, and E. Strache, *Systemtheoretische Ansatze in der Soziologie* (Wiesbaden: Westdeutscher Verlag, 1973).

12. Russell L. Ackoff, *Redesigning the Future: A Systems Approach to Societal Problems* (New York: Wiley, 1974).

13. Ackoff, 8.

14. M. Greenberger, ed., *Computers and the World of the Future* (Cambridge, Mass.: MIT Press, 1962).

15. Zenon W. Pylyshn, ed., *Perspectives on the Computer Revolution* (Englewood Cliffs, N.J.: Prentice-Hall, 1970).

16. Joseph Weizenbaum, *Computer Power and Human Reason* (San Francisco: W. H. Freeman, 1976).

17. R. B. Coats and A. Parker, *Computer Models in the Social Sciences* (London: Arnold Edward, 1978).

18. Abbe Mowshowitz, *The Conquest of Will: Information Processing in Human Affairs* (Reading, Mass. and Don Mills, Ont.: Addison-Wesley, 1976).

19. George Grant, "The Computer Does Not Impose on Us the Ways It Should Be Used," *Beyond Industrial Growth*, ed. Abraham Rotstein (Toronto: University of Toronto Press, 1976).

Contributors

M. Elaine Botha is professor of philosophy at Potchefstroom University for Christian Higher Education, Potchefstroom, Republic of South Africa

A.B. Cramp is senior lecturer in economics at Emmanuel College, Cambridge, England

Roelf Haan has taught economics as ISEDET, Buenos Aires, and is currently on the staff of the Interchurch Co-Ordination Committee for Development Projects, Netherlands

Hendrik Hart is senior member in philosophy at the Institute for Christian Studies, Toronto

Bas Kee is professor of philosophy at Erasmus University, Rotterdam, Netherlands

David Lyon is senior lecturer in social analysis at Bradford and Ilkley College, England

Paul Marshall is senior member in political theory at the Institute for Christian Studies, Toronto

George N. Monsma, Jr. is professor of economics at Calvin College, Grand Rapids, Michigan

Richard J. Mouw is professor of philosophy and ethics at Fuller Theological Seminary, Pasadena, California

Egbert Schuurman is professor of philosophy at the Delft Institute of Technology, Netherlands, and a member of the Dutch Senate

James W. Skillen is Executive Director of the Association for Public Justice, Washington, D.C.

Daniel F.M. Strauss is professor of philosophy at The University of the Orange Free State, Bloemfontein, Republic of South Africa

Johan D. van der Vyver is professor of law at Witwatersrand University, Johannesburg, Republic of South Africa

Maarten Vrieze was professor of philosophy, until his death in 1986, at Trinity Christian College, Palos Heights, Illinois